Table of contents

INTRODUCTION

Instant Pot – new technology on the food market and third generation pressure cooker to make your ration full of vitamins. What are basic features of the product? It is easy to use Instant Pot. Instant Pot uses safe technology of pressure cooking and gives you opportunity to cook in seven times faster than ordinary. Moreover, this pressure cooker remembers cooking technology, so, if you like cooking the same dishes – you won't have to change settings or set time and temperature once more – machine will do it instead of you! However, now let's focus on the opportunities of cooking with Instant Pot!

This cooking machine has been designed by the Canadian company and from the very beginning it were five separate pressure cookers: one for soup cooking, one for rice, one for porridges, one slow cooker and one instant cooker. All the machines were working using the same strategies, but became so popular, that in one year after the release of new cooker machines, Instant Pot company decided to present unique 6-in-1 cooker! In my book. you will find 600 unique recipes for the Instant Pot – starting from the shrimps and up to the three layer cheesecakes! Instant Pot unites opportunities of soup maker, porridge maker, slow cooker for the super tender meat or for the Greek yogurt receipt. Moreover, this cooking machine lets you make smoothie and soft cocktails! You can even make apple cider in the Instant Pot! Does it mean that you cannot bake vegetables or fruits in the Instant Pot? Of course, not! You can make soft soufflé with the crispy layer and bake a cake! In this case, you will need a little bit more time and a few teaspoons of butter! With Instant Pot, you may cook anything you want! Try new cuisines, eat healthy delicious meals and economy your time cooking favorite dishes. Of course, here you should ask the right question – how many energy will Instant Pot need to cook one dish? For example, to make Greek yogurt you need about 7 hours. During this time we can waste a lot of energy, what will cause big money wastes. By the way, Instant Pot works with the energy saving technology and it allows waste seven times less energy during the cooking session. So one Greek yogurt preparing will request the same energy amount as the hot grill in the microwave! We can already feel pluses of Instant Pot not even talking about new methods Instant Pot developers were using to make this construction!

What is the technology? Instant Pot is machine 6-in-1 as we already reminded. However, it doesn't mean that Instant Pot consists of 6 different parts. It has only three levels and one food processor. You may cook several recipes and products during one cooking session. The fist level of the Instant Pot is the Inner Pot. It is the bowl for the products standing on the basic processor of the Instant Pot with the main display and center of management. You will have to place products in the Inner Pot. It is warming up from the float valve. The same time spirals produce pressure and send it to the Inner Pot. Using just pressure and safety waves Instant Pot cooks food. Pressure is getting in the pot and makes products cook in their own juice. Moreover, on the bottom of the pot you may find small hole with the special thin and small tube for the safe and quick pressure reducing while cooking. Let's see action of the Instant Pot on the real example. Let's imagine we want to try delicious and soft oatmeal early in the morning and we don't have much time. First of all, you have to to pour water in the Instant Pot – in almost all the cases it is one of the most important steps. Water on the bottom of the cooker allows make cooking process possible using pressure and safe waves. The next step, if we are cooking porridges or soups, we need to place products right in the water and start cooking, if we want to bake cake, we will be placing products in the special place in the Pot with the dry surface or, the easiest way is to use baking form. Mix all the ingredients and press one button. Leave Instant Pot alone – you need to do nothing during the cooking session. This machine knows methods of the professional cooking. Pressure cooker will make super delicious lunch easy to make. In some recipes, you have to wait until pressure will reduce naturally for 10-15 minutes. However, it doesn't influence much on the dish's taste, so any time you can press reducing button and wait for seconds until all the pressure will be reduced.

The next part of the Instant Pot is Lid Lock. In the case, you are cooking something more complicated than soup or porridge, smoothie and any other liquid dish you need to close the Lid to make cooking process more intensive. Of course, machine can produce as much pressure as required, but still with the closed lid cooking will be quicker. So Lid Lock it is steel ring with the glass on top and you will have an opportunity to control the cooking session. On the Lid you also may find special reducing button. Moreover, Instant Pot company has projected different styles for the Instant Pots and you may choose exactly the style you like the most, including colors and materials.

After discussing the theory, let's come back to one more great advantage of the Instant Pot – opportunity to remember recipes you were using during the cooking session. We can say, that the base of the Instant Pot it is small portable computer with the easy display, where you may choose any regime you need (from the "Poultry" and up to the "Yogurt"). Nevertheless, this small computer has its own memory to memorize the way of cooking. Let's imagine that once you have cooked shrimps in coconut sauce with the garlic tomatoes. To addition, after this cooking session you were using Instant Pot several times. Maybe you have been cooking shrimps three or more months ago. Anyway, machine will memorize the way of cooking and it will understand what the procedure will be after the time and regime choose. Instant Pot can think itself! It is unique quality for the cooking machines! This revolutionary new pressure cooker will make your grey weekdays super easy! By the way, it can cook quickly your favorite healthy dishes and make you happy with the wide choice of recipes you may choose for the cooking in Instant Pot. Pressure Cooker will be memorizing recipes and you will not have even to remind the time needed for the meat or poultry cooking.

In the modern world, healthy lifestyle becomes an object of obsession. Especially among successful people. We can easily say, that people who surround us think about our status just looking at the faces. That is why everyone of us is trying to look better with every new day. Instant Pot will make it several times easier for you. Of course, cooking can be tiring! However, with Instant Pot it is almost impossible. Just collect needed ingredients, mix them right in the Inner Pot and start cooking session.

What about the regimes of cooking. This pressure cooking is that smart, that even has it's own regimes for the every life occasion. On the basic panel where you are setting time, you will see several buttons. One button is for one cooking regime. Depending on the dish, you have decided to cook, you may choose: "Poultry", "Meat", "Yogurt", "Soup", "Porridge". Moreover, there are two basic cooking regimes. If you don't want to set special cooking regime, you have to choose between only two types of cooking: "High Pressure" regime or "Low Pressure" cooking. They differ only with one feature – how intensive will pressure be producing in the Pot. For example, the tender you need to make the dish, the lower pressure should be. However, "Low Pressure" cooking requires more time, than "High Pressure" cooking. Cooking with low distribution of the pressure is suitable for the yogurts, soups and light creamy sauces. The same time, it is better to choose "High Pressure" regime cooking meat or poultry. Cooking on high doesn't mean dishes will be less tender, it only means, pressure will be producing more quickly and there will be more intensive work with the products. Anyway, if you choose "Low" or "High Pressure" cooking regime – you will waste for sure 7 times less time!

Live life in your satisfaction, never care about the time and don't eat only ordinary dishes because they are quick and easy to cook! With Instant Pot you can try drunken mussels and Caribbean salmon, full chicken under the cheesy sauce and homemade low-alcohol drinks! Cook anything you want and everything you have ever dreamed to try. This pressure cooker will make any of your dreams true! Just read this 600 Instant Pot recipes book and make sure!

BREAKFAST

Cut Oats

English traditional breakfast will full you with the vitamins and energy to make the day successful and bright!

Prep time: 5 minutes | **Cooking time:** 5 minutes | **Servings:** 12

Ingredients:

- 3 cups cut oats
- 9 cups water
- Caramelized cherries to serve

Directions:

1. Place cut oats in the Instant Pot.
2. Pour water on the cut oats and leave them for 15 minutes.
3. Turn on Instant Pot and let it come to pressure for 5 minutes on "High Pressure" regime. Place cut oats in the pressure cooker.
4. Cook cut oats for 3 minutes on "High Pressure" regime.
5. Leave cut oats in the Instant Pot after the cooking for 10 minutes for the natural release of pressure.
6. Place cut oats on the plate and top with cherries.

Nutrition:

- Calories: 140
- Fat: 2.5g
- Carbohydrates: 27g
- Protein:6g

Hard Boiled Eggs

Quick, easy and delicious breakfast for those who are always in a hurry! Forget about being late and cook with Instant Pot!

Prep time: 2 minutes | **Cooking time:** 8 minutes | **Servings:** 5

Ingredients:

- 1 cup water
- 5 eggs

Directions:

1. Place eggs in the Instant Pot basket.
2. Pout one cup of water on the eggs.
3. Turn on Pressure Cooker and set "High Pressure" regime. You should cook eggs for 8 minutes.
4. Leave eggs to rest after the cooking for the natural release of pressure. It will take you 5 minutes.
5. Take eggs out, clean and serve!

Nutrition

- Calories: 70
- Fat: 5g
- Carbohydrates: 0g
- Protein:1

Scotch Eggs

Make this morning special without hard moves – just try Scotch eggs in Instant Pot!

Prep time: 4 minutes | **Cooking time:** 12 minutes | **Servings:** 8

Ingredients:
- 8 eggs
- 2 tablespoons vegetable oil
- 2lb country
- style sausages

Directions:
1. Pour water in the Instant Pot basket.
2. Place eggs in the basket and cook on "High Pressure" regime for 6 minutes.
3. Let the pressure release for another 5 minutes after the cooking.
4. Clean eggs.
5. Divide sausages in 8 parts.
6. Place eggs on the sausages and roll up. You should get circle shape rolls with the eggs inside. To fix the form, you may use small wooden sticks.
7. Put scotch eggs in the Instant Pot and cook for 6 minutes on "High Pressure" regime.
8. Serve with fresh herbs!

Nutrition:
- Calories: 266
- Fat: 15g
- Carbohydrates: 19g
- Protein: 12g

Greek Yogurt

Enjoy Greek traditions – try low calories yogurt with toasts this morning!

Prep time: 5 minutes | **Cooking time:** 2 hours | **Servings:** 7

Ingredients:
- ½ gallon milk
- Cuisine yogurt strainer
- 1 tablespoon yogurt "starter"

Directions:
1. Sterilize Instant Pot with the water. Just pour water in the Instant Pot and press "Saute" button. Wait for 7 minutes until water will start boiling. Pour water out of the pressure cooker.
2. Pour milk in the Instant Pot.
3. Close the lid.
4. Press "Yogurt" button.
5. After the signal open the lid, whisk milk and check out temperature – it should be 360oF.
6. Place milk in the fridge for 10 minutes. Whisk milk when it is cold.
7. Mix milk with starter.
8. Place mix in the Instant Pot and press "yogurt" button.
9. When the time is up, place yogurt in the fridge for 2 hours.
10. Serve!

Nutrition:
- Calories: 80
- Fat: 0g
- Carbohydrates: 6g
- Protein: 15g

Casserole with Ham and Cheese

Super satisfying and tasty casserole with ham is exactly what you need this morning!

Prep time: 5 minutes

Cooking time: 4 hours
Servings: 12

Ingredients:
- 64 ounce bag hash browns
- 2 teaspoons pepper
- 2 onions
- 2 teaspoons salt
- 4 cups chopped ham
- 2 cups milk
- 4 cups shredded cheese
- 24 eggs

Directions:
1. Place half of onions, half of cheese and half of ham in the Instant Pot.
2. Mix beaten eggs with some milk, salt and pepper.
3. Pour beaten eggs on the cheese mix.
4. Set "Low Pressure" regime.
5. Set time on 4 hours and cook egg mix on "Low Pressure" regime.
6. Serve casserole with fresh herbs!

Nutrition:
- Calories: 220
- Fat: 14g
- Carbohydrates: 13g
- Protein:11g

Banana Toast in French Style

Crispy toasts with soft sweet bananas and vanilla in Instant Pot – let yourself eat healthy food!

Prep time: 15 minutes | **Cooking time:** 25 minutes | **Servings:** 7

Ingredients:
- 6 slices crumbed French bread
- Maple syrup to serve
- 4 bananas
- ¼ cup pecans
- 2 tablespoons brown sugar
- 2 tablespoons chilled butter
- ¼ cup cream cheese
- ½ teaspoon cinnamon
- 3 eggs
- 1 teaspoon vanilla extract
- ½ cup milk
- 1 teaspoon white sugar

Directions:
1. Cut bread into cubes. It may be big strips or squared shape cubes.
2. Prepare baking form for the Instant Pot.
3. Place half of a bread in the Instant Pot.
4. Cover bread with half of bananas.
5. Put sugar on bananas.
6. Melt some cream cheese in microwave and pour on bananas.
7. Add remaining bread and bananas to the Instant Pot.
8. Cover pie with pecans.
9. Mix eggs with sugar, milk, vanilla and cinnamon in a bowl.
10. Pour egg mix on bananas. Add some water to the mix.
11. Select "High Pressure" on the display and cook for 25 minutes.
12. Serve breakfast with nuts!

Nutrition:
- Calories: 337
- Fat: 17g
- Carbohydrates: 31g
- Protein:14g

Mexican Casserole

Hot, spicy and satisfying Mexican traditional breakfast for you today!

Prep time: 10 minutes | **Cooking time:** 25 minutes | **Servings:** 16

Ingredients:

- 16 eggs
- Cilantro
- 2 pounds ground sausages
- onions
- 2 cups mozzarella cheese
- 1 red onion
- 2 cups Cotija cheese
- 2 bell peppers
- 1 cup flour
- 2 cans black beans
- 1 cup green

Directions:

1. Preheat pressure cooker. Turn on Instant Pot, pour 1 tablespoon of oil in the Lid and turn on "Saute" regime.
2. Place sausages with chopped onions in the Instant Pot.
3. Cook onions with sausages for 6 minutes on "High Pressure" regime.
4. Mix eggs with some flour.
5. Chop vegetables. On the other plate mix beans with Cotija and Mozzarella cheeses. Add eggs mix to the cheesy mixture.
6. Pour flour mix in the Instant Pot.
7. Add chopped vegetables with beans.
8. Set "High Pressure" regime and cook casserole for 20 minutes.
9. Serve with fresh herbs!

Nutrition:

- Calories: 380
- Fat: 16g
- Carbohydrates: 48g
- Protein:12g

Cheesy Breakfast Pie

You will like this 5 ingredients cheesy pie because of its lightness, easiness and taste!

Prep time: 5 minutes | **Cooking time:** 10 minutes | **Servings:** 12

Ingredients:

- 18 slices bacon
- 1 teaspoon pepper
- 6 cups hash browns
- 3 teaspoons kosher salt

- 18 eggs
- 1 cup shredded cheddar cheese
- 1 cup milk

- 3 peppers

Directions:

1. Cut bacon into slices and place in Instant Pot. Cook for 6 minutes on "High Pressure" regime. Set bacon slices aside after the cooking session.
2. Wash and chop peppers, cook for 3 minutes on "High Pressure" regime. Leave peppers in the Instant Pot.
3. Place hash browns in the Instant Pot and cook for 2 more minutes not changing regime settings.
4. Mix milk with eggs. Add pepper, salt and cheese.
5. Pour mix in the Instant Pot on the hash browns and peppers in the Instant Pot. Place bacon on top of the egg mixture. Sprinkle eggs with pepper and salt to taste.
6. Add ½ glass of water.
7. Cook for 10 minutes on "High Pressure" regime.
8. Serve with onion rings in marinade.

Nutrition:

- Calories:490
- Fat: 25g

- Carbohydrates: 33g
- Protein: 32g

Burrito Casserole

Try this special morning burrito and stay happy for all the day!

Prep time: 10 minutes | **Cooking time:** 20 minutes | **Servings:** 6

Ingredients:
- 4 eggs
- ¾ teaspoon taco seasoning
- 2 pound red potatoes
- ¼ teaspoon mesquite seasoning
- ¼ cup chopped onions
- ¼ teaspoon chili powder
- 1 jalapeno
- ½ teaspoon salt
- 6oz steak
- 6 tortillas

Directions:
1. Cut steak in cubes.
2. Mix taco seasoning with salt, pepper, mesquite seasoning, chili powder, eggs and 1 tablespoon of water in a separate bowl.
3. Chop onions and jalapeno. Cut potatoes and ham.
4. Mix onions with seasoning, steak and potato cubes. Place in the Instant Pot.
5. Add water to the Instant Pot.
6. Cook ingredients for 15 minutes on "Manual".
7. Place burrito feeling on tortillas and serve!

Nutrition:
- Calories: 371
- Fat: 16g
- Carbohydrates: 0g
- Protein:20g

Chocolate Chip Pudding

Start this morning with light and satisfying pudding and enjoy new day!

Prep time: 2 minutes | **Cooking time:** 12 minutes | **Servings:** 1

Ingredients:
- 2 cups chopped and cubed challah bread
- 1/3 cup chocolate chunks
- milk
- 1 egg
- ½ teaspoon cinnamon
- ¼ cup milk
- ¼ cup sweetened

Directions:
1. Whisk eggs with some milk.
2. Blend chocolate chunks, cinnamon and bread. Add eggs. You may use mixer to get tender mixture.
3. Pour mix in a baking form suitable for the Instant Pot.
4. Place baking form in the Instant Pot. Cook on "Manual" regime for 12 minutes.
5. Serve with nuts!

Nutrition:
- Calories: 90
- Fat: 1g
- Carbohydrates: 7g
- Protein:15g

Veggie Breakfast Quiche

No odd calories, no odd fat, just vitamins and fresh taste!

Prep time: 10 minutes | **Cooking time:** 30 minutes | **Servings:** 7

Ingredients:
- 8 eggs
- 1 ½ cup shredded cheese
- ½ cup milk
- 2 onions
- ½ cup flour
- 1 cup chopped tomatoes
- ¼ teaspoon salt
- 1 red bell pepper
- ¼ teaspoon salt
- Herbs to serve

Directions:
1. Cover Instant Pot basket with the foil.
2. Pour 1 cup of water in the Instant Pot.
3. Mix beaten eggs, salt, pepper and flour with some milk.
4. Wash and chop vegetables. Mix vegetables with cheese. Top vegie mix with seasoning.
5. Place cheese mix with vegetables in the Instant Pot.
6. Cook mix on the "High Pressure" regime for 30 minutes.
7. Serve with cheese!

Nutrition:
- Calories: 77
- Fat: 3g
- Carbohydrates: 3g
- Protein:9g

Blueberry Breakfast

Cook vitamin boom today – it's much easier than you thought!

Prep time: 2 minutes | **Cooking time:** 6 minutes | **Servings:** 1

Ingredients:
- 1/3 cup oats
- 1 cup water
- 1/3 cup almond milk
- Cinnamon to serve
- 1/3 cup Greek yogurt
- Salt to taste
- 1/3 cup blueberries
- Vanilla to taste
- 1 tablespoon chia seeds
- Sweetener to taste

Directions:
1. Add water to the Instant Pot. The same time cover oats with water and leave for 20 minutes.
2. Mix dried oats, almond milk, cinnamon, yogurt, salt, blueberries, vanilla, cumin seeds and sweetener using blender.
3. Pour mixture in the jar and cover it with the foil.
4. Place jar in the Instant Pot and set "Manual" regime.
5. Cook blueberry dessert for 6 minutes.
6. Serve with nuts!

Nutrition:
- Calories: 230
- Fat: 8g
- Carbohydrates: 36g
- Protein: 4g

Apple Pumpkin Butter

Sweet, healthy and satisfying butter – rich taste for you this morning!

Prep time: 5 minutes | **Cooking time:** 15 minutes | **Servings:** 4

Ingredients:
- 2 cans pumpkin puree
- Salt to taste
- 1 tablespoon pumpkin pie spice
- 1 bottle apple cider
- 3 apples
- ½ cup honey
- 1 cup sugar

Directions:
1. Wash and chop apples.
2. Mix sugar with honey, cider and salt with spices. Add puree to the sugar mix.
3. Cover apple slices with the puree mix.
4. Cook apples in the Instant Pot for 10 minutes on "Manual" regime.
5. Leave apples to rest in the Instant Pot for 15 minutes more for the natural release of pressure.
6. Serve apples with powdered sugar.

Nutrition:
- Calories: 15g
- Fat: 0g
- Carbohydrates: 10g
- Protein: 0g

Almond Yogurt with Peaches

Have you ever tried natural homemade yogurt with almond taste? It's time to do that!

Prep time: 15 minutes | **Cooking time:** 9 hours | **Servings:** 4

Ingredients:
- 2 peaches
- 4 cups almond milk
- 1 teaspoon vanilla
- 1/3 cup raw cashews
- powder
- 1 tablespoon maple syrup
- 2 tablespoons arrowroot powder
- ¼ cup plain almond yogurt
- ¼ teaspoon agar

Directions:
1. Blend almond milk, cashews, arrow powder and agar powder. Pour milky mixture in the Instant Pot and set "Saute" function.
2. Warm up mix for 5 minutes. Remove yogurt from the pressure cooker and put in the fridge to cool down.
3. Mix yogurt with vanilla and maple syrup.
4. Place peach slices in the blender and make fruit puree.
5. Add fruit puree to the yogurt.
6. Pour mix in the jars for the Instant Pot and add one cup of water.
7. Select "Yogurt" regime and cook for 7 hours. Serve with nuts!

Nutrition:
- Calories: 180
- Fat: 11g
- Carbohydrates: 18g
- Protein: 5g

Orange Marmalade

Sweets can make the mood perfect. Marmalade is much better – just try it for the breakfast with crispy toast and get real pleasure!

Prep time: 10 minutes | **Cooking time:** 15 minutes | **Servings:** 7

Ingredients:
- 4 oranges
- 1 ½ weight of fruit sugar
- 1 lemon juice

Directions:
1. Wash and clean oranges. Cut into the slices. You may use blender to get pureed consistence.
2. Place oranges in the Instant Pot, cover with cup of water and lemon juice.
3. Set "Manual" regime and cook for 15 minutes.
4. Add sugar to the cooked oranges. Change regime on "Saute" and cook oranges in the Instant Pot for 5 minutes.
5. Serve in Jars with toasts!

Nutrition:
- Calories: 49
- Fat: 0g
- Carbohydrates: 13g
- Protein: 1g

Spanish Tortilla

Add more passion, taste and colors to the grey weekdays – just try Spanish tortilla!

Prep time: 10 minutes | **Cooking time:** 20 minutes | **Servings:** 12

Ingredients:
- 18 eggs
- 5 cups water
- 12oz French Fries
- 12oz Grated Cheese
- 3 tablespoons melted butter
- 3 teaspoons tomato paste
- 1 cup Spanish onions
- 1 cup milk
- 1 teaspoon sea salt
- 6 tablespoons Bisquick
- 1 teaspoon Fox Point Seasoning
- 3 garlic cloves

Directions:
1. Wash and slice potatoes. You may slice them into cubes or stripes.
2. Mix beaten eggs with seasoning.
3. Blend baking mix with milk and tomato paste.
4. Add beaten eggs to the baking mix.
5. Chop onions with garlic and add to the egg mix.
6. Place potatoes in the Instant Pot, pour egg mix on top and cover with cheese.
7. Set "High Pressure" regime and cook dish for 15 minutes.
8. Leave cooked tortilla for 10 minutes for the natural release of pressure.
9. Serve with grated cheese.

Nutrition:
- Calories: 167
- Fat: 3.5g
- Carbohydrates: 25g
- Protein: 9.6g

Banana Bread

Bananas are full of vitamins and can leave you satisfied for a long time – why not make them main dish this morning, especially baked?

Prep time: 5 minutes | **Cooking time:** 50 minutes | **Servings:** 12

Ingredients:
- 12 bananas
- 3 teaspoons baking powder
- 3 sticks soft butter
- 6 cups flour
- 3 tablespoons vanilla
- 1 cup sugar
- 9 eggs

Directions:
1. Cut and mash bananas.
2. Mix butter, beaten eggs, vanilla and baking powder.
3. Add sugar and flour to the banana mix.
4. Pour banana mix in the Instant Pot and add 1 cup of water.
5. Set "Manual" regime and cook for 50 minutes. If you like crispy desserts more, you may place banana bread in the oven after the Instant Pot. In this case, you need to preheat oven up to 400oF and bake bread for 10 minutes.
6. Quickly remove banana bread of the Instant Pot and serve!

Nutrition:
- Calories: 392
- Fat: 19g
- Carbohydrates: 45g
- Protein:5g

Crustless Quiche

Why not to enjoy delicious and soft meat in the morning? We are sure – this is perfect start of the day!

Prep time: 10 minutes | **Cooking time:** 30 minutes | **Servings:** 12

Ingredients:
- 18 eggs
- 3 cups shredded cheese
- 1 cup milk
- 6 green onions
- 1 teaspoon salt
- 1 cup sliced ham
- 1 teaspoon pepper
- 3 cups ground sausage
- 12 slices bacon

Directions:
1. Pour one cup of water in the Instant Pot.
2. Whisk eggs with milk and salt, pepper. Use blender to get tender mixture.
3. Cut bacon, ham and green onions. Add some cheese.
4. Prepare pan for the Instant Pot and cover with the foil.
5. Mix eggs mixture with a meat mix and place in the Instant Pot.
6. Select "High Pressure" regime and cook for 30 minutes.
7. Leave meat quiche in the Instant Pot and let the pressure release naturally for 10 minutes.
8. Serve with fresh herbs!

Nutrition:
- Calories: 368
- Fat: 24g
- Carbohydrates: 10g
- Protein:30g

Apple Porridge

Make this morning special – try apple porridge in the Instant Pot and open new perspectives!

Prep time: 5 minutes | **Cooking time:** 25 minutes | **Servings:** 6

Ingredients:
- 8 apples
- Salt to taste
- 2 squash
- ½ teaspoon ginger
- 1 cup bone broth
- 1 teaspoon cinnamon
- 6 tablespoons elm
- 4 tablespoons maple syrup
- 4 tablespoons gelatin

Directions:
1. Wash and cut apples.
2. Mix delicate squash with apple chunks.
3. Mix bone broth with ginger and salt.
4. Add a bone mixture to the apples. Use spoon to mix and leave apples in the broth for 5 minutes.
5. Set "Manual" regime and cook porridge for 8 minutes.
6. Leave cooked dish to rest in the Instant Pot for 10 minutes after the cooking for the natural release of pressure.
7. Pour porridge in the blender and blend with elm, syrup and gelatin.
8. Serve with nuts!

Nutrition:
- Calories: 298
- Fat: 6g
- Carbohydrates: 49g
- Protein:7g

Blueberry Jam

Make morning taste extra delicious, sweet and be healthy the same time – make crispy toasts with blueberry jam!

Prep time: 5 minutes | **Cooking time:** 10 minutes | **Servings**: 4

Ingredients:
- 2 pounds blueberries
- 1 pound honey

Directions:
1. Coat blueberries with honey. Place blueberry mix in the blender and crush berries in pureed mix.
2. Pour berry mix in the Instant Pot.
3. Select "Keep Warm" regime.
4. Cook for 2 minutes.
5. Change regime on "Saute Function".
6. Cook for 3 minutes.
7. Leave blueberries in the Instant Pot and let the pressure release naturally for 10 minutes.
8. Serve in jars with toasts!

Nutrition:
- Calories: 36
- Fat: 0g
- Carbohydrates: 8g
- Protein:1g

Buckwheat Porridge

Vegan, easy, delicious and full of minerals – sounds like a perfect breakfast!

Prep time: 4 minutes | **Cooking time:** 6 minutes | **Servings:** 3

Ingredients:

- 1 cup buckwheat groats
- Nuts to serve
- 3 cups rice milk
- ½ teaspoon vanilla
- 1 banana
- 1 teaspoon cinnamon
- ¼ cup raisins

Directions:

1. Pour buckwheat in the Instant Pot.
2. Mix mashed bananas with raisins, milk, cinnamon and vanilla.
3. Add vanilla mix to the Instant Pot.
4. Cook porridge on "Manual" regime for 6 minutes.
5. Leave porridge in the Instant Pot and let the pressure release naturally for 20 minutes.
6. Serve porridge with nuts!

Nutrition:

- Calories:117
- Fat: 1.5g
- Carbohydrates: 22g
- Protein:4g

Coffeecake Oatmeal

Oatmeal can become your favorite breakfast dish – try and you will fall in love with it!

Prep time: 5 minutes | **Cooking time:** 5 minutes | **Servings:** 7

Ingredients:

- 4 ½ cups water
- 1 teaspoon vanilla
- 1 ½ cups oats
- 1 teaspoon allspice
- 1 ½ cups pumpkin puree
- 2 teaspoons cinnamon
- 1 tablespoon cinnamon
- ½ cup coconut sugar
- ¼ cup pecans

Directions:

1. Mix oats, vanilla, pumpkin puree, cinnamon and allspice. In the case, you like extra tender taste – use blender to crush ingredients and get light pureed consistence.
2. Pour water in the Instant Pot and add mixed ingredients.
3. Select "Manual" regime and cook oatmeal for 3 minutes.
4. Blend some sugar with pecans and cinnamon.
5. Pour cinnamon mix on the oatmeal and serve!

Nutrition:

- Calories: 88
- Fat: 3g
- Carbohydrates: 14g
- Protein:1.5g

Berries Cake with Cream

Make a celebration to honor yourself right this morning!

Prep time: 5 minutes   **Cooking time:** 10 minutes   **Servings:** 12

Ingredients:
- 10 eggs
- 3 teaspoons powdered sugar
- ½ cup sugar
- 2 teaspoons milk
- 4 tablespoons butter
- 1 teaspoon vanilla extract
- 1 cup ricotta cheese
- ½ cup yogurt
- 2 cups vanilla yogurt
- 1 cup Berry compote
- 4 teaspoons vanilla extract
- Yogurt glaze
- 2 cups wheat pastry
- 4 teaspoons baking powder
- 1 teaspoon salt

Directions:
1. Warm up some berry compote.
2. Prepare 6 baking cups for the Instant Pot. It is better to use round shape baking forms.
3. Mix beaten eggs with some cheese, vanilla, butter and yogurt.
4. Mix flour with salt and baking powder.
5. Mix flour mix with egg mixture.
6. Pour compote on a batter.
7. Place batter in the cups and add 1 cup of water to the Instant Pot.
8. Select "High Pressure" regime and cook for 25 minutes.
9. Mix some yogurt, vanilla, powdered sugar and milk.
10. Cover cooked cake with yogurt and serve!

Nutrition:
- Calories: 230
- Fat: 12g
- Carbohydrates: 30g
- Protein:3g

Korean Style Eggs

Try eggs with seasoning and scallions – more vitamins and less calories are easy to get with Instant Pot!

Prep time: 5 minutes   **Cooking time:** 5 minutes   **Servings:** 1

Ingredients:
- 1 egg
- Pinch of garlic
- Salt to taste
- Pepper to taste
- 1/3 cup water
- Pinch of sesame seeds
- Chopped scallions

Directions:
1. Whisk egg with water. Use fork or blender to mix ingredients well.
2. Mix scallions, sesame seeds, pepper and salt. Add garlic to the scallions mix.
3. Place an egg in the cup, add sesame mix and put in the Instant Pot. Top an egg with a scallions mix.
4. Cook an egg for 5 minutes on "High Pressure" regime.

Nutrition:
- Calories: 48
- Fat: 3g
- Carbohydrates: 4g
- Protein:0g

Eggs de Provence

Do you like France! Fell yourself somewhere in Paris this morning, trying traditional egg receipt!

Prep time: 5 minutes

Cooking time: 20 minutes
Servings: 6

Ingredients:
- 6 eggs
- 1/8 teaspoon sea salt
- 1 chopped onion
- 1 teaspoon Herbs de Provence
- 1 cup ham
- 1 cup cheddar cheese
- ½ cup heavy creams
- 1 cup kale leaves

Directions:
1. Whisk eggs with some creams.
2. Mix kale leaves, cheese, ham, herbs and chopped onion with sea salt. Use blender to get well-mixed sauce.
3. Mix kale sauce with eggs.
4. Pour eggs in cups and place in the Instant Pot.
5. Cook on "High Pressure" regime for 20 minutes.
6. Serve!

Nutrition:
- Calories: 301
- Fat: 28g
- Carbohydrates: 0g
- Protein:12g

Poached Eggs

Eggs – the easiest breakfast dish we all well know, but even eggs can surprise you!

Prep time: 10 minutes

Cooking time: 15 minutes

Servings: 2

Ingredients:
- 1 cup cubed potatoes
- 1 teaspoon taco seasoning
- 2 eggs
- 1 tablespoon chopped cilantro
- 1 tablespoon bacon
- ½ cup diced onion
- 1 jalapeno

Directions:
1. Pour water (1 cup) in the Instant Pot.
2. Place potatoes in a bowl in the Instant Pot and cook on "High Pressure" regime for 2 minutes.
3. Mix chopped onions, bacon, jalapeno and cilantro.
4. Set potatoes aside.
5. Add some butter to the Instant Pot and change regime on "Saute" to melt butter.
6. Add a bacon, potatoes and cilantro with pepper and seasoning to the Instant Pot.
7. Beat eggs and add to the Instant Pot.
8. Select "High Pressure" regime and cook for 1 minute.
9. Cover dish with the seasoning and serve!

Nutrition:
- Calories: 71
- Fat: 4g
- Carbohydrates: 0g
- Protein:6g

Breakfast Quinoa

Healthy, easy, quick, light and delicious – breakfast for those who care about themselves!

Prep time: 5 minutes | **Cooking time:** 10 minutes | **Servings:** 15

Ingredients:

- 3 cups quinoa
- Salt to taste
- 5 cups water

- 2 teaspoons cinnamon
- 5 tablespoons maple syrup

- 2 teaspoons vanilla

Directions:

1. Mix quinoa, some water, maple syrup, cinnamon, salt and vanilla. Pour mix in the bowl and use mixer to whisk it well. The same time you need to find suitable baking form for the Instant Pot. Pour mix in a baking form.
2. Place mix in the Instant Pot.
3. Cook on "High Pressure" regime for 1 minute.
4. Leave dish in the Instant Pot and let the pressure release naturally for 10 minutes.
5. Serve with fresh berries and almonds!

Nutrition:

- Calories: 400
- Fat: 2g

- Carbohydrates: 22g
- Protein: 7g

Coconut Yogurt

Feel paradise melting on the plate trying this coconut yogurt receipt!

Prep time: 15 minutes | **Cooking time:** 8 hours | **Servings:** 2

Ingredients:

- 2 cans coconut cream
- 3 half pint jars

- 1 package yogurt starter
- 1 tablespoon gelatin

Directions:

1. Place some coconut cream in the Instant Pot and select "Yogurt" regime.
2. Cook yogurt for 5 minutes on the "Yogurt" regime. In 5 minutes place yogurt in the fridge to cool it down.
3. Mix starter with gelatin.
4. Mix yogurt starter with cream.
5. Place yogurt in the Instant Pot and cook for 8 hours on the "Yogurt" regime.
6. Serve cooled down in jars!

Nutrition:

- Calories: 140
- Fat: 0g

- Carbohydrates: 30g
- Protein:4g

Egg Muffins

Easy breakfast in Instant Pot can be not only extra healthy, but also so delicious, that you will have a willing to take it with you to the workplace!

Prep time: 5 minutes | **Cooking time:** 8 minutes | **Servings:** 4

Ingredients:
- 4 eggs
- 4 slices bacon
- ¼ teaspoon lemon pepper seasoning
- 1 onion
- 4 tablespoons cheddar

Directions:
1. Pour 1 cup of water in the Instant Pot.
2. Beat eggs and mix with lemon pepper. Use blender to get tender consistence.
3. Mix chopped onions and a bacon with some cheddar cheese.
4. Mix eggs with a bacon.
5. Place muffins in the special forms and put in the Instant Pot.
6. Cook on "High Pressure" regime for 8 minutes.
7. Serve with fresh herbs!

Nutrition:
- Calories: 115
- Fat: 1g
- Carbohydrates: 22g
- Protein: 5g

Mini Omelets

Feels like France! Try soft and tender omelets in Air Fryer!

Prep time: 2 minutes | **Cooking time:** 10 minutes | **Servings:** 6

Ingredients:

- 6 eggs
- Salt to taste
- 2 cups milk
- 6 slices bacon

Directions:
1. Whisk eggs with milk and add salt. Use mixer on the second speed to get as tender consistence as needed.
2. Cut bacon on slices.
3. Place bacon in the baking forms.
4. Pour whisked eggs on top of the bacon slices.
5. Cook omelets on "Manual" regime in the Instant Pot for 10 minutes.
6. Serve with cherry tomatoes!

Nutrition:
- Calories:67
- Fat: 4g
- Carbohydrates: 0g
- Protein:6g

Giant Pancake

Few minutes and giant pancake for the breakfast is ready – cooking with Instant Pot is always super easy!

Prep time: 5 minutes | **Cooking time:** 45 minutes | **Servings:** 16

Ingredients:

- 4 cups flour
- Maple syrup for serving
- ½ cup sugar
- ½ cup butter
- 4 teaspoons baking powder
- 2 cups milk
- 2 teaspoons baking soda
- 4 eggs
- 2 teaspoons salt

Directions:

1. Mix beaten eggs with sugar in a bowl. Use mixer on the second speed to get tender mix. Add Baking soda, salt and baking powder to the mix. Use mixer one more time.
2. Add flour to the mix and use mixer on the third speed.
3. Place butter in the Instant Pot.
4. Melt butter in the Instant Pot for 4 minutes on the "Sauté" regime.
5. Place batter in the Instant Pot and cook for 45 minutes on "High Pressure" regime.
6. Place cake on a plate and top with maple syrup.

Nutrition:

- Calories: 300
- Fat: 8g
- Carbohydrates: 54g
- Protein:7g

Sausage Gravy

One of the most delicious and satisfying dishes for the breakfast – meaty, creamy and covered with fresh herbs – you will like it for sure!

Prep time: 5 minutes | **Cooking time:** 25 minutes | **Servings:** 16

Ingredients:

- 2 tablespoons olive oil
- Black peppercorns to taste
- 2 pounds Italian sausages
- Sea salt to taste
- 2 cups chopped onions
- 2 teaspoons green chili
- 2 cups chopped mushrooms
- 1 cup flour
- 2 jalapeno peppers
- 1 cup heavy creams
- 1 stick butter
- 6 cups milk
- 2 bell peppers

Directions:

1. Pour olive oil in the Instant Pot and turn on "Sauté" regime. Warm up olive oil for 3 minutes.
2. Wash and cut peppers.
3. Wash and peel mushrooms, cut them into the small slices.
4. Cut sausages into slices.
5. Place sausages in the Instant Pot and cook for 4 minutes on "Sauté" regime.
6. Add chopped onions and cook for 5 minutes on "Sauté" regime in Instant Pot.
7. Add chopped mushrooms and cook for 10 minutes on "Sauté" regime.
8. Pour milk in the Instant Pot and add chopped peppers.
9. Add flour and cream to the Instant Pot. Cook for 5 minutes more on "High Pressure" regime. Add peppercorns and serve hot!

Nutrition:

- Calories: 600
- Fat: 64g
- Carbohydrates: 30g
- Protein:15g

Chocolate Oatmeal

Tender, sweet, delicious and satisfying – chocolate oatmeal is the best breakfast you could ever imagine!

Prep time: 5 minutes | **Cooking time:** 15 minutes | **Servings:** 1

Ingredients:
- 2 cups oatmeal
- Chocolate chips to serve
- 6 cups water
- 10oz bag cherries
- 1 cup milk
- 1 teaspoon vanilla
- 2 tablespoons cocoa powder
- 1 teaspoon cinnamon

Directions:
1. Mix cinnamon with cocoa powder and vanilla.
2. Pour water in the Instant Pot. Turn on "Sauté" regime and warm up water for 3 minutes.
3. Place oatmeal in the Instant Pot.
4. Add cocoa powder mix in the Instant Pot and mix well. Cook oatmeal for 4 minutes on "Sauté" regime.
5. Add cherries and milk to cinnamon and cook for 6 minutes on "High Pressure" regime.
6. Top oatmeal with chips and serve!

Nutrition:
- Calories: 175
- Fat: 9g
- Carbohydrates: 22g
- Protein: 3g

Cranberry Toasts with Mozzarella

Fresh berries with delicious and light cheese – satisfying breakfast!

Prep time: 5 minutes | **Cooking time:** 30 minutes | **Servings:** 5

Ingredients:
- 1 cup cranberries
- ¼ teaspoon salt
- 1 cup shredded Mozzarella cheese
- ¼ cup orange juice
- ¼ teaspoon cinnamon
- ½ cup sugar
- 4 tablespoons butter
- 1 loaf Challah bread
- ½ cup granulated sugar
- ¼ teaspoon sea salt
- 2 cups whole milk
- 1 teaspoon vanilla extract
- 3 eggs
- 1 orange zest

Directions:
1. Mix granulated sugar, cranberries, cinnamon, salt and orange juice.
2. Pour mix on the frying pan and warm up for 3 minutes.
3. Place butter in the Instant Pot and melt on the "Sauté" regime for 4 minutes.
4. Remove melted butter from the Instant Pot and mix with eggs, vanilla, sea salt and orange zest. Add milk to the mix and use blender to whisk ingredients.
5. Pour milk mix on the frying pan over cranberries and fry for 3 minutes more.
6. Pour water in the Instant Pot.
7. Place cranberry mix in the Instant Pot and add cheese.
8. Cook toasts on "High Pressure" regime for 25 minutes.
9. Remove toast from the Instant Pot using quick pressure release function and serve hot!

Nutrition:
- Calories: 218
- Fat: 7g
- Carbohydrates: 26g
- Protein: 13g

Yogurt with Fruits

Natural yogurt with fruits is easy to cook with Instant Pot, saving satisfying taste and juicy texture!

Prep time: 45 minutes | **Cooking time:** 8 hours | **Servings:** 4

Ingredients:

- 1 gallon milk
- 2 cups fruits
- ½ cup Greek yogurt
- 2 tablespoons vanilla bean paste
- 1 cup sugar

Directions:
1. Pour milk in the Instant Pot.
2. Set "Yogurt" regime and cook milk for 45 minutes in the Instant Pot.
3. Remove milk from the Instant Pot and place it in the fridge to cool down for 15 minutes.
4. Mix yogurt with vanilla paste and sugar. Add Greek yogurt to the mix.
5. Cook yogurt in the Instant Pot for 8 hours.
6. Pour yogurt in jars and place in the fridge.
7. Serve yogurt cold!

Nutrition:
- Calories: 160
- Fat: 4g
- Carbohydrates: 4g
- Protein:4g

Triple Berry Pancake Sauce

This super light and super full of vitamins sauce will be perfect addition to any breakfast toast and any pancake receipt!

Prep time: 5 minutes | **Cooking time:** 10 minutes | **Servings:** 3

Ingredients:
- 2 cups rhubarb
- 1 tablespoon water
- 1 cup blueberries
- 1 tablespoon cornstarch
- 1 cup strawberries
- 2 tablespoons lemon juice
- 1 cup raspberries
- ¾ cup sugar

Directions:
1. Mix rhubarb, raspberries and sugar using blender.
2. Add lemon juice to the raspberry mix and add lemon juice. Use blender one more time to get light and tender mixture.
3. Pour mix in the Instant Pot and cook on "High Pressure" regime for 3 minutes.
4. Leave raspberry mix in the Instant Pot. Let pressure release naturally for 10 minutes.
5. Mix water with cornstarch and add to the pressure cooker.
6. In a separate bowl mix strawberries and blueberries using blender.
7. Add berry mix to the Instant Pot.
8. Serve with fresh mint leaves!

Nutrition:
- Calories: 390
- Fat: 3g
- Carbohydrates: 150g
- Protein:5g

Savory Mushroom Thyme Oatmeal

Satisfying, healthy and tender oatmeal with the mushroom slices will be super delicious breakfast!

Prep time: 5 minutes | **Cooking time:** 25 minutes | **Servings:** 8

Ingredients:

- 4 tablespoons butter
- Salt to taste
- Pepper to taste
- 1 onion
- 1 cup smoked gouda
- 4 garlic cloves
- 16oz mushrooms
- 2 cups cut oats
- 4 tablespoons olive oil
- 2 14-ounce cans chicken broth
- ½ teaspoon salt
- 1 cup water
- 6 springs thyme

Directions:

1. Place butter in the Instant Pot. Set "Sauté" regime and melt it for 3 minutes.
2. Wash and chop onions. Place onions in the pressure cooker. Cook on the same regime for 3 minutes to get them golden color.
3. Add garlic to the Instant Pot. Cook on "Sauté" regime for 1 minute.
4. Place oats in the Instant Pot and cook on the same regime for 1 minute.
5. Mix broth, water, salt and thyme. Pour broth mix in the Instant Pot. Cook on "High Pressure" regime for 10 minutes.
6. Cut mushrooms on the small slices and place on the frying pan. Add oil to the frying pan. Cook for 3 minutes until mushrooms slices turn gold.
7. Add mushrooms to the Instant Pot and cook for 10 minutes more on "High Pressure" regime.
8. Serve with seasoning!

Nutrition:

- Calories: 307
- Fat: 15g
- Carbohydrates: 30g
- Protein: 14

Tomato Quiche with Spinach

Vegetable quiche with cheese on top and juicy filling – this breakfast will give you energy for the full day!

Prep time: 5 minutes | **Cooking time:** 20 minutes | **Servings:** 12

Ingredients:

- 24 eggs
- ½ cup Parmesan cheese
- 1 cup milk
- 8 tomato slices
- 1 teaspoon salt
- 6 green onions
- ½ teaspoon pepper
- 2 cups diced tomato
- 6 cups baby spinach

Directions:

1. Place baking form in the Instant Pot.
2. Pour water in the Instant Pot.
3. Mix eggs, salt and pepper using a fork. Add milk to egg mixture and use mixer on the second speed.
4. Wash and chop tomatoes with the spinach.
5. Wash and chop onions.
6. Add tomatoes, onions and spinach to egg mixture. Top mixture with Parmesan cheese.
7. Pour vegetable mix in the baking form and cook on "High Pressure" regime for 20 minutes.
8. Let the pressure release naturally. (10 minutes).

Nutrition:

- Calories: 460
- Fat: 34g
- Carbohydrates: 24g
- Protein:16g

Pumpkin Steel Cut Oats

Fresh pumpkin will add autumn motives to the grey weekdays and cut oats will make you feel light and satisfying the same time!

Prep time: 10 minutes | **Cooking time:** 20 minutes | **Servings:** 8

Ingredients:

- 1 tablespoons butter
- 1/3 teaspoon salt
- 1 cups cut oats

- 1 teaspoons pumpkin pie spice
- 3 cups water
- 2 teaspoons cinnamon

- 1 cups pumpkin puree
- 1/2 cup maple syrup
- 1 tablespoon honey
- 1 tablespoon cheese

Directions:

1. Place butter in the Instant Pot. Set "Sauté" regime. Melt butter in the Instant Pot for 3 minutes. You should get light and tender liquid on the bottom of your pressure cooker – it is your base for the further cooking.
2. Add cut oats to the Instant Pot and cook on "Sauté" regime for 3 minutes. Wait until they turn soft. Add honey and mix well.
3. Pour water in the Instant Pot and add puree with maple syrup.
4. Add spice with cinnamon and pie spice. Cook mix in the Instant Pot for 10 minutes on "High Pressure" regime. Add cheese and wait until it starts melting.
5. Let the pressure release naturally for 10 minutes.
6. Serve oats with additional maple syrup.

Nutrition:

- Calories: 404
- Fat: 6g

- Carbohydrates: 70g
- Protein:20g

Cinnamon Raisin Bread

Super sweet bread with the crispy dough and satisfying taste!

Prep time: 5 minutes | **Cooking time:** 25 minutes | **Servings:** 1 loaf

Ingredients:

- 4 tablespoons butter
- ½ cup raisins
- ½ cup brown sugar
- 7 slices cinnamon bread
- 3 cups milk
- ¼ teaspoon salt
- 3 eggs
- ½ teaspoon cinnamon
- 1 teaspoon vanilla extract
- 1 cup caramel pecan sauce

Directions:

1. Place butter in the Instant Pot and turn on "Sauté" regime. Melt butter in the Instant Pot for 3 minutes.
2. Remove butter from the pressure cooker and mix with brown sugar, milk, eggs and cinnamon using blender.
3. Add salt and vanilla to egg mixture and mix with the fork.
4. Cut bread into cubes.
5. Add bread and raisins to egg mixture. Leave for 20 minutes to rest on the table.
6. Cover Instant Pot with the foil.
7. Prepare baking forms.
8. Pour egg mixture in the baking forms.
9. Place baking forms in the Instant Pot and cook on "High Pressure" regime for 20 minutes.
10. Do a quick release.
11. Remove mixture from the pressure cooker.
12. Preheat oven up to 350oF.
13. Place bread in the oven and bake for 10 minutes.
14. Top bread with caramel sauce and serve hot!

Nutrition:

- Calories: 360
- Fat: 2g
- Carbohydrates: 70g
- Protein:10g

Meat Lovers Quiche

Meat, cheese and juicy, tender vegetables – this quiche will be exactly something you will like!

Prep time: 10 minutes | **Cooking time:** 30 minutes | **Servings:** 16

Ingredients:
- 24 eggs
- 4 cups cheese
- 2 cups milk
- 8 onions
- 1 teaspoon salt
- 1 cup ham
- 1 teaspoon pepper
- 2 cups ground sausage
- 8 slices bacon
- 1/3 cup butter

Directions:
1. Place baking form in the Instant Pot. The same time place butter in the cup and melt up for 1 minute in microwave.
2. Pour water in the pressure cooker. Add melted butter and mix with water.
3. Mix eggs, salt and pepper using a fork.
4. Add milk to egg mixture and mix with the mixer on the second speed.
5. Mix sausages, bacon, chopped onions, ham and cheese.
6. Add meat mix to the baking form in the Instant Pot. Cover meat mix with egg mixture.
7. Cook quiche in the pressure cooker for 30 minutes on "High Pressure" regime.
8. Let the pressure release naturally (10 minutes).
9. Cover quiche with cheese and serve hot!

Nutrition:
- Calories: 150
- Fat: 12g
- Carbohydrates: 32g
- Protein: 9g

Apple Cherry Risotto

Light rice soup with the tender fruits and delicious smell will be both satisfying and extraordinary breakfast!

Prep time: 5 minutes | **Cooking time:** 10 minutes | **Servings:** 1

Ingredients:
- 2 tablespoons butter
- ½ cup cherries
- 1 ½ cups adobo rice
- 3 cups milk
- 2 apples
- 1 cup apple juice
- 1 ½ teaspoons cinnamon
- ½ cup brown sugar
- ¼ teaspoon salt

Directions:
1. Place butter in the Instant Pot. Set "Sauté" regime and melt butter for 3 minutes.
2. Add rice to some melted butter in the Instant Pot and cook for 5 minutes on "Sauté" regime.
3. Mix apples with sugar, cinnamon and salt. Place mix in the Instant Pot.
4. Add water and milk to the pressure cooker.
5. Cook mix for 10 minutes on "High Pressure" regime.
6. Do a quick pressure release and add cherries.
7. Serve with almonds and milk!

Nutrition:
- Calories: 220
- Fat: 6g
- Carbohydrates: 33g
- Protein: 8g

Strawberries and Cream Cut Oats

Beautiful, satisfying, tender and super delicious breakfast in cups – only 10 minutes and sweet cream dish is ready!

Prep time: 5 minutes | **Cooking time:** 10 minutes | **Servings:** 10

Ingredients:
- 10 tablespoon butter
- 10 ½ cups strawberries
- 10 cup cut oats
- 5 cup chia seeds
- 10 cups water
- 5 teaspoon salt
- 5 cup cream
- 15 tablespoons brown sugar
- ½ cup cream

Directions:
1. Place butter in the Instant Pot. Set "Sauté" regime and melt butter for 3 minutes. You should get tender and soft liquid on the bottom of the pressure cooker. It is your base for the cooking.
2. Add oats and cook on the same regime for 3 minutes. It should turn sift and tender.
3. Pour water in the Instant Pot. Add creams to water and mix well.
4. Mix creams with sugar and add to the pressure cooker.
5. Cook cut oats for 10 minutes on "High Pressure" regime.
6. Add chia seeds and strawberries. Do a quick pressure release.
7. Serve hot!

Nutrition:
- Calories: 190
- Fat: 4g
- Carbohydrates: 32g
- Protein: 5g

Lemon Blueberry Cut Oats

Fresh lemon with the tender smell and juicy berries full of vitamins will make morning cut oats special!

Prep time: 5 minutes | **Cooking time:** 20 minutes | **Servings:** 2

Ingredients:
- 1/3 tablespoons soft butter
- 1/6 cup chia seeds
- 1/2 cups cut oats
- 1/2 cups blueberries
- 2 cups water
- 1/6 teaspoon salt
- 1/2 cups half and half
- 1/4 tablespoons lemon zest
- 1 tablespoon sugar

Directions:
1. Place butter in the Instant Pot and melt on "Sauté" regime for 3 minutes. You should melt butter to get light and tender base for baking.
2. Place oats in the Instant Pot and wait until they turn brown and soft. It will take you around 4 minutes. (Regime – "Sauté").
3. Mix half and half with sugar, zest and salt. Use blender to get tender mix.
4. Pour water in the pressure cooker. Add half and half mix to the Instant Pot.
5. Cook cut oats in the pressure cooker for 10 minutes on "High Pressure" regime.
6. Do a quick pressure release and add seeds with blueberries.
7. Serve warm!

Nutrition:
- Calories: 650
- Fat: 26g
- Carbohydrates: 82g
- Protein:2g

Cake Oatmeal

Caramelized, sweet, tender and satisfying oatmeal with the sweet baked carrot – breakfast you won't forget!

Prep time: 5 minutes | **Cooking time**: 15 minutes | **Servings**: 1

Ingredients:

- 1/6 tablespoon butter
- 1/8 cup chia seeds
- 1/6 cup cut oats
- 1/7 cup raisins
- 1/2 cups water
- 1/8 teaspoon salt
- 1/6 cup grated carrots
- 1/6 teaspoon pumpkin pie spice
- 1/2 tablespoons maple syrup
- 1/4 teaspoons cinnamon

Directions:

1. Place butter in the Instant Pot and melt for 3 minutes on the "Sauté" regime. Melt butter to get tender and soft sauce.
2. Add carrots with cut oats in the Instant Pot and cook for 3 minutes more on the "Sauté" regime. It will be your base for the further cooking process.
3. Pour water in the pressure cooker. Mix ingredients with water to get porridge texture.
4. Mix maple syrup, cinnamon, pumpkin pie spice salt and add to the pressure cooker.
5. Cook oatmeal for 10 minutes on the "High Pressure" regime.
6. Let the pressure release naturally (10 minutes).
7. Add raisins and seeds to the mix and leave for 10 minutes to rest.
8. Serve warm!

Nutrition:

- Calories: 740
- Fat: 42g
- Carbohydrates: 130g
- Protein:3g

Strawberry Cheesecake Quinoa

This taste you won't forget – just try!

Prep time: 5 minutes | **Cooking time:** 10 minutes | **Servings:** 10

Ingredients:

- 10 cups quinoa
- 5 cup Greek yogurt
- 20 cups water
- 20 cups slices strawberries
- 20 tablespoons honey
- 4 teaspoon pumpkin pie spice
- 5 teaspoon vanilla

Directions:

1. Mix quinoa, vanilla, honey, sweet spice, Greek yogurt and strawberries. First mix with fork, and after using blender.
2. Pour water in the Instant Pot. Mix ingredients with water.
3. Add quinoa to the pressure cooker and cook on "Manual" for 1 minute.
4. Let the pressure release naturally (10 minutes).
5. Serve warm!

Nutrition:

- Calories: 170
- Fat: 7g
- Carbohydrates: 23g
- Protein: 20g

Blueberry Bowl for Breakfast

Do you want to get maximum vitamins in few minutes?

Prep time: 5 minutes | **Cooking time:** 70 minutes | **Servings:** 10

Ingredients:

- 10 cups white quinoa
- Blueberries to serve
- 10 cups water
- 4 cup chopped pistachios
- 10 cinnamon sticks
- 10 cups yogurt
- 5 cup raisins
- 10 cups apple juice
- 10 tablespoons honey
- 3 cups apple

Directions:

1. Pour water in the Instant Pot. Bring water to boil on "Sauté" regime. It may take up to 5 minutes.
2. Add cinnamon with quinoa to the Instant Pot. Mix ingredients well.
3. Cook quinoa on "Manual" regime for 1 minute. Just make it tender and soft.
4. Let the pressure release naturally for 10 minutes. Prepare bowls for serving.
5. Pour quinoa in a bowl.
6. Pour apple juice with melted honey and yogurt over quinoa.
7. Add apple, raisins, pistachios and blueberries to quinoa.
8. Place bowl in a fridge for 60 minutes.
9. Serve with yogurt on top!

Nutrition:

- Calories: 150
- Fat: 2g
- Carbohydrates: 33g
- Protein:4g

Cornmeal Porridge

Add Jamaican vibes to the grey weekdays!

Prep time: 5 minutes | **Cooking time:** 20 minutes | **Servings:** 12

Ingredients:

- 12 cups water
- 2 cups caramel
- 4 cups milk
- 6 teaspoons nutmeg
- 3 cups yellow cornmeal
- 4 teaspoons vanilla extract
- 8 cinnamon sticks
- 12 pimento berries

Directions:

1. Pour water and milk in the Instant Pot and cook on "Sauté" regime for 6 minutes. You should get boiling water.
2. Mix cinnamon, berries, vanilla and nutmeg. Use blender to get tender and soft mix.
3. Add cornmeal to the Instant Pot with vanilla mix. Mix well ingredients in the pressure cooker.
4. Cook on "High Pressure" regime for 6 minutes.
5. Add caramel and serve hot!

Nutrition:

- Calories: 128
- Fat: 5g
- Carbohydrates: 14g
- Protein:10g

Cinnamon Bread with Apple

Neither pie, nor bread - try what this breakfast is!

Prep time: 5 minutes | **Cooking time:** 20 minutes | **Servings**: 2 loaves

Ingredients:
- 4 cans cinnamon rolls
- 1 cup butter
- 6 green apples
- 2 teaspoons cinnamon
- 1 cup sugar

Directions:
1. Wash and cut apples. Peel using knife and remove seeds.
2. Place butter in the Instant Pot. Melt butter for 3 minutes on "Sauté" regime. You should get soft liquid mix.
3. Mix sugar with cinnamon. Use blender to mix well.
4. Cut cinnamon rolls in pie shapes. They should be hand size and circle.
5. Place cinnamon mix with apples on top of the rolls.
6. Place rolls in the Instant Pot and cook for 20 minutes on "High Pressure" regime.
7. Do a quick pressure release.
8. Serve with powdered sugar!

Nutrition:
- Calories: 110
- Fat: 4g
- Carbohydrates: 20g
- Protein:3g

Egg Custard

This four ingredients Japanese dish will be both interesting and delicious dish!

Prep time: 5 minutes | **Cooking time:** 10 minutes | **Servings:** 1

Ingredients:
- 3 eggs
- 5 tablespoons sugar
- 1 ½ cup milk
- A pinch of salt

Directions:
1. Pour milk in the Instant Pot.
2. Add sugar and salt to the Instant Pot and cook for 5 minutes on "Low Pressure" regime.
3. Beat eggs in a bowl and whisk using blender on the second speed.
4. Add milk mix to the eggs and mix one more time using blender.
5. Prepare baking forms for the Instant Pot.
6. Pour mix in the baking forms.
7. Cook eggs for 1 minute on the "Low Pressure" regime.
8. Let the pressure release naturally (10 minutes).
9. Serve hot!

Nutrition:
- Calories: 60
- Fat: 3g
- Carbohydrates: 6g
- Protein:2g

Apple Bread with Caramel Icing

Taste this bread early in the morning with butter and feel the taste of paradise!

Prep time: 20 minutes | **Cooking time:** 70 minutes | **Servings:** 2 loaves

Ingredients:

- 6 cups apple slices
- 4 cups powdered sugar
- 2 cups sugar
- 2 cups heavy creams
- 4 eggs
- 4 cups brown sugar
- 2 tablespoons vanilla
- 2 sticks butter
- 2 tablespoons apple pie spice
- 2 tablespoons baking powder
- 4 cups flour

Directions:

1. Beat eggs in mixer cup and add sugar, whisk on the second speed. You should get sweet cream. Add apple pie spice and mix dough one more time.
2. Place butter in the Instant Pot and melt on "Sauté" regime. It will take you around 3 minutes. Melt butter to get liquid base for baking.
3. Add egg mix to the Instant Pot and mix with a spoon. It is better to prepare baking form suitable for your pressure cooker.
4. Wash and peel apples. Carefully remove seeds. Add apples to the Instant Pot. Before baking, wash and peel apples.
5. Mix flour with baking powder and vanilla.
6. Add flour to the Instant Pot and cook for 70 minutes on "High Pressure" regime.
7. Do a quick pressure release.
8. Serve with cream!

Nutrition:

- Calories: 110
- Fat: 1g
- Carbohydrates: 24g
- Protein: 3g

Vanilla Latte Cut Oats

Try this coffee taste dessert for the breakfast!

Prep time: 5 minutes | **Cooking time:** 10 minutes | **Servings**: 2

Ingredients:

- 1 cup water
- Grated chocolate
- 1/2 cups milk
- Whipped cream
- 1/4 cups cut oats
- 1 teaspoon vanilla extract
- 1 tablespoon sugar
- 1/6 teaspoon salt
- 1/2 teaspoons espresso powder

Directions:

1. Pot water with milk to the Instant Pot. Mix liquids and bring to boil on "Sauté" regime.
2. Mix oats with sugar and espresso powder. Use spoon to mix spices.
3. Add espresso mix to some milk in the Instant Pot. Mix well with hot milk and water.
4. Cook mix on "High Pressure" regime for 10 minutes.
5. Let the pressure release naturally (10 minutes).
6. Add sugar with vanilla extract to the pressure cooker.
7. Serve with chocolate and creams!

Nutrition:

- Calories: 146
- Fat: 1g
- Carbohydrates: 3g
- Protein:32g

Vanilla Cinnamon Quinoa for the Breakfast

This tender and soft breakfast with juicy apples will be prefect sigh for the breakfast!

Prep time: 2 minutes | **Cooking time:** 10 minutes | **Servings:** 1

Ingredients:
- 1 cup quinoa
- ¼ cup gentle sweet
- 1 ½ cup water
- ½ teaspoon vanilla
- ¼ teaspoon mineral salt
- 2 tablespoons cinnamon
- 1 sliced apple

Directions:
1. Mix apple with cinnamon and salt.
2. Pour water in the Instant Pot.
3. Add apple mix to the pressure cooker.
4. Add vanilla, sweet and quinoa to the pressure cooker.
5. Cook quinoa for 1 minute on "Manual" regime.
6. Let the pressure release naturally for 10 minutes.
7. Serve warm!

Nutrition:
- Calories: 226
- Fat: 10g
- Carbohydrates: 26g
- Protein:8g

Bread Pudding

Hot, caramelized, satisfying and sweet pudding – exactly what you need for the breakfast!

Prep time: 25 minutes | **Cooking time:** 15 minutes | **Servings:** 11

Ingredients:
- 1 bread loaf
- ¼ teaspoons sea salt
- 2 cups milk
- 1 tablespoon vanilla extract
- 4 eggs
- 2 egg yolks
- ½ cup maple syrup
- ½ cup butter

Directions:
1. Cut bread loaf into cubes.
2. Cover Instant Pot with the foil.
3. Mix eggs with yolks using fork.
4. Add milk with syrup, vanilla and salt to egg mixture and mix using mixer on the second speed.
5. Place butter in the Instant Pot and melt on the "Sauté" regime for 3 minutes.
6. Pour water in the Instant Pot.
7. Place baking form in the pressure cooker. Put bread in the baking form.
8. Add egg mix on top of the bread layer.
9. Cook pudding for 15 minutes on "Steam" regime.
10. Let the pressure release naturally (20 minutes).
11. Serve hot!

Nutrition:
- Calories: 392
- Fat: 20g
- Carbohydrates: 45g
- Protein: 5g

Burrito Casserole for Breakfast

Easy, delicious and light receipt for the breakfast – you will like it!

Prep time: 10 minutes | **Cooking time:** 20 minutes | **Servings:** 12

Ingredients:
- 8 eggs
- 1 teaspoon taco seasoning
- 4 red potatoes
- 1 teaspoon chili powder
- 1 cup onion
- 1 teaspoon mesquite seasoning
- 2 jalapeno peppers
- 1 teaspoon salt
- 12 oz ham

Directions:
1. Mix salt with seasoning and eggs using mixer on the second speed.
2. Pour water in the Instant Pot. Add egg mixture to the Instant Pot.
3. Chop onions and cube potatoes, slice ham and chop jalapeno pepper.
4. Ad vegetable mix to the Instant Pot.
5. Cook eggs with vegetables for 20 minutes on "Manual" regime.
6. Let the pressure release naturally.
7. Place egg mix on tacos and serve!

Nutrition:
- Calories: 886
- Fat: 50g
- Carbohydrates:46g
- Protein:50g

Cinnamon Oatmeal with Banana

Super easy, satisfying and delicious oatmeal for the breakfast!

Prep time: 20 minutes | **Cooking time:** 5 minutes | **Servings:** 3

Ingredients:
- 1 cup oatmeal
- 1 tablespoon brown sugar
- 1 cup milk
- 2 teaspoons cinnamon
- 1 cup water
- 2 bananas

Directions:
1. Clean and mash bananas.
2. Pour milk and water in the pressure cooker.
3. Add oatmeal in the Instant Pot.
4. Place bananas and cinnamon with sugar in the Instant Pot.
5. Cook oatmeal on "Manual" regime for 5 minutes.
6. Let the pressure release naturally (20 minutes).
7. Serve with bananas!

Nutrition:
- Calories: 250
- Fat: 7g
- Carbohydrates: 56g
- Protein: 8g

Stuffed Peaches

Juicy peaches full of vitamins – something extra fresh this morning!

Prep time: 15 minutes | **Cooking time:** 5 minutes | **Servings:** 12

Ingredients:
- 36 peaches
- A pinch of salt
- 3 cups flour
- 3 teaspoons almond extract
- 3 cups maple sugar
- 2 teaspoons cinnamon
- 12 tablespoons butter

Directions:
1. Place butter in the Instant Pot and melt for 3 minutes on "Sauté" regime. Melt butter to get tender butter base or baking.
2. Slice peaches and remove seeds. Wash and peel peaches before.
3. Remove butter from the Instant Pot and mix with sugar, cinnamon, extract and flour.
4. Place sugar mix in the peaches. Make it look like peaches filling.
5. Pour water in the Instant Pot.
6. Place peaches in the pressure cooker and cook for 5 minutes on "Manual" regime.
7. Let the pressure release naturally.
8. Serve with creams!

Nutrition:
- Calories: 30
- Fat: 2g
- Carbohydrates: 9g
- Protein: 2g

Maple Oatmeal

This sweet and juicy oatmeal will be one of the most delicious breakfasts in your life!

Prep time: 10 minutes | **Cooking time:** 15 minutes | **Servings:** 1

Ingredients:
- 1/4 cup cut oats
- 1 tablespoon caramel
- 1 tablespoon cherries
- 1/8 tablespoon maple syrup
- 1 cup water
- 1/8 tablespoon brown sugar
- 1/6 teaspoon vanilla
- 1/8 teaspoon salt
- 1/8 teaspoon cinnamon

Directions:
1. Mix cinnamon, salt, vanilla, brown sugar and maple syrup. Set aside. Add caramel to seasoning and get soft sauce. Warm up sauce in microwave to melt it.
2. Pour water in the Instant Pot. Warm up water on "Sauté" regime. It will take you about 4 minutes.
3. Add vanilla mix to the pressure cooker and add cut oats. Mix well with water to get porridge texture.
4. Cook oats on "High Pressure" regime for 15 minutes.
5. Let the pressure release naturally. Top with cherries.
6. Serve hot!

Nutrition:
- Calories: 310
- Fat: 4g
- Carbohydrates: 62g
- Protein: 6g

Monkey Bread

Super delicious bread slices for the real dessert lovers!

Prep time: 5 minutes | **Cooking time:** 20 minutes | **Servings:** 2

Ingredients:
- 1 can Grands biscuits
- ½ cup brown sugar
- ½ cup sugar
- ½ stick butter
- 1 ½ teaspoon cinnamon

Directions:
1. Mix sugar with cinnamon.
2. Make crumbs of the biscuits. Add brown sugar with cinnamon mix.
3. Place butter in the pressure cooker and melt on the "Sauté" regime for 3 minutes.
4. Pour water in the Instant Pot.
5. Place biscuit mix in the Instant Pot and cook on "High Pressure" regime for 20 minutes.
6. Let the pressure release naturally.
7. Serve hot!

Nutrition:
- Calories: 296
- Fat: 15g
- Carbohydrates: 38g
- Protein: 3g

Lemon Ricotta Pancake

Easy to cook and light receipt will be super satisfying breakfast!

Prep time: 10 minutes | **Cooking time:** 50 minutes | **Servings:** 2

Ingredients:
- 1 lemon zest
- 1 cup cream
- 2 cups ricotta cheese
- 3 cups milk
- 2 ½ cup pancake mix

Directions:
1. Pour water in the Instant Pot (1 ¼ cups) and warm up on the "Sauté" regime for 3 minutes.
2. Pour milk in the Instant Pot and cook on "Sauté" regime for 3 minutes.
3. Mix pancake mix with ricotta cheese and lemon zest.
4. Place pancake mix in the Instant Pot and cook on "High Pressure" regime for 30 minutes.
5. Add creams to the mix in the Instant Pot and cook for 10 minutes more on "Manual" regime.
6. Serve hot!

Nutrition:
- Calories: 142
- Fat: 10g
- Carbohydrates: 18g
- Protein: 5g

Lunch Dishes

Honey Garlic Lettuce with Chicken

Fresh and easy rolls with lettuce and chicken meat it is variant of light, easy and satisfying dinner!

Prep time: 30 minutes

Cooking time: 30 minutes

Servings: 5

Ingredients:

- 1/8 cup honey garlic sauce
- Raw honey
- 2 tablespoons coconut aminos
- Garlic cloves
- ¼ teaspoon chilies
- 1 fide jar
- 1 tablespoon minced onion
- 1/8 cup war cashews
- ½ teaspoon salt
- 1 avocado
- 1 teaspoon pepper
- 1 green onion
- 9 chicken thighs
- ½ bell pepper
- Jalapeno

Directions:

1. Cut garlic cloves and cover with some honey. Mix well.
2. Pour honey mix on the frying pan and warm up. Cook honey on low fire for 4 minutes to melt it down and make garlic cloves marinated with some honey.
3. Mix chopped onions, chilies, salt, pepper and coconut aminos.
4. Add honey garlic sauce to the onion mix.
5. Wash and cut chicken meat.
6. Cover chicken meat with the marinade. Leave chicken meat to marinade for 30 minutes.
7. Place chicken in the Instant Pot and cook on "High Pressure" regime for 7 minutes.
8. Wash and cut remaining vegetables.
9. Lay vegetables in the lettuce, add chicken meat and pour sauce on top.
10. Serve with almonds!

Nutrition:

- Calories: 326
- Fat: 15g
- Carbohydrates: 39g
- Protein:32g

Sushi Rice

Prepare sushi rice for the lunch and enjoy both sushi balls and rice pies!

Prep time: 2 minutes

Cooking time: 10 minutes

Servings: 9

Ingredients:

- ½ cup sushi rice
- 1 tablespoon rice wine vinegar
- 1 cup water

Directions:

1. Wash rice. Just pour water on a rice in the plate and leave for 15 minutes.
2. Place sushi rice in the Instant Pot and cook on "High Pressure" regime for 7 minutes.
3. Pour vinegar on sushi rice and place it in the fridge for 10 minutes.
4. Form pies or balls and cover with fresh herbs!
5. Serve!

Nutrition:

- Calories: 170
- Fat: 0g
- Carbohydrates: 37g
- Protein:3g

Vegetable Pot Stickers

What about traditional Chinese lunch? Vegetable stickers are easy to take with you and quick to cook!

| **Prep time:** 45 minutes | **Cooking time:** 20 minutes | **Servings:** 5 |

Ingredients:

- 1 tablespoon canola oil
- 1/3 teaspoon brown sugar
- 1 ounce shitake mushrooms
- 1/3 tablespoon ginger

- 1/6 tablespoon soy sauce
- 1/3 tablespoon sesame oil
- 1/3 scallion
- 1/8 cup rice vinegar
- 1/6 bunch kale

- 1/8 cup soy sauce
- 1/8 teaspoon kosher salt
- 1/6 cup water
- 5 wonton wrappers

Directions:

1. Pour canola oil on the frying pan and warm up for 4 minutes on low fire.
2. Mix scallions with soy sauce and mushrooms. Fry mushroom mix on the frying pan for 4 minutes.
3. Mix a carrot, kale and salt. Add chopped carrot to the mushrooms on the frying pan.
4. Place filling on the wonton wrapper and roll wrappers in the triangles.
5. Mix some vinegar, sesame oil, soy sauce, brown sugar and ginger.
6. Place pot stickers in the Instant Pot and cook for 10 minutes on "High Pressure" regime.
7. Add canola oil and water. Cook wrappers for 3 minutes more not changing the cooking regime.

Nutrition:

- Calories: 130
- Fat: 2g

- Carbohydrates: 23g
- Protein:5g

Sweet Pineapple Chicken

Healthy pineapple sauce with soft and delicious chicken cubes – truly perfect receipt!

| **Prep time:** 5 minutes | **Cooking time:** 7 minutes | **Servings:** 8 |

Ingredients:

- 4 chicken breasts
- 4 tablespoons water
- ½ cup ketchup
- 4 tablespoons cornstarch
- ½ cup honey

- 2 cup pineapple chunks
- 4 tablespoons soy sauce
- 2 tablespoon wine vinegar
- 4 teaspoons minced garlic
- 2 tablespoons sesame oil

- 4 teaspoons ginger
- 4 cups broccoli slaw
- ¼ teaspoon salt
- 4 cups brown rice
- 1 cup rice vinegar

Directions:

1. Mix vinegars with honey, chopped garlic, salt and ginger. Add some ketchup to sauce.
2. Cut chicken meat into cubes.
3. Marinade chicken in sauce.
4. Place chicken meat in the Instant Pot for 7 minutes, cook on "High Pressure" regime.
5. Mix broccoli slaw with sesame oil and vinegar.
6. Mix cornstarch with water and add to the prepared chicken.
7. Serve with broccoli slaw and rice!

Nutrition:

- Calories: 177
- Fat: 0.5g

- Carbohydrates: 37g
- Protein:8g

French Dip Sandwiches

Soft meat melting in your mouse with light buns and vegetables full of vitamins!

Prep time: 15 minutes | **Cooking time:** 1 hour 30 minutes | **Servings**: 12

Ingredients:

- 1/5 pounds beef roast
- 6 slices cheese
- 1 tablespoon olive oil
- Salt to taste
- 2 teaspoons kosher salt
- ¼ teaspoon garlic powder
- Pepper to taste
- 3 tablespoons butter
- ½ teaspoon garlic powder
- 6 soft rolls
- Chopped onion
- 1 bay leaf
- ½ cup of wine
- 1 can beef broth

Directions:

1. Pour olive oil in the Instant Pot.
2. Mix salt with pepper and garlic powder.
3. Cover chicken meat with seasoning.
4. Wash and chop onions.
5. Mix onions with some wine and place in the Instant Pot on "Saute" regime.
6. Add beef broth and bay leaf to the onions in the Instant Pot.
7. Mix beef broth and onions with a meat and cook in the Instant Pot for 100 minutes on "Stew" regime.
8. Mix salt, melted butter and garlic powder.
9. Cover bunches with a butter mix and make toasts.
10. Place meat in the toasts. Add cheese and remaining ingredients. Serve hot!

Nutrition:

- Calories: 629
- Fat: 20g
- Carbohydrates: 59g
- Protein:51g

Thai Chicken Lunch

Small cups with Chinese chicken and seasoning for the lunch – meat lovers will like this receipt for sure!

Prep time: 5 minutes | **Cooking time:** 10 minutes | **Servings:** 2

Ingredients:

- 2 tablespoons olive oil
- Peanuts
- 4 chicken breasts
- Bean sprouts
- 1 cup white rice
- Chopped carrots

- 2 cups broth
- Cilantro
- 1 tablespoon peanut butter
- 1 teaspoon hot sauce
- ½ cup sweet chili sauce

- 1 teaspoon lime juice
- 3 tablespoons soy sauce
- ½ tablespoon garlic
- ½ tablespoon fish sauce
- ½ tablespoon ginger

Directions:

1. Pour olive oil in the Instant Pot.
2. Cook chicken meat for 3 minutes per side on "Poultry" regime and turn off the Instant Pot.
3. Mix ginger, fish sauce, garlic, soy sauce, lime juice, chili sauce, butter and broth.
4. Make sauce of the ingredient mix using blender.
5. Cover chicken with sauce.
6. Place rice with chicken and sauce in the Instant Pot and cook for 10 minutes on "High Pressure" regime.
7. Mix cilantro, peanuts and washed, chopped vegetables.
8. Serve lunch with peanut topping and soy sauce.

Nutrition:

- Calories: 500
- Fat: 10g

- Carbohydrates: 68g
- Protein:30g

Spanish Lasagna

Real Italians know how to cook really satisfying lunch dishes – try this lasagna in Instant Pot and make sure!

Prep time: 5 minutes

Cooking time: 35 minutes

Servings: 12

Ingredients:

- 2 lbs turkey
- 10 lasagna noodles
- 2 cups cottage cheese
- 2 tablespoons garlic salt
- 2 cups Italian cheese blend
- 2 tablespoons onion powder
- 2 cans tomatoes
- 2 teaspoons pepper
- 2 tablespoons oregano
- 2 tablespoons parsley
- 6 cups spinach leaves
- 2 tablespoons thyme
- 1 cup hot sauce
- 1 chili pepper

Directions:

1. Mix cheese with tomatoes, chili pepper, hot sauce, onion powder, garlic salt and parsley, thyme with pepper.
2. Pour cheese on the noodles, cover with turkey and spinach.
3. Make one more layer on the noodle.
4. Cover noodles with some cheese.
5. Pour 3 cups of water in the Instant Pot.
6. Place lasagna in the Instant Pot. Cook lasagna for 35 minutes on "High Pressure" regime.
7. Serve with Bolognese sauce.

Nutrition:

- Calories: 415
- Fat: 35g
- Carbohydrates: 2g
- Protein:23g

Potato Salad

Salad – perfect idea for the really healthy lunch!

Prep time: 5 minutes

Cooking time: 5 minutes

Servings: 8

Ingredients:

- 6 potatoes
- Salt to taste
- Pepper to taste
- 1 ½ cup water
- 1 tablespoon mustard
- 4 eggs
- 1 tablespoon pickle juice
- ¼ cup chopped onion
- 2 tablespoons chopped parsley
- 1 cup mayonnaise

Directions:

1. Mix beaten eggs with cubed potatoes and water. Firstly, whisk eggs with water using mixer. Pour egg mixture over cubed potatoes and mix once more with a spoon.
2. Place egg mix in the Instant Pot and cook for 5 minutes on "High Pressure" regime.
3. Mix mayonnaise, parsley, chopped onion, mustard, pepper and salt using blender to get tender sauce.
4. Pour sauce on a salad and mix well.
5. Serve salad with herbs!

Nutrition:

- Calories: 357
- Fat: 20g
- Carbohydrates: 28g
- Protein:7g

Beef Gyros

Fresh vegetables with soften meat and crispy bun – this roll will make you fall in love with south cuisine!

Prep time: 15 minutes | **Cooking time:** 45 minutes | **Servings:** 15

Ingredients:
- 3 1/2lbs beef roast
- Tomatoes
- 3 onions
- Lettuce
- 6 tablespoons olive oil
- Pita bread
- 3 teaspoons garlic powder
- Salt to taste
- Pepper to taste
- 3 teaspoons oregano
- 1 cup water
- 1 teaspoon salt
- 1 teaspoon pepper
- 6 tablespoons lemon juice

Directions:
1. Mix lemon juice, pepper, salt, oregano, garlic powder and olive oil. Wash and cut meat. Place meat in a zip-bag. Pour marinade on a meat.
2. Marinade meat in the sauce for 20 minutes.
3. Place meat in the Instant Pot and cook for 15 minutes on "High Pressure" regime.
4. Place meat in a pita bread and add chopped vegetables.

Nutrition:
- Calories: 593
- Fat: 12g
- Carbohydrates: 74g
- Protein:44g

Indian Butter Chicken

Soft and healthy meat receipt can be satisfying enough to fill you with the energy for the full day!

Prep time: 15 minutes | **Cooking time:** 10 minutes | **Servings:** 8

Ingredients:
- 2lbs chicken breast
- 1 tablespoon water
- 1 stick of butter
- 2 tablespoons cornstarch
- 2 teaspoons garam masala
- Salt to taste
- 2 teaspoon cayenne pepper
- Cilantro
- 2 teaspoons curry powder
- 5 garlic cloves
- 1 teaspoon cumin
- 1 chopped onion
- 1 teaspoon ginger
- 1 can tomato paste
- 1 can coconut milk
- 1 cup chicken stock

Directions:
1. Place butter in the Instant Pot and melt on "Saute" regime.
2. Mix chopped garlic with onions and chicken stock. Add coconut milk. Use blender to get tender sauce. Add tomato paste to the mix. Mix one more time with the spoon.
3. Mix cumin, curry powder, pepper, ginger, garam masla and salt.
4. Add seasoning mix to tomato paste.
5. Marinade chicken in sauce and cook in the Instant Pot for 10 minutes on "Poultry" regime.
6. Mix cornstarch with water and add to the chicken. Saute for 5 minutes.

Nutrition:
- Calories: 196
- Fat: 13g
- Carbohydrates: 4g
- Protein:15g

Egg Sandwiches

What is perfect lunch? It is something delicious, satisfying, low in calories and full of vitamins the same time – egg sandwiches with mayonnaise will make any work day better!

Prep time: 5 minutes | **Cooking time:** 10 minutes | **Servings:** 12

Ingredients:
- 12 brown baguettes
- Salt to taste
- 36 eggs
- Pepper to taste
- 36 tablespoons mayonnaise
- 6 teaspoons parsley
- 6 carrots
- 6 teaspoons mustard powder
- 1 cup cucumber
- 1 cup cheese
- 1 cup onions

Directions:
1. Pour water in the Instant Pot.
2. Place eggs in the Instant Pot and cook for 5 minutes on "High Pressure" regime.
3. Wash and chop carrot, onion and cucumber. Mix vegetables with salt, pepper and mayonnaise. Add mustard powder and parsley to the vegetable mix.
4. Mash prepared eggs with sauce and vegetables.
5. Halve baguette. You need to cut it the way to get two long slices as like for the ordinary sandwich.
6. Fry vegetable mix on the frying pan for 5 minutes and place on the baguette slices.
7. Serve with fresh herbs!

Nutrition:
- Calories: 245
- Fat: 4g
- Carbohydrates: 42g
- Protein: 16g

Red Beans with Rice

Hot and light red beans with soft rice – special dinner for the special day!

Prep time: 10 minutes | **Cooking time:** 35 minutes | **Servings:** 5

Ingredients:
- ½ onion
- 5 cups rice
- ½ bell pepper
- ½ pound chicken
- 1 celery stalk
- 3 cups water
- 1 clove garlic
- 1 leaves bay
- ½ pound kidney beans
- ½ teaspoon fresh thyme
- ½ teaspoon salt
- ½ teaspoon hot sauce
- ¼ teaspoon white pepper

Directions:
1. Mix pepper, hot sauce, salt, thyme, beans, leaves bay, garlic, celery and bell pepper with onion.
2. Place ingredients in the Instant Pot and cook for 28 minutes on "High Pressure" regime.
3. Add chicken to the Instant Pot and cook for 15 more minutes on the same regime.
4. Boil rice. Just pour hot water in a bowl and put it on the fire. Add rice to bowling water and cook for 10 minutes.
5. Serve beans with rice!

Nutrition:
- Calories: 327
- Fat: 2g
- Carbohydrates: 66g
- Protein: 13g

Tavern Sandwiches

Why sandwich is the best lunch variant? It is easy to take to the office, delicious and full of vitamins!

Prep time: 5 minutes | **Cooking time:** 15 minutes | **Servings:** 8

Ingredients:
- 2 pounds beef
- Sandwich buns
- 3 chopped onions
- 8 slices cheese
- ½ teaspoon salt
- 1 tablespoon ketchup
- ¼ teaspoon pepper
- 2 tablespoons mustard
- 10 ounce can chicken soup

Directions:
1. Place beef in the Instant Pot and saute until it turns pink color.
2. Mix mustard, pepper, ketchup, salt, cheese and chopped onions. Add sauce to the Instant Pot. Pour chicken soup on top of the mix in the pressure cooker.
3. Cook chicken with sauce for 7 minutes on "High Pressure" regime.
4. Pour beef mix on the sandwich buns.
5. Cover beef with cheese slices.
6. Serve with fresh herbs!

Nutrition:
- Calories: 464
- Fat: 259g
- Carbohydrates: 30g
- Protein:21g

Jacket Potato

Potato is one of the most favorite vegetables in USA – follow native American traditions!

Prep time: 5 minutes | **Cooking time:** 20 minutes | **Servings:** 8

Ingredients:
- 8 potatoes
- Salt to taste
- 2 tablespoons butter
- Pepper to taste

Directions:
1. Pour water in the Instant Pot.
2. Wash potatoes and add seasoning.
3. Cook potatoes for 20 minutes on "High Pressure" regime.
4. Leave potatoes to rest in the Instant Pot for 6 minutes for the natural release of pressure.
5. Serve hot with herbs!

Nutrition:
- Calories: 93
- Fat: 1g
- Carbohydrates: 21g
- Protein:2g

Paleo Kielbasa with Sauerkraut

Southern cuisine with Asian vibes – super delicious lunch full of taste!

Prep time: 5 minutes | **Cooking time:** 10 minutes | **Servings**: 8

Ingredients:
- 2 cups water
- 3 cups sauerkraut
- 1 pound kielbasa
- 4 potatoes
- 3 onions

Directions:
1. Pour half of water in the Instant Pot. Chop onions and place in the Instant Pot. Set "Saute" regime and cook onions for 4 minutes until they turn golden color. Leave onions in the Instant Pot.
2. Mix sauerkraut with kielbasa.
3. Cook sauerkraut for 6 minutes on "Saute" regime.
4. Add more water to the Instant Pot.
5. Cook sauerkraut with kielbasa on "Steam" regime for 5 minutes more.
6. Serve!

Nutrition:
- Calories: 750
- Fat: 61g
- Carbohydrates: 14g
- Protein:34g

Lasagna for the Lunch

Make this day tastes like Italy!

Prep time: 5 minutes | **Cooking time**: 5 minutes | **Servings:** 15

Ingredients:
- 3 cox pasta
- 36oz water
- 24oz ricotta cheese
- 50oz jar Pasta sauce
- 24oz Mozzarella cheese
- 1 pound sausage
- 1 pound beef

Directions:
1. Place sausage and beef in the Instant Pot and cook until them turn brown.
2. Mix pasta, sauce and water.
3. Add sauce mix to the Instant Pot.
4. Cook meat in Instant Pot for 3 minutes on "High Pressure" regime.
5. Add ricotta and mozzarella to the Instant Pot and cook for 3 minutes more on the same regime.
6. Serve with rosemary!

Nutrition:
- Calories: 350
- Fat: 1g
- Carbohydrates: 41g
- Protein:373g

Hawaiian Fried Rice

Fried Rice it is traditional Hawaiian receipt – try it right now!

Prep time: 10 minutes | **Cooking time:** 30 minutes | **Servings:** 12

Ingredients:
- 2 tablespoons olive oil
- Chopped scallions
- 2 onions
- 2 cups chopped pineapple
- 2 red peppers
- 4 tablespoon soy sauce
- 12oz ham
- 4 cups water
- 6 eggs
- 2 cups brown rice

Directions:
1. Mix chopped pepper, onion and olive oil. Place onion mix in the Instant Pot and saute for 4 minutes. Eave onions in the pressure cooker.
2. Mix ham with beaten eggs. Place egg mix in the Instant Pot and cook for 3 minutes.
3. Mix water, brown rice, soy sauce, pineapple and place in the Instant Pot.
4. Cook rice with ham on "High Pressure" regime for 24 minutes.
5. Let rice in the Instant Pot and let the pressure release naturally for 5 minutes! Serve with scallions!

Nutrition:
- Calories: 200
- Fat: 70g
- Carbohydrates: 27g
- Protein:3g

Beef Stew

Enjoy satisfying beef mea with seasoning and light sauce full of taste!

Prep time: 10 minutes | **Cooking time:** 20 minutes | **Servings:** 12

Ingredients:
- 6 pounds beef stew
- ½ cup chopped parsley
- 1 cup flour
- 4 cups beef stock
- Salt to taste
- 2 tablespoons tomato paste
- 6 tablespoons vegetable oil
- 2lbs red potatoes
- 1 cup red wine
- 4 celery stalks
- 2 onions
- 6 carrots
- 4 garlic cloves

Directions:
1. Mix stew with salt, pepper and flour.
2. Pour oil in the Instant Pot.
3. Place beef with wine in the Instant Pot and cook for 5 minutes on "High Pressure" regime.
4. Mix chopped onions, garlic, carrots, celery, potatoes, tomato paste and beef stock.
5. Place beef with vegetable mix in the Instant Pot.
6. Cook meat for 20 minutes on the same regime.
7. Serve with parsley!

Nutrition:
- Calories: 300
- Fat: 13g
- Carbohydrates: 13g
- Protein:20g

Chicken Carnitas

Crispy, soft and sweet chicken meat on your lunch plate – not only delicious dinner, but real vitamin boom!

Prep time: 15 minutes | **Cooking time:** 25 minutes | **Servings:** 2

Ingredients:

- 2 pounds chicken breasts
- 2 tablespoons oil
- 1 tablespoon cumin
- 1 bay leaf
- ½ teaspoon chili powder
- ½ bunch cilantro
- Salt to taste
- 1 chipotle pepper
- Pepper to taste
- Juice of 1 orange
- 1 onion
- ¼ cup lime juice
- 5 garlic cloves
- ¼ cup chicken broth
- ½ cup mayo
- 2 chipotle peppers
- 1 tablespoon milk

Directions:

1. Mix garlic cloves, pepper, cilantro, chili powder, bay leaf with cumin. Put seasoning on the chicken breasts.
2. Pour oil in the Instant Pot and place chicken meat inside the Pot.
3. Add onions and garlic to the meat and saute for 6 minutes.
4. Mix orange juice, zest, lime juice, broth, sauce, and one chipotle pepper. Cover chicken with sauce.
5. Cook chicken meat in the Instant Pot for 10 minutes on "High Pressure" regime.
6. Pour oil on the chicken meat and boil it for 12 minutes more.
7. Mix mayo, milk, 2 chipotle peppers and powder.
8. Serve chicken with mayo sauce.

Nutrition:

- Calories:105
- Fat: 5g
- Carbohydrates: 1g
- Protein:12g

Cheesy Egg Bake

Only 10 minutes, 7 ingredients and satisfying lunch is on your plate!

Prep time: 5 minutes | **Cooking time:** 10 minutes | **Servings:** 8

Ingredients:

- 12 slices bacon
- 1 teaspoon pepper
- 4 cups hash browns
- 2 teaspoons salt
- 12 eggs
- 1 cup cheddar cheese
- ½ cup milk

Directions:

1. Cut bacon in slices and place in the Instant Pot.
2. Saute bacon in the Instant Pot until it turns crispy. You need to pour 1-2 tablespoons of oil on the bacon to get more crispy taste.
3. Add hash browns and saute for 3 minutes more.
4. Prepare baking form for the Instant Pot.
5. Mix beaten eggs, milk, shredded cheese, salt, pepper and hash browns mix.
6. Place egg mixture in the baking forms.
7. Pour water in the Instant Pot and place baking form there.
8. Cook egg pie for 10 minutes on "High Pressure" regime.
9. Serve with cheese and onions!

Nutrition:

- Calories: 202
- Fat: 12g
- Carbohydrates: 7g
- Protein:16g

Pot Pork Carnitas

Light and healthy cornitas with satisfying melting meat and colorful vegetables – something you definitely will like!

Prep time: 15 minutes | **Cooking time**: 50 minutes | **Servings:** 6

Ingredients:

- 11/2 pounds boneless pork
- ¼ teaspoon garlic powder
- 1 teaspoon kosher salt
- 1/8 teaspoon adobo seasoning
- Pepper to taste
- 1 bay leave
- 3 garlic cloves
- 1 chipotle pepper
- 6 teaspoons cumin
- ¼ cup chicken broth
- ¼ teaspoon sazon
- 1/8 teaspoon dry oregano

Directions:

1. Place pork on the frying pan and fry with salt and pepper for 5 minutes.
2. Place garlic cloves into the meat. Make holes garlic clove size with the knife in the meat.
3. Mix cumin, sazon, oregano, garlic power and adobo. Cover meat with seasoning.
4. Add chipotle peppers to the meat and place mix in the Instant Pot.
5. Cook meat for 50 minutes on "High Pressure" regime.
6. Serve with the bunches and avocado slices.

Nutrition:

- Calories: 109
- Fat: 2g
- Carbohydrates: 3g
- Protein:17g

Buffalo Chicken with Sweet Potatoes

This light and colorful salad will make any lunch extra delicious and full of vitamins!

Prep time: 15 minutes | **Cooking time:** 30 minutes | **Servings:** 24

Ingredients:

- 6 pounds chicken breast
- Salt to taste
- 8 onions
- Pepper to taste
- 18 tablespoons butter
- 2 teaspoons garlic powder
- 18 tablespoons buffalo sauce
- 2 teaspoons onion powder
- 36 ounces mini potatoes

Directions:

1. Melt butter in the Instant Pot and cook chopped onion for 3 minutes on "Saute" regime.
2. Mix shredded chicken meat, mini potatoes, seasoning and buffalo sauce in the Instant Pot.
3. Bake chicken for 30 minutes on "Poultry" regime.
4. Place chicken meat in the preheated up to 400oF oven for 3 minutes.
5. Serve with hot sauce!

Nutrition:

- Calories: 319
- Fat: 10g
- Carbohydrates: 28g
- Protein:30g

Butternut Risotto

Sweet, easy to cook and healthy rice lunch – add more Asian vibes!

Prep time: 5 minutes | **Cooking time:** 10 minutes | **Servings:** 4

Ingredients:
- Olive oil
- 1 tablespoon nutritional yeast
- ½ cup of chopped onion
- 1 handful of parsley
- 3 cloves garlic
- ¼ teaspoon oregano
- 1 bell pepper
- ½ teaspoon coriander
- 2 cups butternut squash
- 1 teaspoon pepper
- 1 cup rice
- 1 teaspoon salt
- 3 cups vegetable broth
- 1 pack mushrooms
- ½ cup white wine

Directions:
1. Pour oil in the Instant Pot and warm up on the "Saute" regime.
2. Mix chopped onion, garlic, butternut squash and bell pepper. Saute on the frying pan for 5 minutes.
3. Mix onion mix with some rice.
4. Mix wine, broth, mushrooms, pepper, salt, oregano and coriander.
5. Pour mix in the Instant Pot with rice mix and cook on "High Pressure" regime for 5 minutes.
6. Mix with yeast and parsley.
7. Serve!

Nutrition:
- Calories: 143
- Fat: 1g
- Carbohydrates: 31g
- Protein:4g

Lentil Tacos

Spanish tacos with delicious meat and hot sauce – it will be one of your most favorite lunches!

Prep time: 5 minutes | **Cooking time:** 15 minutes | **Servings:** 18

Ingredients:
- 12 cups brown lentils
- 2 teaspoons cumin
- 12 cups water
- 6 teaspoons salt
- 12oz tomato sauce
- 6 teaspoons garlic powder
- 3 teaspoons chili powder
- 3 teaspoons onion powder

Directions:
1. Mix onion powder, chili powder, garlic powder, tomato sauce, salt, cumin and lentils.
2. Put ingredients in the Instant Pot. Pour water on top of the mix.
3. Cook lentils in the Instant Pot for 15 minutes on "High pressure" regime.
4. Leave lunch in the Instant Pot and let the pressure release naturally for 10 minutes.
5. Serve with tacos and vegetables!

Nutrition:
- Calories: 247
- Fat: 4g
- Carbohydrates: 38g
- Protein:14g

Tomato Chicken Cacciatore

Can chicken plate with vegetables be perfect lunch? With Instant Pot it can!

Prep time: 5 minutes | **Cooking time:** 15 minutes | **Servings:** 13

Ingredients:

- 2 teaspoons olive oil
- 1 cup green olives
- 8 pounds chicken legs
- 3 springs basil leaves
- 2 pounds cherry tomatoes
- 3 cups water
- 6 garlic cloves
- 1 cup red wine
- 1 teaspoon pepper flakes
- 1 teaspoon oregano
- 1 teaspoon salt

Directions:

1. Pour olive oil in the Instant Pot.
2. Place chicken meat in the Instant Pot and cook for 6 minutes on "High Pressure" regime.
3. Add cherry tomatoes to the Instant Pot. Sprinkle tomatoes with salt and pepper.
4. Mix oregano, pepper flakes, red wine, garlic cloves, olive oil, basil leaves and olives.
5. Cover chicken meat with seasoning and vegetables.
6. Place chicken in the Instant Pot and cook with sauce for 15 minutes on "Poultry" regime.
7. Serve with herbs!

Nutrition:

- Calories: 312
- Fat: 15g
- Carbohydrates: 17g
- Protein:29g

Burrito Bowl

Satisfying burrito bowl with meat, porridge, vegetables and extra delicious sauce!

Prep time: 5 minutes | **Cooking time:** 7 minutes | **Servings:** 13

Ingredients:

- 2 tablespoon olive oil
- 1 ½ lime zest
- 1 ½ lime juice
- 3 boneless chicken breasts
- 1 ½ cups water
- 5 red onions
- 3 ½ cups rice
- 1 bell pepper
- 2 cups cabbage
- 4 cup black beans
- 5 bay leaves
- 3 ½ cup water
- 1 teaspoon garlic powder
- 1 ½ teaspoon salt
- 4 teaspoon marjoram
- 1 teaspoon cumin powder
- 4 teaspoon cayenne pepper

Directions:

1. Mix rice, zest, juice and water.
2. Pour olive oil in the Instant Pot and cook chicken for 5 minutes on "High Pressure" regime.
3. Mix onion, pepper, beans, seasoning and water with a bay leaf.
4. Place vegetable mix in the Instant Pot.
5. Put chicken meat on the vegetable mix.
6. Place rice mixture on top of the chicken mix.
7. Cook rice mix for 7 minutes in Instant Pot on the same regime.
8. Mix the dish well and serve!

Nutrition:

- Calories: 445
- Fat: 10g
- Carbohydrates: 79g
- Protein:15g

Chicken Fajitas with Peppers

Fajitas – low in calories, soft, crispy and full of vitamins lunch cooked without oil!

Prep time: 5 minutes | **Cooking time:** 15 minutes | **Servings:** 8

Ingredients:
- 8 chicken breasts
- 1 ½ cup chicken broth
- 2 tablespoons fajita seasoning
- 4 cloves garlic
- Salt to taste
- 2 onions
- Pepper to taste
- 4 peppers
- 8 tortillas
- 2 red onions

Directions:
1. Mix chicken meat with fajita sauce and seasoning with chopped onion and garlic cloves.
2. Place chicken in the Instant Pot.
3. Cook meat mix for 5 minutes on "High Pressure" regime.
4. Cut red peppers and onion.
5. Place chicken with vegetables on tortillas and roll up.
6. Serve!

Nutrition:
- Calories: 251
- Fat: 10g
- Carbohydrates: 43g
- Protein: 18g

Pepper Salad

Really creative and delicious tomato salad in Instant Pot will be juicy and really bright in taste!

Prep time: 10 minutes | **Cooking time:** 10 minutes | **Servings:** 7

Ingredients:
- 1 cup water
- Salt to taste
- 5 bell peppers
- Pepper to taste
- 2 pounds tomatoes
- ¼ teaspoon garlic powder
- 3 eggs
- 2 tablespoons cider vinegar
- ½ cup mayonnaise
- 1 tablespoon honey
- ¼ cup pickle relish
- ¼ cup Dijon mustard

Directions:
1. Pour water in the Instant Pot.
2. Mix pepper and eggs with tomatoes and place in the Instant Pot.
3. Cook potato mix on "High Pressure" regime for 5 minutes.
4. Mix mayo, apple cider vinegar, mustard, relish, honey, salt and pepper. Set mix aside.
5. Top tomatoes and eggs with sauce and serve!

Nutrition:
- Calories: 55
- Fat: 2g
- Carbohydrates: 8g
- Protein: 1g

Sweet Potatoes

Really soft and extremely delicious potatoes with the seasoning – satisfying lunch both for the ordinary day and special occasion!

Prep time: 5 minutes | **Cooking time:** 30 minutes | **Servings:** 8

Ingredients:
- 4 sweet potatoes
- 1.5 cup water

Directions:
1. Wash and peel potatoes. Cover potatoes with salt and pepper.
2. Pour water in the Instant Pot. Bring water to boil on "Saute" regime.
3. Place potatoes in the Instant Pot.
4. Cook potatoes for 20 minutes on "High Pressure" regime.
5. Serve with herbs!

Nutrition:
- Calories: 24
- Fat: 0g
- Carbohydrates: 5g
- Protein:1g

Goulash

Instant Pot meat with macaroni in Czech style – something that won't leave you unmoved!

Prep time: 5 minutes | **Cooking time:** 5 minutes | **Servings:** 10

Ingredients:

- 2lb beef
- Salt to taste
- 2 onions
- Pepper to taste
- 5 garlic cloves
- 5 bay leaves
- 5 cans tomato sauce
- 5 cups water
- 5 cans tomatoes
- 3 cups noodles
- 5 tablespoons Italian seasoning
- 4 tablespoons soy sauce

Directions:
1. Mix beef with chopped onion, salt and pepper.
2. Mix tomatoes, tomato sauce, Italian seasoning, water, soy sauce, bay leaves and noodles.
3. Coat beef with sauce.
4. Place beef mix in the Instant Pot and cook on "High Pressure" regime for 5 minutes.
5. Coat beef with Parmesan and serve!

Nutrition:
- Calories: 330
- Fat: 2g
- Carbohydrates: 66g
- Protein:9g

Chicken Skewers with Lemon Dill Pilaf

Super light and tender lunch with chicken – pleasure for the real food lovers!

Prep time: 5 minutes | **Cooking time:** 15 minutes | **Servings:** 2

Ingredients:
- 2 chicken breasts
- 1 tablespoon dried dill
- ½ cup chicken broth
- ½ carrot
- 1 tablespoon oregano
- 1 lemon zest
- ½ teaspoon dried thyme
- 1 cup water
- ½ teaspoon rosemary
- 1 cup basmati rice
- 1 tablespoon Dijon mustard
- Salt to taste
- Pepper to taste
- 1 lemon juice
- 2 garlic cloves

Directions:
1. Wash and chicken meat on cubes.
2. Mix lemon juice with chicken broth.
3. Mix rosemary, oregano, salt, pepper, thyme, garlic, mustard and dried dill.
4. Mix herbs with lemon juice and broth.
5. Pour marinade in to a zip-bag.
6. Place chicken slices into a bag and leave for 15 minutes to marinade.
7. Place chicken in the bowl. Add rice, lemon zest and water with carrot.
8. Place all the ingredients in the Instant Pot and cook on "Manual" regime for 6 minutes.
9. Let the pressure release naturally (10 minutes).
10. Place carrots, chicken and dill on the skewers. Serve!

Nutrition:
- Calories: 110
- Fat: 2g
- Carbohydrates: 1g
- Protein: 22g

Spanish Rice

Try hot, full of taste and unordinary Spanish rice from the Instant Pot!

Prep time: 10 minutes | **Cooking time:** 25 minutes | **Servings:** 2

Ingredients:
- 4 tablespoons broth
- 4 ½ cups water
- 1 onion
- 2 teaspoons salt
- 4 garlic cloves
- 28oz can tomatoes
- 4 cups brown rice

Directions:
1. Wash and chop onion.
2. Mix chopped onion with garlic and broth.
3. Add rice to the mix.
4. Pour broth mix into the Instant Pot and cook on "Sauté" regime for 5 minutes.
5. Mix tomatoes with water and salt.
6. Add tomatoes to the pressure cooker and cook on "High Pressure" regime for 25 minutes.
7. Let the pressure release naturally (10 minutes).

Nutrition:
- Calories: 215
- Fat: 4g
- Carbohydrates: 45g
- Protein: 5g

Drumstick Soup

Can easy and satisfying the same time soup be perfect lunch? With Instant Pot it can!

Prep time: 10 minutes | **Cooking time:** 50 minutes | **Servings:** 3

Ingredients:
- 1 ½ pounds chicken drumsticks
- 1 quart chicken broth
- 2 ribs celery
- ½ teaspoon pepper
- 2 carrots
- 2 bay leaves
- 1 parsnip
- 1 onion
- 1 rutabaga

Directions:
1. Pour water in the Instant Pot – you will need 3 cups.
2. Mix parsnip with chopped onion, rutabaga, bay leaves, cut carrots, pepper and celery.
3. Cover drumsticks with herb mix.
4. Pour broth in the Instant Pot.
5. Place drumsticks in the pressure cooker.
6. Cook on "Soup" regime for 50 minutes.
7. Serve hot with fresh green onion!

Nutrition:
- Calories: 250
- Fat: 4g
- Carbohydrates: 27g
- Protein: 7g

Onion Soup

Quick, easy and low calories receipt will be both delicious and healthy lunch!

Prep time: 15 minutes | **Cooking time:** 10 minutes | **Servings:** 12

Ingredients:
- 8 tablespoons avocado oil
- 8 springs of fresh thyme
- 24 cups chopped onions
- 8 bay leaves
- 4 tablespoon balsamic vinegar
- 4 teaspoon salt
- 24 cups stock

Directions:
1. Pour oil in the Instant Pot.
2. Warm up oil on the "Sauté" regime for 3 minutes. Do not bring it to boil.
3. Place onions in the Instant Pot and cook for 15 minutes on "Sauté" regime. Onions should be cleaned and chopped.
4. Mix vinegar with bay leaves and salt. Add to the Instant Pot.
5. Pour stock over the onion mix in the pressure cooker.
6. Add thyme to the pressure cooker and cook soup on "High Pressure" regime for 10 minutes.
7. Let the pressure release naturally (10 minutes).
8. Serve hot!

Nutrition:
- Calories: 170
- Fat: 5g
- Carbohydrates: 23g
- Protein: 7g

Cob Wrapped in Bacon

Juicy, baked and satisfying cob wrapped in fried bacon slices!

Prep time: 1 minute | **Cooking time:** 15 minutes | **Servings:** 3

Ingredients:
- 3 corns on the cobs
- Salt to taste
- Pepper to taste
- 3 slices bacon
- 1 tablespoon butter

Directions:
1. Pour water in the Instant Pot.
2. Cover corns with salt and pepper.
3. Wrap corns in the bacon slices.
4. Place corns in the Instant Pot and cook for 12 minutes on "Steam" regime.
5. Pour melt butter over the corns and serve hot!

Nutrition:
- Calories: 285
- Fat: 21g
- Carbohydrates: 17g
- Protein: 8g

Spanish Chorizo with Potato Hash

Spicy, juicy and satisfying – this receipt has everything a good lunch needs!

Prep time: 5 minutes | **Cooking time:** 10 minutes | **Servings:** 12

Ingredients:
- 18 potatoes
- Salt to taste
- Pepper to taste
- 3 sausages
- 9 tablespoons basil
- 12 slices bacon
- 9 tablespoons rosemary
- 3 peeled onions
- 3 cups stock
- 3 cups soft cheese
- 3 tablespoons oil
- 6 tablespoons yogurt
- 3 tablespoons garlic puree

Directions:
1. Wash and chop onion.
2. Mix chopped onion with oil and garlic.
3. Place onion mix in the Instant Pot. Cook on "Sauté" regime for 5 minutes.
4. Peel potatoes and cut on cubes. Cut sausages. Add potatoes with meat in the Instant Pot.
5. Slice bacon and add to the pressure cooker.
6. Mix garlic puree, yogurt, soft cheese and salt. Set aside.
7. Mix rosemary, pepper and basil.
8. Place seasoning in the pressure cooker. Add puree mix.
9. Cook soup on "Soup" regime for 10 minutes.
10. Let the pressure release naturally (10 minutes).
11. Serve hot!

Nutrition:
- Calories: 230
- Fat: 8g
- Carbohydrates: 35g
- Protein: 7g

Braised Lamb Shanks

Tender and delicious butternut squash on your plate – soft and tender lunch!

Prep time: 10 minutes | **Cooking time:** 60 minutes | **Servings:** 12

Ingredients:

- 16 ounces shallots
- 1/4teaspooncayenne pepper
- 8 tablespoon ghee
- ½ teaspoon cardamom
- 2 tablespoons olive oil
- 1 teaspoon paprika
- 4 lamb shanks

- 1 teaspoon cumin
- 2 carrots
- 1 teaspoon cinnamon
- 2 onions
- 2 teaspoons curry powder
- 12 ounce can tomato paste
- 4 tablespoons ghee

- 2 tablespoons rosemary
- 2 teaspoons sea salt
- 8 springs thyme
- 2 butternut squashes
- 2 cups red wine
- 1 teaspoon pepper
- 4 cups stock
- 2 teaspoons salt

Directions:

1. Turn on oven and warm up to 400oF.
2. Pour ghee on the baking form.
3. Mix shallots and cook in the oven for 20 minutes.
4. Pour oil in the Instant Pot.
5. Place lamb shanks in the pressure cooker and cook for 3 minutes on "Sauté" regime.
6. Wash and chop carrot with onion. Place to the Instant Pot.
7. Mix wine, pepper, stock, salt, thyme, sea salt, rosemary, tomato paste, curry powder, cinnamon, cumin, paprika and cardamom. Add to the Instant Pot.
8. Add shanks to the pressure cooker.
9. Cook for 35 minutes on "High Pressure" regime.
10. Let the pressure release naturally.
11. Place all the ingredients in the oven and bake for 30 minutes.

Nutrition:

- Calories:473
- Fat: 26.8g

- Carbohydrates: 35.2g
- Protein:20g

Ribs with Creamy Coleslaw

Tender, sweet and creamy rubs will be perfect lunch both for the meat lovers and for those who follow a diet!

Prep time: 30 minutes | **Cooking time:** 35 minutes | **Servings:** 12

Ingredients:

- 7lbs baby back ribs
- 2 teaspoons paprika
- 2 teaspoons chili
- 2 teaspoons garlic powder
- 2 teaspoons salt
- 2 teaspoons dry mustard
- 3 teaspoons pepper
- 3 teaspoons onion powder
- 6 slices bacon
- 3 tablespoons cooking fat
- 2 onions
- 2 teaspoons cayenne pepper
- 6 garlic cloves
- 2 teaspoons smoked paprika
- 2 cups tomato sauce
- 1 cup apple cider vinegar
- 18oz tomato paste
- 3 cups natural apple juice
- 2 cups aminos
- 9 cups cabbage
- 2 cups mayonnaise
- 3 cups red cabbage
- 6 teaspoons caraway seeds
- 6 carrots
- 3 cups raisins
- 6green onions

Directions:

1. Mix salt, paprika, pepper, onion powder, dry mustard, garlic powder and chili.
2. Place seasoning in a zip-bag and add baby back ribs.
3. Leave ribs to marinate mix for 20 minutes.
4. Mix bacon with chopped onion, garlic cloves, tomato sauce and tomato paste. Use blender to get creamy mix.
5. Mix apple juice, coconut aminos, smoked paprika and cayenne pepper. Add to blended sauce and use blender one more time to get creamy sauce.
6. In the other bowl mix chopped cabbage, red cabbage, carrots, onions, raisins and top with the caraway seeds and mayonnaise.
7. Place marinated meat in the Instant Pot and cook for 15 minutes on "High Pressure" regime.
8. Add chopped vegetables to the meat and cook for 10 minutes more on the "High Pressure" regime.
9. Add sauce to the pressure cooker and cook for 25 minutes more on "High Pressure" regime.
10. Serve hot!

Nutrition:

- Calories: 180
- Fat: 88g
- Carbohydrates: 67g
- Protein:52g

Roast and Gravy

One hour roast and gravy will be both satisfying and light lunch for those who like delicious meals!

Prep time: 5 minutes | **Cooking time:** 60 minutes | **Servings:** 5

Ingredients:

- 4 pounds chick roast
- Chopped parsley to taste
- A pinch of salt
- 6 garlic cloves
- Pepper to taste
- 4 chopped carrots
- 2 cups beef broth
- 2 parsnips
- 2 tablespoons balsamic vinegar
- 4 springs thyme
- 2 teaspoons fish sauce
- 1 spring rosemary

Directions:

1. Cover meat with salt, pepper, rosemary, vinegar and parsley. Leave meat to marinate for 20 minutes.
2. Place marinated meat in the marinade in the Instant Pot.
3. Add fish sauce to the meat.
4. Add parsnip and chopped carrots to the pressure cooker.
5. Cook meat with the vegetables for 60 minutes on "High Pressure" regime.
6. Let the pressure release naturally (15 minutes).
7. Serve with mashed potatoes!

Nutrition:

- Calories: 108
- Fat: 9g
- Carbohydrates: 3g
- Protein: 1g

Chicken Faux Pho

Try light and satisfying shredded chicken with healthy vegetables and tender seasoning!

Prep time: 15 minutes | **Cooking time:** 30 minutes | **Servings:** 4

Ingredients:

- 4lbs chicken pieces
- Sea salt to taste
- 2 onions
- 1 daikon root
- 1 inch ginger
- 1 head bok choy
- 1 tablespoons coriander seeds
- 1 cup fresh cilantro
- 1 teaspoon cardamom pops
- ¼ cup fish sauce
- 1 cardamom pods
- 1 lemon glass stalk
- 1 cinnamon stick
- 4 garlic cloves

Directions:

1. Pour water in the Instant Pot and add coriander seeds. Cook seeds for 5 minutes on "Sauté" regime.
2. Wash and cut chicken into cubes.
3. Place chicken meat in the Instant Pot.
4. Mix garlic, cinnamon, lemon glass stalk, fish sauce, cardamom, cilantro, root, ginger, bok choy, salt and chopped onion.
5. Add seasoning mix to the chicken slices in the pressure cooker.
6. Cook ingredients for 30 minutes on "High Pressure" regime.
7. Let the pressure release naturally.

Nutrition:

- Calories: 301
- Fat: 7g
- Carbohydrates: 33g
- Protein: 25g

Lemon Olive Chicken

Tender chicken slices in the lemon sauce with the seasoning full of vitamins – try this healthy lunch and get everything needed for the successful day!

Prep time: 10 minutes | **Cooking time:** 10 minutes | **Servings:** 12

Ingredients:

- 12 chicken breasts
- 2 cups sliced onions
- 2 teaspoons organic cumin
- 3 cans green olives
- 3 teaspoons sea salt
- 3 cups chicken bone-in-broth
- 2 teaspoons pepper
- 3 lemons
- 2 cups butter

Directions:

1. Wash and place chicken breasts in the Instant Pot.
2. Mix salt, cumin, chopped onions, olives, pepper, and lemons.
3. Add lemon mix in the pressure cooker.
4. Pour broth over the meat and add butter.
5. Cook meat for 10 minutes on "High Pressure" regime.
6. Serve hot with fresh herbs!

Nutrition:

- Calories: 271
- Fat: 7g
- Carbohydrates: 10g
- Protein: 12g

Beefless Stew

Full of vitamins, satisfying and colorful stew – perfect lunch to try any when!

Prep time: 30 minutes | **Cooking time:** 45 minutes | **Servings:** 10

Ingredients:

- 1 ½ onion
- 3 carrots
- ½ cup parsley
- 3 ribs celery
- 1 ½ cups cooked peas
- 2 portabella mushrooms
- 2 teaspoons rosemary
- 1 ½ tablespoon garlic
- 1 tablespoon paprika
- 5 cups water
- 1 tablespoon Italian seasoning
- 2 pound white potatoes
- ½ cup tomato paste

Directions:

1. Wash and peel potatoes.
2. Wash and chop onions.
3. Pour water in the pressure cooker.
4. Add chopped onions to the Instant Pot. Cook for 3 minutes on "Sauté" regime.
5. Mix carrots, celery and seasoning with garlic, rosemary, parsley and mushrooms. Cook for 8 minutes on "Sauté" regime.
6. Add water and cook mushroom mix for 5 minutes more on "Sauté" regime.
7. Add tomato paste, paprika, potatoes and peas to the pressure cooker.
8. Cook vegetable mix in the Instant Pot for 30 minutes on "Low Pressure" regime.
9. Let the pressure release naturally (15 minutes).
10. Serve with fresh herbs!

Nutrition:

- Calories: 238
- Fat: 4g
- Carbohydrates: 39g
- Protein: 15g

Vegan Posole

Lunches in Instant Pot are always easy to cook, juicy and healthy!

Prep time: 10 minutes | **Cooking time:** 40 minutes | **Servings:** 8

Ingredients:

- 1 14oz red chili puree
- 6 cups vegetable broth
- 2 25oz cans hominy
- 2 20oz cans of jackfruit
- 1 onion
- 1 tablespoon oil
- 8 garlic cloves

Directions:

1. Pour oil in the Instant Pot.
2. Add chopped onion and garlic in the Instant Pot and cook for 5 minutes on "Sauté" regime.
3. Add jackfruit and puree to the pressure cooker and cook on "Sauté" regime for 3 minutes more.
4. Remove cooked mix from the Instant Pot and place in a bowl.
5. Add hominy, broth and puree. Blend mix in a bowl, using blender.
6. Place mix back to the pressure cooker.
7. Cook for 10 minutes on "Manual" regime.
8. Let the pressure release naturally (20 minutes).
9. Serve with fresh orange juice!

Nutrition:

- Calories: 115
- Fat: 5g
- Carbohydrates: 21g
- Protein: 10g

Refried Beans

Can beans be juicy and super tender? With Instant Pot they can!

Prep time: 15 minutes | **Cooking time:** 45 minutes | **Servings:** 12

Ingredients:

- 12 pounds pinto beans
- 12 teaspoons sea salt
- 6 cups chopped onion
- 24 cups water
- 30 garlic cloves
- 24 cups chicken broth
- 6 jalapeno
- 18 tablespoons lard
- 12 teaspoons oregano
- 3 teaspoon pepper
- 6 teaspoon cumin

Directions:

1. Pour water over the beans and leave for 15 minutes. Beans should soak in the water. In 15 minutes dry beans.
2. Place chopped onions with garlic cloves and cut jalapeno with cumin and oregano to the Instant Pot.
3. Add lard, pepper, water and broth to the Instant Pot.
4. Use blender to blend all the ingredients together.
5. Mix all the ingredients with the beans using blender.
6. Place blended mix in the pressure cooker and cook for 45 minutes on "Chili" regime.
7. Let the pressure release naturally for 20 minutes.
8. Serve hot!

Nutrition:

- Calories: 720
- Fat: 12g
- Carbohydrates: 100g
- Protein: 36g

Pizza Casserole

Low carb, easy to cook and tender pizza casserole in pressure cooker – juicy lunch you will like!

Prep time: 10 minutes | **Cooking time:** 10 minutes | **Servings:** 2

Ingredients:
- 2 cups tomatoes
- ½ teaspoon onion powder
- 1lbs ground turkey
- ½ teaspoon pepper
- 1 pack pepperoni
- 2 garlic cloves
- ½ cup mozzarella
- ½ teaspoon salt
- ½ cup cheddar cheese
- 1 tablespoon oregano

Directions:
1. Mix tomatoes with oregano, salt, garlic, pepper, onion powder and use blender to get tender mix of the ingredients.
2. Place pepperoni in the Instant Pot, add sauce, add turkey and cheese on top. Make 3 more layers.
3. Cook pizza on "High Pressure" regime for 10 minutes.
4. Let the pressure release naturally for 20 minutes.
5. Serve hot!

Nutrition:
- Calories: 371
- Fat: 19g
- Carbohydrates: 25g
- Protein: 25g

No Noodle Lasagna

Another lasagna idea for the lunch – no noodle receipt!

Prep time: 10 minutes | **Cooking time:** 25 minutes | **Servings:** 8

Ingredients:
- 1 pound beef
- 8 ounces mozzarella
- 2 garlic cloves
- 1 jar marinara sauce
- 1 onion
- 1 egg
- 1 ½ cups ricotta cheese
- ½ cup parmesan cheese

Directions:
1. Wash and chop onion.
2. Mix onion with beef and garlic.
3. Mix egg with two types cheese using blender.
4. Add marinara sauce to ricotta mix and use blender one more time.
5. Mix onion with garlic with cheese mixture using a fork.
6. Pour half of sauce in the Instant Pot. Add beef meat to the Instant Pot. Top beef with sauce.
7. Cook meat with sauce on "High Pressure" regime for 10 minutes.
8. Let the pressure release naturally.
9. Serve!

Nutrition:
- Calories: 1050
- Fat: 5g
- Carbohydrates: 220g
- Protein: 35g

Lime Steak Bowl with Chili

Soft and tender steak with lime juice and tender seasoning on your plate for the lunch – something you will like for sure!

Prep time: 5 minutes | **Cooking time:** 15 minutes | **Servings:** 12

Ingredients:
- 4 pounds steak strips
- 9 diced avocados
- 3 tablespoons water
- 3 teaspoons Cholula
- 3 teaspoons minced garlic
- 2 teaspoons cracked pepper
- 3 tablespoons EVOO
- 3 teaspoons sea salt
- 6 teaspoons lime juice
- 3 teaspoons chili powder

Directions:
1. Pour oil in the Instant Pot and warm up on the "Sauté" regime for 3 minutes.
2. Place garlic in the pressure cooker and cook on "Sauté" regime for 3 minutes more.
3. Mix lime juice with chili powder, sea salt, EVOO, pepper, Cholula and avocados.
4. Place steak in the Instant Pot.
5. Place avocado mix over the meat.
6. Cook meat on "High Pressure" regime for 10 minutes.
7. Let the pressure release naturally (15 minutes).
8. Serve hot with avocados.

Nutrition:
- Calories: 340
- Fat: 8g
- Carbohydrates: 30g
- Protein: 37g

Jamaican Jerk Pork Roast

Add more colors and bright taste to the grey weekdays with this lunch receipt!

Prep time: 15 minutes | **Cooking time:** 45 minutes | **Servings:** 12

Ingredients:
- 4lb pork shoulder
- ½ cup beef broth
- ¼ cup Jamaican Jerk spice blend
- 1 tablespoon olive oil

Directions:
1. Pour oil in the Instant Pot.
2. Add spice blend to the Instant Pot and cook on "Sauté" regime for 3 minutes.
3. Pour beef broth in the Instant Pot and cook on "Sauté" regime for 4 minutes.
4. Place meat in the pressure cooker.
5. Cook meat for 45 minutes on "High Pressure" regime.
6. Serve hot!

Nutrition:
- Calories: 271
- Fat: 13g
- Carbohydrates: 3g
- Protein:33g

Green Chili Pork Taco Bowl

So tender, crispy and satisfying taco bowl – everyone will like it for sure!

Prep time: 20 minutes | **Cooking time:** 45 minutes | **Servings:** 1

Ingredients:
- 1/4lbs pork roast
- 3oz tomatillo salsa
- 1/4 teaspoons ground cumin
- 1/4 tablespoon olive oil
- 1/4 teaspoons garlic powder
- 1/8 teaspoon pepper
- 1/8 teaspoon salt
- 1 tomato
- 1 bunch kale leaves
- 1 tablespoon heavy creams

Directions:
1. Pour oil in the Instant Pot and cook on "Sauté" regime. It6 will take you around 3 minutes. Just warm up oil, but do not bring it to boil.
2. Mix garlic powder with salt, pepper, cumin and salsa. Use spoon to mix spices well.
3. Cover meat with salsa sauce. You should coat all the sides of meat. Add creams to the meat.
4. Place meat in sauce in the pressure cooker.
5. Cook meat for 45 minutes on "High Pressure" regime.
6. Let the pressure release naturally (20 minutes). The same time wash and cut tomato on slices. Place tomato over the meat.
7. Serve hot with fresh herbs!

Nutrition:
- Calories:340
- Fat: 12g
- Carbohydrates: 35g
- Protein: 23g

Salsa Verde Chicken

Melting shredded chicken meat with fresh herbs and vegetables full of vitamins – this lunch won't leave you unmoved!

Prep time: 10 minutes | **Cooking time:** 25 minutes | **Servings:** 12

Ingredients:
- 8lbs chicken breasts
- 42 ounces salsa verde
- 4 teaspoons cumin
- 4 teaspoons salt
- 4 teaspoons smoked paprika

Directions:
1. Mix paprika with salt, cumin and salsa verde. Use spoon to mix ingredients well.
2. Pour sauce over the chicken meat. Coat mix with sauce from all sides.
3. Place chicken meat in the pressure cooker and cook on "High Pressure" regime for 25 minutes.
4. Let the pressure release naturally (20 minutes).
5. Serve hot with fresh vegetables and bright herbs!

Nutrition:
- Calories: 145
- Fat: 2g
- Carbohydrates: 5g
- Protein: 26g

Rigate Paste

Try super satisfying rigate pasta for the lunch today!

Prep time: 5 minutes | **Cooking time:** 20 minutes | **Servings:** 12

Ingredients:

- 8 cups pasta
- 4 onions
- Olive oil
- 4 small shallots
- A pinch of basil
- 12 garlic cloves
- 4 pinches of oregano
- 12 mushrooms
- 4 dashes of sherry wine
- 4 zucchinis
- 4 cups chicken stock
- 4 tablespoons fish sauce
- 4 cups tomato paste
- 4 tablespoons Worcestershire sauce
- 8 tablespoons soy sauce

Directions:

1. Mix Worcestershire sauce with fish sauce, soy sauce, tomato paste and chicken stock.
2. Use blender to get extra tender sauce.
3. Pour oil in the Instant Pot and warm up for 3 minutes on "Sauté" regime. Just warm up oil and do not bring it to boil.
4. Mix chopped onion, shallots, garlic, mushrooms, oregano, zucchini, wine, basil and place in the Instant Pot.
5. Cook onion mix in the pressure cooker for 5 minutes on "High Pressure" regime.
6. Add pasta and sauce to the Instant Pot and cook for 5 minutes on "High Pressure" regime.
7. Serve hot!

Nutrition:

- Calories: 350
- Fat: 1g
- Carbohydrates: 75g
- Protein: 11g

Lettuce Wraps with Pork

Get maximum of vitamins with this easy and satisfying lettuce wraps!

Prep time: 15 minutes | **Cooking time:** 75 minutes | **Servings:** 12

Ingredients:

- 3 cups wheat berries
- 6 heads lettuce
- 3 tablespoons peanut oil
- 3 teaspoons oelek
- 3 pounds pork loin
- 6 tablespoons brown sugar
- 24 scallions
- 6 tablespoons fish sauce
- 1 cup cilantro
- 1 cup lime juice

Directions:

1. Pour water in the Instant Pot and add wheat berries.
2. Cook berries on "High Pressure" regime for 30 minutes.
3. Remove berries from the Instant Pot.
4. Pour oil in the Instant Pot.
5. Mix scallions with cilantro, lime juice, cooked wheat berries, fish sauce, scallions, sugar, pork loin, oelek and place in the Instant Pot.
6. Cook mix in the pressure cooker for 15 minutes on "High Pressure" regime.
7. Serve meat on the lettuce leaves.

Nutrition:

- Calories: 625
- Fat: 17g
- Carbohydrates: 35g
- Protein: 68g

Honey Sesame Chicken

Tender chicken in honey with sesame seeds can be super tender and satisfying lunch dish!

Prep time: 10 minutes | **Cooking time:** 20 minutes | **Servings:** 12

Ingredients:
- 12 chicken breasts
- Sesame seeds to serve
- Salt to taste
- Pepper to taste
- 12 teaspoons cornstarch

- 3 cups honey
- 1 teaspoon red pepper flakes
- 1 cup soy sauce
- 6 garlic cloves

- 1 cup onion
- 6 tablespoons oil
- 1 cup ketchup

Directions:
1. Place chicken in the Instant Pot. Wash and shred meat before this.
2. Mix honey, salt, pepper, cornstarch, red pepper flakes, soy sauce, garlic, chopped onion and ketchup. Use blender to get tender sauce.
3. Pour sauce over the chicken meat. Cover chicken from all sides.
4. Add oil to the pressure cooker.
5. Cook chicken meat on "Meat" regime for 20 minutes.
6. Let the pressure release naturally (15 minutes).
7. Serve hot!

Nutrition:
- Calories: 260
- Fat: 5g

- Carbohydrates: 28g
- Protein: 27g

Carrots with Mint

Small baby carrots with fresh mint will add taste to your life!

Prep time: 5 minutes | **Cooking time:** 5 minutes | **Servings:** 2

Ingredients:
- 1 pound Baby Carrots
- Sea salt to taste

- 1 cup water
- 1 tablespoon mint leaves

- 1 tablespoon butter

Directions:
1. Pour water in the Instant Pot.
2. Place carrots in the pressure cooker.
3. Add butter, mint leaves and salt to the pressure cooker.
4. Cook carrots on "High Pressure" regime.
5. Let the pressure release naturally.
6. Serve hot with butter!

Nutrition:
- Calories: 83
- Fat: 1g

- Carbohydrates: 20g
- Protein: 2g

Pizza Pasta

Italian traditional lunch can be super satisfying meal for you today!

Prep time: 5 minutes | **Cooking time**: 10 minutes | **Servings:** 6

Ingredients:
- 1lb sausage
- 1 tablespoon butter
- 8oz pizza sauce
- Salt to taste
- Pepper to taste
- 16oz pasta sauce
- 1 teaspoon Italian seasoning
- 28oz water
- 2 teaspoons garlic
- 8oz mozzarella
- 1lb pasta
- 20 slices pepperoni

Directions:
1. Place butter and garlic in the Instant Pot.
2. Add cut sausage with seasoning to the pressure cooker.
3. Cook ingredients on "Sauté" regime for 5 minutes.
4. Add sauces and pasta to the Instant Pot. Cook for 5 minutes on "Manual" regime.
5. Add pepperoni, mozzarella and cook for 1 minute on "High Pressure" regime.
6. Let the pressure release naturally.
7. Serve!

Nutrition:
- Calories: 480
- Fat: 14g
- Carbohydrates: 66g
- Protein:21g

Stuffed Cabbage

Soft and delicious vegetables with delicious and tender filling!

Prep time: 20 minutes | **Cooking time:** 15 minutes | **Servings:** 8

Ingredients:
- 1 ½ pounds turkey
- Cream
- 1 ½ pounds chicken
- 1 tablespoon olive oil
- 1 cup rice
- 1 cabbage
- 12 carrots
- 2 tablespoons dill
- 4 onions
- 1 can tomatoes
- 1 cup sour cream

Directions:
1. Place cabbage in the Instant Pot and warm up for 15 minutes on "Low Pressure" regime.
2. Wash and cut onions with tomatoes and carrots.
3. Pour creams in the Instant Pot and cook for 2 minutes on "Sauté" regime.
4. Add chopped vegetables and dill with rice to the pressure cooker.
5. Cook for 10 minutes on "High Pressure" regime.
6. Add chicken and turkey to the Instant Pot.
7. Cook meat on "Meat" regime for 20 minutes.
8. Serve hot with additional creams!

Nutrition:
- Calories: 298
- Fat: 17g
- Carbohydrates: 24g
- Protein:13g

Thai Chicken Rice Bowls

Satisfing rice bowl with vegetables and chicken tender meat!

Prep time: 15 minutes | **Cooking time:** 10 minutes | **Servings:** 1

Ingredients:

- 1/2 tablespoons olive oil
- Peanuts to serve
- 1 chicken breast
- Bean sprouts
- 1/4 cup white rice
- Shredded carrots
- 1/2 cups broth
- Shredded zucchini
- 1/2 tablespoons peanut butter
- Cilantro
- 1/8 cup Thai sauce
- 1/4 teaspoon sriracha
- 1 tablespoon soy sauce
- 1/4 teaspoons lime juice
- 1/8 tablespoons fish sauce
- 1/4 tablespoons garlic
- 1/8 tablespoon ginger

Directions:

1. Pour oil in the Instant Pot and warm up on "Sauté" regime for 3 minutes. Just warm up oil. Do not bring it to boil.
2. Wash and shred chicken meat. Place chicken meat in the Instant Pot.
3. Cook chicken for 6 minutes in the Instant Pot.
4. Mix ginger, Thai sauce, soy sauce, fish sauce, garlic, lime juice and sriracha sauce. Use blender to get well mixed sauce.
5. Pour sauce on the chicken meat.
6. Add rice to the pressure cooker.
7. Pour broth in the Instant Pot.
8. Cook ingredients on "High Pressure" regime for 10 minutes.
9. Let the pressure release naturally.
10. Serve chicken with vegetables, peanuts and cilantro.

Nutrition:

- Calories: 709
- Fat: 20g
- Carbohydrates: 92g
- Protein:33g

Red Beans with Rice

Super satisfying red beans with tender and light rice for the lunch – always great idea!

Prep time: 15 minutes | **Cooking time:** 30 minutes | **Servings:** 10

Ingredients:

- 1 onion
- 10 cups rice
- 1 bell pepper
- 1 pound chicken
- 3 celery stalks

- 7 cups water
- 3 garlic cloves
- 2 bay leaves
- 1 pound red bens
- 1 teaspoon thyme

- 1 teaspoon salt
- 1 teaspoon hot sauce
- ½ teaspoon pepper
- ¼ teaspoon white pepper

Directions:

1. Pour water in the Instant Pot and warm up for 3 minutes on "Sauté" regime.
2. Mix pepper, white pepper, hot sauce, salt, thyme, garlic, celery and set aside.
3. Wash and chop bell pepper. The same time place rice in a bowl with boiling water and boil for 10 minutes. Set aside.
4. Place chicken, pepper, beans, seasoning in the pressure cooker and cook for 30 minutes on "High Pressure" regime.
5. Add water and cook for 15 minutes more on "High Pressure" regime.
6. Let the pressure release naturally (20 minutes).
7. Serve with rice!

Nutrition:

- Calories: 327
- Fat: 2g

- Carbohydrates: 66g
- Protein: 13g

Beef Shawarma

Try super delicious and soft shawarma today!

Prep time: 5 minutes | **Cooking time:** 70 minutes | **Servings:** 2

Ingredients:
- 2 pounds beef chunk
- 1 cup beef broth
- 5 garlic cloves
- 2 tablespoons olive oil
- 3 tablespoons shawarma seasoning
- 4 tablespoons white vinegar
- ½ teaspoon salt

Directions:
1. Mix salt, seasoning and garlic.
2. Cut beef into slices.
3. Top beef with seasoning mix.
4. Pour vinegar over the meat.
5. Pour oil in the Instant Pot and warm up for 3 minutes on "Sauté" regime.
6. Place meat in the Instant Pot. Cook on "Stew" regime for 30 minutes.
7. Pour broth over the meat and cook for 35 minutes more on "Stew" regime.
8. Serve on tacos with onions and fresh vegetables.

Nutrition:
- Calories: 280
- Fat: 15g
- Carbohydrates: 2g
- Protein: 34g

Poblano White Beans

Juicy, tender and soft poblano beans for the lunch is delicious and satisfying dish!

Prep time: 5 minutes | **Cooking time:** 35 minutes | **Servings:** 12

Ingredients:
- 4 cups tomatoes
- Salt to taste
- Pepper to taste
- 2 cups chopped poblano
- 4 teaspoons dried oregano
- 2 cups chopped onion
- 2 cups water
- 1 jalapeno
- 2 cups beans
- 2 teaspoons cumin

Directions:
1. Wash vegetables attentively. Mix chopped onions with tomatoes, poblano and jalapeno.
2. Use blender to mix vegetables. You should get sauce texture mix.
3. Mix cumin, beans, oregano, pepper and salt.
4. Put seasoning over the blended vegetables. Coat vegetables with seasoning well.
5. Add water to the pressure cooker.
6. Cook vegetables for 35 minutes on "High Pressure" regime.
7. Let the pressure release naturally (15 minutes).
8. Serve hot!

Nutrition:
- Calories: 225
- Fat: 6g
- Carbohydrates: 15g
- Protein: 27g

SIDE DISHES

Garlic Mashed Potatoes

Satisfying addition to the main dish full of taste and vitamins!

Prep time: 60 minutes | **Cooking time:** 15 minutes | **Servings:** 5

Ingredients:

- 1 batch garlic sour cream
- Black peppercorns
- 1 cup vegetable stock
- ¼ teaspoon salt
- 2 pounds gold potatoes
- ½ teaspoon onion powder
- 1 celery root
- 1 teaspoon dill
- ½ teaspoon thyme
- 3 tablespoons yeast
- 1 onion
- ½ cup water
- 1 garlic bulb
- 2 tablespoons rice vinegar
- 1 cup raw cashews

Directions:

1. Turn on oven and preheat up to 400oF.
2. Roast garlic cloves for the 40 minutes.
3. Blend cooked garlic cloves with cashew nuts, rice vinegar, yeast, water, onion powder, salt, pepper and dill.
4. Pour water and stock in the Instant Pot and add some thyme.
5. Cook potatoes in the Instant pot with the blended ingredients for 12 minutes on "High Pressure" regime.
6. Serve with herbs!

Nutrition:

- Calories: 228
- Fat: 14g
- Carbohydrates: 30g
- Protein:5g

Sicilian Medley

Plate full of vitamins, colors and taste – these roasted vegetables will be even better that the main dish!

Prep time: 10 minutes | **Cooking time:** 45 minutes | **Servings:** 3

Ingredients:

- 1 cubed eggplant
- Pepper to taste
- 1 teaspoon salt
- 1 bunch basil
- ¼ cup olive oil
- ¼ cup olives
- 1 pepper
- 1 tablespoon raisins
- 2 zucchinis
- 2 tablespoons nuts
- 1 onion
- 1 tablespoon capers
- 2 potatoes
- 10 cherry tomatoes

Directions:

1. Cook eggplant in a strainer for 30 minutes.
2. Place all the vegetables, oil, potatoes and eggplant in the Instant Pot and cook for 3 minutes on "High Pressure" regime.
3. Add chopped onions, peppers and zucchini to the Instant Pot. Cook vegetables for 3 more minutes on the same regime.
4. Mix basil, nuts, capers, raisins, olives, pepper and salt. Add seasoning mix to the vegetables.
5. Cook vegetables with seasoning for 6 minutes not changing the regime.
6. Serve vegetables with some basil and nuts!

Nutrition:

- Calories: 593
- Fat: 36g
- Carbohydrates: 63g
- Protein:10g

Mashed Potatoes

Soft milky potatoes in Instant Pot – light and creamy addition both to the fish, poultry and meat!

Prep time: 5 minutes | **Cooking time:** 20 minutes | **Servings:** 17

Ingredients:
- 17 potatoes
- Pepper to taste
- 12 cups water
- Salt to taste
- 12 teaspoons salt
- 3 cups cream

Directions:
1. Wash and peel potatoes. Cut potatoes into slices.
2. Place vegetables in the Instant Pot.
3. Coat potatoes with salt and water.
4. Cook dish in the Instant Pot for 20 minutes on "High Pressure" regime.
5. Mash potatoes with cream.
6. Add salt and pepper to the mashed potatoes and serve!

Nutrition:
- Calories: 113
- Fat: 4g
- Carbohydrates: 17g
- Protein:2g

Basmati Rice

Try best ever rice receipt to get delicious and satisfying dinner!

Prep time: 15 minutes | **Cooking time:** 5 minutes | **Servings:** 13

Ingredients:
- 7 cups Basmati rice
- Seasoning to taste
- 4 jalapeno peppers
- 9 cups water

Directions:
1. Pour water in the Instant Pot.
2. Place rice with peeled pepper in the Instant Pot and cook for 5 minutes on "High Pressure" regime.
3. Leave rice with seasoning in the Instant Pot for 10 more minutes for the natural release of pressure.
4. Add herbs to taste and butter to taste.
5. Serve with the vegetables!

Nutrition:
- Calories: 191
- Fat: 0.6g
- Carbohydrates: 39g
- Protein:6g

Spanish-Style Brown Rice

Do you want to try perfect addition to the main course, but afraid of the odd calories? Try Spanish-Style rice!

Prep time: 5 minutes | **Cooking time:** 20 minutes | **Servings:** 15

Ingredients:

- 15 white onions
- 6 teaspoons sea salt
- 7 tablespoons rosemary
- 14 garlic cloves
- 14 cups water
- 3 cups lime juice
- 14 teaspoons oregano
- 7 basil leaves
- 13 cups brown rice
- 9 tablespoons tomato paste

Directions:

1. Pour oil and place cut onions in the Instant Pot. Cook for 5 minutes on "High Pressure" regime.
2. Mix minced garlic, basil, rosemary, oregano with tomato paste. Add tomato mix to the Instant Pot and cook for 2 more minutes on the same regime.
3. Put brown rice to the Instant Pot.
4. Add chicken and salt to the Instant Pot. Pour lime juice on top.
5. Cook rice in the Instant Pot for 16 minutes on "High Pressure" regime.
6. Serve with herbs!

Nutrition:

- Calories: 140
- Fat: 3g
- Carbohydrates:26g
- Protein:3g

Kabocha Squah Soup

Creamy kabocha soup is not only bright, but also full of vitamins!

Prep time: 10 minutes | **Cooking time:** 10 minutes | **Servings:** 15

Ingredients:

- 14 cups kabocha squash
- 7 cups almond milk
- 7 cups water
- 1 ¼ teaspoon turmeric
- 1 ¼ cup oats
- 1 ¼ teaspoon ginger
- 5 cups onions
- 6 teaspoons curry powder
- 10 garlic cloves
- 5 teaspoons smoked paprika
- 5 tablespoon seasoning

Directions:

1. Place squash in the Instant Pot and cook for 10 minutes on "High Pressure" regime.
2. Mix seasoning, smoked paprika, garlic cloves, chopped onions, ginger, oats, turmeric and put in the Instant Pot. Pour water in the Instant Pot.
3. Cook ingredients for 5 minutes on the same regime.
4. Add almond milk to the ingredients.
5. Place cooked ingredients in the blender and make a pure.
6. Serve with fresh basil!

Nutrition:

- Calories: 57
- Fat: 0g
- Carbohydrates: 15g
- Protein:0g

Avgolemono Soup

Light lemon cream-soup – don't you want to try it?

Prep time: 5 minutes | **Cooking time:** 20 minutes | **Servings**: 15

Ingredients:
- 15 cups chicken stock
- Handful Italian parsley
- 3 cups rice
- 6 tablespoons herb blend
- 6 lemons
- 7 chicken breasts

Directions:
1. Mix rice with chicken stock and boil in the Instant Pot for 5 minutes on "High Pressure" regime.
2. Add shredded chicken and herbs to the lid.
3. Mix beaten eggs with lemon juice.
4. Add some pepper and some salt to egg mixture.
5. Pour mixture in the Instant Pot and cook until soup will turn white.
6. Serve with the lemon slices!

Nutrition:
- Calories: 269
- Fat:7g
- Carbohydrates:26g
- Protein:25g

Broccoli Soup

Perfect start of the full dinner or satisfying enough cream-coup for the broccoli lovers!

Prep time: 5 minutes | **Cooking time:** 10 minutes | **Servings**: 5

Ingredients:
- 1 cup chopped onion
- ¼ cup parsley
- 2 garlic cloves
- 1 tablespoon yeast
- ½ cup carrot
- 1 can white beans
- 2 heads Broccoli
- 1 cups water
- 1 teaspoon salt
- 1 teaspoon thyme

Directions:
1. Mix onion, garlic, broccoli and carrot. Add some thyme and salt to the mix.
2. Cook broccoli mix in the Instant Pot for 3 minutes on "High Pressure" regime.
3. Cook broccoli for 4 minutes more after the signal.
4. Add white beans and yeast to the Pot. Cook for 10 minutes on the same regime.
5. Blend cooled soup and serve!

Nutrition:
- Calories: 160
- Fat: 7g
- Carbohydrates: 17g
- Protein:8g

Jasmine Rice

Quick and easy addition to the poultry, fish or meat – white rice with the seasoning and sauce!

Prep time: 5 minutes | **Cooking time:** 15 minutes | **Servings:** 14

Ingredients:
- 9 cups water
- 4 teaspoon salt
- 3 cup Italian herbs
- 2 drops lime extract
- 12 cups rice

Directions:
1. Mix rice, water and salt.
2. Place rice in the Instant Pot.
3. Cook rice in the Instant Pot for 9 minutes on "Saute" regime.
4. Add some butter to the rice.
5. Serve rice with herbs and lime!

Nutrition:
- Calories: 352
- Fat: 0.4g
- Carbohydrates: 78g
- Protein:7g

Chive Potatoes with Garlic

Soft mashed potatoes with the bight taste – what can be easier and more delicious for the dinner?

Prep time: 10 minutes | **Cooking time**: 10 minutes | **Servings:** 5

Ingredients:
- 2 cups chicken stock
- ¼ cup chives
- 2 pounds potatoes
- ½ teaspoon salt
- 4 cloves garlic
- ½ cup whole milk
- 1 cup yogurt

Directions:

1. Mix broth, garlic and potatoes.
2. Place potato mix in the Instant Pot and cook for 9 minutes on "High Pressure" regime.
3. Mash potato with some milk, yogurt and salt.
4. Add chives to the mashed potatoes.
5. Serve soup with herbs!

Nutrition:
- Calories: 160
- Fat: 6g
- Carbohydrates: 25g
- Protein:3g

Oxtail Ragout

Soft meat with sauce and satisfying vegetables – neither soup not meat – this dish will be good for everybody!

Prep time: 15 minutes | **Cooking time:** 35 minutes | **Servings:** 12

Ingredients:
- 4 tablespoons butter
- 4 tablespoons water
- 2 onions
- 4 tablespoons arrowroot
- 4 stalks celery
- 4 teaspoons red wine
- 4 carrots
- 6 oxtails
- 4 cups beef broth
- 6 peppercorns
- 1 cans tomatoes
- 1 teaspoon salt
- 4 bay leaves
- 1 teaspoon rosemary
- 4 teaspoons thyme

Directions:
1. Mix butter with onions, celery and carrots.
2. Cook vegetable mix in the Instant Pot for 2 minutes on "Saute" regime.
3. Mix beef broth with thyme, rosemary, salt, tomatoes, bay leaves and peppercorns.
4. Add oxtails to the thyme mix.
5. Cook vegetable mix for 30 minutes in the Instant Pot on "High Pressure" regime.
6. Add water and serve!

Nutrition:
- Calories: 280
- Fat: 24g
- Carbohydrates: 27g
- Protein:30g

Coconut Soup with Carrot

Bright, healthy and delicious creamy coconut soup will be something special!

Prep time: 15 minutes | **Cooking time:** 25 minutes | **Servings:** 6

Ingredients:
- 1 tablespoon coconut oil
- ¼ cup basil
- 1 onion
- ½ teaspoon pepper
- 1 pound carrots
- 1 teaspoon salt
- 2 garlic cloves
- ¼ teaspoon red pepper
- 1 tablespoon Thai curry paste
- 1 tablespoon lime juice
- 4 cups vegetable broth
- 1 cup coconut milk
- 1 teaspoon honey

Directions:
1. Pour coconut oil in the Instant Pot.
2. Chop onion and cut carrots.
3. Add vegetables to the Instant Pot and cook for 5 minutes on "Saute" regime.
4. Add garlic and curry paste to the Instant Pot.
5. Mix remaining ingredients and combine with soup in the Instant Pot.
6. Change regime settings on "High Pressure". Cook soup for 20 minutes.
7. Leave soup for 10minutes to rest after the cooking for the natural release of pressure.
8. Serve with basil!

Nutrition:
- Calories: 140
- Fat: 10g
- Carbohydrates: 10g
- Protein:0g

Spicy Black Chili

Do you want to try something really hot? Cook this soup!

Prep time: 15 minutes | **Cooking time:** 20 minutes | **Servings:** 18

Ingredients:

- 12 cups black beans
- Vegan cheese
- 12 tablespoons olive oil
- Jicama
- 13 red onions
- Cilantro
- 14 garlic cloves
- Avocado

- 12 tablespoons chili powder
- Green chilies
- 11 teaspoons ground cumin
- 13 tablespoons canola oil
- 11 teaspoons oregano
- 11 cans chipotle peppers
- 1 ½ teaspoons sea salt

- 11 tablespoons wine vinegar
- 12 cups water
- 9 ounces bitter greens
- 12 teaspoons chipotle chile oil
- 1 ½ cup red salsa
- 17 ounces green chilies

Directions:

1. Pour oil in the Instant Pot.
2. Place onions and garlic in the Instant Pot.
3. Saute garlic with an onion for 5 minutes.
4. Mix all other ingredients and blend using blender.
5. Place remaining ingredients in the Instant Pot and cook for 15 minutes on "High Pressure" regime.
6. Add greens to the puree soup and cook for 5 minutes more on the same regime.
7. Add vinegar to the soup.
8. Serve soup with the avocado, cream, corn, cilantro and cheese!

Nutrition:

- Calories: 160
- Fat: 2g

- Carbohydrates: 29g
- Protein: 8g

Carrot Bacon Soup

Enjoy crispy bacon slices in the creamy carrot sweet soup!

Prep time: 20 minutes | **Cooking time:** 5 minutes | **Servings:** 6

Ingredients:

- 2 pounds carrots
- White vinegar
- 4 cups broth

- ½ cup apple cider vinegar
- ½ onion
- Maple syrup

- ½ pack bacon
- Salt to taste

Directions:

1. Fry onions and bacon for 3 minutes on the frying pan.
2. Slice carrots and mix with white vinegar.
3. Pour broth on the carrots and place vegetables in the Instant Pot.
4. Cook carrots for 5 minutes on "High Pressure" regime.
5. Blend ingredients into soup.
6. Add a bacon, salt, vinegar, syrup and onions to the blended carrots.
7. Serve!

Nutrition:

- Calories: 143
- Fat: 2g

- Carbohydrates: 28g
- Protein: 14g

Beet Borscht

Try national Ukrainian soup with delicious meat and soft vegetables!

Prep time: 20 minutes | **Cooking time:** 45 minutes | **Servings:** 8

Ingredients:
- 8 cups beets
- ½ cup coconut yogurt
- ½ cup celery
- ¼ cup dill
- ½ cup carrots
- ½ tablespoon thyme
- 2 garlic cloves
- 1 tablespoon salt
- 1 onion
- 1 bay leaf
- 2 cups cabbage
- 6 cups stock

Directions:
1. Coat beets with water and cook in the Instant Pot for 7 minutes on "Saute" regime.
2. Mix peeled beets and carrots, celery, cabbage, onions, garlic, stock, bay leaf, thyme and salt.
3. Place mix in the Instant Pot.
4. Cook vegetable mix in the Instant Pot for 45 minutes on "High Pressure" regime.
5. Serve with coconut yogurt on top and dill!

Nutrition:
- Calories: 78
- Fat: 4g
- Carbohydrates: 8g
- Protein:3g

Clam Chowder

National England white soup – are you interested? Just try!

Prep time: 5 minutes | **Cooking time:** 10 minutes | **Servings:** 15

Ingredients:
- 22oz clams
- 10 tablespoons flour
- 9 cups clam juice
- 8 tablespoon butter
- 10 cups bacon
- 9 cups cream
- Onion
- 9 cups milk
- 5 ½ cups white wine
- 7 pinches cayenne pepper
- 9 potatoes
- 6 sprig thyme
- 7 bay leaves

Directions:
1. Cube bacon.
2. Cook bacon in the Instant Pot until it turns brown.
3. Add onion, salt and pepper to the bacon.
4. Mix wine with washed and cubed potatoes, cayenne pepper, thyme and remaining ingredients and add to the soup.
5. Cook soup for 10 minutes on "High Pressure" regime.
6. Add flour and butter, mix soup on the low heat.
7. Serve with creams!

Nutrition:
- Calories: 160
- Fat: 9g
- Carbohydrates: 13g
- Protein:4g

Tomato Soup with Roasted Vegies

Spicy tomatoes with roasted slices of vegetables and hot seasoning – try Spanish sides!

Prep time: 15 minutes | **Cooking time:** 45 minutes | **Servings:** 7

Ingredients:

- 3lbs cherry tomatoes
- Basil leaves
- 14 garlic cloves
- ½ cup parmesan cheese
- 2 tablespoons olive oil
- 1 cup creams
- Salt to taste
- Pepper to taste
- ½ teaspoon pepper flakes
- ½ teaspoon dried basil leaves
- Onion
- 1 teaspoon onion powder
- Bell pepper
- 1 teaspoon garlic powder
- 2 celery ribs
- 2 cups chicken broth
- 3 tablespoons tomato paste

Directions:

1. Firstly, we need to prepare roasted tomatoes for the soup. Turn on oven and preheat it up to 425oF.
2. Halve cherry tomatoes.
3. Cover tomatoes with the olive oil, salt, pepper, garlic cloves and red pepper flakes.
4. Bake tomatoes for 25 minutes on "High Pressure" regime.
5. Pour 2 tablespoons of olive oil in the Instant Pot.
6. Mix chopped onion, garlic powder, celery, bell pepper, onion powder, salt, pepper and dried basil. Add basil mix to the Instant Pot and saute for 3 minutes.
7. Add tomato paste with the roasted tomatoes to the soup.
8. Mix chicken broth with salt and pepper. Pour chicken broth in the Instant Pot. Change regime settings from "Saute" to the "High Pressure" regime.
9. Cook soup for 10 minutes.
10. Leave soup in the Instant Pot and let the pressure release naturally for 10 minutes.
11. Mash soup in cream and serve with fresh basil leaves and cheese!

Nutrition:

- Calories: 59
- Fat: 1g
- Carbohydrates: 0g
- Protein:1g

Tortellini Soup

Creams, meat and fresh herbs – Italians know how to surprise you!

Prep time: 20 minutes | **Cooking time:** 8 hours | **Servings:** 9

Ingredients:

- 5 sausages
- 1 cup heavy creams
- 2 tablespoons olive oil
- 5 cups fresh kale
- 1 onion
- 9 ounces cheese tortellini
- 2 carrots
- 3 cans milk
- 2 stalks celery
- ¼ cup cornstarch
- 10 garlic cloves
- ½ teaspoon red pepper flakes
- 1 tablespoon Italian seasoning
- ½ teaspoon black pepper
- 2 teaspoons chicken boullion powder
- ½ teaspoon salt
- 4 cups chicken broth
- 1 cup water

Directions:

1. Fry sausages on the frying pan with the oil.
2. Mix chopped onions, celery, carrots, sausages and garlic. Place mix in the Instant Pot and add remaining ingredient apart from creams, tortellini, milk and cornstarch.
3. Cook soup for 4 hours on "Low Pressure" regime.
4. Change pressure on low and cook for 7 hours more on the same regime.
5. Mix cornstarch with water, milk and tortellini.
6. Combine ingredients well.
7. Add tortellini mix to the soup and cook for 45 minutes more on "High Pressure" regime.
8. Add creams to the cooked soup and mix well.
9. Serve with herbs!

Nutrition:

- Calories: 250
- Fat: 18g
- Carbohydrates: 53g
- Protein:22g

Easy Chicken Soup

Chicken boullion it is the best source of vitamins and trusted treatment for the cold or even flu!

Prep time: 10 minutes | **Cooking time:** 60 minutes | **Servings:** 8

Ingredients:
- 1 onion
- Chopped green onions
- 2 carrots
- 5 cups water
- 1 ½ cup green beans
- Black pepper
- 4 garlic cloves
- 1 tablespoon sea salt
- 1 inch ginger
- 4 lb chicken

Directions:
1. Mix seasoning with vegetables.
2. Place veggie mix in the Instant Pot.
3. Put chopped chicken meat on the vegetables.
4. Pour water on the future soup.
5. Set Soup regime and cook for 30 minutes on "High Pressure" regime.
6. Leave soup in the Instant Pot and let the pressure release naturally for 10 minutes.
7. Serve with green chopped onions!

Nutrition:
- Calories: 140
- Fat: 4g
- Carbohydrates: 15g
- Protein:9g

Lentil Soup

Meat lovers will like this receipt – two kinds meat and nothing odd!

Prep time: 10 minutes | **Cooking time:** 25 minutes | **Servings**: 5

Ingredients:
- 1 tablespoon olive oil
- ½ teaspoon pepper
- ½ onion
- ½ teaspoon salt
- 2 stalks celery
- 2 cups spinach
- 2 carrots
- 1 can diced tomatoes
- ½ pound chicken sausages
- 1 cup lentils
- 1 cups beef broth
- 2 teaspoons garlic

Directions:
1. Mix chopped carrots with an onion and celery.
2. Pour olive oil in the Instant Pot.
3. Place vegetable mix in the Instant Pot.
4. Saute vegies for 6 minutes in the Instant Pot.
5. Cut chicken sausage.
6. Place sausages in the Instant Pot.
7. Cook sausages for 5 minutes on "High Pressure" regime.
8. Mix garlic, spinach, celery, lentils and add to the Instant Pot.
9. Cook soup for 25 minutes on the same regime.
10. Serve soup with Parmesan cheese!

Nutrition:
- Calories: 68
- Fat: 1g
- Carbohydrates: 16g
- Protein:5g

Cauliflower Soup

Don't you want more healthy food in your ration? Welcome low in calories soup!

Prep time: 10 minutes | **Cooking time:** 10 minutes | **Servings:** 15

Ingredients:

- 6 ½ onions
- 8 ½ cups half and half
- 12 tablespoons olive oil
- 10 cups cheddar cheese

- 3 heads cauliflower
- 9oz cream cheese
- 12 cups chicken stock
- 9 teaspoons salt

- 4 teaspoons garlic powder
- 8 slices bacon

Directions:

1. Wash and cup all the vegetables.
2. Mix cauliflower with an onion.
3. Saute cauliflower with an onion and olive oil for 4 minutes in the Instant Pot.
4. Add chicken stock, salt and garlic powder to the Instant Pot. Cook for 5 minutes on "High Pressure" regime.
5. Mix cheese with some half and half.
6. Fry bacon on the frying pan and cut in cubes.
7. Mix soup with the cheese mix and blend.
8. Serve soup with the bacon slices!

Nutrition:

- Calories: 120
- Fat: 9g

- Carbohydrates: 10g
- Protein:9g

Meatball Soup with Kale

Healthy and tender meat balls with fresh and light herbs – perfect side for the satisfying lunch!

Prep time: 10 minutes | **Cooking time:** 20 minutes | **Servings:** 2

Ingredients:

- 1/4 lbs chicken breast
- 1 egg
- 1/4 tablespoons arrowroot powder
- 1/4 tablespoons olive oil
- 1/8 teaspoons salt
- 1/8 teaspoon red pepper
- 1/6 teaspoons pepper
- 1 garlic cloves
- 1 teaspoon basil
- 1 teaspoons garlic powder
- 1 teaspoons onion powder
- 1 tablespoons yeast
- 1/8 tablespoon diced oregano
- 2 cups vegetable stock
- 1/2 teaspoons thyme
- 1 celery stalk
- 1/4 bunches kale
- 1/2 onion
- 1 carrot

Directions:

1. Mix celery, onions and carrots.
2. Pout olive oil to the Instant Pot.
3. Place onion mix in the Instant Pot.
4. Saute vegetables in the Instant Pot for 3 minutes.
5. Mix garlic, salt, rep pepper and thyme.
6. Add kale and seasoning to the vegetables.
7. Mix chicken breast, arrowroot powder, yeast, basil, salt, pepper, oregano, onion powder, red pepper and garlic powder. Form balls of the meat mix and place them in the Instant Pot to the soup.
8. Cook soup on "High Pressure" regime for 15 minutes.
9. Serve with herbs!

Nutrition:

- Calories: 168
- Fat: 3g
- Carbohydrates: 22g
- Protein:13g

Italian Vegetable Soup

Italian herbs with bright vegetables and boom of vitamins in the plate – what can be better for the dinner?

Prep time: 10 minutes | **Cooking time:** 15 minutes | **Servings:** 8

Ingredients:
- 2 tablespoons olive oil
- Lemon zest
- 2 onions
- 2 bay leaf
- 1 teaspoon salt
- 8 cups chicken stock
- 1 red chili
- 2 cups tomatoes
- 4 celery sticks
- 2 zucchinis
- 4 carrots
- 8oz kale
- 12 button mushrooms
- 2 handfuls porcini mushrooms
- 8 cloves garlic

Directions:
1. Mix chopped onion with olive oil, celery, salt and carrots. Saute mix in the Instant Pot for 4 minutes.
2. Mix chili with sliced mushrooms. Add garlic, porcini mushrooms and kale to the mix. Cook for 2 minutes more on "Saute" regime.
3. Add remaining ingredients to soup and cook on "High Pressure" regime for 10 minutes.
4. Leave soup in the Instant Pot and let the pressure release naturally for 10 minutes.
5. Serve soup with green onions!

Nutrition:
- Calories: 106
- Fat: 4g
- Carbohydrates: 7g
- Protein:10g

Enchilada Chicken Soup

Natural enchilada sauce with soft chicken meat and vegetables full of calories – light and satisfying soup is easy to cook with Instant Pot!

Prep time: 10 minutes | **Cooking time:** 40 minutes | **Servings:** 15

Ingredients:
- 12 chicken breasts
- Olive oil
- 8 teaspoons salt
- 4 cups chicken broth
- 6 teaspoon oregano
- 5 ¼ cups enchilada sauce
- 4 teaspoons cumin
- 3 cans diced tomatoes
- 9 onions
- 12 cans black beans
- 12 cloves garlic
- 6 cans corn
- 4 ½ cups quinoa
- 2 cans diced green chilies

Directions:
1. Turn on Instant Pot and pour olive oil in it.
2. Wash and chop meat.
3. Chop an onion.
4. Mix quinoa, green chilies, corn, garlic, meat, chopped onion, black beans, tomatoes, cumin, sauce, oregano, salt and broth. Add water.
5. Cook soup on "High Pressure" regime for 25 minutes.
6. Leave soup to rest after the cooking for 10 minutes for the natural release of pressure and serve!

Nutrition:
- Calories: 360
- Fat: 24g
- Carbohydrates: 22g
- Protein:13g

Potato Soup with Cheese

If you like cheddar and cream soups – this receipt will become your favorite one!

Prep time: 15 minutes | **Cooking time:** 10 minutes | **Servings:** 8

Ingredients:
- 2 tablespoons butter
- 1/3 cup cheddar
- 3 leeks
- 1 ½ cups creams
- 1 teaspoon salt
- 4 potatoes
- 4 garlic cloves
- 5 cups vegetable broth
- 4 springs thyme
- ¾ cups white wine
- 1 ½ teaspoon dried oregano
- 2 bay leaves

Directions:
1. Place butter in the Instant Pot and turn on "Saute" regime.
2. Mix leeks with salt and garlic. Saute for 1 minute in the Instant Pot.
3. Add all remaining ingredients to the Instant Pot instead of creams.
4. Cook soup on "High Pressure" regime for 10 minutes.
5. Add creams to the cooked soup and blend.
6. Serve soup with cheese.

Nutrition:
- Calories: 276
- Fat: 9g
- Carbohydrates: 27g
- Protein:16g

Beef Soup with Barley

Beef boulion is one of the most delicious – try it with porridge and vegetables!

Prep time: 15 minutes | **Cooking time:** 90 minutes | **Servings:** 17

Ingredients:
- 8 ½ pounds stew meat
- 7 cups barley
- Salt to taste
- 4 potatoes
- Pepper to taste
- 1 chicken breast
- 1 cup milk
- 8 ½ teaspoon thyme
- 8 tablespoons oil
- 4 bay leaves
- 20 mushrooms
- 5 cups water
- 3 cups mixed celery with onions and carrots
- 17 cups beef broth
- 7 garlic cloves

Directions:
1. Fry meat with salt and pepper for 6 minutes on the frying pan.
2. Place meat with shredded in blender chicken and mushrooms in the Instant Pot and saute for 2 minutes.
3. Add garlic and vegetable mix to the Pot and cook for 6 minutes more on "Saute" regime.
4. Add remaining ingredients to the Instant Pot and cook for 15 minutes on "High Pressure" regime.
5. Serve with fresh onions!

Nutrition:
- Calories:89
- Fat: 2g
- Carbohydrates: 10g
- Protein:5g

Taco Soup

Do you want to realize what is real Spanish soup? Try this receipt!

Prep time: 10 minutes | **Cooking time:** 20 minutes | **Servings:** 10

Ingredients:

- 2 ½ tablespoons ghee
- 9 ounces green chilies
- 6 onions
- 9 ounces coconut milk
- 6 bell peppers
- 24 ounces beef broth
- 4 pounds beef
- 28 ounces diced tomatoes
- 7 tablespoons chili powder
- 5 ¼ teaspoon cayenne pepper
- 8 tablespoons cumin
- 6 ½ teaspoon onion powder
- 7 teaspoons salt
- 4 ½ teaspoon garlic powder
- 5 teaspoons black pepper
- 7 teaspoons cinnamon
- 5 teaspoons paprika

Directions:

1. Place ghee, onions and bell peppers in the Instant Pot.
2. Saute vegetables for 6 minutes.
3. Add beef to the Instant Pot.
4. Cook soup ingredients for 6 minutes more on "High Pressure" regime.
5. Mix cinnamon, paprika, black pepper, garlic powder, salt, onion powder, cumin and cayenne pepper. Put seasoning in the Instant Pot.
6. Cook soup on the same regime for 25 minutes.
7. Serve with the chopped avocado and heavy creams!

Nutrition:

- Calories: 280
- Fat: 13g
- Carbohydrates:20g
- Protein:18g

Ramen

How about Middle Asia cuisine? Soup with egg and herbs will make you feel happy and full of energy the same time!

Prep time: 5 minutes | **Cooking time:** 20 minutes | **Servings:** 14

Ingredients:

- 10 tablespoons sesame oil
- Sesame seeds
- 10 teaspoons ginger
- Boiled eggs
- 13 garlic cloves
- 8 cups baby spinach
- 15oz mushrooms
- 7 carrots
- 3 pounds chicken
- 15 ounces ramen
- 8 tablespoons soy sauce
- Salt to taste
- 16 cups water

Directions:

1. Pour 1 cup of water in the Instant Pot.
2. Place eggs in the Instant Pot.
3. Sauté eggs for 3 minutes.
4. Remove eggs and put oil, ginger and garlic in the Instant Pot.
5. Saute seasoning for 2 minutes.
6. Mix mushrooms with water, salt, soy sauce, chopped chicken and pepper.
7. Place mushroom mix in the Instant Pot.
8. Cook ingredients on "High Pressure" regime for 20 minutes.
9. Place noodles in the Instant Pot and add carrots and spinach.
10. Cook soup for 10 minutes more on the same regime.
11. Serve with eggs!

Nutrition:

- Calories: 793
- Fat: 37g
- Carbohydrates: 66g
- Protein:41g

Buffalo Chicken Soup

Creamy, satisfying and healthy – the soup you will like for sure!

Prep time: 5 minutes | **Cooking time:** 10 minutes | **Servings:** 12

Ingredients:
- 12 chicken breasts
- 10 cups heavy creams
- 13 cups chicken bone-broth
- 12 cups cheddar cheese
- 9 ½ cups celery
- 5 cups hot sauce
- 6 ¼ cup onion
- 12 tablespoons ghee
- 8 garlic cloves
- 7 tablespoons dressing mix

Directions:
1. Turn on Instant Pot and set Soup Function.
2. Mix cheese with creams and set aside.
3. Place dressing, garlic cloves, ghee, chopped onion, hot sauce, celery, chicken breasts and bone-broth in the Instant Pot.
4. Cook soup ingredients on "High Pressure" regime for 10 minutes.
5. Blend soup with cream and cheese.
6. Serve with herbs!

Nutrition:
- Calories: 313
- Fat: 25g
- Carbohydrates: 4g
- Protein:29g

Chicken Soup with Corn

Are you tired of routine soup receipts? It's time to try bright corn soup!

Prep time: 10 minutes | **Cooking time:** 20 minutes | **Servings:** 1

Ingredients:
- 1/4 tablespoon coconut oil
- 1/4 teaspoon salt
- 1/2 chicken breasts
- 1/6 teaspoon white pepper
- 1 scallion
- 1/2 garlic cloves
- 1/3 potato
- 1/4 tablespoon tamari sauce
- Knob of ginger
- 1/2 tablespoon fish sauce
- 1 cob of fresh corn
- 1 cup chicken stock
- 1 tablespoon arrowroot powder
- Handful of cilantro
- 1 handfuls baby spinach
- Juice of ½ lime
- 1 egg

Directions:
1. Pour coconut oil in the Instant Pot.
2. Mix chicken meat with onion, potato and ginger.
3. Saute potato mix in the Instant Pot for 5 minutes.
4. Add 1 cup of corns and 1 cup chicken stock to the Instant Pot.
5. Cook for 1 minute on "Saute" regime.
6. Add all corn and all the remaining ingredients apart from cilantro, eggs, lime, arrowroot powder and spinach leaves.
7. Cook soup on "High Pressure" regime for 15 minutes.
8. Whisk eggs in the soup and cook for 1 more minute.
9. Serve with fresh basil leaves!

Nutrition:
- Calories: 189
- Fat: 1g
- Carbohydrates: 23g
- Protein:21g

Pork Stew with Hominy

Light broth with satisfying and tender pork meat and fresh vegetables with easy topping!

Prep time: 10 minutes | **Cooking time:** 30 minutes | **Servings:** 7

Ingredients:

- 2 tablespoons olive oil
- ¼ cup water
- Salt to taste
- 2 tablespoons cornstarch
- 1 ½ pounds pork shoulder
- Avocado slices for topping
- 1 onion
- 2 cans hominy
- 4 garlic cloves
- 4 cups chicken broth
- 2 tablespoons chili powder

Directions:

1. Wash pork meat and cover with salt.
2. Pour oil in the Instant Pot and warm up for 3 minutes on "Sauté" regime.
3. Place pork in the Instant Pot and cook for 6 minutes on "High Pressure" regime.
4. Wash and chop onion with garlic. Place onion mix in the Instant Pot, add chili powder. Cook onions with pork meat on "Sauté" regime for 5 minutes.
5. Pour broth in the pressure cooker.
6. Cook mix for 30 minutes on "High Pressure" regime.
7. Let the pressure release naturally (10 minutes).
8. Remove meat from the Instant Pot and shred into small slices.
9. Place cornstarch with water and hominy in the Instant Pot.
10. Cook hominy in the pressure cooker for 4 minutes on "Sauté" regime.
11. Do a quick release and serve hominy with pork and avocado slices with lime.

Nutrition:

- Calories: 300
- Fat: 9g
- Carbohydrates: 26g
- Protein: 29g

Chunky Cheese Soup with Potatoes

Creamy, light and tender soup for the dinner in bet Italian traditions!

Prep time: 15 minutes | **Cooking time:** 10 minutes | **Servings:** 7

Ingredients:

- 2 tablespoons butter
- 6 slices bacon
- ½ cup onion
- 1 cup corn
- 6 cups potatoes (cubed)
- 2 cups half and half

- 2 cans chicken broth
- 1 cup cheddar cheese
- 1 teaspoon salt
- 3oz creamy cheese
- ½ teaspoon pepper
- 2 tablespoons water

- 1/8 teaspoon pepper flakes
- 2 tablespoons cornstarch
- 2 tablespoons parsley

Directions:

1. Place butter in the Instant Pot. Melt it up for 2 minutes on the "Sauté" regime.
2. Wash and chop onions, add to the pressure cooker and sauté on the same regime for 5 minutes.
3. Mix salt with pepper, parsley, flakes and add to the onions.
4. Pour broth in the Instant Pot.
5. Place cubes potatoes in the pressure cooker and cook for 5 minutes on "High Pressure" regime.
6. Do a quick release and remove potatoes from the Instant Pot.
7. Mix cornstarch with water. Pour creamy cheese with cheddar and cornstarch with water in the Instant Pot.
8. Mix half and half with bacon. Add to the pressure cooker.
9. Add potatoes to the Instant Pot and cook on "Soup" regime for 10 minutes.
10. Serve hot!

Nutrition:

- Calories: 210
- Fat: 8g

- Carbohydrates: 25g
- Protein: 7g

Asopado

Best side receipt with natural Spanish flavor!

Prep time: 10 minutes | **Cooking time:** 10 minutes | **Servings:** 7

Ingredients:

- 1 chili pepper
- 3 tablespoons olive oil
- 1 onion
- 1 bunch cilantro
- 10 garlic cloves

- 6 cups water
- Avocado for topping
- 2 tablespoons tomato seasoning
- White rice

- 8 chicken thighs
- 3 tablespoons cider vinegar

Directions:

1. Wash and chop onion.
2. Mix onion with garlic and cilantro. Cut pepper into slices and add to the onion mix.
3. Pour oil in the Instant Pot and add onion mix.
4. Cook onion mix for 5 minutes on "Sauté" regime.
5. Pour water in the bowl and bring to boil. Place rice in the bowling water and boil for 10 minutes.
6. Pour water in the pressure cooker.
7. Cover chicken with seasoning and vinegar.
8. Place chicken in the Instant Pot and cook for 10 minutes on "High Pressure" regime.
9. Let the pressure release naturally (10 minutes).
10. Serve with rice and avocado slices.

Nutrition:

- Calories: 138
- Fat: 2g

- Carbohydrates: 9g
- Protein: 20g

Creamy Wild Rice Soup

Served in bread loaves with bright vegetables and light taste will be perfect side for today!

Prep time: 10 minutes | **Cooking time:** 10 minutes | **Servings:** 7

Ingredients:

- 2 tablespoons butter
- 1 cup half and half
- 1 cup onion
- 1 cup milk
- 1 cup carrots
- 4oz cream cheese
- 1 cup celery
- 2 tablespoons water
- 28oz chicken broth
- 2 tablespoons cornstarch
- 2 chicken breasts
- 1 tablespoons parsley
- 6oz wild rice
- Dash pepper flakes
- 1 teaspoon salt
- ½ teaspoon pepper

Directions:

1. Wash and chop carrots with celery and onion.
2. Place butter in the Instant Pot.
3. Add onion, carrot and celery to the pressure cooker.
4. Cook vegetable mix on "Sauté" regime for 5 minutes.
5. Pour broth in the Instant Pot.
6. Mix chicken meat with rice and pepper. Add salt and parsley to the rice mix.
7. Place chicken mix in the Instant Pot and cook for 5 minutes on "High Pressure" regime.
8. Let the pressure release naturally (5 minutes).
9. Cover cornstarch with water.
10. Place cornstarch with cream cheese and half and half in the Instant Pot. Add milk.
11. Cook half and half mix for 10 minutes on "Soup" regime.
12. Serve soup warm!

Nutrition:

- Calories: 140
- Fat: 4g
- Carbohydrates: 2g
- Protein: 2g

Lentils and Rice

Satisfying lentils and rice will be perfect addition to any meat dinner!

Prep time: 10 minutes | **Cooking time:** 15 minutes | **Servings:** 3

Ingredients:

- 3 cups water
- 1 cup chicken stock
- 1 cup heavy creams
- 1 cup halves cherry tomatoes
- 1/3 tablespoons yeast
- 1/6 cups white rice

- Salt to taste
- 1 tablespoon butter
- 1/4 cup lentils
- 1/4 teaspoon garlic powder
- 1/4 cup green lentils

- 1/4 teaspoon onion powder
- 1/2 teaspoons cumin
- 1/2 teaspoons cinnamon
- 1 teaspoon turmeric
- 1 teaspoon coriander

Directions:

1. Mix onion and garlic powder with coriander, turmeric, cinnamon, cumin sat and yeast. Use spoon to mix seasoning well. Onion and garlic should be chopped. The same time place butter in cup and preheat in microwave (1 min). Pour butter sauce over onion mix.
2. Pour water in the pressure cooker. Mix water with heavy creams in the Instant Pot to get milky mix. Add chicken stock and bring mix to boil.
3. Place two types lentils and rice in the pressure cooker.
4. Add seasoning mix to the Instant Pot and mix well. Add halved tomatoes on top.
5. Cook on "High Pressure" regime for 15 minutes.
6. Let the pressure release naturally (10 minutes).
7. Serve!

Nutrition:

- Calories: 290
- Fat: 3g

- Carbohydrates: 49g
- Protein: 15g

Vegetable Rice in Indian Style

Feel real India with this easy to cook receipt!

Prep time: 5 minutes | **Cooking time:** 20 minutes | **Servings:** 1

Ingredients:

- 1/5 tablespoon olive oil
- 1/5 cup peas
- ¼ cup shallot
- 1 cup heavy creams
- 1 tablespoon sea salt

- 1/2 cups chicken broth
- 1/4 garlic clove
- 1/3 teaspoons curry powder
- 1/4 cups brown rice

- 1/4 teaspoon salt
- 1/8 cup chopped carrot
- 1 cup crumbs
- 1 cup parmesan
- Pepper to taste

Directions:

1. Wash carrot and peel it using knife. Cut carrot on 1 cm cubes. Mix carrots with garlic. Garlic should be minced.
2. Pour oil in the Instant Pot and add garlic mix. You should warm up oil on "Sauté" regime. It will take around 3 minutes.
3. Add salt, curry powder and pepper to the Instant Pot.
4. Cook on "Sauté" regime. It will take you 4 minutes. Add heavy creams and mix well.
5. Pour chicken broth in the Instant Pot. Ass cheese.
6. Add rice, shallot and peas to the pressure cooker. Add sea salt and mix well.
7. Cook rice mix for 20 minutes on "High Pressure" regime.
8. Let the pressure release naturally (15 minutes). Mix with crumbs.
9. Serve hot!

Nutrition:

- Calories: 302
- Fat: 2g

- Carbohydrates: 66g
- Protein:9g

Ribollita

Do you want to try super tender and satisfying Tuscan soup today?

Prep time: 15 minutes | **Cooking time:** 15 minutes | **Servings:** 9

Ingredients:

- ½ pounds beans
- ½ cup Parmesan cheese
- 3 tablespoons olive oil
- 8 slices bread
- 1 onion

- 5 ounce Kale leaves
- 2 carrots
- ½ teaspoon pepper
- 2 celery stalks
- 2 springs thyme leaves

- 4 garlic cloves
- 2 sage leaves
- 15 ounce tomatoes
- 1 bay leaf
- 4 cans chicken broth

Directions:

1. Pour water in the Instant Pot.
2. Cook on "High Pressure" regime for 5 minutes to sterilize.
3. Add beans and cook for 5 minutes more.
4. Let the pressure release naturally (60 minutes).
5. Remove beans with water from the pressure cooker.
6. Pour oil in the Instant Pot.
7. Chop onions, mix with cubes carrots and celery. Place onion mix in the pressure cooker.
8. Add garlic with sage, bay leaf, thyme, salt and pepper to the Instant Pot. Cook on "Sauté" regime for 5 minutes.
9. Pour broth in the Instant Pot.
10. Add beans and tomatoes to the Instant Pot. Cook on "High Pressure" regime for 5 minutes.
11. Let the pressure release naturally (10 minutes).
12. Add cheese and bread to the Instant Pot and cook for 10 minutes on "Sauté" regime.
13. Serve soup hot!

Nutrition:

- Calories: 343
- Fat: 6g

- Carbohydrates: 54g
- Protein: 16g

Chicken Corn Chowder

Colorful, bright and tender soup for you today!

Prep time: 15 minutes | **Cooking time:** 5 minutes | **Servings:** 1

Ingredients:

- 1/3 tablespoons butter
- Salt to taste
- Pepper to taste
- 1/6 cup onion
- 1/8 cup half and half
- 1/6 garlic clove

- 1/3 cups corn
- 1/4 cans chicken broth
- 1/3 chicken breasts
- 1/6 can Pumpkin puree
- 1/3 potatoes
- 1/8 teaspoon seasoning

- 1/8 teaspoon nutmeg
- ¼ teaspoon pepper
- 1/8 teaspoon pepper flakes

Directions:

1. Place butter in the Instant Pot. Melt butter for 1 minute on "Sauté" regime to get tender liquid for the further cooking.
2. Add onion to the Instant Pot. Cook on "Sauté" regime for 5 minutes. Cook until vegetables turn golden brown color.
3. Add garlic, pepper, salt pepper flakes, nutmeg, seasoning and half and half to the pressure cooker. Cook for 1 minute more on "Sauté" regime.
4. Pour broth in the Instant Pot. Mix ingredients with broth.
5. Mix pumpkin puree, chicken and potatoes.
6. Cook for 5 minutes on "High Pressure" regime.
7. Do a quick release and serve with corn!

Nutrition:

- Calories: 320
- Fat: 17g

- Carbohydrates: 28g
- Protein: 15g

Edamame Salad

Fresh vegetables with herbs and hot seasoning can be greatest ever addition to the dinner!

Prep time: 10 minutes | **Cooking time:** 5 minutes | **Servings:** 2

Ingredients:

- 1/4 cup quinoa
- 1/2 cups red cabbage
- 1/8 cups water
- 1/3 onions
- 1/8 teaspoon salt
- 1/4 cup edamame

- 1/3 carrot
- 1/4 cucumber
- 1/4 tablespoon soy sauce
- 1/2 tablespoons basil
- 1/8 cup lime juice
- 1/8 cup cilantro

- 1/4 tablespoons sugar
- 1/8 cup peanuts
- 1/4 tablespoon olive oil
- Pinch of pepper flakes
- 1/4 tablespoon ginger
- 1/4 tablespoon sesame oil

Directions:

1. Pour water in the Instant Pot. Turn on "Sauté" function to warm up water (add salt to taste and do not overcook water).
2. Mix cucumber, carrot, edamame, salt, chopped onions and cabbage with quinoa.
3. Place vegetable mix in the pressure cooker and cook for 5 minutes on "Sauté" regime. Cook until they turn gold color.
4. Let the pressure release naturally (10 minutes).
5. Mix sesame oil with oil, soy sauce and sugar. Pour over the vegetables in the pressure cooker and mix well. You may mix sauces with blender to get extra tasty sauce.
6. Mix basil, cilantro, peanuts, pepper flakes, ginger and lime juice.
7. Place vegetables with sauce on the plate and add seasoning. Mix well.
8. Serve!

Nutrition:

- Calories: 170
- Fat: 9g

- Carbohydrates: 11g
- Protein: 11g

Tomato Herbed Polenta

Do you like creamy and tender tomato sides? Try right now!

Prep time: 5 minutes | **Cooking time:** 20 minutes | **Servings:** 12

Ingredients:

- 4 tablespoons olive oil
- 2 cups polenta
- 1 cup onion
- 4 tablespoons parsley
- 4 teaspoons garlic
- 6 tablespoons basil
- 8 cups water
- 2 teaspoons rosemary
- 1 cup tomatoes
- 4 teaspoons oregano
- 2 teaspoons salt
- 2 bay leaves

Directions:

1. Pour oil in the Instant Pot. Warm up oil for 2 minutes on "Sauté" regime. Do not bring oil to boil. Just warm it up.
2. Mix onion with garlic and place in the Instant Pot. Cook on "Sauté" regime for 1 minute. Wait until vegetables turn golden color.
3. Pour water in the pressure cooker. Mix water with melted oil and onions.
4. Mix salt, bay leaf, oregano, rosemary and tomatoes. Add basil and parsley. Place tomatoes in the Instant Pot and to with polenta.
5. Cook tomatoes on "High Pressure" regime for 5 minutes.
6. Let the pressure release naturally (10 minutes).
7. Serve hot!

Nutrition:

- Calories: 153
- Fat: 2g
- Carbohydrates: 31g
- Protein: 7g

Poblano Corn Chowder

Creamy soup with bright and tender vegetables boiled in the pressure cooker – what can be healthier?

Prep time: 20 minutes | **Cooking time:** 5 minutes | **Servings:** 8

Ingredients:

- 1 tablespoon olive oil
- A dash of hot sauce
- 1 onion
- 4 cups corn
- 2 carrots
- 2 cups half and half

- 2 celery stalks
- 3 tablespoon water
- 1 pepper
- 3 tablespoon cornstarch
- 2 garlic cloves
- 4 cups potatoes

- 2 cans chicken broth
- ½ teaspoon pepper
- ½ teaspoon thyme
- 1 teaspoon salt

Directions:

1. Pour oil in the Instant Pot. Add onion, garlic, salt, thyme, pepper, celery and corn to the Instant Pot.
2. Cook for 6 minutes on "Sauté" regime.
3. Pour water over cornstarch.
4. Mix chopped potato with pepper and carrots. Top with hot sauce.
5. Place vegetables mix in the Pressure cooker and add cornstarch.
6. Cook for 5 minutes on "High Pressure" regime.
7. Let the pressure release naturally (10 minutes).
8. Serve hot!

Nutrition:

- Calories: 150
- Fat: 7g

- Carbohydrates: 18g
- Protein: 5g

Creamy Enchilada Soup

Light shredded chicken meat with colorful vegetables and tender broth!

Prep time: 10 minutes | **Cooking time:** 20 minutes | **Servings:** 16

Ingredients:

- 8 cups chicken broth
- 2 cans beans
- 6 chicken breasts
- 4 tablespoons taco seasoning
- 2 cans green chilies
- 2 cans tomato sauce
- 2 onions
- 4 teaspoons cumin
- 6 russet potatoes
- 3 teaspoons salt
- 2 bell pepper s
- 6 garlic cloves
- 16 cups butternut squash

Directions:

1. Pour broth in the Instant Pot. Warm up broth for 3 minutes on "Sauté" regime. Do not overcook broth – it should not start boiling.
2. Mix chicken meat with chilies, onion, cubed potatoes, pepper, squash, salt, garlic and cumin with tomato sauce and taco seasoning.
3. Place chicken mix in the pressure cooker.
4. Cook on "High Pressure" regime for 20 minutes.
5. Let the pressure release naturally (10 minutes).
6. Remove chicken from soup and shred carefully.
7. Add beans to soup and use blender to get tender mix.
8. Shred chicken meat and add back to soup.
9. Serve hot!

Nutrition:

- Calories: 127
- Fat: 1g
- Carbohydrates: 16g
- Protein: 14g

Pho Ga

Asian soup for the delicious and tender lunch!

Prep time: 20 minutes | **Cooking time:** 10 minutes | **Servings:** 5

Ingredients:

- 2 tablespoon canola oil
- 2 tablespoons rock sugar
- 2 yellow onions
- ¼ cup fish sauce
- 1 hand ginger
- 7 chicken drumsticks
- 1 bunch cilantro
- 1 teaspoon coriander seeds
- 3 star anise pods
- 1 teaspoon fennel seeds
- 1 cinnamon stick
- 4 garlic cloves

Directions:

1. Pour oil in the Instant Pot.
2. Mix garlic, cinnamon, fennel seeds, anise pods, coriander seeds, cilantro, ginger, onions and sugar.
3. Place seasoning mix in the pressure cooker. Cook on "Sauté" regime for 5 minutes.
4. Add drumsticks with fish sauce to the Instant Pot.
5. Cook for 20 minutes on "High Pressure" regime.
6. Let the pressure release naturally (10 minutes).
7. Serve hot!

Nutrition:

- Calories: 950
- Fat: 12g
- Carbohydrates: 116g
- Protein: 88g

Bok Choy Chicken Soup

Noodles with chicken meat in Asian style – something you need for the lunch today!

Prep time: 15 minutes | **Cooking time:** 20 minutes | **Servings:** 12

Ingredients:

- 24 chicken drumsticks
- 12 cups water
- 3 pounds Somen
- 1cup shredded turkey
- 3 cups chicken stock
- 3 pounds bok choy
- 6 teaspoons salt

Directions:

1. Cover chicken drumsticks with salt. Carefully place salt over meat to coat it from all sides.
2. Pour chicken broth in the Instant Pot. Warm up broth on "Sauté" regime. Do not overcook. Add salt to taste. To warm up broth with salt you will need around 3 minutes.
3. Place chicken meat and shredded turkey in the pressure cooker and cook for 10 minutes on "High Pressure" regime.
4. Let the pressure release naturally. Shred chicken meat after the cooking.
5. Boil noodles in hot water for 5 minutes.
6. Add Somen and bok choy to the chicken in the Instant Pot. Add noodles and water.
7. Cook mix for 5 minutes on "High Pressure" regime.
8. Let the pressure release naturally (10 minutes).
9. Serve hot!

Nutrition:

- Calories: 466
- Fat: 26g
- Carbohydrates: 11g
- Protein: 46g

Fruit Soup

Creamy and tender fruit soup full of vitamins – perfect dinner idea!

Prep time: 10 minutes | **Cooking time:** 5 minutes | **Servings:** 12

Ingredients:
- 3 cantaloupes
- 3 tablespoons chia seeds
- 3 oranges
- 3 tablespoons powdered sugar
- 6 peaches
- 2 teaspoons vanilla
- 3 16oz pineapple juice
- 3 8oz Greek yogurt

Directions:
1. Place peaches, pineapple juice, cantaloupes and vanilla to the Instant Pot.
2. Cook fruits for 5 minutes on "High Pressure" regime.
3. Add oranges and chia seeds to the Instant Pot.
4. Cook for 2 minutes on "High Pressure" regime. Let the pressure release naturally (10 minutes).
5. Remove mix from the pressure cooker and mix with yogurt using blender.
6. Serve in cups with powdered sugar and chia seeds.

Nutrition:
- Calories: 550
- Fat: 4g
- Carbohydrates: 20g
- Protein: 0g

Mushroom Stock

Light mushroom stock with minimum calories!

Prep time: 5 minutes | **Cooking time:** 20 minutes | **Servings:** 9

Ingredients:
- 6 ounces mushrooms
- 12 cups water
- 6 carrots
- 6 bay leaves
- 6 celery stalks
- 6 springs thyme

Directions:
1. Wash and peel mushrooms. Carefully leave only heads. Slice mushrooms.
2. Place mushrooms in the Instant Pot.
3. Add thyme, celery, bay leaves, chopped carrots and water to the Instant Pot. Mix ingredients well and mix with mushrooms in the Pot.
4. Cook on "High Pressure" regime for 20 minutes.
5. Let the pressure release naturally (10 minutes).
6. Serve hot!

Nutrition:
- Calories: 40
- Fat: 0g
- Carbohydrates: 5g
- Protein:1g

Chunky Corn Soup

Try this soup full of vitamins and color!

Prep time: 10 minutes | **Cooking time:** 10 minutes | **Servings:** 7

Ingredients:

- 2 tablespoons butter
- 6 slices bacon
- ½ cup onion
- 1 cup corn
- 2 cans broth
- 2 cups half and half

- 1 teaspoon salt
- 1 cup cheddar cheese
- ½ teaspoon pepper
- 3oz cream cheese
- 1/8 teaspoon pepper flakes

- 2 tablespoons water
- 2 tablespoons parsley
- 2 tablespoons cornstarch
- 3 cups sweet potatoes
- 3 cups russet potatoes

Directions:

1. Wash and peel potatoes. Slice into cubes.
2. Pour oil in the Instant Pot.
3. Wash and chop onion. Mix onion with pepper, pepper flakes, parsley, corn and bacon.
4. Cook bacon mix on "Sauté" regime for 5 minutes.
5. Pour water over the cornstarch.
6. Mix half and half with cream cheese, cheddar cheese, potatoes and add to the pressure cooker.
7. Pour broth over the vegetable mix.
8. Add cornstarch to the pressure cooker.
9. Cook on "High Pressure" regime for 10 minutes.
10. Let the pressure release naturally.
11. Blend soup mix and serve hot!

Nutrition:

- Calories: 190
- Fat: 10g

- Carbohydrates: 20g
- Protein:5g

Zuppa Toscana

Feel Italy near you with this light and easy receipt!

Prep time: 5 minutes | **Cooking time:** 10 minutes | **Servings:** 4

Ingredients:

- 3 bacon slices
- 1 cups fresh spinach
- 1/2 pound chicken sausage
- 1/2 cup parmesan cheese
- 1/2 tablespoon butter
- 1/2 can milk
- 1/2 cup chopped onion
- 1 tablespoon cornstarch
- 1 1/2 garlic cloves
- 1 1/2 russet potatoes
- 1 1/2 cans chicken broth
- 1/4 teaspoon red pepper flakes
- 1 teaspoon salt
- 1 teaspoon pepper

Directions:

1. Place butter in the Instant Pot. Melt it up to get tender sauce on the bottom of the Instant Pot.
2. Mix pepper, salt, red pepper flakes, garlic and onion. Place onion mix in the pressure cooker.
3. Cook onion mix on "Sauté" regime for 5 minutes. Wait until onions turn golden color.
4. Pour water over cornstarch. Let it soak.
5. Mix cubes potatoes, spinach and sausages.
6. Pour broth in the Instant Pot. Mix ingredients with broth.
7. Add vegetable mix to the pressure cooker.
8. Cook on "High Pressure" regime for 5 minutes.
9. Let the pressure release naturally.
10. Mix cornstarch with milk and cream cheese.
11. Add to the Instant Pot. Cook for 5 minutes on "High Pressure" regime.
12. Let the pressure release naturally (10 minutes).
13. Serve hot!

Nutrition:

- Calories: 170
- Fat: 4g
- Carbohydrates: 24g
- Protein: 10g

Tomailo Soup with Hominy

Try easy and tender tomatillo soup with lime slices and shredded meat!

Prep time: 15 minutes | **Cooking time:** 10 minutes | **Servings:** 3

Ingredients:

- 1/2 tablespoon olive oil
- Salt to taste
- Pepper to taste
- 1/2 onion
- 1/2 teaspoon red pepper flakes
- 1 garlic cloves
- 7ounce white hominy
- 1/2 can tomatillos
- 7ounce yellow hominy
- 1/2 teaspoon cumin
- 8unce salsa
- 1 cup chicken meat
- 1 can chicken broth

Directions:

1. Pour oil in the Instant Pot. Warm up oil in the pressure cooker. Do not bring it to boil.
2. Mix salt, pepper, red pepper flakes, cumin and onion. Place onion mix in the pressure cooker and cook for 5 minutes on "Sauté" regime. Wait until ingredients turn golden color.
3. Mix hominies with salsa, chicken meat and tomatillos.
4. Pour broth in the Instant Pot. Add chicken mix to the Instant Pot.
5. Cook for 5 minutes on "High Pressure" regime.
6. Let the pressure release naturally (20 minutes).

Nutrition:

- Calories: 188
- Fat: 6g
- Carbohydrates: 15g
- Protein: 16

Minestrone with Basil Pesto

Tomato soup with cheese and fresh herbs!

Prep time: 15 minutes | **Cooking time:** 10 minutes | **Servings:** 5

Ingredients:

- 1/2 tablespoons olive oil
- 2 tablespoons basil pesto
- 1/2 onion
- 1/4 teaspoon pepper
- 2 garlic cloves
- 1/2 can beans
- 1 cup heavy creams
- 1 cucumber
- 1 carrot
- 1 cup baby spinach
- 1/2 cup celery
- 1 cup pasta
- 1 can tomato
- 1/2 teaspoon salt
- 2 cups vegetable stock
- 1 bay leaf

Directions:

1. Pour oil in the Instant Pot. Warm up on "Sauté" regime.
2. Mix onion, garlic, carrots and celery. Cook on "Sauté" regime for 5 minutes. Let ingredients turn golden color.
3. Pour stock in the Instant Pot.
4. Wash and cut vegetables carefully. Place cucumber, tomatoes, bay leaves and salt in the Instant Pot. Cook on "High Pressure" regime for 5 minutes.
5. Let the pressure release naturally (10 minutes).
6. Add pasta, spinach, beans add pepper with pesto to the Pressure Cooker. Mix and leave to rest. It will take about 5 minutes.
7. Serve with Parmesan cheese on top.

Nutrition:

- Calories: 110
- Fat: 6g
- Carbohydrates: 13g
- Protein:5g

Amish Macaroni Salad

Light and satisfying salad the same time will be perfect side!

Prep time: 15 minutes | **Cooking time:** 10 minutes | **Servings:** 8

Ingredients:
- 1 ½ cups macaroni
- Salt to taste
- Pepper to taste
- 3 eggs
- ¼ cup onion
- 2 ½ cups water
- ½ cup celery
- 1 teaspoon salt
- 2 tablespoons mustard
- ¾ cup mayonnaise
- ¼ cup vinegar
- 1/3 cup sugar

Directions:
1. Mix macaroni with beaten eggs.
2. Pour water in the Instant Pot.
3. Sprinkle salt over the macaroni.
4. Place macaroni in the pressure cooker and cook for 5 minutes on "High Pressure" regime.
5. Let the pressure release naturally (10 minutes).
6. Add pepper, onion, celery, mustard, vinegar, sugar, mayonnaise and pepper to the macaroni mix.
7. Mix well.
8. Serve hot!

Nutrition:
- Calories: 270
- Fat: 15g
- Carbohydrates: 28g
- Protein: 5g

Farro Pilaf with Wild Rice

Something really Indian is easy to cook with Instant Pot!

Prep time: 15 minutes | **Cooking time:** 25 minutes | **Servings:** 10

Ingredients:
- A drizzle olive oil
- Fresh herbs to serve
- 1 shallot
- ½ cup hazelnuts
- 1 teaspoon garlic
- ¾ cup cherries
- ¾ cup wild rice
- 1 teaspoon sea salt
- 1 ½ cup grain farro
- 1 tablespoon fresh herbs
- 6 cups broth

Directions:
1. Pour oil in the Instant Pot.
2. Mix onion, rice, farro, salt, garlic and hazelnuts. Place onion mix in the pressure cooker.
3. Add cherries and broth to the Instant Pot. Add hazelnuts.
4. Cook mix on "Rice" regime for 25 minutes.
5. Let the pressure release naturally (20 minutes).
6. Serve with fresh herbs!

Nutrition:
- Calories: 160
- Fat: 0g
- Carbohydrates: 33g
- Protein: 6g

Cherry Salad

Do you like cherry salad with the steaks and rice? Try and you will love it for sure

Prep time: 10 minutes | **Cooking time:** 40 minutes | **Servings:** 5

Ingredients:
- 1 cup grain farro
- 2 cups cherries
- 1 tablespoon apple cider vinegar
- 10 mint leaves
- 1 teaspoon lemon juice
- ¼ cup chives
- 1 tablespoon olive oil
- ½ cup dried cherries
- ¼ teaspoon sea salt

Directions:
1. Pour water in the Instant Pot.
2. Place farro in the Instant Pot and cook for 40 minutes on "High Pressure" regime.
3. Do a quick release.
4. Mix salt with cherries, oil, chives, lemon juice, mint leaves, vinegar and farro.
5. Serve!

Nutrition:
- Calories: 289
- Fat: 13g
- Carbohydrates: 37g
- Protein: 5g

Cornbread

You can eat cornbread with butter or try it with bacon – anyway it will be delicious dinner!

Prep time: 15 minutes | **Cooking time:** 20 minutes | **Servings:** 2

Ingredients:
- 1/2 packages Corn Muffin mix
- 1 egg
- 1 cup sesame seeds
- 1 teaspoon honey
- 1 tablespoon butter
- 2 tablespoons butter
- 1/2 cup milk
- 1 cup nuts

Directions:
1. Mix eggs with milk using mixer. You should get tender creamy sauce. Place butter in the Instant Pot and melt up. It will take you 3 minutes. Pour butter in milky mixture and mix well.
2. Add muffin mix to egg mixture and mix using mixer. Add honey and warm up mix in microwave for 1 minute.
3. Pour water in the Instant Pot. Mix with ingredients in the pressure cooker.
4. Mix ingredients well with milk mixture and add nuts. Pour more butter to the ingredients.
5. Cook on "High Pressure" regime. It will take you 20 minutes to prepare bread. The same time melt up honey. Just pour honey in a cup and place in the microwave. Cook for 1 minute.
6. Let the pressure release naturally (10 minutes). Pour honey over the bread.
7. Serve hot!

Nutrition:
- Calories: 220
- Fat: 1g
- Carbohydrates: 0g
- Protein: 2g

Blue Cheese Cheesecake

Try first vegetable cheese cheesecake!

Prep time: 15 minutes | **Cooking time:** 30 minutes | **Servings:** 1

Ingredients:
- 1/3 cup bread crumbs
- Salt to taste
- Pepper to taste
- 1/3 pecans
- 1/6 tablespoon rosemary
- 1/3 tablespoon butter
- 1/6 clove garlic

- 1oz cream cheese
- 1 egg
- 1oz blue cheese
- Spinach
- Pecans
- Sliced strawberries
- 1/2 tablespoons olive oil

- Salt and pepper to taste for the salad
- 1/2 tablespoons vinegar
- 1/6 garlic clove
- 1/2 tablespoons honey

Directions:
1. Wash fruits and vegetables. Carefully clean ingredients of leaves. Mix spinach with pecans and strawberries. Use blender to get soft and tender mixture.
2. Mix salt, pepper, garlic clove, honey, vinegar and olive oil. Pour vinegar mix over spinach salad. Mix well to coat all the ingredients.
3. Place butter in the Instant Pot and melt it up for 4 minutes on "Sauté" regime.
4. Mix crumbs with melted butter. You should get sauce texture mix, but do not overmix – there should be full crumbs in the mix.
5. Place crumbs layer on the bottom of the Instant Pot.
6. Mix eggs with cream cheese, pepper, salt, rosemary, garlic and pecans using blender.
7. Place cheese mix on the crumbs layer. Add blue cheese.
8. Cook cheesecake on "High Pressure" regime for 20 minutes.
9. Let the pressure release naturally (10 minutes).

Nutrition:
- Calories: 470
- Fat: 8g
- Carbohydrates: 59g
- Protein: 30g

Mexican Green Rice

Try Mexican herbs with tender rice and feel special taste today!

Prep time: 15 minutes | **Cooking time:** 10 minutes | **Servings:** 3

Ingredients:
- 1 ¼ cups vegetable broth
- Salt to taste
- Pepper to taste

- 1 cup long-grain rice
- ¼ cup green salsa
- ½ avocado

- ½ cup cilantro

Directions:
1. Pour broth in the Instant Pot.
2. Place rice in the pressure cooker and cook on "High Pressure" regime for 3 minutes.
3. Let the pressure release naturally for 10 minutes.
4. Blend avocado, cilantro, salsa, pepper and salt.
5. Mix rice with salsa mix and serve!

Nutrition:
- Calories: 600
- Fat: 0g
- Carbohydrates: 136g
- Protein: 12g

Rosemary Garlic Potatoes

Try really juicy potatoes for this dinner!

Prep time: 5 minutes | **Cooking time:** 5 minutes | **Servings:** 1

Ingredients:

- 1/3 pounds potatoes
- 1/2 springs rosemary
- 1/3 tablespoon olive oil
- 1/3 garlic cloves

Directions:

1. Pour water in the Instant Pot. Warm up water for 3 minutes on "Sauté" regime. Do not overcook – it should not start boiling.
2. Place slices potatoes in the pressure cooker and cook for 5 minutes on "High Pressure" regime.
3. Let the pressure release naturally (10 minutes).
4. Remove potato from the Instant Pot.
5. Pour oil in the pressure cooker and add rosemary with garlic.
6. Cook on "Sauté" regime for 5 minutes. Wait until ingredients will be soft enough. Place seasoning over potatoes.
7. Serve potato with rosemary mix!

Nutrition:

- Calories: 142
- Fat: 7g
- Carbohydrates: 18g
- Protein: 2g

Stuffing

The most satisfying receipt for the dinner today!

Prep time: 15 minutes | **Cooking time:** 25 minutes | **Servings:** 12

Ingredients:

- 4 cups chicken broth
- 1 teaspoon pepper
- 2 cups butter
- 4 teaspoons poultry seasoning
- 4 cups celery
- 1 cup shredded turkey meat
- 4 teaspoons sage
- 4 onions
- 8 teaspoons salt
- 4 loaves bread (toasted)

Directions:

1. Cut bread into cubes. They should be one cm size.
2. Mix butter with broth, pepper, salt, seasoning, celery and onion with sage. Use fork to mix seasoning well.
3. Add cubes loaf to seasoning mix. Cubes should be covered. Add shredded turkey meat and mix well with seasoning.
4. Place in the Instant Pot and cook on "High Pressure" regime for 15 minutes.
5. Let the pressure release naturally (10 minutes).
6. Place mix on the baking form and bake in the oven (preheated up to 350oF) for 10 minutes.
7. Serve hot!

Nutrition:

- Calories: 350
- Fat: 17g
- Carbohydrates: 43g
- Protein: 6g

BLT Potato Salad

Try satisfying salad with the creamy sauce and tender cheese!

Prep time: 10 minutes | **Cooking time:** 5 minutes | **Servings:** 12

Ingredients:

- 12 russet potatoes
- Salt to taste
- Pepper to taste
- 2 cups water
- 2 cups parsley
- 6 eggs
- 10 tomatoes
- 2 cups mayonnaise
- 12 bacon slices
- 2 tablespoons dill pickle juice
- 6 green onions
- 2 tablespoons mustard

Directions:

1. Pour water in the Instant Pot. Warm up water for 3 minutes on "Sauté" regime, but be careful – do not bring water to boil.
2. Wash and peel potatoes carefully using knife. Wash peeled potatoes one more time and cube potatoes. Peel them using knife.
3. Mix potatoes with beaten eggs. Use mixer to get well mixed mixture.
4. Place potatoes in the pressure cooker and cook on "High Pressure" regime. It will take you 5 minutes to finish cooking session.
5. Let the pressure release naturally (10 minutes).
6. Mix juice, mayonnaise, mustard, onions, bacon slices, tomatoes, salt, pepper and parsley. Place sauce over potatoes.

Nutrition:

- Calories: 210
- Fat: 15g
- Carbohydrates: 17g
- Protein: 4g

Goat Cheese Risotto

Goat cheese is several times more tender and super healthy – try it right now!

Prep time: 10 minutes | **Cooking time:** 10 minutes | **Servings:** 16

Ingredients:

- 4 tablespoons olive oil
- 1 cup toasted pecans
- 1 cup onion
- 8 ounces goat cheese
- 4 garlic cloves
- 4 tablespoons lemon juice
- 2 cups rice
- Pepper to taste
- 1 cup wine
- 24 ounces spinach leaves
- 6 cups vegetable broth

Directions:

1. Pour oil in the Instant Pot. Warm up oil for 2 minutes on "Sauté" regime. It should not start bulbing.
2. Wash and clean onion. Cut onion on cubes. Mix chopped onions with garlic.
3. Place onion mix with rice, pepper and pecans in the pressure cooker.
4. Cook on "Sauté" regime for 5 minutes.
5. Mix spinach leaves with goat cheese. Use mixer on the second speed to get well mixed sauce.
6. Pour wine, broth and juice to the pressure cooker. Add cheese mix to the Instant Pot.
7. Cook risotto for 5 minutes on "High Pressure" regime.
8. Let the pressure release naturally (10 minutes).

Nutrition:

- Calories: 242
- Fat: 7g
- Carbohydrates: 35g
- Protein: 8g

MAIN DISHES

Shredded Chicken

Soft, tender and low in calories chicken receipt is common and easy to cook in Instant Pot!

Prep time: 15 minutes | **Cooking time:** 20 minutes | **Servings:** 4

Ingredients:
- 4 pounds chicken breast
- ½ teaspoon black pepper
- ½ cup water
- 1 teaspoon salt

Directions:
1. Chop chicken meat. Cover chicken meat with pepper and salt.
2. Place chicken in the Instant Pot.
3. Cover chicken with water.
4. Cook meat on "Poultry" regime for 20 minutes.
5. Serve with herbs!

Nutrition:
- Calories: 230
- Fat: 9g
- Carbohydrates: 0g
- Protein: 46g

Whole Chicken

Juicy, spicy and really delicious whole chicken will be extremely with Instant Pot!

Prep time: 10 minutes | **Cooking time**: 40 minutes | **Servings**: 8

Ingredients:
- 4 pounds chicken
- Pepper
- 1 tablespoon coconut oil
- Italian herbs
- Salt to taste

Directions:
1. Pour coconut oil in the Instant Pot.
2. Saute chicken in the Instant Pot for 6 minutes.
3. Add seasoning and water to the chicken.
4. Cook chicken on "Poultry" regime for 25 minutes.
5. Serve with lemon juice!

Nutrition:
- Calories: 140
- Fat: 7g
- Carbohydrates: 0.5g
- Protein: 19g

Potato Chili

Truly vegetarian, low in calories and healthy chili receipt! Potato Chili is traditional southern receipt, that won't leave you unmoved for sure!

Prep time: 5 minutes | **Cooking time:** 15 minutes | **Servings:** 2

Ingredients:

- 1/4 bell peppers
- 1 cup vegetable broth
- 2 onions
- 1/2 tablespoons chili powder
- 1/2 potatoes
- 3 tomatoes
- 5 tablespoons oil
- 2 teaspoon cumin
- 2 garlic cloves
- 1/2 teaspoon cinnamon
- 2 tablespoon coconut oil
- 1/4 teaspoons cocoa powder
- 2 teaspoons garlic
- 1/4 can diced tomatoes
- 2 cans black beans
- 1 pack chips

Directions:

1. Turn on "Saute" regime on Instant Pot.
2. Mix chopped tomatoes, dried beans after soaking them in water for 15 minutes, garlic cloves, cubed potatoes, chopped onions with oil and saute for 3 minutes.
3. Add remaining ingredients to the Instant Pot. Mix well in the Instant Pot to get salad conscience.
4. Cook chili on "High Pressure" for 15 minutes.
5. Turn on frying pan and pour oil on it.
6. Wash and cut tomatoes.
7. Fry tomatoes on the frying pan for 6 minutes.
8. Add chips to the vegetable mix and tomatoes!

Nutrition:

- Calories: 1110
- Fat: 78g
- Carbohydrates: 55g
- Protein:49g

White Bean Chili

Chicken, healthy white beans and super quick receipt for Instant Pot – now you have all the necessary reasons to call this day successful!

Prep time: 10 minutes | **Cooking time:** 30 minutes | **Servings:** 17

Ingredients:

- 5 pounds northern beans
- Salt to taste
- 4 cups onion
- 13 tablespoons vegetable shortening
- 8 garlic cloves

- 9 chicken thighs
- 12 tablespoons flour
- 4 cups chicken broth
- 2 teaspoons chili powder
- 8 ounces green chilies
- 1 teaspoon cumin

- 17 ounces diced tomatoes
- 4 ½ teaspoon coriander
- 3 ½ teaspoon black pepper
- 3 ½ teaspoon oregano

Directions:

1. Coat beans with water and set aside.
2. Mix chopped onion, flour, garlic, chili powder, coriander, cumin, pepper, oregano, chilies, tomatoes and chicken broth.
3. Place chicken mix in the Instant Pot.
4. Add beans to the Instant Pot.
5. Add remaining ingredients to the Pot.
6. Cook on "Chili" regime for 30 minutes.
7. Let chili in the Instant Pot and let the pressure release naturally for 10 minutes!

Nutrition:

- Calories: 241
- Fat: 11g

- Carbohydrates: 25g
- Protein:16g

Mississippi Pot-Roast

Meat in Instant Pot is super delicious! Full of juice, taste and with hot seasoning – you will like it for sure!

Prep time: 10 minutes | **Cooking time:** 90 minutes | **Servings:** 5

Ingredients:
- 5lb arm roast
- 7 pepperoncinis
- ½ cup beef broth
- ¼ cup butter
- ½ cup pepperoncini sauce
- 1 envelope gravy mix
- 1 envelope dressing mix

Directions:
1. Mix juice with broth and pour in the Pressure Cooker.
2. Place roast in the Instant Pot.
3. Cover roast with seasoning.
4. Place butter and pepperoncini on top.
5. Cook meat for 90 minutes on "Meat" regime.
6. Serve with herbs!

Nutrition:
- Calories: 300
- Fat: 17g
- Carbohydrates: 3g
- Protein:32g

Steak Meatballs

Meatballs with juice and broth will be both satisfying and super tender!

Prep time: 5 minutes | **Cooking time:** 20 minutes | **Servings:** 9

Ingredients:
- 3 teaspoons olive oil
- Parsley
- 1 cup minced onions
- 1 cup beef broth
- 1 lb beef
- 8oz mushrooms
- 1 lb turkey
- 1 teaspoon mustard powder
- 1 cup breadcrumbs
- 4 teaspoons Worcestershire sauce
- 3 eggs
- 2 teaspoons red vinegar
- 4 tablespoons tomato paste
- 3 tablespoons flour
- Salt to taste
- Pepper to taste

Directions:
1. Mix chopped mushrooms with onions and saute in the Instant Pot for 5 minutes.
2. Mix flour and broth with vinegar, sauce, mustard powder and tomato paste. Set aside.
3. Mix remaining ingredients.
4. Form meatballs.
5. Place meatballs in the Instant Pot and cover with tomato sauce mix.
6. Add mushrooms and onions.
7. Cook for 20 minutes on "High Pressure" regime.
8. Serve with fresh green onion!

Nutrition:
- Calories: 260
- Fat: 22g
- Carbohydrates: 5g
- Protein:12g

Chicken in Milk

Poultry dinner with creams and milk will make your lunch unforgettable!

Prep time: 20 minutes | **Cooking time:** 5 hours | **Servings:** 15

Ingredients:
- 5-pound chicken
- 6 ¼ cups milk
- Salt
- Lemon zest
- 5 ½ tablespoon pepper
- 3 ½ cinnamon stick
- 6 tablespoon olive oil
- 3 ¼ cup sage leaves
- 10 garlic cloves

Directions:
1. Wash and clean chicken from the insights.
2. Pour oil on the frying pan and fry chicken from the all sides.
3. Place chicken in the Instant Pot and add juice.
4. Mix garlic cloves, apple juice, sage leaves, olive oil, cinnamon, pepper, lemon zest and salt and add to the chicken.
5. Cover chicken with milk. Cook poultry in the Instant Pot for 5 hours on "Low Pressure" regime.
6. Serve with herbs!

Nutrition:
- Calories: 400
- Fat: 7g
- Carbohydrates: 18g
- Protein:34g

Carnitas

Mexican style pork with fresh herbs and juice vegetables will make your dinner satisfying and light the same time!

Prep time: 10 minutes | **Cooking time:** 75 minutes | **Servings:** 15

Ingredients:
- 5 pounds pork meat
- Lime
- 2 cups chicken stock
- Salsa to taste
- 6 garlic cloves
- 13 tortillas
- 3 onions
- Pepper to taste
- 3 teaspoons cumin
- Salt to taste
- 3 teaspoons cinnamon powder
- 1 cup juice
- 2 bay leaves
- 1 tablespoon soy sauce

Directions:
1. Wash and cut meat.
2. Place meat in the Instant Pot.
3. Mix salt, pepper, garlic, onion, cumin, cinnamon powder, soy sauce, bay leaves, juice and chicken stock.
4. Pour marinade on the meat.
5. Cook meat in the Instant Pot for 30 minutes on "High Pressure" regime.
6. Roast pork in the oven for 10 minutes (450oF).
7. Serve with the tortillas!

Nutrition:
- Calories: 47
- Fat: 3g
- Carbohydrates: 0.5g
- Protein: 5g

Turkey in Mushroom Sauce

Soft and tender mushrooms in creams with satisfying pork meat melting in your mouse – something extra delicious!

Prep time: 15 minutes | **Cooking time:** 35 minutes | **Servings:** 13

Ingredients:

- 6lbs turkey
- 4 tablespoons water
- 13 cremini mushrooms
- 5 tablespoons cornstarch
- 3 onions
- 4 tablespoons soy sauce

- 13 garlic cloves
- 5 tablespoons Worcestershire sauce
- 1 shallot
- 3 cups chicken stock
- Dash of sherry wine

- Salt to taste
- Pepper to taste
- 2 tablespoons peanut oil
- 1 cup heavy creams

Directions:

1. Pour oil in the Instant Pot and preheat it until hot.
2. Place turkey meat in the Instant Pot for 15 minutes and cook on "Poultry" regime. Remove and set aside pork meat after the cooking.
3. Place mushrooms and onions in the Instant Pot and cook for 7 minutes on "High Pressure" regime.
4. Mix seasoning with garlic and shallot. Add mix to the mushrooms and cook for 2 more minutes on the same regime.
5. Mix Worcestershire sauce with soy sauce and chicken stock.
6. Place meat with sauce in the Instant Pot and cook for 5 minutes not changing the regime.
7. Serve immediately!

Nutrition:

- Calories: 127
- Fat: 15g
- Carbohydrates:25g
- Protein: 13g

Turkey with Tomato Sauce

Tender pork can be hot and spicy with real tomato sauce – try this receipt and make sure!

Prep time: 10 minutes | **Cooking time:** 20 minutes | **Servings:** 3

Ingredients:

- 4lbs turkey
- 1 ½ tablespoon cornstarch
- ½ teaspoon white sugar
- Salt to taste
- Pepper to taste
- ¼ teaspoon sesame oil

- 1 cup water
- 1 tablespoon soy sauce
- 1 teaspoon Worcestershire sauce
- ½ tablespoon dark soy sauce
- 1 tablespoon peanut oil

- 1 onion
- 2 tablespoon ketchup
- 4 garlic cloves
- 1/3 cup tomato paste
- 1 shallot
- 8 mushrooms

Directions:

1. Mix sugar, salt, oil and two types of soy sauce.
2. Marinade turkey in soy sauce for 15 minutes.
3. Wash and cut mushrooms.
4. Pour peanut oil in the Instant Pot and place pork chops in it.
5. Cook pork chops for 8 minutes.
6. Mix shallot and onions with garlic. Place onion mix in the Instant Pot and add mushrooms. Cook for 3 minutes on "High Pressure" regime.
7. Add water to the meat.
8. Mix ketchup, sugar and Worcestershire sauce with tomato paste. Add to the pork.
9. Cook meat for 3 minutes more on "Meat" regime.
10. Serve pork with tomato sauce on top!

Nutrition:

- Calories: 203
- Fat: 7g

- Carbohydrates: 4g
- Protein:23g

Bolognese Pasta

Traditional Bolognese pasta is tender, satisfying and can become your favorite lunch – just follow right receipt!

Prep time: 5 minutes | **Cooking time:** 25 minutes | **Servings:** 4

Ingredients:

- ½ pound beef
- 1 tablespoon Worcestershire sauce
- 16oz penne rigate
- 1 tablespoon fish sauce
- 12 mushrooms

- 2 tablespoons light soy sauce
- 3 garlic cloves
- 5.5 fl oz tomato paste
- 1 celery
- 1 cup chicken stock
- 1 onion

- Olive oil
- Dash of sherry wine
- Salt to taste
- Pepper to taste
- Pinch of dried oregano
- Pinch of dried basil

Directions:

1. Pour olive oil in the Instant Pot.
2. Cover beef meat with salt and pepper.
3. Mix seasoning with garlic and onions, mushrooms, oregano, celery and basil. Saute vegetable mix in the Instant Pot for 3 minutes.
4. Remove vegetables from the Instant Pot and brown beef meat in it.
5. Pour chicken stock, water, soy sauce, fish sauce and Worcestershire sauce in the Instant Pot. Add vegetable mix to the meat.
6. Cook for 2 minutes on "High Pressure" regime.
7. Add remaining ingredients to the Instant Pot and cook on "High Pressure" regime for 4 minutes.
8. Leave pasta in the Instant Pot and let the pressure release naturally for 5 minutes!

Nutrition:

- Calories: 650
- Fat: 10g

- Carbohydrates: 55g
- Protein:26g

Penne Pasta

Can pasta be super healthy dinner? With Instant Pot it can!

Prep time: 5 minutes | **Cooking time:** 20 minutes | **Servings:** 13

Ingredients:

- 18oz penne
- 3 tablespoons fish sauce
- 4 onions
- 3 tablespoons Worcestershire sauce
- Dash of sherry wine

- 5 shallot s
- 6 tablespoons light soy sauce
- 5 garlic cloves
- 7fl oz tomato paste

- 18 mushrooms
- 4 cups chicken stock
- 4 zucchini squash
- Olive oil

Directions:

1. Pour olive oil in the Instant Pot.
2. Mix shallot, onion, salt, pepper, mushrooms and zucchini squash.
3. Place zucchini mix in the Instant Pot and cook for 3 minutes on "High Pressure" regime.
4. Mix sherry wine, chicken stock, water and sauces in the Instant Pot.
5. Add pasta and tomato paste to the Instant Pot.
6. Cook pasta on "High Pressure" regime for 6 minutes.
7. Leave pasta in the Instant Pot and let the pressure release naturally for 7 minutes.
8. Serve with zucchini!

Nutrition:

- Calories: 220
- Fat: 1g

- Carbohydrates: 43g
- Protein:8g

Chicken Congee

Chicken porridge with herbs in Instant Pot will be juicy, fresh and soft!

Prep time: 5 minutes | **Cooking time:** 60 minutes | **Servings:** 7

Ingredients:
- 1 cup rice
- Salt to taste
- 7 cups water
- Green onions
- 6 drumsticks
- 1 tablespoon ginger

Directions:
1. Pour water in the Instant Pot.
2. Add rice to the Instant Pot.
3. Mix ginger, onions and salt with meat and put in the Instant Pot.
4. Cook meat with rice for 30 minutes on "High Pressure" regime.
5. Serve porridge with herbs!

Nutrition:
- Calories: 318
- Fat: 5g
- Carbohydrates: 23g
- Protein:41g

Pork Chops

Real meat with juice, herbs and fresh vegetables – meat lovers will go crazy about this receipt!

Prep time: 20 minutes | **Cooking time:** 3 hours | **Servings:** 5

Ingredients:
- 5 pork chops
- 8 ¼ cup water
- ½ cup salt
- Celery
- Bay leaf
- Chopped vegetables to taste

Directions:
1. Mix herbs with salt and place in the fridge for 2 hours.
2. Fry washed and chopped vegetables on the frying pan for 3 minutes.
3. Pour water in the Instant Pot.
4. Add marinated pork chops in the Instant Pot and cook for 3 hours on "Low Pressure" regime.
5. Serve with the fried vegetables!

Nutrition:
- Calories: 102
- Fat: 5g
- Carbohydrates: 0g
- Protein:13g

Pork Carnitas

Spanish rolls with pork and onions – easy, super soft and super juicy dinner!

Prep time: 20 minutes | **Cooking time:** 8 hours | **Servings:** 20

Ingredients:
- 1 pound pork
- 3 cups water
- 2 tablespoons salt
- 1 can tomatoes
- 1 tablespoon cumin
- 4 peppers
- 1 tablespoon pepper
- 8 garlic cloves
- 1 tablespoon oregano
- 1 teaspoon cayenne pepper
- 2 teaspoons cinnamon

Directions:
1. Mix cinnamon, cayenne pepper, oregano, garlic cloves, pepper, cumin, salt.
2. Place pork in the seasoning mix and top with tomatoes.
3. Place meat in the Instant Pot.
4. Cook meat on "Low Pressure" regime for 8 hours.
5. Serve in tortillas with pineapple and onion!

Nutrition:
- Calories: 150
- Fat: 10g
- Carbohydrates: 5g
- Protein:11g

Korean Ribs

What is Korean cuisine famous for? Spices and herbs! Try them in your ration right today!

Prep time: 20 minutes | **Cooking time:** 9 hours | **Servings:** 5

Ingredients:
- 6 pounds beef ribs
- Handful cilantro
- Salt to taste
- 1 cup chicken broth
- Pepper to taste
- 1 tablespoon coconut vinegar
- 1 pear
- 2 teaspoons fish sauce
- ½ cup coconut aminos
- 1 piece ginger
- 6 garlic cloves
- 3 scallions

Directions:
1. Cover meat with pepper.
2. Pour water into the bowl and preheat it.
3. Place ribs in boiling water and cook for 10 minutes.
4. Place ribs in the Instant Pot.
5. Add remaining ingredients to the Instant Pot and cook meat for 9 hours on "Low Pressure" regime.
6. Serve with sauce and cilantro!

Nutrition:
- Calories: 379
- Fat: 25g
- Carbohydrates: 3g
- Protein:31g

Brisket

Tender and spicy meat with colorful onions will be both independent dinner and perfect satisfying to the sides!

Prep time: 20 minutes | **Cooking time:** 9 hours | **Servings:** 12

Ingredients:
- 2 tablespoons olive oil
- 2 tablespoon soy sauce
- 3 pounds red onions
- 4 tablespoon Worcestershire sauce
- 7 pounds beef brisket
- 4 cups broth
- Salt to taste
- 12 garlic cloves
- Pepper to taste

Directions:
1. Fry meat with onions on the frying pan for 20 minutes.
2. Mix remaining ingredients and cover meat with marinade.
3. Place meat with onions in the Instant Pot and cook on "Low Pressure" regime for 8 hours.
4. Leave meat in the Instant Pot and let the pressure release naturally for 30 minutes.
5. Serve with herbs!

Nutrition:
- Calories: 44
- Fat: 2g
- Carbohydrates: 0g
- Protein:6g

Barbacoa Beef

Try something new today and do nothing the same time – just put ingredients in the Instant Pot and wait! Just imagine tender and soft beef cooked in its own juice melting on your tongue!

Prep time: 20 minutes | **Cooking time:** 9 hours | **Servings:** 3

Ingredients:
- 1/4 cans chipotles
- 1 bay leaf
- 1/4 bunch cilantro
- 1/2 cups chicken stock
- 1/6 onion
- 1 pound beef brisket
- 1/4 head garlic
- 1/6 cup vinegar
- 1/4 teaspoon ground cloves
- 2 lime juice
- Salt to taste

Directions:
1. Place lime juice, salt, minced garlic cloves, vinegar, cleaned garlic head, bay leaf, cilantro and chopped onion in the Instant Pot.
2. Top vegie mix with the beef brisket.
3. Cover meat with water. You will need 3 cups water to get juicy meat!
4. Cook meat on "Low Pressure" regime for 9 hours.
5. Serve with cilantro and tortillas!

Nutrition:
- Calories: 165
- Fat: 7g
- Carbohydrates: 2g
- Protein:24g

Chicken Burrito Bowls

Satisfying and tender burrito bowls on the dinner table is not complicated to cook – Instant Pot will make everything instead of you!

Prep time: 20 minutes | **Cooking time:** 8 hours | **Servings:** 2

Ingredients:
- 1/2 pound chicken breasts
- 1/2 cup frozen corn
- 1/3 can tomatoes
- 1/2 can black beans
- 1 cup chicken stock
- 1/4 cup brown rice
- 1 teaspoons chili powder
- 1/3 teaspoon cumin
- 1 teaspoon salt

Directions:
1. Mix chicken meat with tomatoes.
2. Mix remaining ingredients (apart from corn, beans and rice).
3. Place ingredients in the Instant Pot and cook on low pressure for 4 hours.
4. Add rice, corn and beans to the Instant Pot and cook on "Low Pressure" regime for 4 hours more.
5. Serve with avocado!

Nutrition:
- Calories:472
- Fat: 12g
- Carbohydrates: 67g
- Protein:52g

Spinach Ragatoni with Mozzarella

National Italian cuisine is always satisfying and healthy the same time – try Italian style pasta with soft and tender mozzarella cheese!

Prep time: 20 minutes | **Cooking time:** 4 hours | **Servings:** 7

Ingredients:
- 7 cups tomato sauce
- ½ cup parmesan
- 1 pack penne
- 1/8 teaspoon red pepper flakes
- 1 container ricotta cheese
- ½ teaspoon sugar
- 2 cups mozzarella cheese
- 2 ½ teaspoon salt
- 1 ball mozzarella
- 2 tablespoons olive oil
- 1 pack spinach
- 4 garlic cloves

Directions:
1. Mix cheese with olive oil, seasoning and tomato sauce.
2. Add pasta to the cheesy mix.
3. Cook pasta for 3 ½ hours on "Low Pressure" regime in the Instant Pot.
4. Cook pasta for 20 minutes more on "High Pressure" regime.
5. Top with more cheese and serve!

Nutrition:
- Calories: 200
- Fat: 1g
- Carbohydrates:41g
- Protein:7g

Ratatouille

Famous French vegetables with seasoning and sauce – tender dinner for real vegetable lovers!

Prep time: 30 minutes | **Cooking time:** 6 hours | **Servings:** 9

Ingredients:

- 4 tablespoons olive oil
- ¼ cup chopped basil leaves
- 2 onions
- ½ teaspoon salt
- 1 pound eggplant
- 2 tablespoons tomato paste
- 1 pound zucchini squash
- 4 garlic cloves
- 2 red bell peppers
- 1 pound tomatoes

Directions:

1. Fry onions with salt on the frying pan for 30 minutes.
2. Wash and cut vegetables.
3. Place vegetables with garlic in the Instant Pot and cover with onions.
4. Add olive oil and tomato paste to the vegetable mix and sprinkle with pepper.
5. Cook vegetable mix for 4 hours on "High Pressure" regime.
6. Serve with fresh basil leaves!

Nutrition:

- Calories:154
- Fat: 3g
- Carbohydrates: 12g
- Protein:2g

Sloppy Joes

Can we cook burger in the Instant Pot quickly? Of course we can! What is sloppy? It is your easy, healthy and satisfying dinner full of juice and taste!

Prep time: 20 minutes | **Cooking time:** 30 minutes | **Servings:** 1

Ingredients:

- 1/2 pounds turkey
- 1 hamburger bun
- 1/3 onion
- 1/8 teaspoon pepper
- 1/2 bell pepper
- 1/4 teaspoon salt
- 1/2 can tomato sauce
- 1/2 teaspoon paprika
- 1/3 tablespoons tomato paste
- 1/2 teaspoon garlic powder
- 1 tablespoon honey
- 1/4 tablespoon mustard
- 1 tablespoon apple cider vinegar

Directions:

1. Mix vinegar, mustard, honey, powder, tomato paste and pepper.
2. Coat meat with honey mix and add tomato sauce.
3. Add chopped onion to the mix.
4. Place meaty mix in the Instant Pot apart from buns.
5. Cook burger filling for 30 minutes on "High Pressure" regime. After the Instant Pot, place meaty mix with sauce on the frying pan and make it crispy frying for 5 minutes.
6. Place buns in the Pot and cook separately for 5 minutes on "High Pressure" regime (with no water).
7. Place meat on the buns and cover with sauce.
8. Serve as burgers!

Nutrition:

- Calories: 371
- Fat: 19g
- Carbohydrates: 22g
- Protein:29g

Tikka Masala

Asian cuisine can be super soft and delicious – just avoid odd one spices and save juicy taste!

Prep time: 20 minutes | **Cooking time:** 8 hours | **Servings:** 15

Ingredients:

- 3 pounds chicken thighs
- 6 cups cooked rice
- 3 onions
- Cilantro
- 3 garlic cloves
- 1 cup heavy creams
- 3-inch ginger
- 2 cans tomatoes
- 6 tablespoons tomato paste
- 5 teaspoons salt
- 6 teaspoons garam masala
- 6 teaspoons salt
- 4 teaspoons paprika

Directions:

1. Wash and cut chicken.
2. Mix onion, garlic, tomato paste, ginger, salt, paprika and garam masala with tomatoes.
3. Coat chicken with marinade.
4. Place chicken in the Instant Pot and cook on "Low Pressure" regime for 8 hours.
5. Add creams a few minutes before the end of cooking session.
6. Serve chicken with rice!

Nutrition:

- Calories: 483
- Fat: 22g
- Carbohydrates: 28g
- Protein:7g

Ham with Maple-Honey Sauce

Bone in meat always more juicy and soft – what a perfect taste it will be after the Instant Pot!

Prep time: 5 minutes | **Cooking time:** 25 minutes | **Servings**: 3

Ingredients:

- ½ cup maple sauce
- 1 bone-in ham
- ½ cup honey
- 1 teaspoon nutmeg
- ¼ cup brown sugar
- 1 teaspoon cinnamon
- 2 teaspoons orange juice

Directions:

1. Mix orange juice, cinnamon, sugar, nutmeg, honey and sauce.
2. Marinade ham in the sauce for 15 minutes.
3. Place ham in the Instant Pot for 15 minutes. Cook on "High Pressure" regime.
4. Add more honey to the meat.
5. Serve with fresh herbs!

Nutrition:

- Calories: 100
- Fat: 30g
- Carbohydrates: 0g
- Protein:0g

Panade with Sausage and Beans

One of the easiest and quickest dinners you can cook!

Prep time: 20 minutes | **Cooking time:** 5 hours | **Servings:** 7

Ingredients:
- 1 pound country bread
- 4 cups chicken broth
- 1 tablespoon olive oil
- 2 cups mozzarella cheese
- 8 ounces pork sausage
- 2 cans cannellini beans
- 1 onion
- 1 teaspoon thyme
- 1 Swiss chard
- 2 garlic cloves

Directions:
1. Make breadcrumbs of the bread.
2. Fry onion slices with the sausage on the frying pan for 10 minutes.
3. Mix chard for 5 minutes using blender.
4. Mix garlic, thyme and chards and cook for 4 minutes more.
5. Add salt and pepper to the chards.
6. Place bread cubes in the Instant Pot.
7. Add chard mix and bread to the Instant Pot.
8. Top chards with cheese and remaining ingredients.
9. Cook on "High Pressure" regime for 5 hours.
10. Serve with fresh lettuce!

Nutrition:
- Calories:319
- Fat: 4g
- Carbohydrates: 63g
- Protein:11g

Mac and Cheese

Baked macaroni with cheese and seasoning in the Instant Pot is possible to cook saving juice and taste!

Prep time: 20 minutes | **Cooking time:** 3 hours | **Servings:** 9

Ingredients:
- 3 cups cheese
- 3 teaspoon mustard
- 2 pounds macaroni
- 4 teaspoon salt
- 2 cups milk
- 3 cans evaporated milk

Directions:
1. Mix milk with cheese.
2. Mix salt with mustard.
3. Add mustard to the mac.
4. Add milk mixture to the mac.
5. Place pasta in the Instant Pot and cook for 3 minutes on "Low Pressure" regime.
6. In the end of cooking session top mac with cheese.
7. Leave mac in the Instant Pot and let the pressure release naturally for 10 minutes.
8. Serve mac with creams!

Nutrition:
- Calories: 240
- Fat: 9g
- Carbohydrates: 25g
- Protein:15g

Vindaloo

So many spices and herbs on pork tender meat – make this day special and guarantee happiness for yourself!

| **Prep time:** 20 minutes | **Cooking time:** 3 hours 30 minutes | **Servings:** 21 |

Ingredients:

- 3 piece ginger
- 3 tablespoons vinegar
- 9 tablespoons canola oil
- 6 tablespoons tamarind paste
- 1 teaspoon fenugreek seeds
- 3 teaspoons sugar

- 9 onions
- 3 pieces cassia
- 8 pounds pork shoulder
- 20 peppercorns
- 16 cloves garlic
- 12 cardamom pods
- 12 sarrano chilies

- 2 teaspoons brown mustard seeds
- 2 teaspoons turmeric
- 3 teaspoons cumin seeds
- 2 teaspoons red chile
- 6 teaspoons coriander seeds
- 2 teaspoons salt

Directions:

1. Mince ginger.
2. Fry seeds with onion on the frying pan for 10 minutes.
3. Mix ginger, onions, garlic, turmeric, chiles, salt and chilie.
4. Add mix to the Instant Pot and cook for 3 hours on "Low Pressure" regime.
5. Mix remaining ingredients and add in the Instant Pot.
6. Cook mix on "Low Pressure" regime for 30 minutes.
7. Serve with ginger!

Nutrition:

- Calories: 230
- Fat: 6g

- Carbohydrates: 16g
- Protein: 26g

Chana Masala

Indian traditions mixed with Chinese style – there is never enough Asia!

Prep time: 20 minutes | **Cooking time:** 5 hours | **Servings:** 7

Ingredients:

- 2 cups chickpeas
- 1 ½ teaspoon salt
- 5 cups water
- ¼ teaspoons Indian red chile
- 2 cardamom pods
- ¼ teaspoon turmeric

- 2 pieces cassia
- 2 bay leaves
- 6 cloves
- 3 tablespoons canola oil
- 2 serrano leaves
- 1 onion
- ½ teaspoon pepper

- 6 garlic cloves
- ¾ teaspoon mango powder
- 3 peeled tomatoes
- 2 teaspoons cumin
- 1 ½ tablespoons coriander

Directions:

1. Mix chickpeas with water, cardamom, bay leaves, chile, cassia, garlic cloves and salt with turmeric.
2. Cook seasoning mix on "High Pressure" regime for 10 minutes.
3. Fry onions with garlic for 10 minutes.
4. Blend tomatoes.
5. Place chickpea, cassia, pods, seasoning with onion in the Instant Pot.
6. Cook mix for 5 hours on "High Pressure" regime.
7. Serve with fresh herbs!

Nutrition:

- Calories: 423
- Fat: 14g

- Carbohydrates: 60g
- Protein:19g

Lemon Dal

Can Asian cuisine be super satisfying? With Instant Pot it can!

Prep time: 20 minutes | **Cooking time:** 3 hours | **Servings:** 14

Ingredients:
- 2 cups lentils
- 12 kari
- 10 cups water
- 2 teaspoon brown mustard seeds
- 1 onion
- 2 tablespoons ghee
- 8 cloves garlic
- 2 tablespoons milk
- 1 piece ginger
- 4 tablespoons lemon juice
- 5 serrano chiles
- 2 teaspoons salt

Directions:
1. Place lentils in the Instant Pot.
2. Cover lentils with the onions and remaining ingredients apart from kari leaves.
3. Cook dish for 2 hours on "High Pressure" regime.
4. Add water to the Instant Pot and cook dish for 30 minutes more on the same regime.
5. Serve hot with kari leaves!

Nutrition:
- Calories: 220
- Fat: 5g
- Carbohydrates: 29g
- Protein:11g

Biryani

No one can cook rice better than Middle East habitats – we are ready to prove this fact with this receipt!

Prep time: 20 minutes | **Cooking time:** 60 minutes | **Servings:** 7

Ingredients:
- 2 cups basmati rice
- 4 serrano chiles
- 6 cups water
- ¼ cups golden raisins
- 3 teaspoons salt
- ¼ cup cashews
- 3 tablespoons milk
- 1 Cornish
- 1 teaspoons threads
- ½ teaspoon turmeric
- 2 onions
- 1 teaspoon red chile
- 2 tablespoons ghee
- 1 tablespoon coriander
- 1 piece ginger
- 2 tablespoons garam masala
- 8 garlic cloves
- 1 tablespoon yogurt
- 1 tomato

Directions:
1. Wash rice and soak it in water for 30 minutes.
2. Mix onion with milk and fry on the frying pan for 10 minutes.
3. Add ghee and onions to the frying pan and cook for 7 minutes on "High Pressure" regime.
4. Mix remaining ingredients and place with the fried onions in the Instant Pot.
5. Cook rice with seasoning and vegetables for 15 minutes on "High Pressure" regime.
6. Serve with fresh herbs!

Nutrition:
- Calories: 640
- Fat: 22g
- Carbohydrates: 80g
- Protein:10g

Spaghetti Dinner

Italian, satisfying, healthy and tender – perfect dinner in Instant Pot!

Prep time: 5 minutes | **Cooking time:** 5 minutes | **Servings:** 12

Ingredients:

- 4 tablespoons olive oil
- 2 pounds spaghetti
- 1 onion
- 4 garlic cloves
- 28 ounces diced tomatoes
- Parmesan to serve
- 6 ounces tomato paste
- 2 teaspoons fennel seeds
- 20 ounces tomato sauce
- 1 teaspoon pepper
- 4 cups chicken stock
- 1 teaspoon red pepper flakes
- 4 teaspoons basil
- 2 teaspoons sea salt
- 2 teaspoons oregano
- 2 teaspoons brown sugar
- 4 teaspoons parsley flakes

Directions:

1. Pour oil in the Instant Pot.
2. Warm it up for 4 minutes in the Instant Pot on "Sauté" regime. Be careful not to bring oil to boil.
3. Wash and clean onions. Cut onions on small cubes. Chop onions and place in the pressure cooker.
4. Mix onions with garlic and cook for 1 minute on "Sauté" regime.
5. Break spaghetti on halves. Place spaghetti in the Instant Pot.
6. Mix tomatoes, tomato paste, tomato sauce, chicken stock, basil, oregano, parsley flakes, brown sugar, sea salt, red pepper flakes, pepper and fennel seeds. Use blender to get tender sauce.
7. Pour tomato sauce over pasta. Mix well to coat all pasta.
8. Cook for 5 minutes on "High Pressure" regime.
9. Let the pressure release naturally (5 minutes).

Nutrition:

- Calories: 496
- Fat: 8g
- Carbohydrates: 86g
- Protein: 27g

Broccoli and Cheddar Pasta

Tender veggie sauce over satisfying and easy to cook pasta will be your favorite lunch receipt!

Prep time: 2 minutes | **Cooking time:** 5 minutes | **Servings:** 12

Ingredients:

- 3 pounds pasta
- 3 cups milk
- 12 cups water
- 3 cups frozen broccoli
- 2 oz Parmesan cheese
- 1 teaspoon rosemary
- 16 oz cheddar cheese

Directions:

1. Pour water in the Instant Pot. Warm up water. Be careful not to bring it to boil.
2. Break pasta. Place pasta in the pressure cooker.
3. Wash broccoli. Cut broccoli on slices. Mix broccoli with rosemary.
4. Place broccoli over pasta.
5. Cook for 5 minutes on "High Pressure" regime.
6. Do a quick release.
7. Mix milk with cheese using mixer.

Nutrition:

- Calories: 263
- Fat: 21g
- Carbohydrates: 36g
- Protein: 9g

Enchilada Pasta

Try soft, meaty pasta in best Spanish traditions! Enjoy tender and light lunches!

Prep time: 5 minutes | **Cooking time:** 5 minutes | **Servings:** 4

Ingredients:

- 8oz pasta
- ½ cup sour cream
- 2lbs beef
- 1 can black olives
- 1 ½ cups broth
- 2 cups cheese
- 2 tablespoons taco seasoning
- 12oz enchilada sauce

Directions:

1. Wash and shred beef.
2. Mix meat with taco seasoning.
3. Place meat in the Instant Pot and cook for 6 minutes on "High Pressure" regime.
4. Pour broth in the pressure cooker.
5. Place pasta in the Instant Pot.
6. Add enchilada sauce to the Instant Pot.
7. Cook for 5 minutes on "High Pressure" regime.
8. Do a quick release.
9. Chop olives.
10. Mix olives with cream and cheese.
11. Add cheese with olives to pasta and serve!

Nutrition:

- Calories: 430
- Fat: 12g
- Carbohydrates: 67g
- Protein: 26g

Bow Tie Pasta

Juicy, spicy, tasty pasta for you right now!

Prep time: 10 minutes | **Cooking time:** 15 minutes | **Servings:** 12

Ingredients:

- 3 tablespoons olive oil
- 16 oz bow tie pasta
- 3 pounds ground sausage
- 9 cups water
- 1 tablespoon butter
- 3 onions
- 1 teaspoon salt
- 1 teaspoon red salt
- 6 garlic cloves
- 1 teaspoon red pepper flakes
- 28 oz tomatoes
- 3 teaspoons basil

Directions:

1. Mix butter with oil. Pour oil with butter in the Instant Pot.
2. Warm it up on "Sauté" regime for 4 minutes. Do not overcook. It should not start bulbing.
3. Clean sausages of the skin. Mix sausages with chopped onion and garlic. Add red salt to the mix.
4. Place onion mix in the Instant Pot and cook on "Sauté" regime. You need to make onions brown color. It will take you around 10 minutes.
5. Wash and peel vegetables. Mix tomatoes with basil, red pepper flakes, salt and add to the Instant Pot.
6. Break pasta. Place pasta in the pressure cooker.
7. Cook for 5 minutes on "High Pressure" regime.
8. Do a quick release.

Nutrition:

- Calories: 113
- Fat: 1g
- Carbohydrates: 21g
- Protein: 4g

Parmesan Risotto

Healthy and satisfying risotto can become perfect dinner variant – just try this receipt!

Prep time: 10 minutes | **Cooking time:** 15 minutes | **Servings:** 8

Ingredients:
- 2 tablespoons butter
- ½ teaspoon salt
- ½ cup shallots
- 2 ounces cheese
- 3 garlic cloves
- 3 cups broth
- 1 1/3 cups Arborio rice
- 1 cup white wine

Directions:
1. Place butter in the Instant Pot.
2. Melt it up for 4 minutes on "Sauté" regime.
3. Place shallots in the pressure cooker.
4. Add garlic to the pressure cooker.
5. Place rice in the pressure cooker.
6. Pour wine over the rice.
7. Cook for 1 minute on "High Pressure" regime.
8. Add broth with salt to the pressure cooker.
9. Add parmesan to the Instant Pot.
10. Cook for 10 minutes on "High Pressure" regime.
11. Do a quick release.
12. Serve with cheese.

Nutrition:
- Calories: 369
- Fat: 8g
- Carbohydrates: 5g
- Protein: 8g

Spaghetti Squash

Try cooked spaghetti squash in the pressure cooker – you will find it tasty for sure!

Prep time: 10 minutes | **Cooking time:** 10 minutes | **Servings:** 3

Ingredients:
- 1 small spaghetti squash
- 1 cup water

Directions:
1. Wash and cut spaghetti in 2 halves.
2. Pour water in the Instant Pot.
3. Place squash in the pressure cooker.
4. Cook for 10 minutes on "High Pressure" regime. Do a quick release.
5. Mash spaghetti squash cooked filling.
6. Serve spaghetti squash warm!

Nutrition:
- Calories: 59
- Fat: 4g
- Carbohydrates: 8g
- Protein:1g

Honey Ginger Carrots

Try sweet carrots with spicy hot sauce for the dinner today!

Prep time: 2 minutes | **Cooking time:** 2 minutes | **Servings:** 4

Ingredients:
- 7 carrots
- ¼ cup water
- 3 tablespoons honey
- 1 teaspoon salt
- 1 teaspoon ginger

Directions:
1. Wash and cut carrots into cubes.
2. Pour water in the Instant Pot.
3. Mix honey with ginger and salt.
4. Pour sauce over the carrots.
5. Place carrots with sauce in the pressure cooker.
6. Cook for 2 minutes on "High Pressure" regime.
7. Do a quick release.
8. Serve warm!

Nutrition:
- Calories: 122
- Fat: 8g
- Carbohydrates: 14g
- Protein: 1g

Brown Sugar Carrots

Sweet dinner can not only improve your mood but also make your grey weekdays brighter!

Prep time: 5 minutes | **Cooking time:** 5 minutes | **Servings:** 12

Ingredients:
- 32oz bag carrots
- 1 teaspoon salt
- 1 cup water
- 8 tablespoons butter
- 1 cup brown sugar

Directions:
1. Wash and peel carrots using knife carefully. Wash carrots one more time and cut carrots into cubes. You should get around 1cm size cubes.
2. Place butter in the Instant Pot. Melt butter to get tender sauce on the bottom of the Instant Pot. Do not overcook.
3. Chop onion and add to the cooking basket.
4. Cook for 2 minutes on "Sauté" regime. Wait until ingredients turn golden color.
5. Add carrots with sugar to the pressure cooker.
6. Pour water over the ingredients.
7. Cook on "High Pressure" regime. It will take you 5 minutes to finish cooking session.
8. Do a quick release.
9. Serve hot!

Nutrition:
- Calories: 110
- Fat: 4g
- Carbohydrates: 16g
- Protein: 1g

Chicken Stock

Prepare heathy must have soup for the dinner!

Prep time: 10 minutes | **Cooking time:** 120 minutes | **Servings:** 12

Ingredients:
- 4 chicken carcass
- Water
- 4 onions
- 8 tablespoons cider vinegar
- 8 bay leaves
- 15 peppercorns
- 1 egg

Directions:
1. Place chicken carcass in the Instant Pot. The same time place egg in boiling water (not in the Instant Pot). Boil egg for 6 minutes. Clean boiled egg and set aside.
2. Wash, peel and chop onion. You should get small onion cubes.
3. Place onion and bay leaves with peppercorns in the pressure cooker.
4. Pour cider vinegar over the ingredients in the Instant Pot. Mix well with ingredients.
5. Set "Soup" regime and cook for 120 minutes.
6. Let the pressure release naturally (20 minutes). Cut boiled onn on 2 halves – place on soup.
7. Serve warm!

Nutrition:
- Calories:86
- Fat: 3g
- Carbohydrates: 4g
- Protein: 1g

Creamy Tomato Soup

Soft and tender tomato soup with healthy herbs and satisfying seasoning!

Prep time: 10 minutes | **Cooking time:** 20 minutes | **Servings:** 4

Ingredients:
- 1 can tomatoes
- 15 basil leaves
- 1 can diced tomatoes
- 1 cup heavy creams
- 1 tablespoons garlic
- 1/3 cup butter
- 1 can chicken broth
- 2 tablespoons sugar

Directions:
1. Pour broth in the Instant Pot.
2. Mix garlic with tomatoes and diced tomatoes.
3. Place tomato mix in the pressure cooker.
4. Add basil leaves and sugar to soup.
5. Cook for 20 minutes on "High Pressure" regime.
6. Do a quick release.
7. Mix soup with creams and serve!

Nutrition:
- Calories: 450
- Fat: 32g
- Carbohydrates: 33g
- Protein: 8g

Broccoli and Potato Soup

Full of vitamins, vegetables and colors – this soup will be the reason to smile today!

Prep time: 10 minutes | **Cooking time:** 15 minutes | **Servings:** 24

Ingredients:

- 16 tablespoons butter
- Chopped green onion
- 16 garlic cloves
- 24 slices bacon
- 8 broccoli heads

- 8 cups cheddar cheese
- 1 cup heavy creams
- 2 tortillas
- 1 rosemary flower
- 8lbs gold potatoes

- 8 cups half and half
- 12 cups vegetable broth
- Salt to taste
- Pepper to taste

Directions:

1. Place butter in the Instant Pot cooking busket.
2. Melt butter for 3 minutes on "Sauté" regime. You should get t6ender liquid on the bottom of the Instant Pot. Mix it to cover all the bottom with butter. Pour creams to the ingredients. Remove ingredients from the Instant Pot and place in blender cup. Blend well.
3. Wash and peel potatoes using knife. Wash peeled potatoes one more time. Cut potatoes into cubes. Place garlic with broccoli, potatoes and broth in the pressure cooker. Potatoes and garlic should be cut into cubes.
4. Cook on "High Pressure" regime. It will take you 5 minutes to finish cooking session.
5. Let the pressure release naturally (10 minutes). The same time make crumbs of tortillas and add to soup.
6. Add cheese, bacon, half and half, basic seasoning to soup. Mix well.
7. Serve hot with rosemary flower on top!

Nutrition:

- Calories: 276
- Fat: 9g

- Carbohydrates: 27g
- Protein: 16g

Rich and Creamy Pork Chops

Sauce with juicy tender taste and satisfying pork chops will make you wait for this dinner all day!

Prep time: 10 minutes | **Cooking time:** 30 minutes | **Servings:** 4

Ingredients:

- 6 pork chops
- 1 tablespoon fresh parsley
- 3 tablespoons oil
- 1 ½ cup sour cream
- 1 ½ cups water
- 1 can cream of mushroom soup
- 2 teaspoons chicken bouillon powder

Directions:

1. Pour oil in the Instant Pot and warm up for 4 minutes on "Sauté" regime.
2. Place pork chops in the Instant Pot.
3. Cook pork chops for 6 minutes on "High Pressure" regime.
4. Pour water in the pressure cooker.
5. Pour bouillon over the ingredients in the Instant Pot.
6. Mix creams with mushroom soup and parsley.
7. Place creamy mix over the meat.
8. Cook for 10 minutes on "High Pressure" regime.
9. Let the pressure release naturally (15 minutes).
10. Serve with herbs!

Nutrition:

- Calories: 193
- Fat: 9g
- Carbohydrates: 0g
- Protein: 17g

Pork Adobo

Try this juicy and tender pork meat with sweet sauce and delicious smell!

Prep time: 10 minutes | **Cooking time:** 10 minutes | **Servings:** 12

Ingredients:

- 6lbs short ribs
- 3 tablespoons cornstarch
- 18 garlic cloves
- 3 tablespoons water
- 1 tablespoon sugar
- Salt to taste
- Pepper to taste
- 1 cup soy sauce
- 12 bay leaves
- 3 cups vinegar
- 2 tablespoons pepper corn

Directions:

1. Pour oil in the Instant Pot.
2. Warm up oil for 4 minutes in the pressure cooker. Do not bring it to boil.
3. Add garlic to the Instant Pot. Cook for 4 minutes on "Sauté" regime. Garlic should start smelling nice and turn golden color.
4. Wash and shred meat. Place meat in the Instant Pot.
5. Add salt and pepper over the meat. Coat meat well.
6. Cook for 6 minutes on "High Pressure" regime.
7. Add soy sauce, sugar, cornstarch, bay leaves, pepper corn, vinegar and cook for 15 minutes on "High Pressure" regime.
8. Let the pressure release naturally (10 minutes).
9. Serve hot!

Nutrition:

- Calories: 251
- Fat: 18g
- Carbohydrates: 2g
- Protein: 18g

Spaghetti Sauce

This light and meaty sauce for pasta will make any dinner satisfying and delicious!

Prep time: 10 minutes | **Cooking time:** 10 minutes | **Servings:** 6

Ingredients:

- 2 pounds Italian sausage
- Parmesan for topping
- 6 ounces tomato paste
- 2 teaspoons fennel seeds
- 30 ounces tomato sauce
- ½ cup water
- 3 teaspoons basil
- ½ cup red wine
- 2 teaspoons parsley flakes
- ¼ teaspoons pepper

Directions:

1. Pour oil in the Instant Pot. Warm it up for 4 minutes on "Sauté" regime.
2. Place cut sausage in the Instant Pot.
3. Cook sausage for 5 minutes on "High Pressure" regime.
4. Add pepper, pepper flakes, basil, parsley, fennel seeds, water, wine and se salt to the meat.
5. Top mix with sugar, tomato paste and tomato sauce. Mix well.
6. Cook meat for 10 minutes on "High Pressure" regime.
7. Let the pressure release naturally (15 minutes).
8. Serve meat with cheese topping and pasta.

Nutrition:

- Calories: 440
- Fat: 16g
- Carbohydrates: 50g
- Protein: 24g

Cordon Blue Casserole

Cheesy pasta with meat and sauce – this extra satisfying dish will be pleasure for everybody who likes delicious dinners!

Prep time: 10 minutes | **Cooking time:** 25 minutes | **Servings:** 4

Ingredients:

- 16oz Rotini pasta
- 1 cup breadcrumbs
- 1 pound chicken breast
- 2 tablespoons butter
- 1 pound ham
- 1 tablespoon spicy mustard
- 16oz Swiss cheese
- 2 cups chicken broth
- 8oz Gouda cheese
- 8oz heavy cream

Directions:

1. Pour broth in the Instant Pot.
2. Place pasta in the Instant Pot.
3. Shred chicken mix.
4. Place chicken meat in the pressure cooker.
5. Cook for 25 minutes on "High Pressure" regime.
6. Mix ham with mustard, cheese and creams.
7. Add to the Instant Pot.
8. Wait for 5 minutes.
9. Serve hot!

Nutrition:

- Calories: 447
- Fat: 37g
- Carbohydrates: 5g
- Protein: 25g

Tex-Mex Chili Mac

Enjoy easy and delicious recipes with maximally bright taste and tender texture!

Prep time: 5 minutes | **Cooking time:** 15 minutes | **Servings:** 4

Ingredients:

- 1 tablespoon vegetable oil
- ¼ teaspoon cayenne pepper
- Pound ground sausage
- 1 teaspoon salt
- 1 onion
- 1 tablespoon chili powder
- 3 garlic cloves
- 1 can green chilies
- 2 cups water
- 1 can tomato sauce
- 2 cups macaroni
- 1 cup corn
- 2 tablespoons cilantro

Directions:

1. Pour oil in the Instant Pot.
2. Warm up oil for 4 minutes on "Sauté" regime.
3. Place meat, onions and garlic in the Instant Pot.
4. Cook for 10 minutes on "High Pressure" regime.
5. Pour water over the ingredients.
6. Add macaroni, tomato sauce, chilies and chili powder to the pressure cooker.
7. Add salt and cayenne pepper to the Instant Pot.
8. Cook for 5 minutes on "High Pressure" regime.
9. Do a quick release.
10. Mix cheese with cream and chips. Serve!

Nutrition:

- Calories: 276
- Fat: 7g
- Carbohydrates: 30g
- Protein: 25g

Apple Butter Chops

Sweet and spicy, hot and tender, juicy and crispy – this receipt will surprise you!

Prep time: 10 minutes | **Cooking time:** 25 minutes | **Servings:** 12

Ingredients:

- 6lbs pork chops
- 3 cups apple sauce
- Salt to taste
- Pepper to taste

- 28oz apple butter
- 6 tablespoons oil
- 8 garlic cloves
- 3 chopped onions

- ½ cup chopped red onion
- 1 cup heavy creams

Directions:

1. Cover meat with basic seasoning (mix salt with pepper and cover meat from all sides with hands). Pour creams over chicken meat and leave chicken for 10 minutes to marinade.
2. Pour oil in the Instant Pot.
3. Place onion and garlic in the Instant Pot. Add red onion to the mix in the pressure cooker.
4. Cook onion mix on "Sauté" regime. It will take you around 4 minutes to make vegetables brown colored.
5. Place meat in the Instant Pot.
6. Pour apple sauce with apple butter to the Instant Pot. Mix meat with the sauce and make sauce coat all the meat slices.
7. Cook for 20 minutes on "High Pressure" regime.
8. Do a quick release.
9. Serve!

Nutrition:

- Calories: 245
- Fat: 7g

- Carbohydrates: 14g
- Protein: 28g

Sausage and Mash

Double dinner is always better – get maximum vitamins and pleasure with this easy to cook receipt!

Prep time: 10 minutes | **Cooking time:** 10 minutes | **Servings:** 2

Ingredients:

- 4 potatoes
- Salt to taste
- Pepper to taste
- 1 cup milk

- 1 tablespoon cornflour
- Knob of butter
- ½ cup water
- 1 teaspoon mustard

- ½ cup red wine
- 2 tablespoons cheddar
- ½ cup onion jam
- 6 sausages

Directions:

1. Wash and peel potatoes.
2. Mix pepper with salt, cornflour, red wine, onion jam.
3. Pour oil in the Instant Pot.
4. Warm up oil for 4 minutes on "Sauté" regime.
5. Place sausages in the pressure cooker.
6. Cook for 6 minutes on "High Pressure" regime.
7. Add sauce to the meat.
8. Pour water over sausages.
9. Cook for 4 minutes more on "High Pressure" regime.
10. Do a quick release.
11. Remove sausages from the Instant Pot.
12. Place butter in the Instant Pot. Melt it up for 4 minutes on "Sauté" regime.
13. Mix mustard with cheddar.
14. Place potatoes in the Instant Pot.
15. Cook potatoes for 10 minutes on "High Pressure" regime.
16. Mash cooked potatoes with milk.
17. Add mustard sauce and mix potatoes well.
18. Serve potatoes with sausages!

Nutrition:

- Calories: 470
- Fat: 23g

- Carbohydrates: 17g
- Protein: 25g

Italian Sausages with Onions and Peppers

Add more herbs and taste to the grey weekdays, and try really soft and tender meat receipt!

Prep time: 10 minutes | **Cooking time:** 6 minutes | **Servings:** 12

Ingredients:

- 6 tablespoons olive oil
- 8 Italian sausages
- ¼ cup white wine
- 9 garlic cloves
- 3 teaspoon Italian herbs

- 6 onions
- 6 yellow bell peppers
- 6 red bell peppers
- 3 cups chicken broth

- 1 cup halves tomato cherries
- 1 tablespoon sesame seeds

Directions:

1. Pour oil in the Instant Pot.
2. Place cut sausages in the pressure cooker. Mix sausages with halves cherry tomatoes.
3. Cook sausages and tomatoes for 5 minutes on "High Pressure" regime.
4. Do a quick release.
5. Remove sausages from the Instant Pot.
6. Place garlic in the Instant Pot.
7. Add onions to the pressure cooker.
8. Cook for 5 minutes on "Sauté" regime.
9. Wash and cut bell pepper.
10. Place pepper with herbs in the pressure cooker.
11. Add broth and wine to the Instant Pot.
12. Mix sausages with sauce and garlic in the Instant Pot.
13. Cook for 6 minutes on "High Pressure" regime.
14. Let the pressure release naturally (15 minutes). Cover sausages with sesame seeds. You may add mozzarella cheese to taste for serving.
15. Serve hot!

Nutrition:

- Calories: 280
- Fat: 18g
- Carbohydrates: 10g
- Protein: 14g

Tenderloin Teriyaki

Fresh, juicy and satisfying pork meat in sweet spicy sauce!

Prep time: 10 minutes | **Cooking time:** 30 minutes | **Servings:** 12

Ingredients:

- 6 tablespoons canola oil
- 6 green onions
- 6 pork tenderloins
- Sesame seeds

- Salt
- 1 tablespoon butter
- Pepper
- 6 cups teriyaki sauce

- 1 cup hot sauce
- 1 cup creams

Directions:

1. Wash pork meat.
2. Coat pork with basil seasoning (mix salt and pepper, coat meat with hands). Add creams to the pork meat. Seasoning mix should cover all the sides.
3. Mix butter with oil. Pour oil mixture in the Instant Pot.
4. Warm up oil for 4 minutes on "Sauté" regime. Just warm up oil, do not overcook and don't bring it to boil.
5. Add onions to the Instant Pot (cook for 5 minutes on "Sauté" regime).
6. Cut pork chops in halves. Add hot sauce.
7. Place meat in the pressure cooker and add sauce.
8. Cook or 25 minutes on "High Pressure" regime.
9. Let the pressure release naturally (20 minutes).
10. Serve hot!

Nutrition:

- Calories: 193
- Fat: 8g

- Carbohydrates: 2g
- Protein: 33g

Kalua Pork

Enjoy Hawaiian recipe and improve your weekdays!

Prep time: 10 minutes | **Cooking time**: 1 hour | **Servings:** 8

Ingredients:

- 2 tablespoons oil
- 1/2 tablespoons butter
- 2 tablespoons salt
- 2 tablespoons sea salt
- 2lbs shredded boiled pork
- 2lbs pork roast

- 1 cup chopped cherry tomatoes
- 1 cup parmesan
- 4 tablespoons brown sugar
- 2 tablespoon honey

- 1 cup water
- 2 tablespoons soy sauce
- 2 tablespoons Liquid Smoke

Directions:

1. Pour oil in the Instant Pot. Add creams and mix well. Warm up mixture on the bottom of the pressure cooker to get tender sauce. It will be your base for the further cooking.
2. Place pork meat in the Instant Pot. Now you need only pork roast, without shredded pork meat.
3. Cook pork meat for 6 minutes on "High Pressure" regime. Add chopped cherries and mix meat with more butter.
4. Pour water, soy sauce, liquid smoke in the Instant Pot. Add honey with sugar and butter to the meat.
5. Add brown sugar to the Instant Pot.
6. Cover pork with salt. Mix pork with shredded meat.
7. Place pork in the pressure cooker and cook for 1 hour.
8. Let the pressure release naturally (20 minutes).
9. Serve with rice!

Nutrition:

- Calories: 140
- Fat: 9g

- Carbohydrates: 3g
- Protein:13g

Apple Cider Pork

You have never tasted this juicy pork meat before – check it out!

Prep time: 10 minutes | **Cooking time:** 25 minutes | **Servings:** 12

Ingredients:

- 3 pounds pork loin
- 1 tablespoon onion powder
- 1 tablespoon ginger powder
- 1 tablespoon garlic powder
- 2 tablespoons olive oil
- 1 tablespoons melted butter
- 1 tablespoon pepper
- 1 tablespoon red pepper flakes
- 6 cups cider
- 1 tablespoon sea salt
- 1 onion
- 1 red onion
- 2 apples

Directions:

1. Wash and peel apples. Cut apples on slices. Mix apples with ginger and garlic powder. Add cubed red onion and red pepper flakes.
2. Mix powder with salt and pepper. Add butter to the seasoning mix with apples.
3. Cover meat with seasoning.
4. Pour oil in the Instant Pot.
5. Warm up oil on "Sauté" regime. It will take you around 4 minutes just to warm up, do not bring it to boil.
6. Place chopped onions in the pressure cooker.
7. Cook for 5 minutes on "Sauté" regime.
8. Place meat in the Instant Pot.
9. Pour cider over the meat.
10. Add apple slices to the meat in the pressure cooker.
11. Cook meat for 25 minutes on "High Pressure" regime.
12. Do a quick release.
13. Serve hot!

Nutrition:

- Calories: 188
- Fat: 15g
- Carbohydrates: 4g
- Protein: 9g

Boneless Pork Chops

Sweet and hot meat without bones but with a bright vitamins cocktail for you right now!

Prep time: 5 minutes | **Cooking time:** 5 minutes | **Servings:** 10

Ingredients:

- 2 tablespoons coconut oil
- 2 cups water
- 1 cup heavy creams
- 1 cup shredded cheese to taste

- 1 cup halved cherry tomatoes
- 10 boneless pork chops
- 2 packs of ranch mix
- 2 sticks of butter

- 1 tablespoon olive oil
- 1 tablespoon Italian herbs

Directions:

1. Pour oil in the Instant Pot. Add ½ butter stick and coconut oil to the pressure cooker. Pour creams over oil. Mix using spoon creams with oil in the cooking basket.
2. Warm up oil for 4 minutes on "Sauté" regime. You need to get liquid tender sauce on the bottom of the Instant Pot.
3. Wash pork chops and cover with ranch mix. The same time wash tomatoes and mash in blender. Add tomatoes to the meat.
4. Place pork chops in the Instant Pot. Sprinkle meat with cheese.
5. Pour water over the meat. Add Italian herbs to the meat.
6. Add butter to the pressure cooker.
7. Cook meat for 5 minutes on "High Pressure" regime.
8. Do a quick release.
9. Serve hot!

Nutrition:

- Calories: 130
- Fat: 5g

- Carbohydrates: 0g
- Protein: 23g

Potato Cheese Soup

Chunky cheese soup with herbs is easy to cook using pressure cooker!

Prep time: 10 minutes | **Cooking time:** 10 minutes | **Servings:** 14

Ingredients:

- 4 tablespoons butter
- 4 cups half and half
- 1 cup chopped onion
- 1 cup cheddar cheese
- 1 cup mozzarella
- 6 cups cubed potatoes
- 2 cups cubed cauliflower
- 2 tablespoons water
- 2 cans chicken broth
- 2 tablespoons cornstarch
- 1 teaspoon salt
- 2 tablespoons parsley
- ½ teaspoon pepper
- 1/8 teaspoon red pepper flakes
- 1 cup corn
- 6 slices bacon

Directions:

1. Place butter in the Instant Pot.
2. Melt butter for 4 minutes on "Sauté" regime. You should get soft and tender liquid on the bottom of the pressure cooker. It will be your base for cooking.
3. Add onion and salt, pepper, red pepper flakes, parsley, chicken broth to the Instant Pot.
4. Cook for 5 minutes on "Sauté" regime. Add cauliflower to the pressure cooker.
5. Place potatoes in the Instant Pot.
6. Cook for 4 minutes on "High Pressure" regime.
7. Pour water over the cornstarch.
8. Add cornstarch to the pressure cooker. Add mozzarella cheese and mix ingredients well.
9. Mix creams cheese with cheese and add to the Instant Pot.
10. Mix all the ingredients with bacon and half and half, bring to boil.
11. Do a quick release.
12. Serve!

Nutrition:

- Calories: 276
- Fat: 9g
- Carbohydrates: 27g
- Protein: 16g

Ham White Bean Soup

Try light and satisfying the same time soup that will give you both vitamins and energy!

Prep time: 15 minutes | **Cooking time:** 15 minutes | **Servings:** 8

Ingredients:

- 1lb beans
- 1 teaspoon paprika
- 1 tablespoon olive oil
- 1 teaspoon thyme
- 1 chopped carrot

- 1 teaspoon mint
- 1 onion
- 1 teaspoon pepper
- 3 garlic cloves
- 2 teaspoons salt

- 1 peeled tomato
- 2 cups water
- 1lb ham
- 4 cups vegetable broth

Directions:

1. Pour oil in the Instant Pot.
2. Add carrots, chopped onion, tomato, garlic and cook for 5 minutes on "Sauté" regime in the Instant Pot.
3. Mix beans with ham and place in the pressure cooker.
4. Pour stock and water over the ingredients.
5. Mix salt, pepper, mint, thyme and paprika.
6. Place seasoning mix over the meat in the Instant Pot.
7. Cook meat for 15 minutes on "High Pressure" regime.
8. Let the pressure release naturally (10 minutes).
9. Serve warm!

Nutrition:

- Calories: 129
- Fat: 1g

- Carbohydrates: 27g
- Protein: 14g

Cabbage Roll Soup

Easy, quick and super satisfying soup for the great dinner!

Prep time: 5 minutes | **Cooking time:** 20 minutes | **Servings:** 12

Ingredients:

- 3 onions
- 3 tablespoons garlic powder
- 9 garlic cloves
- 3 tablespoons Worcestershire sauce
- 1lb beef
- 1lb chicken
- 1 ½ cup vegetable juice
- ½ lb pork
- 4 cups beef broth
- ¾ cup rice
- 2 tablespoons tomato paste
- 1 cabbage
- 1 can tomatoes
- 1 cucumber
- 1 tablespoon onion powder
- 1 tablespoon oil
- 1 teaspoon oregano
- Salt
- Pepper
- 1 teaspoon thyme
- 1 bay leaf
- 1 teaspoon cayenne pepper

Directions:

1. Pour oil in the Instant Pot.
2. Warm up oil for 2 minutes on "Sauté" regime. You need to get tender liq2uid on the bottom of the pressure cooker. Do not bring oil to boil.
3. Place onions with garlic in the pressure cooker. Add cucumbers to the onion mix.
4. Cook for 3 minutes on "Sauté" regime. Wait until vegetables turn golden color.
5. Mix pork with beef and chicken meat and place in the Instant Pot.
6. Cook for 6 minutes on "High Pressure" regime.
7. Add pepper, salt, bay leaf, thyme. Oregano, onion powder, garlic powder, sauce, vegetable juice, beef broth, tomato paste, tomatoes, cabbage and rice to the Instant Pot. Mix ingredients well.
8. Cook soup for 20 minutes on "High Pressure" regime.
9. Do a quick release.
10. Serve!

Nutrition:

- Calories: 188
- Fat: 7g
- Carbohydrates: 15g
- Protein: 16g

Smoked Sausage with White Bean and Vegetable Soup

Satisfying, healthy and super delicious – this receipt will be something you fall in love with!

Prep time: 10 minutes | **Cooking time**: 20 minutes | **Servings:** 12

Ingredients:

- 3lbs beans
- 1 teaspoon pepper
- 6 tablespoons olive oil
- 3 teaspoon salt
- 14oz turkey sausage

- 14oz chicken sausage
- 3 cups baby spinach
- ½ onion
- ½ red onion
- 8 cups vegetable broth

- 2 garlic cloves
- 2 teaspoons rosemary
- 3 carrots
- 1 teaspoon thyme
- 2 celery stalk

Directions:

1. Pour oil in the Instant Pot. The same time clean sausages of the skin and mix chicken with turkey sausages.
2. Warm up for 3 minutes on "Sauté" regime.
3. Place onions in the pressure cooker. Add red onion to the pressure cooker. You may add 1 tablespoon water to get more tender onions with brighter taste.
4. Add garlic to the Instant Pot.
5. Cook on "Sauté" regime for 2 minutes.
6. Add beans, sausages, carrots, celery, thyme, rosemary, baby spinach, salt and pepper. Pour broth over the ingredients in the Instant Pot.
7. Cook soup for 20 minutes on "High Pressure" regime.
8. Do a quick release.
9. Serve!

Nutrition:

- Calories: 250
- Fat: 8g

- Carbohydrates: 33g
- Protein: 12g

Copycat Chili

Juicy, tender, spicy, interesting receipt for those who like trying something new!

Prep time: 5 minutes | **Cooking time:** 25 minutes | **Servings:** 8

Ingredients:

- 1 tablespoon vegetable oil
- Salt
- Pepper
- 2 teaspoons garlic
- 1 can tomato sauce

- 1lb beef
- 1 can diced tomatoes
- 1 onion
- 1 can red beans
- 1 bell peppers

- 1 can Rotel
- 6 celery stalks
- 1 can beans
- 1 pack chili seasoning

Directions:

1. Pour oil in the Instant Pot.
2. Warm up oil for 3 minutes in the Instant Pot.
3. Place garlic in the pressure cooker.
4. Cook garlic for 4 minutes on "Sauté" regime.
5. Place beef in the Instant Pot and add celery, onion, bell pepper.
6. Cook beef for 10 minutes on "High Pressure" regime.
7. Pour water, rotel and tomato sauce over the ingredients in the pressure cooker.
8. Place beans, salt, pepper, diced tomatoes, red beans and seasoning in the Instant Pot.
9. Cook for 10 minutes on "High Pressure" regime.
10. Do a quick release.
11. Serve!

Nutrition:

- Calories: 144
- Fat: 1g

- Carbohydrates: 258g
- Protein: 10g

Vegetable Beef Soup

Make your menu brighter and more interesting with this exiting receipt!

Prep time: 10 minutes | **Cooking time:** 5 minutes | **Servings:** 4

Ingredients:
- 2lbs beef
- ½ teaspoon oregano
- 1 onion
- 2 teaspoons parsley flakes
- 2 teaspoons garlic
- ½ teaspoon pepper
- 1 can tomatoes
- ½ teaspoon salt
- 3 cups beef broth
- 3 tablespoons tomato paste
- 4 carrots
- 4 potatoes
- 3 celery stalks

Directions:
1. Place chopped onion with beef and garlic in the Instant Pot.
2. Cook ingredients for 4 minutes on "Sauté" regime.
3. Pour broth with tomato sauce and tomatoes in the pressure cooker.
4. Add carrots, celery, potatoes, salt, pepper and parsley flakes with oregano to the mix.
5. Cook for 5 minutes on "High Pressure" regime.
6. Do a quick release.
7. Serve!

Nutrition:
- Calories: 90
- Fat: 1g
- Carbohydrates: 15g
- Protein: 4g

Pulled Pork

The quickest and the easiest receipt you have ever tries to cook for the lunch in your Instant Pot!

Prep time: 2 minutes | **Cooking time:** 50 minutes | **Servings:** 12

Ingredients:
- 6 cups Dr. Pepper
- 3 tablespoons salt
- 1 tablespoon sea salt
- 1 cup BBQ sauce
- 1 cup hot sauce
- 1 tablespoon garlic powder
- 4 pounds pork roast
- 1 tablespoon onion powder
- 1 onion

Directions:
1. Wash and cut meat in to 5 slices.
2. Mix salt, onion powder, garlic powder and cover mix with seasoning. Mix seasoning with hot sauce to get tender marinade. Cover pork meat with marinade and leave for10 minutes to marinate.
3. Add chopped onion to the Instant Pot.
4. Add Dr. Pepper and BBQ sauce. Add sea salt to the meat.
5. Place pork roast in the pressure cooker.
6. Cook meat for 50 minutes on "High Pressure" regime.
7. Do a quick release.
8. Serve hot!

Nutrition:
- Calories: 335
- Fat: 5g
- Carbohydrates: 49g
- Protein:21g

APPETIZERS

Chicken Wings

Softy and tender chicken wings will be perfect appetizer to make celebration better and your day easier!

Prep time: 5 minutes | **Cooking time:** 30 minutes | **Servings:** 3

Ingredients:
- 2 pounds chicken wings
- ½ cup BBQ sauce

Directions:
1. Pour water in the Instant Pot.
2. Place chicken in the Instant Pot cooking basket.
3. Cook chicken on "High Pressure" regime for 5 minutes.
4. Dry chicken wings.
5. Add more BBQ sauce to the chicken wings and bake in the oven for 10 minutes on 450oF.

Nutrition:
- Calories: 150
- Fat: 9g
- Carbohydrates: 3g
- Protein:14g

Umami Meatballs

Small and tender meatballs can be super satisfying and healthy appetizer!

Prep time: 30 minutes | **Cooking time:** 10 minutes | **Servings:** 1

Ingredients:
- 1/3 pound beef
- 1/3 teaspoon oregano
- 1 strip bacon
- 1/2 teaspoon basil
- Onion
- ½ cup tomato paste
- 1 garlic clove
- 1 cup tomato sauce
- 1 egg
- 1 cup chicken stock
- 1 teaspoon dried oregano
- ½ cup shredded cheese
- 1/3 teaspoon fennel seed
- ¼ cup milk
- ½ teaspoon Worcestershire sauce
- ½ cup panko
- ½ teaspoon salt
- ¼ teaspoon pepper

Directions:
1. Mix beef, bacon slices, chopped and washed onion, minced garlic, beaten egg, oregano, fennel seed, Worcestershire sauce, salt, pepper, panko, milk and cheese.
2. Separately, mix chicken stock, tomato paste and tomato sauce with basil and oregano. Place tomato mix in the Instant Pot and cook on "High Pressure regime for 5 minutes.
3. Turn on oven and preheat up to 450oF.
4. Roll meatballs of the meat mix.
5. Bake meatballs for 15 minutes in the oven.
6. Place meatballs in the Instant Pot to tomato sauce and cook for 5 more minutes.
7. Serve with fresh herbs!

Nutrition:
- Calories: 45
- Fat: 0g
- Carbohydrates: 10g
- Protein:0g

Chicken Pot Breast

Small chicken rolls with asparagus in the center will be not only beautiful, but also delicious appetizer!

Prep time: 10 minutes | **Cooking time:** 35 minutes | **Servings:** 1

Ingredients:

- 1 chicken breast
- 1 cup water
- 1/2 piece cooked ham
- Salt to taste
- 1 fresh asparagus spear
- Pepper to taste
- 1/2lb bacon
- 2 slices Mozzarella cheese

Directions:

1. Wash and slice chicken breasts on small slices.
2. Turn on blender and place chicken meat inside it to get smaller slices.
3. Mix salt with water. Place chicken in the salted water and marinade for 30 minutes.
4. Place 1 slice mozzarella on the dried chicken breast, add ham, 2 asparagus and roll up chicken.
5. Top chicken meat with seasoning.
6. Pour water in the Instant Pot and place chicken breasts in the cooking basket.
7. Cook chicken in the Instant Pot for 15 minutes on the "Poultry" regime with oil.
8. Serve with cheesy sauce!

Nutrition:

- Calories: 229
- Fat: 6g
- Carbohydrates: 29g
- Protein:15g

Devided Eggs

Quick and hot devided eggs will be good looking and tender addition to any lunch! You may place eggs on the toasts or serve it with the meat – as you wish!

Prep time: 5 minutes | **Cooking time:** 25 minutes | **Servings**: 3

Ingredients:

- 2 eggs
- Pepper to taste
- Salt to taste
- 1/4 cup water
- ½ teaspoon sriracha
- Paprika to taste
- 5 basil leaves
- 1/4 teaspoon white vinegar
- 1/3 tablespoons mayonnaise
- 1/8 teaspoon Dijon mustard
- 1/6 tablespoon olive oil

Directions:

1. Pour cold water in the Instant Pot. It should be cold to make eggs stay special shape. However, you need to bring water to boil for 5 minutes.
2. Place eggs in the Instant Pot and cook on "High Pressure" regime for 12 minutes. Add salt and pepper to eggs to make them super delicious.
3. Slice cooked eggs and remove yolks.
4. Mix mayonnaise, olive oil, mustard, white vinegar, sriracha and yolks. Place mayonnaise mix in the eggs on the yolks places.
5. The same time pour vinegar on the basil leaves and leave them in vinegar to marinade for 10 minutes as minimum.
6. Place dried basil leaves on the eggs to get more interesting smell and taste!

Nutrition:

- Calories: 71
- Fat: 5g
- Carbohydrates: 0g
- Protein:6g

Beef Snack

Can fast snack be easy and meaty? Of course it can with Instant Pot!

Prep time: 15 minutes | **Cooking time:** 45 minutes | **Servings:** 3

Ingredients:
- 1 pound beef snack
- 1 ½ cup Chinese master stock

Directions:
1. Pour water in the bowl and bring to boil.
2. Boil beef snack in hot water for 5 minutes.
3. Top snack with master stock and place in the Instant Pot.
4. Cook on "High Pressure" regime for 35 minutes.
5. Place snack in the fridge and leave to cool down.
6. Slice and serve cold!

Nutrition:
- Calories: 155
- Fat: 14g
- Carbohydrates: 1.5g
- Protein: 6g

Boiled Peanuts

One of the loveliest and most popular appetizers - peanuts! It is not only perfect addition to the main courses, but also great snack!

Prep time: 5 minutes | **Cooking time:** 75 minutes | **Servings:** 4

Ingredients:
- 1 pound peanuts
- 1 teaspoon sugar
- ½ cup salt
- 1 tablespoon BBQ seasoning
- Water
- Jalapeno pepper
- 1 tablespoon Cajun seasoning
- Garlic

Directions:
1. Place peanuts in the bowl with cold water for 5 minutes.
2. Place peanuts with water and salt in the Instant Pot.
3. Cook peanuts for 75 minutes on "High Pressure" regime.
4. Mix sugar, salt, BBQ seasoning, jalapeno pepper and Cajun seasoning with garlic.
5. Serve peanuts with the sauce.

Nutrition:
- Calories: 27
- Fat: 2g
- Carbohydrates: 2g
- Protein: 1g

Cupcakes Frittata

Small cupcakes with satisfying frittata and fresh green onions will be colorful addition to any celebration! Easy, lovely, healthy and tender frittata is the best friend of those who want to be happy and healthy the same time!

Prep time: 5 minutes | **Cooking time:** 5 minutes | **Servings:** 2

Ingredients:

- 3 eggs
- 2 jars
- 1/4 teaspoon salt
- 1/2 cup water
- ¼ cup sliced bacon
- 1/2 scallion
- ½ cup cheese
- ½ cup potatoes
- 1/2 tablespoon whipping cream

Directions:

1. Mix beaten eggs with creams. Use blender to get as tender mix as possible. Add salt to the mix. Pour eggs in the cupcake baking forms. Prepare circle shape forms – it is the best variant for the cooking in the Instant Pot.
2. Place bacon in the oven with scallions (400oF) and cook for 3 minutes. It will make these ingredients crispy and golden colored.
3. Pour oil over the eggs in the jars. Place bacon on top to make the dish look more beautiful.
4. Wash and cut potato into cubes. Mix cubed potato with cheese, chopped scallion and cooked sliced bacon.
5. Pour water in the Instant Pot.
6. Place jars in the Instant Pot and cook on "High Pressure" regime for 5 minutes.
7. Leave egg mix in the Instant Pot and let the pressure release naturally for 10 minutes.

Nutrition:

- Calories: 85
- Fat: 5g
- Carbohydrates: 0.5g
- Protein:7g

Sesame Noodles

Everybody loves sesame noodles! You will love they even more after trying this Instant Pot receipt!

Prep time: 5 minutes | **Cooking time:** 1 minute | **Servings:** 12

Ingredients:

- 32 ounces egg noodles
- 2 tablespoons chili oil
- 6 cups water
- 8 tablespoons sugar
- 16 scallions
- 8 tablespoons seasoned rice
- 1 tablespoon toasted sesame oil
- 7 tablespoons pure sesame oil
- 9 tablespoons canola oil
- 1cup soy sauce
- 15 cloves garlic

Directions:

1. Mix chili oil, sugar, scallions, rice, sesame oil, canola oil, soy sauce and garlic in one bowl.
2. Pour water in the Instant Pot.
3. Place noodles in the Instant Pot.
4. Coat noodles with the sauce.
5. Cook noodles in the Instant Pot for 1 minute on "High Pressure" regime and leave for natural release of pressure for 2 minutes.

Nutrition:

- Calories: 104
- Fat: 3g
- Carbohydrates: 16g
- Protein:3g

Garlic Noodles

The quickest appetizer ever – one minute and voila – noodles are ready!

Prep time: 5 minutes | **Cooking time:** 1 minute | **Servings:** 10

Ingredients:

- 6 pounds Chinese noodles
- 9 teaspoons cornstarch
- 8 teaspoons canola oil
- 9 teaspoon sea salt
- 4 tablespoons garlic
- 4 teaspoons oyster sauce
- 1 teaspoons vinegar
- 3 teaspoons sugar
- 5 teaspoons sambal oelek
- 5 teaspoons shoaxing
- 1 teaspoon sugar
- 1/4 cup chicken broth
- 1/4 teaspoon pure sesame oil
- 6 cucumbers
- 9 cups water
- 5 tablespoons cilantro

Directions:

1. Mix chicken broth and cornstarch.
2. Pour oil in the Instant Pot.
3. Choose meat function on the Instant Pot display.
4. Pour canola oil in the Instant Pot and warm up.
5. Mince garlic and place it in the Instant Pot and cook for 1 minute.
6. Mix oelek with chili paste and cook for 1 more minute in the Instant Pot on "High Pressure" regime.
7. Mix shoaxing, sugar, oyster sauce, sea salt and remaining ingredients.
8. Place mix in the Instant Pot and cook for 1 minute on "High Pressure" regime. Leave for natural release for 2 minutes.
9. Place cucumber in the blender and crush it with the sea salt. Serve with the noodles!

Nutrition:

- Calories: 244
- Fat: 7.5g
- Carbohydrates: 40g
- Protein:6g

Gefilte Fish

Small fish balls – both tender appetizer and goof lunch idea!

Prep time: 40 minutes | **Cooking time**: 25 minutes | **Servings**: 15

Ingredients:

- 3 ½ pounds whitefish
- ¼ teaspoon pepper
- 2 carrots
- 1 teaspoon salt
- 2 onions

- 2 teaspoons sugar
- ¼ teaspoon pepper
- ½ cup Matzo Meal
- 2 quarts water
- 1 carrot

- 1,75 pounds whitefish
- Onion
- 3 eggs

Directions:

1. Mix pepper, chopped onion, salt, 3.5 pounds fish fillets, water and sugar. Place fish mix in the Instant Pot.
2. Cook mix for 15 minutes on "High Pressure" regime.
3. Mix chopped onion, cut carrot, 3 egg whites, salt, pepper and sugar with Matzo Meal. Use blender to mix ingredients.
4. Add remaining fish fillets and blend.
5. Place blended mix in the fridge.
6. Mix cooled mix with the cooked fish and cook in the Instant Pot for 10 more minutes not changing regime settings.
7. Form balls of the fish mix and add remaining ingredients.
8. Cook for 5 minutes more in the Instant Pot on "High Pressure" regime.
9. Remove fish balls, cool down and serve!

Nutrition:

- Calories: 38
- Fat: 1g

- Carbohydrates: 6g
- Protein:3g

Artichoke Dip with Spinach

Artichoke dip can taste super delicious with tostadas, tacos and even ordinary chips!

Prep time: 2 minutes | **Cooking time:** 5 minutes | **Servings**: 1

Ingredients:
- 2oz cream cheese
- 1/4 teaspoon onion powder
- 4oz box Frozen spinach
- 1/4 garlic clove
- 4oz Shredded Parm cheese
- ½ cup mayo
- 2oz mozzarella
- ½ cup sour cream
- ½ cup chicken broth
- 2oz artichoke hearts

Directions:
1. Wash and cut artichokes.
2. Pour chicken broth in the Instant Pot.
3. Place garlic cloves in the Instant Pot.
4. Mix creams, spinach and mozzarella with the remaining ingredients.
5. Place ingredients in the Instant Pot and cook on "High Pressure" regime for 5 minutes.
6. Quickly serve with chips!

Nutrition:
- Calories: 30
- Fat: 1.5g
- Carbohydrates: 2g
- Protein:2g

Syracuse Potatoes

Small and hot potatoes can both replace sides and become perfect appetizer on the dinner table!

Prep time: 20 minutes | **Cooking time:** 5 minutes | **Servings:** 8

Ingredients:
- 3lbs bite-sized potatoes
- ½ cup ghee
- 1 cup salt
- 6 cups water

Directions:
1. Wash potatoes and clean skin.
2. Mix salt with water.
3. Pour water in the Instant Pot.
4. Place potatoes in the Instant Pot.
5. Cook potatoes on "High Pressure" for 2 minutes.
6. Serve potatoes with ghee.

Nutrition:
- Calories: 495
- Fat: 20g
- Carbohydrates: 45g
- Protein:0g

Steak Tacos

Small tacos with satisfying tender meat and fresh vegetables! Tacos are crispy, tender, juicy and satisfying the same time! Perfect dish for any life occasion!

Prep time: 5 minutes | **Cooking time:** 5 minutes | **Servings:** 1

Ingredients:

- 4oz sirioin steak
- Pepper to taste
- 1/4 cup chopped onion
- Spanish herbs

- 1/8 cup chopped tomatoes
- 1/3 tablespoons chopped cilantro
- 1/6 cup Mexican cheese

- 1/5 tablespoon olive oil
- 1/5 tablespoons sour cream
- 2 tablespoons salsa

Directions:

1. Pour olive oil in the Instant Pot and set saute function. It will take you 5 minutes to bring oil to the pre-boiling consistence.
2. Add salsa, cream, cilantro, herbs and chopped onion to the oil. You may add salt and pepper to taste if you like.
3. Put steaks into warmed up sauce mix and leave for 10 minutes to marinade. After turn on Instant Pot again and cook for 10 minutes on the "Meat" regime.
4. Cover steaks with cheese and place on tacos.
5. Place steak in the hot oven (400oF) and bake for 3 more minutes.
6. Add cheese after the baking and wash fresh vegetables.
7. Serve with herbs and vegetables to taste!

Nutrition:

- Calories: 200
- Fat: 6g

- Carbohydrates: 21g
- Protein: 12g

Scampi Shrimp

Light and easy to cook shrimp will be perfect addition to any celebration – you will like this easy and healthy receipt!

Prep time: 5 minutes | **Cooking time:** 3 minutes | **Servings:** 1

Ingredients:

- 1/5 lb shrimp
- Pepper to taste
- ½ lemon

- Salt to taste
- 1/2 tablespoons butter
- Parsley to taste

- 1 garlic cloves
- 1/6 cup chicken broth
- ¼ cup white wine

Directions:

1. Turn on "Saute" regime on Instant Pot.
2. Melt butter. Pour melted liquid in the Instant Pot.
3. Mince garlic and add it in the Instant Pot.
4. Pour wine to the Instant Pot.
5. Cover shrimp with chicken broth, add salt and pepper.
6. Cook prawns on "High Pressure" regime for 3 minutes.
7. Serve with lemon juice and parsley!

Nutrition:

- Calories: 90
- Fat: 5g

- Carbohydrates: 2g
- Protein: 15g

Hummus in Instant Pot

Satisfying, healthy and easy receipt for your super quick lunch!

Prep time: 10 minutes | **Cooking time:** 35 minutes | **Servings:** 8

Ingredients:
- 4 cups chickpeas
- Olive oil
- 12 cups hot water
- 2 cup cooking liquid
- 3 teaspoons salt
- Salt to taste
- 4 cubes vegetable stock
- 3 teaspoons cumin powder
- 12 tablespoons light tahini
- 8 garlic cloves
- 1 cup lemon juice

Directions:
1. Mix water with salt.
2. Place chickpeas in water.
3. Pour water in the Instant Pot and add chickpeas.
4. Pour vegetable stock in the Instant Pot.
5. Cook chickpeas for 35 minutes on "High Pressure" regime.
6. Mix chickpeas with lemon juice, garlic cloves, tahini, cumin powder and other ingredients and blend until smooth.
7. Serve with olive oil and paprika.

Nutrition:
- Calories: 35
- Fat: 4g
- Carbohydrates: 1g
- Protein:0g

Ranch Potatoes

Cubes colorful and satisfying - ranch potatoes is the best variant of quick and healthy appetizer!

Prep time: 10 minutes | **Cooking time:** 5 minutes | **Servings:** 12

Ingredients:
- 9 yellow potatoes
- Salt to taste
- Pepper to taste
- 6 tablespoons seasoning mix
- 1 cup water
- 6 tablespoons butter

Directions:
1. Wash and cube potatoes.
2. Cover potatoes with seasoning.
3. Pour water in the Instant Pot. Add butter.
4. Cook potatoes on "High Pressure" regime for 5 minutes.
5. Serve with pepper.

Nutrition:
- Calories: 60
- Fat: 0g
- Carbohydrates: 13g
- Protein:2g

Chili Con Queso

Hot, easy and delicious both with chips and with tacos – super nice appetizer for those who like bright taste!

Prep time: 5 minutes | **Cooking time:** 5 minutes | **Servings:** 10

Ingredients:
- 3 lbs ground chuck
- 4lb velveeta cheese
- 2 onions
- 1 cup water
- 5 garlic cloves
- 2 tablespoons chili powder
- 10oz can rotel
- 2 pocket staco seasoning
- 2 cans tomatoes

Directions:
1. Add meat and chopped onion to the Instant Pot.
2. Place garlic in the Instant Pot and cook on "High Pressure" regime for 1 minute.
3. Add remaining ingredients.
4. Pour water in the Instant Pot.
5. Cook chili for 10 minutes on "Chili" regime. Use blender to crush ingredients.
6. Blend cooked chili to get smooth mix.
7. Serve with the chips!

Nutrition:
- Calories: 160
- Fat: 13g
- Carbohydrates: 3g
- Protein:8g

Corn on the Cob

Favorite kids receipt – make your family happy with the light and easy appetizer!

Prep time: 3 minutes | **Cooking time:** 5 minutes | **Servings:** 1

Ingredients:
- 1 corn on the cob
- 1/2 cups water
- 1 cup melted butter
- Salt to taste

Directions:
1. Turn on Instant Pot and add 2 cups of water.
2. Halve corns on cob and clean of the leaves.
3. Place halved corns on cob in the Instant Pot and cook on "High Pressure" regime for 2 minutes.
4. Add salt and butter to the cobs to taste.
5. Serve hot with butter on top!

Nutrition:
- Calories: 80
- Fat: 0.5g
- Carbohydrates: 20g
- Protein:3g

Green Beans

Delicious, healthy and colorful beans can become your favorite receipt – try it with the rice or with the meat!

Prep time: 5 minutes | **Cooking time:** 20 minutes | **Servings:** 5

Ingredients:
- 2 pounds green beans
- 1 cup water
- Onion
- 3 slices bacon

Directions:
1. Wash and cut beans.
2. Wash and chop onion.
3. Cut bacon on slices.
4. Place bacon and water in the Instant Pot.
5. Place beans and chopped onion in the Instant Pot.
6. Cook ingredients for 20 minutes in the Instant Pot on "High Pressure" regime.
7. Serve with seafood or shrimps!

Nutrition:
- Calories: 34
- Fat: 0.2g
- Carbohydrates: 8g
- Protein: 2g

Cocktail Sausages

Small, covered with the sweet sauce and crispy the same time – you will like these sausages for sure!

Prep time: 5 minutes | **Cooking time:** 1 minute | **Servings:** 8

Ingredients:
- 2 packages cocktail sausages
- 4 ounces beer
- ½ bottle barbeque sauce
- 1 tablespoon honey
- ¼ cup brown sugar
- 1 tablespoon white vinegar

Directions:
1. Mix sausages with sauce.
2. Place covered with sauce sausages in the Instant Pot.
3. Add beer, honey and sugar with vinegar to the Instant Pot.
4. Cook meat for 1 minute on "High Pressure" regime.
5. Leave sausages in the Instant Pot and let the pressure release naturally for 5 minutes!

Nutrition:
- Calories: 120
- Fat: 9g
- Carbohydrates:6g
- Protein:6g

Popcorn in Instant Pot

Do you like watching movies with the corn? Now you can do this any time you want!

Prep time: 10 minutes | **Cooking time:** 5 minutes | **Servings:** 6

Ingredients:
- 2 tablespoons olive oil
- ½ cup popcorn kernels
- Paprika to serve

Directions:
1. Pour oil in the Instant Pot.
2. Turn on "Saute" regime on the Instant Pot.
3. Place popcorn in the Instant Pot and cook until they pop.
4. Top popcorn with paprika or melted caramel.
5. Serve cold!

Nutrition:
- Calories: 510
- Fat: 29g
- Carbohydrates: 55g
- Protein:8g

Bread with Herb and Parmesan

Easy baked bread with herbs and cheese topping – easy and delicious recipes for you!

Prep time: 30 minutes | **Cooking time:** 4 hours | **Servings:**3

Ingredients:
- 3 cups bread flour
- ½ teaspoon garlic powder
- ¼ teaspoon instant yeast
- ½ teaspoon thyme
- ¾ tablespoon salt
- ½ teaspoon oregano
- 1 ½ cups warm water
- ½ cup Parmesan cheese

Directions:
1. Mix ingredients and form dough.
2. Cook dough for 3 hours on "Yogurt" regime.
3. Preheat oven up to 450oF.
4. Bake bread for 30 minutes in the oven after the Instant Pot.
5. Bake bread for 20 minutes on 210oF.
6. Serve with cheesy topping!

Nutrition:
- Calories: 131
- Fat: 2g
- Carbohydrates: 23g
- Protein:4g

Garlic Dip with Mustard

Artichokes with the garlic dip – something extra healthy and full of vitamins for you!

Prep time: 15 minutes | **Cooking time**: 20 minutes | **Servings:** 20

Ingredients:
- 20 artichokes
- 5 teaspoons cayenne pepper
- 4 cups water
- 10 garlic cloves
- 10 tablespoon olive oil
- 7 tablespoon Dijon mustard
- 5 teaspoon pepper
- 8 tablespoon mayonnaise
- 5 teaspoon salt

Directions:
1. Cut one third part of the artichoke.
2. Pour water in the Instant Pot.
3. Place artichokes in the instant Pot and cook on "High Pressure" regime for 20 minutes.
4. Mix remaining ingredients in the blender.
5. Pour sauce mix on the artichokes and serve with seasoning!

Nutrition:
- Calories: 140
- Fat: 14g
- Carbohydrates: 1g
- Protein:1g

Brussels Sprouts in the Instant Pot

Have you even seen receipt easier and quicker? Try healthy and satisfying Brussels Sprouts right now! Even children will fall in love with Brussels Sprouts with this receipt!

Prep time: 5 minutes | **Cooking time:** 7 minutes | **Servings:** 1

Ingredients:
- 1/2 tablespoons olive oil
- Butter to taste
- 1 cup onion
- Salt to taste
- Pepper to taste
- 1 teaspoon garlic
- ½ cup water
- 1 slices bacon
- ½ lb Brussels sprouts

Directions:
1. Pour oil in the Instant Pot and turn on "Saute" regime. Warm up oil and wait until it starts boiling. It will take you 5 minutes.
2. Wash vegetables and chop them with the knife, not using blender.
3. Place blended onion and garlic in the Instant Pot. Pour oil over the garlic mix and warm up for 5 minutes on "Saute" regime to get them golden colored.
4. Mix garlic with bacon cubes and place in the preheated up to 400oF oven. Bake for 3 minutes.
5. Place Brussels sprouts in the Instant Pot and add water. Add more salt and pepper to make vegies taste brighter.
6. Top Brussels sprouts with the onions, garlic, cooked bacon and more oil.
7. Cook vegetables on "High Pressure" regime for 10 minutes.
8. Serve with melted cheese to taste and butter!

Nutrition:
- Calories: 43
- Fat: 2g
- Carbohydrates: 5g
- Protein:2g

Ham and Cheddar French Style Potatoes

Satisfying potatoes with tender ham slices and soft cheese on top – appetizer for those who love delicious meals!

Prep time: 15 minutes | **Cooking time:** 35 minutes | **Servings:** 20

Ingredients:

- 20 potatoes
- Salt to taste
- Pepper to taste
- Chopped onion
- 4 cups water
- 4 cups sliced ham
- 1 teaspoon butter
- 5 cups heavy cream
- 13oz cheese
- 12oz Monterey Jack

Directions:

1. Mix butter with onion and place in the Instant Pot. Saute onions for 2 minutes.
2. Add heavy creams to the Instant Pot and cook for 3 more minutes on "Saute" regime.
3. Add cheese to the cream mix and set aside.
4. Wash and peel potatoes. Place potatoes in the Instant Pot.
5. Add ham and cheese sauce to the potatoes. Top with seasoning.
6. Pour water in the Instant Pot and cook potatoes for 35 minutes on "High Pressure" regime.
7. Serve with Montery Jack and butter.

Nutrition:

- Calories: 290
- Fat: 11g
- Carbohydrates: 35g
- Protein:14g

Artichokes with Cheese

Healthy food can be delicious – just try this artichokes receipt!

Prep time: 10 minutes | **Cooking time:** 10 minutes | **Servings:** 22

Ingredients:

- 22 artichokes
- 12 cup olive oil
- 4 cups panko
- 3 cups chopped parsley
- 2 cups grated parmesan
- 2 teaspoons pepper
- 12 garlic cloves
- 14 teaspoon salt

Directions:

1. Cut one third part of the artichokes.
2. Pour water in the Instant Pot.
3. Place artichokes in the Instant Pot.
4. Cook artichokes on "High Pressure" regime for 5 minutes.
5. Mix salt, garlic cloves, pepper, parmesan, parsley, panko and olive oil and add to the artichokes.
6. Cook artichokes with the cheese and breadcrumbs for 4 minutes more on "High Pressure" regime.
7. Serve with more cheese!

Nutrition:

- Calories: 100
- Fat: 8g
- Carbohydrates: 0g
- Protein:8g

Buffalo Chicken Dip

Tender and soft meat mix to eat with tacos and chips quickly!

Prep time: 5 minutes | **Cooking time:** 15 minutes | **Servings:** 4

Ingredients:
- 1 pound chicken breast
- 8oz cream cheese
- 1 packet ranch dip
- 16oz cheddar cheese
- 1 cup Hot Sauce
- 1 stick butter

Directions:
1. Wash and slice chicken meat.
2. Mix chicken with sauce, cheese and dip.
3. Place butter in the Instant Pot and melt.
4. Place mixed chicken in the Instant Pot and cook for 15 minutes on "High Pressure" regime.
5. Serve with cheese!

Nutrition:
- Calories: 100
- Fat: 8g
- Carbohydrates: 1g
- Protein:11g

Mushrooms with Balsamic Sauce

It is hard to imagine easier appetizer receipt with such a bright taste!

Prep time: 5 minutes | **Cooking time:** 5 minutes | **Servings:** 10

Ingredients:
- 1 cup olive oil
- 6 tablespoons balsamic vinegar
- 6 garlic cloves
- 2lb mushrooms
- 2 cups cheddar

Directions:
1. Wash and slice mushrooms.
2. Pour olive oil in the Instant Pot.
3. Place garlic cloves and sliced mushrooms in the oven (400oF) and bake for 3 minutes. Place baked mix in the Instant Pot.
4. Cook mushrooms on "Saute" regime for 3 minutes. Add cheese on top.
5. Pour vinegar in the Pot.
6. Cook for 2 more minutes in the Instant Pot on "High Pressure" regime.
7. Serve with salt and pepper!

Nutrition:
- Calories: 482
- Fat: 33g
- Carbohydrates: 6g
- Protein:42g

Baked Vegies in the Instant Pot

Is it possible to cook baked pineapples in the Instant Pot? Or course!

Prep time: 30 minutes | **Cooking time:** 60 minutes | **Servings:** 14

Ingredients:

- 4 cups pineapples
- 1 can marinated mushrooms
- 2 cups water
- 2 cups bacon
- 2 cups chicken stock
- 1 ½ onions
- 1 ½ cups mayonnaise
- 2 teaspoons salt
- 1 ½ cups brown sugar
- 2 teaspoons pepper
- 2 tablespoons tomato paste
- 2 tomatoes
- 2 limes juice
- 2 teaspoons mustard
- 2 tomatoes
- 3 tablespoons white wine
- 2 tablespoons balsamic vinegar
- 2 tablespoons Worcestershire sauce

Directions:

1. Add lime juice and sliced tomatoes to the blender. Blend ingredients and add to the Instant Pot.
2. Pour chicken stock in the Instant Pot and saute baconslices for 3 minutes.
3. Add chopped onions to the bacon in the Instant Pot. Cook for 3 more minutes on "Saute" regime. Pour wine on top.
4. Mix remaining products from the list and blend with tomatoes using blender. Add to the Instant Pot.
5. Place pineapples in the Instant Pot and cook for 15 minutes on "High Pressure" regime. Add marinated mushrooms to the Pot and cook for 5 minutes more not changing regime settings.
6. After the cooking, leave dish in the Instant Pot and let the pressure release naturally for 10 minutes.

Nutrition:

- Calories: 340
- Fat: 6g
- Carbohydrates: 55g
- Protein:16g

Queso Dip

Try Spanish dip – cheese with garlic and milk will taste so sweet and soft!

Prep time: 10 minutes | **Cooking time:** 20 minutes | **Servings:** 10

Ingredients:

- 3/4 lb cheese
- 1 cup water
- 1 cup queso cheese mix
- 1 teaspoon oregano
- 1 tablespoon butter
- 1 tablespoon milk
- 8oz cream cheese
- 1 can Rotel
- 1 tablespoon garlic

Directions:

1. Pour water in the Instant Pot.
2. Mix garlic, cheese, queso, oregano, butter, milk and Rotel.
3. Cover pot with the foil from the inside.
4. Pour mix in the Instant Pot.
5. Cook dip for 20 minutes on "High Pressure" regime.
6. Mix cooked dip to get smooth mix and serve!

Nutrition:

- Calories: 150
- Fat: 13g
- Carbohydrates: 5g
- Protein:6g

Cough Syrup

Try easy and delicious syrup to taste with cookies and pancakes!

Prep time: 10 minutes | **Cooking time:** 10 minutes | **Servings:** 1bottle

Ingredients:
- ¼ cup raw honey
- ¼ cup fresh ginger
- ¼ teaspoon cayenne pepper
- ¼ cup thyme springs
- 2 cups water
- 1 lemon juice

Directions:
1. Mince ginger, but leave skin.
2. Pour water in the Instant Pot.
3. Place thyme with ginger in the pressure cooker and cook for 10 minutes on "Sauté" regime.
4. Let the pressure release naturally for 10 minutes.
5. Blend ginger and thyme to get mixture.
6. Mix lemon juice with honey and cayenne pepper.
7. Pour juice mix in a bowl and add ginger mix. Blend well.
8. Pour jam in the bowls and place in the fridge for 2 months.
9. Serve with cookies!

Nutrition:
- Calories: 25
- Fat: 0g
- Carbohydrates: 7g
- Protein: 0g

Asparagus

Try steamed asparagus in Instant Pot and enjoy healthy dishes!

Prep time: 5 minutes | **Cooking time:** 1 minute | **Servings:** 7

Ingredients:
- 7 asparagus
- 1 cup water

Directions:
1. Pour water in the Instant Pot.
2. Cut asparagus on thin slices.
3. Wash asparagus carefully.
4. Place asparagus in the pressure cooker.
5. Cook on "Steam" for 1 minute.
6. Let the pressure release naturally (5 minutes).
7. Serve with creamy cheese.

Nutrition:
- Calories: 27
- Fat: 1g
- Carbohydrates: 5g
- Protein: 3g

Apple Butter

Only 60 minutes and extra delicious and satisfying apple butter is ready!

Prep time: 15 minutes | **Cooking time:** 60 minutes | **Servings:** 6 bottles

Ingredients:
- 9lb apples
- 4 cups water
- ½ cup brown sugar
- ½ cup honey
- 1 cup caramel
- 1 tablespoons vanilla extract
- ¼ teaspoon ground cloves
- 2 tablespoons apple cider vinegar
- ½ teaspoon nutmeg
- Pinch of salt
- 2 tablespoons cinnamon

Directions:
1. Mix cinnamon with nutmeg, ground cloves and sugar.
2. Pour water in the Instant Pot. Add caramel and honey to the pressure cooker. Mix well.
3. Add nutmeg mix in the pressure cooker.
4. Place vinegar and vanilla extract with salt in the Instant Pot.
5. Cook butter for 60 minutes on "High Pressure" regime.
6. Let the pressure release naturally (60 minutes).
7. Blend cooked ingredients and pour in jars.
8. Serve cold!

Nutrition:
- Calories: 50
- Fat: 0g
- Carbohydrates: 8g
- Protein: 0g

Cabbage

Steamed cabbage – it is difficult to imagine something lighter and better to try as appetizer!

Prep time: 15 minutes | **Cooking time:** 10 minutes | **Servings:** 4

Ingredients:
- 1 head of cabbage
- ½ cup water
- 1/3 cup onion
- Salt to taste
- Pepper to taste
- 2 teaspoons garlic

Directions:
1. Wash and cut cabbage on slices.
2. Pour water in the pressure cooker.
3. Top cabbage with salt and pepper.
4. Place cabbage in the Instant Pot.
5. Add garlic and chopped onion to the cabbage.
6. Cook for 10 minutes on "High Pressure" regime in the pressure cooker.
7. Let the pressure release naturally (10 minutes).
8. Serve cold!

Nutrition:
- Calories: 23
- Fat: 1g
- Carbohydrates: 5g
- Protein: 1g

Artichokes

Try how real artichokes without odd stuffing taste – enjoy healthy lifestyle!

Prep time: 5 minutes | **Cooking time:** 15 minutes | **Servings:** 2

Ingredients:
- 2 artichokes
- 1 lemon juice
- 4 garlic cloves
- Salt to taste
- 2 tablespoons garlic

Directions:
1. Wash artichokes.
2. Cut artichokes on parts and clean from the insights.
3. Clean artichokes of the odd skin.
4. Pour lemon juice over the artichokes in the Instant Pot.
5. Add garlic cloves and garlic with salt.
6. Cook for 15 minutes on "High Pressure" regime.
7. Let the pressure release naturally (10 minutes).

Nutrition:
- Calories: 14
- Fat: 0g
- Carbohydrates: 2g
- Protein: 1g

Shrimp and Grits

Shrimp with grits – the best appetizer for the special day: easy to cook, nice looking and super light!

Prep time: 10 minutes | **Cooking time:** 45 minutes | **Servings:** 4

Ingredients:
- 1lb shrimps
- ¼ cup scallions
- 2 teaspoons old bay seasoning
- ¼ cup heavy cream
- 3 strips smoked bacon
- ¼ teaspoon pepper
- 1/3 cup onion
- ½ teaspoon salt
- ½ cup bell pepper
- ¼ teaspoon tabasco sauce
- 1 tablespoon garlic
- ¼ cup chicken broth
- 2 tablespoons dry wine
- 2 tablespoons lemon juice
- 1 ½ cups tomatoes
- ½ cup grits
- 1 tablespoon butter
- 1 cup milk
- Salt to taste
- Pepper to taste
- 1 cup water

Directions:
1. Cover shrimps with seasoning (old bay) and set aside to marinate.
2. Place bacon strips in the Instant Pot.
3. Cook bacon strips for 3 minutes. You should get crispy and golden colored meat.
4. Wash and chop onions.
5. Place onions in the pressure cooker and add bell peppers.
6. Cook chopped vegetables for 3 minutes on "Sauté" regime.
7. Add garlic to the Instant Pot. Place wine, lemon juice, tomatoes, broth, hot sauce, salt, pepper, grits, milk, water, and cook for 10 minutes on "High Pressure" regime.
8. Let the pressure release naturally (10 minutes).
9. Remove grits and set aside.
10. Place butter and shrimp in the pressure cooker. Cook on 'Keep Warm' regime until the shrimp is ready.

Nutrition:
- Calories: 230
- Fat: 16g
- Carbohydrates: 21g
- Protein: 17g

Cheeseburger Macaroni

Try healthy, soft and satisfying appetizer with macaroni and cheese!

Prep time: 15 minutes | **Cooking time:** 13 minutes | **Servings:** 10

Ingredients:

- 1 cup macaroni
- 1 cup salad macaroni black color
- 1 cup cheddar cheese
- 1 cup mozzarella
- 1 cup water
- 1 cup chicken stock
- 1 cup sour cream
- 1lb turkey
- 1 can cheddar cheese soup
- 3 tablespoons olive oil
- 1 tablespoon salt
- 1 tablespoon butter
- 1/3 onion

Directions:

1. Pour oil in the Instant Pot. Place butter in the pressure cooker. Warm up oil mixture for 4 minutes on "Sauté" regime. Mix well. You should get tender oil mixture on the bottom of your pressure cooker.
2. Shred turkey. Mix turkey with black macaroni.
3. Place turkey in the pressure cooker.
4. Cook for 6 minutes on "High Pressure" regime.
5. Wash and chop onions. Place onion in the Instant Pot. Cook on "Sauté" regime for 3 minutes.
6. Pour water in the pressure cooker.
7. Add soup and macaroni to the pressure cooker. Add mozzarella to the Instant Pot.
8. Cook macaroni for 3 minutes on "High Pressure" regime.
9. Add creams with cheese and cook for 1 minute more.
10. Do a quick release.

Nutrition:

- Calories: 180
- Fat: 4g
- Carbohydrates: 27g
- Protein: 8g

Candied Chickpea

Mix of nuts in Instant Pot will be not only fresh, but also light appetizer!

Prep time: 2 minutes | **Cooking time:** 20 minute | **Servings:** 5

Ingredients:

- 1 ½ cup raw pecans
- 6 ounces dried mango
- 1 cup raw almonds
- Pinch of salt
- 1 cup dried chickpeas
- Pinch of pepper
- ½ cup cashews
- 1 tablespoon seasoning mix
- ¼ cup sunflower seeds
- ½ cup maple syrup
- 3 tablespoons butter
- 1 tablespoon water

Directions:

1. Place butter in the Instant Pot. Melt it up for 1 minute on "High Pressure" regime.
2. Mix pecans with almonds and chickpeas. Place in the pressure cooker.
3. Pour water over nut mix.
4. Mix syrup with seeds, seasoning, cashews and pepper with salt.
5. Add to the pressure cooker.
6. Cook for 10 minutes on "High Pressure" regime.

Nutrition:

- Calories: 321
- Fat: 1g
- Carbohydrates: 83g
- Protein: 1g

Caramelized Popcorn

Do you like watching movies? With this receipt, you will like it even more!

Prep time: 2 minutes | **Cooking time:** 5 minute | **Servings:** 1

Ingredients:
- ½ cup corn
- 1 cup milk
- 2 teaspoons coconut oil
- 2 teaspoons sugar
- 2 tablespoons butter

Directions:
1. Pour oil and ½ butter in the Instant Pot.
2. Sauté oil for 3 minutes in the Instant Pot.
3. Add corn and cook for 3 minutes on "High Pressure" regime until pops.
4. Add sugar with water and milk – cook for 3 minutes on "High Pressure" regime. Add butter.
5. Do a quick release of pressure and place popcorn in the fridge.
6. Serve cold!

Nutrition:
- Calories: 130
- Fat: 3g
- Carbohydrates: 22g
- Protein: 2g

Vegan Hummus

Try new hummus version and get as many vitamins as possible!

Prep time: 25 minutes | **Cooking time:** 35 minutes | **Servings:** 12

Ingredients:
- 1 pound garbanzo beans
- ¼ cup olive oil
- 12 cups water
- ¼ teaspoon paprika
- ½ teaspoon cumin
- ½ cup warm bean
- 1 teaspoon salt
- ¼ cup tahini
- 1 lemon juice
- 2 garlic cloves

Directions:
1. Pour water over the beans and leave for 25 minutes.
2. Dry beans.
3. Pour oil in the pressure cooker.
4. Place garlic cloves in the Instant Pot and cook on "Sauté" regime for 3 minutes.
5. Remove garlic cloves from the Instant Pot.
6. Place garlic cloves with dried beans, tahini, juice, salt, warm bean, cumin and paprika blender and mix to get tender smooth.
7. Place mix in the Instant Pot and cook on "High Pressure" regime for 30 minutes.
8. Let the pressure release naturally (20 minutes).
9. Serve hot!

Nutrition:
- Calories: 74
- Fat: 5g
- Carbohydrates: 7g
- Protein: 2g

Baked Beans

Easy to cook baked beans with light and tender sauce!

Prep time: 10 minutes | **Cooking time:** 60 minutes | **Servings:** 16

Ingredients:

- 16oz beans
- 5oz red beans
- 5oz black beans
- 1 ½ tablespoon Worcestershire sauce
- 1 tablespoon hot sauce
- 6 cups water

- ½ teaspoon chili powder
- 8 bacon slices
- 4 ham slices
- 1 ½ teaspoon white vinegar
- 1 chopped onion
- ½ teaspoon garlic salt

- ¾ cup molasses
- ½ teaspoon salt
- ½ cup brown sugar
- 1 tablespoon butter
- ¾ cup ketchup
- 1 ½ teaspoon dry mustard

Directions:

1. Pour water in the Instant Pot. Add butter to the pressure cooker. Mix butter with water and warm up on "Sauté" regime. It will take you around 2 minutes.
2. Mix beans together. Place beans in the Instant Pot.
3. Add salt to the beans.
4. Cook beans on "Manual" for 60 minutes.
5. Remove beans from the Instant Pot and set aside.
6. Mix onions with bacon and set aside.
7. Mix mustard, ketchup, sugar, salt, molasses, salt, vinegar, chili powder and sauce.
8. Pour oil in the Instant Pot.
9. Cook bacon with onions for 3 minutes on "Sauté" regime.
10. Place beans in the pressure cooker and mix with bacon.
11. Pour sauce over the beans in the Instant Pot.
12. Cook on "Manual" for 30 minutes.
13. Let the pressure release naturally (15 minutes).
14. Serve in cups!

Nutrition:

- Calories: 340
- Fat: 1g

- Carbohydrates: 58g
- Protein: 4g

Apple Dumplings

Try easy and quick fruit dumplings for the special evening!

Prep time: 10 minutes | **Cooking time:** 10 minutes | **Servings:** 8

Ingredients:

- 8ounces crescent rolls
- ¾ cup apple cider
- 1 apple
- Pinch nutmeg
- 4 tablespoons butter
- 1 teaspoon cinnamon
- ½ cup brown sugar
- ½ teaspoon vanilla extract

Directions:

1. Turn on Instant Pot and set "Sauté" function.
2. Roll on the floured surface crescent rolls.
3. Wash and cut apple on slices.
4. Place 1 slice apple in each roll.
5. Place butter in the Instant Pot.
6. Roll up dumplings.
7. Place dumplings in the Instant Pot.
8. Place sugar, vanilla extract, cinnamon and nutmeg over the rolls.
9. Pour cider over the rolls.
10. Cook dumplings for 10 minutes on "High Pressure" regime.
11. Let the pressure release naturally (10 minutes).
12. Serve with powdered sugar!

Nutrition:

- Calories: 450
- Fat: 22g
- Carbohydrates: 61g
- Protein: 4g

Black Beans

Super full of vitamins, tender and healthy black beans – appetizer you will like for sure!

Prep time: 10 minutes | **Cooking time:** 20 minutes | **Servings:** 4

Ingredients:

- 1 pound black beans
- 2 teaspoons Worcestershire sauce
- 3 cups water
- 2 bay leaves
- ½ onion
- 2 teaspoons salt
- 2 garlic cloves
- ½ teaspoon cumin

Directions:

1. Pour water in the pressure cooker.
2. Place beans in the Instant Pot.
3. Add cumin, garlic, salt, chopped onion and bay leaves with sauce.
4. Mix beans well in the Instant Pot.
5. Cook for 20 minutes on "Manual" regime.
6. Let the pressure release naturally (10 minutes).
7. Serve hot!

Nutrition:

- Calories: 98
- Fat: 2g
- Carbohydrates: 16g
- Protein: 5g

Beets

Beet – easy, heathy, colorful and full of vitamins. Try it with cheese and nuts!

Prep time: 5 minutes | **Cooking time:** 20 minutes | **Servings:** 1

Ingredients:

- 1 ½ cup water
- Beet

Directions:

1. Wash beet carefully.
2. Clean beet of the skin.
3. Cut beet into slices.
4. Pour water in the Instant Pot.
5. Place sliced beet in the pressure cooker.
6. Cook for 15 minutes on "High Pressure" regime.
7. Let the pressure release naturally (10 minutes).
8. Serve hot!

Nutrition:

- Calories: 37
- Fat: 0g
- Carbohydrates: 9g
- Protein: 2g

Cinnamon Apples

Try light and easy receipt for those who care about their health!

Prep time: 15 minutes | **Cooking time:** 2 hours | **Servings:** 4

Ingredients:

- 6 apples
- 2 tablespoons butter
- ½ cup sugar
- Pinch salt
- ½ cup brown sugar
- 3 tablespoons cornstarch
- 1 Tablespoon cinnamon

Directions:

1. Wash and peel apples.
2. Cut apples on slices.
3. Place butter in the Instant Pot and melt it up for 1 minutes on "Sauté" regime.
4. Place apples in the pressure cooker.
5. Add salt, sugar, brown sugar, cinnamon, cornstarch and cook apples for 2 hours on "High Pressure" regime.
6. Let the pressure release naturally (25 minutes).
7. Serve hot!

Nutrition:

- Calories: 257
- Fat: 7g
- Carbohydrates: 45g
- Protein: 5g

Baba Ghanoush

Try middle Asia cuisine and get as much vitamins as possible!

Prep time: 5 minutes | **Cooking time:** 10 minutes | **Servings:** 2

Ingredients:

- 1/6 eggplant
- Cumin to taste
- ½ onion
- 1 red onion
- 1 tablespoon butter
- 1/6 cup creams
- 1 cup shredded cheese for topping
- Sesame seeds to serve
- Parsley to taste
- 1 garlic clove
- 1/8 tablespoon sesame oil
- ½ teaspoon cumin
- 2 tablespoons olive oil
- 2/4 teaspoons lemon juice
- 2 tablespoons sesame seeds
- 1/8 teaspoon salt
- Dash pepper
- 1 cup chopped cherry tomatoes

Directions:

1. Pour water in the Instant Pot. Add butter to the pressure cooker. Melt butter for 3 minutes on "Sauté" regime. You should get tender oil mixture on the bottom of the pressure cooker. It will be your base for cooking.
2. Wash and cut eggplant into slices. Mix eggplant with cherry tomatoes.
3. Place eggplant in the Instant Pot. Add red onion to the Instant Pot.
4. Cook eggplant for 10 minutes on "High Pressure" regime.
5. Do a quick release. Remove eggplant from the Instant Pot.
6. Add sesame seeds, oil, onion and garlic to the pressure cooker.
7. Sauté onions for 4 minutes in the Instant Pot. Open lid and sprinkle ingredients with cheese.
8. Add eggplant, lemon juice, parsley and cumin back to the pressure cooker.
9. Cook for 3 minutes on "Sauté" regime.
10. Place ingredients in blender and mix well to get tender sauce. Mix with sesame seeds and put on table to rest after the cooking.
11. Serve hot!

Nutrition:

- Calories: 155
- Fat: 14g
- Carbohydrates: 8g
- Protein: 2g

Paleo Stuffed Grape Leaves

Full of vitamins grape leaves with light and satisfying stuffing will be something you want to try today!

Prep time: 10 minutes | **Cooking time:** 15 minutes | **Servings:** 7

Ingredients:
- 1 can grape leaves
- Lemon slices to serve
- 1 cauliflower
- 2 lemons juice
- 2lbs beef
- ½ cup water
- 2 tablespoons mint
- 1 teaspoon sea salt
- 2 tablespoons parsley
- 1 teaspoon onion powder
- 1 cup golden raisins
- 1 teaspoon garlic
- 2 teaspoons minced garlic
- 2 teaspoons oregano
- 2 teaspoons cinnamon

Directions:
1. Mix oregano, cinnamon, garlic, onion powder, parsley, salt, mint and lemon juice. Set seasoning mix aside.
2. Mix rice, cauliflower, raisins with beef.
3. Add seasoning mix to the beef mix.
4. Place grapes on the table.
5. Place 1 teaspoon meat mix to the grape leaves.
6. Roll grape leaves up.
7. Pour water in the pressure cooker.
8. Place rolled grape leaves in the Instant Pot.
9. Cook for 15 minutes on "High Pressure" regime.
10. Let the pressure release naturally (10 minutes).
11. Serve hot!

Nutrition:
- Calories: 298
- Fat: 21g
- Carbohydrates: 20g
- Protein: 13g

Colored Greens

Try light greens with 0 fat! This receipt will give you energy, powder and health

Prep time: 5 minutes | **Cooking time:** 60 minutes | **Servings:** 4

Ingredients:
- 2lbs Collared greens
- ¼ teaspoon red pepper flakes
- 1 smoked turkey wing
- 6 cups chicken broth

Directions:
1. Place turkey in the Instant Pot.
2. Mix greens with broth and pepper flakes.
3. Add greens to the pressure cooker.
4. Cook for 60 minutes on "Manual" regime.
5. Do a quick release.
6. Serve!

Nutrition:
- Calories: 25
- Fat: 0g
- Carbohydrates: 5g
- Protein: 1g

Cranberry Ketchup

Try super light and sweet ketchup! It will be perfect addition to any dish – from meat and up to chicken wings!

Prep time: 5 minutes | **Cooking time:** 10 minutes | **Servings:** 2

Ingredients:

- 2 cups cranberries
- 2 pinches sea salt
- ¼ cup honey
- 2 pinches nutmeg
- ¼ cup vine vinegar
- 2 pinches allspice
- ¼ cup water
- 2 pinches garlic cloves powder

Directions:

1. Mix powder with allspice, nutmeg and salt.
2. Blend cranberries in blender.
3. Pour cranberry mix in the pressure cooker.
4. Add allspice mix to the Instant Pot.
5. Add vinegar and honey to the pressure cooker.
6. Pour water over cranberry mix.
7. Mix ingredients in the Instant Pot well.
8. Cook for10 minutes on "High Pressure" regime.
9. Let the pressure release naturally (10 minutes).
10. Pour in jars and serve cold!

Nutrition:

- Calories: 40
- Fat: 1g
- Carbohydrates: 10g
- Protein: 1g

Palak Paneer

Try Asian version of dip and taste it with chips for the lunch!

Prep time: 20 minutes | **Cooking time:** 10 minute | **Servings:** 3

Ingredients:

- 10oz spinach
- ½ teaspoon salt
- 10oz paneer cheese
- ¼ teaspoon turmeric powder
- 1 onion
- 1 teaspoon coriander
- 1 tomato
- ½ teaspoon red chili
- 1 green chili
- 1 teaspoon cumin
- 5 garlic cloves
- Cream to serve
- 1 inch ginger
- 1 tablespoon oil

Directions:

1. Pour oil in the Instant Pot.
2. Place cumin seeds in the pressure cooker and cook on "Sauté" regime for 3 minutes.
3. Mix ginger, green chili, garlic and chopped onions.
4. Place onion mix in the Instant Pot.
5. Cook onion mix for 4 minutes on "Sauté" regime.
6. Add ginger, red chili, coriander, salt, turmeric powder and tomato to the Instant Pot.
7. Add spinach and cook ingredients on "Manual" regime for 2 minutes.
8. Add creams and cheese to the spinach mix and use blender to get tender mix.
9. Serve with tostadas!

Nutrition:

- Calories: 300
- Fat: 11g
- Carbohydrates: 38g
- Protein: 12g

Boston Brown Bread

Easy, super sweet and juicy bread with honey sauce and grapes!

Prep time: 20 minutes | **Cooking time:** 50 minutes | **Servings:** 1 loaf

Ingredients:
- 1 cup buttermilk
- 1 cup raisins
- 2/3 cup milk
- 1 teaspoon sea salt
- 2 tablespoons sourdough starter
- ¾ cup cornmeal
- ½ cup molasses
- ¾ cup wheat flour
- 3 tablespoons butter
- ¾ cup rye flour

Directions:
1. Mix buttermilk, starter and milk.
2. Mix molasses with butter.
3. Add molasses to milk mixture and whisk well.
4. Add salt and flour to the mix.
5. Add raisins and mix well.
6. Leave dough to rest for 8 hours.
7. Pour water in the pressure cooker.
8. Place dough in the Instant Pot.
9. Cook dough for 50 minutes on "High Pressure" regime.
10. Do a quick release and serve!

Nutrition:
- Calories: 55
- Fat: 1g
- Carbohydrates: 12g
- Protein: 2g

Strawberry Jam

Try granny receipt strawberry jam to try anywhere with toasts and desserts!

Prep time: 3 minutes | **Cooking time:** 5 minutes | **Servings:** 2 jars

Ingredients:
- 1lb organic strawberries
- 1 cup honey

Directions:
1. Wash and cut strawberries into slices.
2. Pour honey in the Instant Pot.
3. Melt honey for 2 minutes on "Sauté" regime.
4. Add strawberries in the pressure cooker.
5. Cook for 3 minutes with honey on "High Pressure" regime.
6. Blend cooked strawberries.
7. Pour jam in jars.
8. Place jam in the fridge and cool down.
9. Serve cold!

Nutrition:
- Calories: 75
- Fat: 0g
- Carbohydrates: 12g
- Protein: 1g

Rosemary Bread

Try satisfying bread with butter in the morning or with olives and cheese for the lunch – you will like it anyway!

Prep time: 95 minutes | **Cooking time:** 120 minutes | **Servings:** 1 loaf

Ingredients:
- 3 ½ cups flour
- 1 teaspoon salt
- 1 pack yeast
- 1 teaspoon sugar
- 1 ¼ cups water
- 3 tablespoons olive oil
- ¼ cup rosemary

Directions:
1. Mix sugar with yeast.
2. Mix flour with rosemary and salt.
3. Add olive oil to salt mix.
4. Mix yeast with rosemary mix and roll up satisfying dough.
5. Leave dough to rest for 95 minutes.
6. Pour water in the Instant Pot.
7. Place dough in the pressure cooker.
8. Cook bread for 2 hours on the "High Pressure" regime.
9. Do a quick release.
10. Serve hot!

Nutrition:
- Calories: 72
- Fat: 1g
- Carbohydrates: 0g
- Protein: 2g

Roasted Garlic

Full heads of roasted garlic will be great addition to the dinner dishes!

Prep time: 20 minutes | **Cooking time:** 5 minutes | **Servings:** 4

Ingredients:
- 8 heads garlic
- 2/3 cup water
- 2 tablespoons olive oil
- 1 teaspoon salt

Directions:
1. Clean garlic heads of the odd skin and separate garlic cloves.
2. Pour oil in the pressure cooker.
3. Place garlic cloves in the Instant Pot.
4. Sate garlic for 4 minutes.
5. Pour water over garlic and add salt.
6. Cook garlic on "Poultry" regime for 5 minutes.
7. Let the pressure release naturally (10 minutes).
8. Serve hot!

Nutrition:
- Calories: 120
- Fat: 4g
- Carbohydrates: 20g
- Protein: 3g

Cheesy Grits

Cheesy appetizer in southern style will be perfect addition to any meal!

Prep time: 5 minutes | **Cooking time:** 10 minutes | **Servings:** 12

Ingredients:
- 2 cups grits
- Butter to serve
- 3 cups water
- 2 teaspoons salt
- 1 ½ cup milk
- 1 cup creams
- 1/3 cup melted butter
- 4 ounces cheddar cheese
- 2 teaspoons butter
- 1 chunk cheese
- 1 cup shredded mozzarella
- ½ teaspoon salt
- 4 tablespoons bacon grease
- 1 cup stone grits

Directions:
1. Pour oil in the Instant Pot. Add melted butter to the Instant Pot.
2. Place grits in the oil and cook on "Sauté" regime for 5 minutes. Just wait until they turn soft and golden color. Add creams over ingredients.
3. Add bacon grease, salt, cheese. Butter, cheddar, milk, salt and reminded grits.
4. Mix ingredients well in the pressure cooker.
5. Cook for 10 minutes on "High Pressure" regime.
6. Let the pressure release naturally (15 minutes).
7. Serve cold!

Nutrition:
- Calories: 203
- Fat: 10g
- Carbohydrates: 20g
- Protein: 9g

Smothered Burritos

Try small and nice looking burritos with sauce you like to get satisfying and light dinner!

Prep time: 20 minutes | **Cooking time:** 35 minutes | **Servings:** 4

Ingredients:
- 3lbs beef roast
- 2 cups cheese
- 16oz enchilada sauce
- 12 burrito tortillas
- 2 beef bullion cubes
- ½ cup water

Directions:
1. Pour water in the Instant Pot.
2. Mix bullion with sauce and beef.
3. Add beef mix in the Instant Pot.
4. Cook for 30 minutes on "High Pressure" regime.
5. Add cheese and cook for 5 minutes more on "Sauté" regime.
6. Let the pressure release naturally (10 minutes).
7. Serve with tortillas!

Nutrition:
- Calories: 650
- Fat: 28g
- Carbohydrates: 67g
- Protein: 34g

Green Chilies

Colorful and bright green chilies with sauce and tender taste!

Prep time: 2 minutes | **Cooking time:** 2 minutes | **Servings:** 4

Ingredients:
- 1 pound green chilies
- ¼ teaspoon garlic powder
- 1 /2 cups apple cider vinegar
- 1 ½ teaspoons sugar
- 1 teaspoon salt

Directions:
1. Place chopped chilies in the Instant Pot.
2. Cover chilies with sugar, salt and powder.
3. Pour vinegar over chili peppers.
4. Cook peppers for 2 minutes on "High Pressure" regime.
5. Leave on "Keep Warm" regime for 20 minutes.
6. Serve in jars!

Nutrition:
- Calories: 10
- Fat: 0g
- Carbohydrates: 1g
- Protein: 0g

Sushi

Small and delicious sushi will be greatest appetizer ever!

Prep time: 3 minutes | **Cooking time:** 7 minutes | **Servings:** 12

Ingredients:
- 4 cups sushi rice
- 8 tablespoons wine vinegar
- 3 cups water
- 12 nori rolls
- 6 cucumbers
- 4 slices ham

Directions:
1. Wash and chop cucumber. Cut ham on slices.
2. Set cucumber aside.
3. Roll nori on the table and cut into strips. Leave to rest.
4. Pour water in the pressure cooker.
5. Add rice and vinegar to the Instant Pot.
6. Cook for 7 minutes on "High Pressure" regime.
7. Let the pressure release naturally (5 minutes).
8. Let rice cool down.
9. Place rice on nori strips and add cucumber. Place ham over cucumber and roll up sushi.
10. Roll sushi and serve with soy sauce!

Nutrition:
- Calories: 310
- Fat: 0g
- Carbohydrates: 8g
- Protein:2g

Ricotta Cheese

Try easy and tender cheese in Instant Pot today and enjoy healthy lifestyle any when!

Prep time: 2 minutes | **Cooking time:** 30 minutes | **Servings:** 8

Ingredients:
- 1 quart milk
- 2 pinches salt
- 1 lemon

Directions:
1. Pour milk in the Instant Pot.
2. Cook milk on "Yogurt" regime for 30 minutes.
3. Add salt and lemon – cook for 3 minutes more on "High Pressure" regime.
4. Let the pressure release naturally (15 minutes).
5. Remove cheese from the pressure cooker and leave to rest in the fridge for 5 days.
6. Serve with bread!

Nutrition:
- Calories: 50
- Fat: 4g
- Carbohydrates: 1g
- Protein: 3g

Drunken Peas

Easy, full of vitamins and healthy peas will be great addition to any meat and green mix!

Prep time: 2 minutes | **Cooking time:** 6 minutes | **Servings:** 2

Ingredients:
- 2oz pancetta
- Salt to taste
- Pepper to taste
- 1 onion
- 1 tablespoon butter
- 1/2lb peas
- 1 cup tomatoes
- 1 tablespoon mint
- 1/2cup beer
- 1 cup heavy creams
- 1 basil leaves bunch

Directions:
1. Pour water in the Instant Pot. Warm up water in the pressure cooker. It will take you around 3 minutes to make water hot. Do not overcook and do not let it bring to boil. Pour creams in water and mix well.
2. Place pancetta and onions with mint in the Instant Pot. The same time wash tomatoes well and cut on small slices.
3. Cook on "High Pressure" regime for 3 minutes.
4. Add peas with beer and butter to the Instant Pot. The same time place tomatoes in blender and blend. Pour tomatoes to the pressure cooker.
5. Add salt and pepper to the Instant Pot.
6. Cook on "High Pressure" regime. It will take you around 5 minutes.
7. Let the pressure release naturally (10 minutes).
8. Serve with lemon slices! Add basil leaves for serving!

Nutrition:
- Calories: 240
- Fat: 10g
- Carbohydrates: 14g
- Protein:23g

POULTRY

Turkey with Sweet Potato

Satisfying melting turkey with light and easy to cook potato will be both perfect lunch and quick dinner!

Prep time: 10 minutes | **Cooking time:** 20 minutes | **Servings:** 6

Ingredients:

- 1 onion
- Brown rice to serve
- 3 garlic cloves
- Salt to taste
- Pepper to taste
- 1lb turkey
- ½ teaspoon chili powder
- 1 can tomatoes
- 1 teaspoon paprika
- 1 can tomato sauce
- 1 teaspoon cumin
- 1 can chickpeas
- 1 cup stock
- 1 red bell pepper
- 1 cup sweet potato

Directions:

1. Pour oil in the Instant Pot.
2. Set Saute function in the Instant Pot.
3. Place minced garlic with chopped onion in the Instant Pot and saute for 5 minutes.
4. Add turkey mince to the Instant Pot.
5. Cook for 4 minutes more on "High Pressure" regime.
6. Mix tomato sauce with tomatoes, beans, potatoes, peppers and remaining ingredients.
7. Pout broth in the Instant Pot.
8. Place tomato mix in the Instant Pot.
9. Cook ingredients for 10 minutes not changing the regime.
10. Serve with boiled rice and creams!

Nutrition:

- Calories: 235
- Fat: 8g
- Carbohydrates: 14g
- Protein:23g

Chicken Caesar Wraps

Cook chicken with healthy vegetables and crispy tacos – make this day taste super light!

Prep time: 5 minutes | **Cooking time:** 25 minutes | **Servings:** 20

Ingredients:

- 4lbs chicken breasts
- 20 tortillas
- 4 cups chicken stock
- 2 cups cheese
- 2 cups Caesar dressing
- 12 cups lettuce
- 1 cup parsley
- 1 teaspoon salt
- 1 teaspoon pepper

Directions:

1. Pour chicken broth in the Instant Pot.
2. Place chicken in the Instant Pot.
3. Cook chicken for 25 minutes on "High Pressure" regime.
4. Cover chicken with cheese and add salt with pepper and parsley.
5. Place lettuce on the tortillas and add chicken in cheese with Caesar dressing.
6. Serve with cheesy sauce.

Nutrition:

- Calories: 482
- Fat: 19g
- Carbohydrates: 41g
- Protein:31g

Chicken Marsala

Cook tender chicken cubes in sweet sauce with fresh herbs and enjoy healthy lifestyle!

Prep time: 5 minutes | **Cooking time:** 10 minutes | **Servings:** 4

Ingredients:
- 4 chicken breasts
- Egg noodles cooked
- Salt to taste
- Pepper to taste
- Parsley to taste
- 2 garlic cloves
- ¼ cup cornstarch
- 1 cup mushrooms
- ½ cup chicken stock
- 1 cup cooking wine

Directions:
1. Top chicken with salt and pepper.
2. Mix garlic with wine and mushrooms.
3. Place chicken in the Instant Pot.
4. Pour wine mix over the chicken.
5. Add remaining ingredients to the Instant Pot, apart from noodles.
6. Cook chicken for 10 minutes on "Poultry" regime.
7. Serve with the noodles.

Nutrition:
- Calories: 215
- Fat: 6g
- Carbohydrates: 4g
- Protein:28g

Chicken Pot Pie

Crispy chicken pie with the juicy filling in the Instant Pot will make any day special!

Prep time: 20 minutes | **Cooking time:** 5 minutes | **Servings:** 6

Ingredients:
- 2lbs chicken breasts
- ¼ teaspoon pepper
- ¼ cup onion
- 1 teaspoon herbs de Provence
- 1lb vegetables
- 1 ½ teaspoons salt
- 8oz biscuit dough
- ½ cup water
- 3 cups chicken stock
- 1 can cream
- 3 potatoes
- 1 ½ teaspoons bouillon
- 1 ½ cup milk
- 2 tablespoons butter
- 2 tablespoons potato starch

Directions:
1. Mix milk, potato starch, butter, salt, bouillon, herbs de Provence, pepper, water and cream.
2. Use blender to get light tender sauce.
3. Pour broth in the Instant Pot.
4. Add chopped onion with the chicken to the Instant Pot.
5. Add potatoes and vegetables with seasoning to the Pot.
6. Cook chicken for 5 minutes on "High Pressure" regime.
7. Serve chicken with sauce!

Nutrition:
- Calories: 380
- Fat: 19g
- Carbohydrates: 33g
- Protein:12g

Frozen Chicken in the Instant Pot

How to cook frozen chicken meat in the Instant Pot with minimal amount of ingredients? Check it out!

Prep time: 5 minutes | **Cooking time:** 15 minutes | **Servings:** 21

Ingredients:
- 6lbs frozen chicken
- Salt to taste
- Pepper to taste
- 1 cup water

Directions:
1. Wash chicken meat and slice on the small parts.
2. Pour water in the Instant Pot.
3. Cover chicken with salt and pepper.
4. Place shredded chicken in the Instant Pot.
5. Cook chicken slices on "High Pressure" regime for 15 minutes.
6. Serve with herbs!

Nutrition:
- Calories: 332
- Fat: 10g
- Carbohydrates: 38g
- Protein:24g

Peruvian Chicken with Herbs

Try exotic meat recipes – you won't stay unmoved!

Prep time: 10 minutes | **Cooking time:** 20 minutes | **Servings:** 4

Ingredients:
- 5 jalapeno peppers
- Salt to taste
- Onion
- 1/3 cup canola oil
- 1 garlic clove
- 1 tablespoon lime juice
- 1/3 cup feta cheese
- 1 yellow onion
- ¼ cup olive oil
- 1 garlic clove
- 1/3 cup feta cheese
- 1 tablespoon lime juice
- ½ teaspoon huacatay paste
- ¼ cup Amarillo paste
- 3lb chicken
- ½ cup water
- 3 tablespoons paprika
- ¼ cup chopped cilantro
- 2 tablespoons cumin
- 1 teaspoon pepper
- 1 ½ tablespoons garlic
- 4 tablespoons canola oil
- 2 tablespoons lime juice

Directions:
1. Mix 5 jalapeno peppers with feta cheese, salt, garlic, lime juice, oil and chopped onion.
2. Use blender to get tender sauce. Set aside.
3. Mix 1 garlic clove, yellow onion with 2 types paste, salt, lime juice, feta cheese and olive oil.
4. Use blender to get sauce and set aside.
5. Wash chicken fillets.
6. Pour oil in the Instant Pot.
7. Mix paprika, cumin, garlic, lime juice, pepper and cilantro.
8. Top chicken meat with marinade. Leave chicken to marinate for 10 minutes.
9. Place chicken in the Instant Pot and cook for 20 minutes on "Poultry" regime.
10. Serve chicken with two sauces on top!

Nutrition:
- Calories: 321
- Fat:20g
- Carbohydrates: 0g
- Protein:34g

Asian Sesame Chicken

Add more Asian vibes to the grey weekdays – start cooking special chicken with the Instant Pot!

Prep time: 5 minutes | **Cooking time:** 15 minutes | **Servings:** 12

Ingredients:
- 1 cup water
- 12 tablespoons water
- 1 cup ketchup
- 3 tablespoons cornstarch
- 1 cup soy sauce
- 6 chicken breasts
- 6 tablespoons honey
- 3 teaspoons minced garlic
- 6 tablespoons sesame oil
- 3 teaspoons rice wine vinegar

Directions:
1. Mix ½ cup water with ketchup, soy sauce, honey, sesame oil, wine vinegar and ginger.
2. Use blender to get light sauce and set aside.
3. Place chicken meat in the Instant Pot.
4. Top chicken with sauce.
5. Pour 3 tablespoons water and cornstarch on top.
6. Cook chicken on "High Pressure" regime for 7 minutes.
7. Serve with fresh herbs!

Nutrition:
- Calories: 130
- Fat:2g
- Carbohydrates: 2g
- Protein: 25g

Cashew Chicken

Satisfying nuts with tender chicken meat and sweet sauce will be something special for you today!

Prep time: 10 minutes | **Cooking time:** 5 minutes | **Servings:** 18

Ingredients:
- 6lbs chicken breasts
- 3 cups water
- 6 cups fresh broccoli
- 6 garlic cloves
- 3 bell peppers
- 6 tablespoons lemon juice
- 2 tablespoons honey
- 1 teaspoon minced ginger
- 3 cups roasted cashews
- 12 tablespoons brown sugar
- 12 tablespoons olive oil
- 3 tablespoons rice vinegar
- 12 tablespoons soy sauce
- 4 tablespoon sesame seeds
- 4 tablespoon hoisin sauce

Directions:
1. Pour oil in the Instant Pot. Pour honey with lemon juice to the Instant Pot.
2. Set "Saute" regime in the Instant Pot. Warm up honey until melt for 5 minutes.
3. Place chicken in the hot Instant Pot.
4. Top chicken with mixed soy sauce, hoisin sauce, sugar, vinegar and seasoning with herbs.
5. Cook chicken with the remaining ingredients for 5 minutes on "High Pressure" regime.
6. Serve chicken meat with roasted cashew nuts.

Nutrition:
- Calories: 591
- Fat: 32g
- Carbohydrates: 29g
- Protein: 32g

Bruschetta Chicken

Only ten minutes and soft, tender chicken meat with veggie topping!

Prep time: 5 minutes | **Cooking time:** 10 minutes | **Servings:** 4

Ingredients:
- 4 chicken cutlets
- 2 cups roma tomatoes
- 1 tablespoon olive oil
- 1 teaspoon parsley
- 4 garlic cloves
- 1 teaspoon basil
- 2 carrots
- Mozzarella cheese
- Balsamic glaze

Directions:
1. Pour oil in the Instant Pot.
2. Set "Saute" regime on the Instant Pot.
3. Add herbs and seasoning on chicken meat.
4. Place chicken meat in the Instant Pot.
5. Top chicken with carrots, glaze, cheese and tomatoes.
6. Cook chicken on "Meat" regime for 10 minutes.
7. Serve with fresh herbs!

Nutrition:
- Calories: 340
- Fat: 10g
- Carbohydrates: 14g
- Protein: 48g

Adobo Chicken

Tender and healthy chicken meat with spices and delicious herbs!

Prep time: 5 minutes | **Cooking time:** 25 minutes | **Servings:** 12

Ingredients:
- 4 pounds chicken breasts
- 1 cup water
- 4 tablespoons seasoning to taste
- 3 cans tomatoes
- 4 tablespoons turmeric

Directions:
1. Wash and slice chicken meat.
2. Pour water in the Instant Pot.
3. Place chicken meat in the Instant Pot.
4. Top chicken with tomatoes.
5. Cook chicken on "High Pressure" regime for 25 minutes.
6. Serve chicken with fresh herbs!

Nutrition:
- Calories: 245
- Fat: 9g
- Carbohydrates: 12g
- Protein: 28g

Verde Chicken

Spanish passions on the plate – with verde chicken receipt it is easy!

Prep time: 5 minutes | **Cooking time:** 25 minutes | **Servings:** 4

Ingredients:
- 2 pounds chicken breasts
- ½ cup chopped cilantro
- 15 ounces salsa verde
- 1 teaspoon cumin

Directions:
1. Wash chicken breasts.
2. Mix cilantro with salsa verde and cumin.
3. Top chicken with cumin mix.
4. Place chicken in the Instant Pot.
5. Cook chicken for 25 minutes on "High Pressure" regime.
6. Serve with garlic.

Nutrition:
- Calories: 250
- Fat: 15g
- Carbohydrates: 25g
- Protein:25g

Chicken with Cheese and Broccoli

Mix baked broccoli with tender melting cheese and light chicken meat to get satisfying soup!

Prep time: 10 minutes | **Cooking time:** 15 minutes | **Servings:** 4

Ingredients:
- 1 head broccoli
- Cheese to serve
- ¼ onion
- Salt to taste
- Pepper to taste
- 4 drumsticks
- 1 teaspoon oregano
- 1 can cheese soup
- 2 cups water

Directions:
1. Pour water in the Instant Pot.
2. Mix cheese soup, oregano, pepper, salt and chopped onion.
3. Place washed chicken meat in the Instant Pot.
4. Top chicken meat with oregano mix.
5. Add broccoli to the Instant Pot.
6. Cook dish on "High Pressure" regime for 15 minutes.
7. Top chicken with cheese and serve!

Nutrition:
- Calories: 143
- Fat:9g
- Carbohydrates: 5g
- Protein:42g

Ginger Garlic Drumsticks

Easy to cook drumsticks have never been this tasty!

Prep time: 5 minutes | **Cooking time:** 20 minutes | **Servings:** 16

Ingredients:
- 28 chicken drumsticks
- 2 chopped onion
- 1 cup water
- 4 teaspoons ginger
- 2 cups soy sauce
- 8 garlic cloves
- 8 teaspoons vinegar
- 8 tablespoons honey
- 8 tablespoons brown sugar

Directions:
1. Wash drumsticks.
2. Pour water in the Instant Pot.
3. Mix sugar with honey, vinegar, garlic cloves, soy sauce, ginger and chopped onion.
4. Place onion mix in the Instant Pot.
5. Cook sauce for 2 minutes on "High Pressure" regime.
6. Add drumsticks to the Instant Pot.
7. Cook chicken for 10 minutes on "Poultry" regime.
8. Serve with fresh herbs!

Nutrition:
- Calories: 155
- Fat: 8g
- Carbohydrates: 1g
- Protein:21g

BBQ Chicken with Potatoes

Crispy chicken in its own juice with satisfying potatoes will be perfect dinner!

Prep time: 10 minutes | **Cooking time:** 15 minutes | **Servings:** 15

Ingredients:
- 10 pounds chicken
- 5 onions
- 5 cups BBQ sauce
- 15 potatoes
- 5 tablespoons Italian seasoning
- 5 tablespoons minced garlic

Directions:
1. Pour water in the Instant Pot.
2. Wash and peel potatoes.
3. Mix chopped onion with seasoning and garlic.
4. Place chicken with potatoes in the Instant Pot.
5. Add onion garlic mix.
6. Cook chicken on "Poultry" regime for 15 minutes.
7. Serve with BBQ sauce.

Nutrition:
- Calories: 350
- Fat: 19g
- Carbohydrates: 27g
- Protein:17g

Chicken Piccata

Chicken in its own juice with lemon sauce and fresh herbs!

Prep time: 5 minutes | **Cooking time:** 5 minutes | **Servings:** 1

Ingredients:
- 1/2 chicken breasts
- 1/8 cup chopped parsley
- 1/8 cup potato starch
- 1/2 tablespoons capers
- 1/4 teaspoon salt
- 1/8 cup water
- 1/8 teaspoon pepper
- 1/6 cup dry wine
- 2 tablespoons butter
- 1/3 lemons
- 1/3 tablespoons olive oil
- 1 shallot

Directions:
1. Cut chicken fillets in halves.
2. Cover chicken meat with the salt and pepper.
3. Place butter in the Instant Pot.
4. Set "Saute" regime in the Instant Pot.
5. Mix shallots with olive oil, lemons, wine and capers.
6. Place chicken in the Instant Pot.
7. Top chicken with potato starch and parsley.
8. Cook chicken on "High Pressure" regime for 3 minutes.
9. Add remaining ingredients to the Instant Pot and cook for 5 minutes more on the same regime.
10. Serve with fresh lemon slices.

Nutrition:
- Calories: 264
- Fat: 12g
- Carbohydrates:4g
- Protein:40g

Firecracker Chicken

Can small chicken slices in their own juice be really crispy and satisfying? Just try this receipt!

Prep time: 10 minutes | **Cooking time:** 10 minutes | **Servings:** 12

Ingredients:
- 6lb chicken thighs
- 3 teaspoons red pepper flakes
- 6 tablespoons cornstarch
- 2 cups sugar snap peas
- 1 cup chicken broth
- 3 onions
- 12tablespoons soy sauce
- 3 bell peppers
- 9 tablespoons dry sherry
- 3 teaspoons garlic
- 6 teaspoons sesame oil
- 3 teaspoons ginger

Directions:
1. Mix broth with sesame oil, dry sherry and soy sauce.
2. Mix ginger, red pepper flakes, garlic, snap peas, bell pepper and chopped onion.
3. Pour sauce in the Instant Pot.
4. Set "Saute" regime on the Instant Pot.
5. Top chicken meat with cornstarch.
6. Place chicken in the Instant Pot and cook for 5 minutes on "High Pressure".
7. Add vegetables to the chicken meat and cook for 3 more minutes on the same regime.
8. Serve hot with herbs!

Nutrition:
- Calories: 600
- Fat: 32g
- Carbohydrates:28g
- Protein:55g

Moo Goo Gai Pan

Make it taste like Asia!

Prep time: 10 minutes | **Cooking time:** 6 minutes | **Servings:** 16

Ingredients:

- 4lbs chicken thighs
- 24oz water
- 4 tablespoons olive oil
- 24oz bamboo shoots
- 3 cups chicken stock
- 4 cups snow peas
- 3 tablespoons soy sauce
- 24oz mushrooms
- 4 tablespoons dry sherry
- 4 carrots
- 4 tablespoons cornstarch
- 8 garlic cloves
- 4 inch ginger

Directions:

1. Wash and chop vegetables.
2. Wash and cut chicken meat.
3. Pour oil in the Instant Pot and turn on "Saute" regime.
4. Place chicken meat in the Instant Pot and cook for 7 minutes.
5. Add chicken stock and cook for 1 minute on "High Pressure" regime.
6. Add cornstarch and seasoning with herbs to the Instant Pot. Cook for 3 minutes on the same regime.
7. Add vegetables to the Instant Pot.
8. Cook for 7 minutes on "High Pressure" regime.
9. Serve chicken with soy sauce!

Nutrition:

- Calories: 272
- Fat: 19g
- Carbohydrates: 12g
- Protein:15g

Chicken with Dumplings

Tender and healthy chicken with satisfying dumplings will be perfect quick lunch and delicious dinner with the side dish!

Prep time: 10 minutes | **Cooking time:** 20 minutes | **Servings:** 12

Ingredients:

- 9 chicken breasts
- 2 teaspoons pepper
- 9 carrots
- 3 teaspoons thyme
- 6 celery stalks
- 3 teaspoons oregano
- 1 onion
- 3 teaspoons salt
- 3 cups chicken broth
- 9 biscuits
- 1 cup milk

Directions:

1. Pour chicken broth in the Instant Pot.
2. Wash and cut vegetables.
3. Place vegetables with the chicken in the Instant Pot.
4. Cook chicken on "High Pressure" regime for 13 minutes.
5. Cut biscuits and place in the Instant Pot instead of meat.
6. Cook biscuits for 1 minute on the same regime.
7. Add celery, thyme, oregano, salt, chopped onion, thyme, carrots and pepper. Cook for 5 more minutes with the chicken and vegetables on "Poultry" regime.
8. Serve with fresh herbs!

Nutrition:

- Calories: 363
- Fat: 4g
- Carbohydrates: 39g
- Protein:42g

Mongolian Chicken

Middle Asian receipt will make chicken tender and satisfying the same time – just try!

Prep time: 10 minutes | **Cooking time:** 20 minutes | **Servings:** 10

Ingredients:
- 5 chicken breasts
- 5 teaspoon sesame seeds
- 4 tablespoons olive oil
- 4 tablespoon garlic powder
- 4 cup sugar
- 4 teaspoon pepper flakes
- 8 garlic cloves
- 3 cups carrot
- 3 tablespoons ginger
- 3 cups water
- 3 cups soy sauce

Directions:
1. Pour water in the Instant Pot and set "Saute" regime. Add ½ soy sauce and salt. Warm up mix in the Instant Pot for 5 minutes.
2. Wash and cube chicken meat.
3. Place chicken in the Instant Pot.
4. Add cornstarch with the chicken to the Instant Pot and cook on "High Pressure" regime for 3 minutes.
5. Add remaining ingredients to the Instant Pot.
6. Cook on "High Pressure" regime for 10 minutes.
7. Top meat with onions and serve!

Nutrition:
- Calories: 110
- Fat: 2g
- Carbohydrates: 0g
- Protein:25g

Chicken Tacos

Only five minutes and crispy, juicy and tender chicken tacos is on your plate!

Prep time: 10 minutes | **Cooking time:** 5 minutes | **Servings:** 4

Ingredients:
- 1 ½ jar BBQ sauce
- Avocado to serve
- 1 can pineapple
- 1 can jack cheese
- 3 chicken breasts
- 1 pack flour tortillas
- 2 tablespoons soy sauce

Directions:
1. Wash and cut chicken breasts.
2. Separate BBQ sauce on two parts.
3. Top chicken with the first part of the BBQ sauce.
4. Add pineapple, cheese and soy sauce and place in the Instant Pot.
5. Cook meat on "High Pressure" regime for 15 minutes.
6. Add another half to the chicken mix and serve!

Nutrition:
- Calories: 190
- Fat: 3g
- Carbohydrates: 2g
- Protein: 22g

Orange Chicken

Quick, tender and juicy receipt to get as many vitamins as possible!

Prep time: 10 minutes | **Cooking time:** 5 minutes | **Servings:** 12

Ingredients:
- 6 chicken breasts
- Onion to serve
- 3 cups BBQ sauce
- 1 onion
- 5 tablespoons orange juice
- 1 orange zest
- 9 tablespoons soy sauce
- 1 cup orange marmalade
- 3 tablespoons cornstarch
- 2 tablespoons honey

Directions:
1. Wash and cut chicken into cubes.
2. Wash and chop onion. Place onion on the frying pan and cook for 4 minutes on the strong fire.
3. Mix marmalade with soy sauce, cornstarch and BBQ sauce.
4. Pour water in the Instant Pot and add onions. Mix orange juice with honey and pour in the Instant Pot.
5. Cook for 2 minutes on "Poultry" regime.
6. Place chicken with orange zest and marinade sauce in the Instant Pot.
7. Cook for 5 minutes on "High Pressure" regime.
8. Serve with herbs!

Nutrition:
- Calories: 380
- Fat: 17g
- Carbohydrates: 27g
- Protein:28g

Spicy Honey Chicken

Tender meat in the sweet sauce with fresh topping!

Prep time: 15 minutes | **Cooking time:** 5 minutes | **Servings:** 12

Ingredients:
- 8 chicken breasts
- 4 tablespoons cornstarch
- 1 tablespoon sugar
- 4 onions
- 6 tablespoons honey
- 1 tablespoon sesame seeds
- 1 tablespoon minced garlic
- 1 onion
- 1 teaspoon Worcestershire sauce
- 1 tablespoon sriracha

Directions:
1. Wash and cut chicken meat.
2. Chop onion and add to the chicken meat.
3. Put chicken with onions in the Instant Pot.
4. Mix cornstarch, sugar, honey, sesame seeds, garlic, soy sauce, Worcestershire sauce and sriracha.
5. Place seasoning mix on top of the chicken meat.
6. Cook chicken for 5 minutes on "High Pressure" regime.
7. Serve with hot sauce!

Nutrition:
- Calories: 181
- Fat: 5g
- Carbohydrates: 18g
- Protein:17g

Chicken Cacciatore

Italians know how to cook delicious poultry – check it out!

Prep time: 10 minutes | **Cooking time:** 3 minutes | **Servings:** 6

Ingredients:

- 1 jar spaghetti sauce
- 1 teaspoon garlic salt
- 4 chicken breasts
- ½ teaspoon chili powder
- ½ onion
- 3 bell peppers

Directions:

1. Wash and cut chicken into cubes.
2. Place chicken in the Instant Pot.
3. Pour sauce on top of the chicken meat.
4. Cut peppers with onions and add to the Instant Pot.
5. Sprinkle meat with powder and garlic salt.
6. Cook meat on "High Pressure" regime for 3 minutes.
7. Serve with fresh herbs!

Nutrition:

- Calories: 312
- Fat: 15g
- Carbohydrates: 17g
- Protein:29g

Faux-Tisserie Chicken

Try full chicken with the tender sauce and delicious herbs!

Prep time: 5 minutes | **Cooking time:** 25 minutes | **Servings:** 12

Ingredients:

- 12 pounds whole chicken
- 8 tablespoons seasoning mix
- 8 tablespoons olive oil
- 3 cups chicken stock
- Salt to taste
- Pepper to taste
- 1 teaspoon basil
- 1 onion
- 1 teaspoon cumin
- 12 garlic cloves
- 1 teaspoon paprika
- 1 teaspoon garlic powder
- 1 teaspoon chili powder
- 1 teaspoon onion powder

Directions:

1. Cover chicken with the oil, salt and pepper.
2. Mix chopped onion with minced garlic.
3. Place chicken in the Instant Pot.
4. Pour stock on top.
5. Add onion mix to the Instant Pot.
6. Cook for 5 minutes on "Saute" regime.
7. Add olive oil, salt, pepper, basil, chopped onion, cumin, garlic cloves, paprika, garlic powder, chili powder and onion powder to the Instant Pot.
8. Cook chicken for 25 minutes on "High Pressure" regime.
9. Serve with fresh herbs!

Nutrition:

- Calories: 210
- Fat: 4g
- Carbohydrates: 17g
- Protein:28g

Buffalo Chicken

Easy, tender and delicious chicken in one cup – great appetizer and perfect dinner with the satisfying side!

Prep time: 5 minutes | **Cooking time:** 15 minutes | **Servings:** 3

Ingredients:
- 4 chicken breasts
- 2 tablespoons Tabasco sauce
- 4 tablespoons butter
- 2 teaspoons cider vinegar
- ½ bottle Hot sauce
- 2 tablespoons honey

Directions:
1. Mix honey with hot sauce, vinegar and Tabasco sauce.
2. Place butter in the Instant Pot and select "Saute" regime.
3. Place chicken in the Instant Pot.
4. Add sauces, vinegar and honey to the chicken and cook on "High Pressure" regime for 10 minutes.
5. Leave chicken for the natural pressure release after the cooking for 5 minutes.
6. Serve with herbs!

Nutrition:
- Calories: 365
- Fat: 11g
- Carbohydrates:42g
- Protein:24g

Café Rio Chicken

Welcome to Brazil and try something extra delicious!

Prep time: 30 minutes | **Cooking time:** 15 minutes | **Servings:** 15

Ingredients:
- 2lbs chicken breasts
- 1 teaspoon salt
- 2lbs chicken thighs
- 1 tablespoon garlic powder
- 1 cup Italian seasoning
- 1 tablespoon cumin
- 1 tablespoon chili powder

Directions:
1. Mix powders with cumin, seasoning and salt.
2. Wash and cut meat.
3. Cover meat with seasoning mix.
4. Place meat in the Instant Pot.
5. Cook on "High Pressure" regime for 15 minutes.
6. Serve with soy sauce!

Nutrition:
- Calories: 180
- Fat: 2g
- Carbohydrates: 23g
- Protein:14g

Mississippi Chicken

Can you imagine boiled but crispy chicken? With Instant Pot it is possible!

Prep time: 15 minutes | **Cooking time:** 10 minutes | **Servings:** 6

Ingredients:
- 3lbs chicken thighs
- 7 pepperoncinis
- 1 envelope dressing mix
- ½ cup pepperoncini juice
- 1 envelope gravy mix
- ½ cup broth
- ½ stick butter

Directions:
1. Mix juices with seasoning, herbs and broth.
2. Place chicken in the Instant pot.
3. Add sauce to the chicken meat.
4. Top chicken with the vegetables and butter.
5. Cook chicken on "High Pressure" regime for 10 minutes.
6. Serve with fresh herbs!

Nutrition:
- Calories: 336
- Fat: 13g
- Carbohydrates: 28g
- Protein:27g

Salsa Chicken

The more Spanish seasoning and taste, the better!

Prep time: 5 minutes | **Cooking time:** 10 minutes | **Servings:** 8

Ingredients:
- 8 chicken breasts
- 4 cups salsa
- Sea salt
- Mexican seasoning

Directions:
1. Wash chicken meat.
2. Cover chicken breasts with salt and seasoning.
3. Place chicken in the blender and blend well to get shredded.
4. Place chicken breasts in the Instant Pot.
5. Top chicken with salsa.
6. Cook chicken meat for 10 minutes on "High Pressure" regime.
7. Serve chicken with herbs and tacos!

Nutrition:
- Calories: 287
- Fat: 13g
- Carbohydrates:7g
- Protein:36g

Fettuccini Alfredo

Try how real Italy tastes! You may feel taste of red wine in your mouse, smell of the fresh baguette and cheese with olives just pronouncing the name of the plate!

Prep time: 5 minutes | **Cooking time:** 10 minutes | **Servings:** 10

Ingredients:

- 5 tablespoon olive oil
- Basil to serve
- 4 teaspoon salt
- 3 cup cheese
- 4 teaspoon pepper

- 5lbs fettuccini noodles
- 4 chicken breasts
- 5 pinch nutmeg
- 7 tablespoons butter
- 4 teaspoon salt

- 15 garlic cloves
- 5 cups chicken broth
- 6 cups heavy creams

Directions:

1. Pour oil in the Instant Pot and select "Saute" regime. It may take up to 5 minutes to warm up oil and make it almost boil.
2. Top chicken meat with salt and pepper. Coat it with your hands to make salt with pepper get in the chicken skin.
3. Place chicken in the Instant Pot and cook for 6 minutes on "Poultry" regime.
4. Add butter to the Instant Pot and melt. Place it on the chicken to make meat more juicy and tasty.
5. Add garlic to the Instant Pot. Place garlic cloves on the chicken or add minced garlic to the melted butter.
6. Add nutmeg, cream and garlic to the Instant Pot and cook for 2 minutes on "Saute" regime.
7. Add remaining ingredients and cook meat for 5 minutes on "High Pressure" regime.
8. Serve meat with fresh herbs!

Nutrition:

- Calories: 250
- Fat: 2g

- Carbohydrates: 46g
- Protein:10g

Chicken with Bacon Sauce

Have you ever tried chicken with meaty sauce and fresh herbs in mustard? It is time to do that!

Prep time: 10 minutes | **Cooking time:** 20 minutes | **Servings:** 15

Ingredients:

- 5 cups Dijon mustard
- 9 cups chicken broth
- 6 teaspoons paprika

- 7 chicken breasts
- 5 teaspoons salt
- 6 tablespoons olive oil

- 1 teaspoon pepper
- 5 cups chopped onion
- 30 bacon slices

Directions:

1. Mix mustard, salt and pepper.
2. Place bacon in the oven (400oF) and bake for 5 minutes with oil.
3. Top chicken with sauce.
4. Add bacon to the chicken in sauce.
5. Cook chicken in the Instant Pot for 2 minutes on "High Pressure" regime.
6. Add remaining ingredients to the Instant Pot.
7. Cook chicken meat in the Instant Pot for 20 minutes more on "Poultry" regime.
8. Serve with fresh herbs!

Nutrition:

- Calories: 440
- Fat: 17g

- Carbohydrates: 38g
- Protein:35g

Chicken Olive 30-minutes Lunch

Tender and satisfying chicken with light black olives and satisfying tomato soup!

Prep time: 10 minutes | **Cooking time:** 15 minutes | **Servings:** 5

Ingredients:
- 1 cup chicken stock
- ½ cup black olives
- 1 teaspoon salt
- 1 can pureed tomatoes
- 1 bay leaf
- 1 teaspoon oregano
- 7 drumsticks
- 1 teaspoon garlic powder
- 1 onion

Directions:
1. Pour stock in the Instant Pot and turn on "Sauté" regime to warm up chicken broth. It will take 3 minutes.
2. Mix chopped bay leaf with salt and add chopped onions, garlic powder, oregano and olives.
3. Place seasoning mix in a zip-bag.
4. Place drumsticks in a zip-bag with marinade.
5. Leave chicken meat to marinade for 15 minutes.
6. Place chicken in the Instant Pot and top with pureed tomatoes.
7. Cook chicken on "High Pressure" regime for 15 minutes.
8. Let the pressure release naturally (10 minutes).
9. Serve hot!

Nutrition:
- Calories: 182
- Fat: 5g
- Carbohydrates: 4g
- Protein: 26g

Taco Ranch Chili with Chicken

Quick and easy taco ranch receipt for satisfying dinner!

Prep time: 10 minutes | **Cooking time:** 35 minutes | **Servings:** 12

Ingredients:
- 12 cans White Chili Beans
- 4 1/2lbs chicken breasts
- 3 cans Rotel
- 3 packets seasoning mix
- 3 packets taco seasoning

Directions:
1. Mix taco seasoning with seasoning mix.
2. Place seasoning mix in a bowl.
3. Add Rotel to a bowl.
4. Place chicken meat in a bowl with seasoning.
5. Add white beans to a bowl and mix well.
6. Leave meat to marinate for 10 minutes.
7. Place mix in the Instant Pot and cook for 15 minutes on "High Pressure" release.
8. Do a quick release and serve!

Nutrition:
- Calories: 289
- Fat: 5g
- Carbohydrates: 0g
- Protein: 29g

Chicken Taco Bowls

Taco bowl – satisfying lunch with meat, vegetables and crispy tacos!

Prep time: 10 minutes | **Cooking time:** 15 minutes | **Servings:** 7

Ingredients:

- 5 chicken breasts
- Sour cream to serve
- 2 packs taco seasoning
- Cilantro to serve
- 1 can black beans
- Cheddar cheese to serve
- 1 bag corn
- 3 cups water
- 1 jar salsa
- 3 cups jasmine rice

Directions:

1. Wash chicken meat and cut on slices. Shred chicken meat on the small slices.
2. Place chicken meat in the Instant Pot.
3. Pour water in the pressure cooker.
4. Place beans and corn in the Instant Pot.
5. Add taco seasoning and rice.
6. Pour more water over the ingredients in the pressure cooker.
7. Add salsa sauce on top of the mix and mix well.
8. Cook meat with rice for 15 minutes on "High Pressure" regime.
9. Do a quick release.
10. Add creams and cilantro with cheddar cheese to the chicken meat.
11. Serve!

Nutrition:

- Calories: 401
- Fat: 21g
- Carbohydrates: 29g
- Protein: 25g

Shredded Chicken with Mexican Herbs

Try hot and delicious Mexican chicken!

Prep time: 15 minutes | **Cooking time:** 35 minutes | **Servings:** 24

Ingredients:

- 8lbs chicken breasts
- 4 teaspoons liquid smoke
- 4 tablespoons olive oil
- 12 drops essential oil
- 4 cup salsa
- 6 teaspoons salt
- ¼ cup heavy creams

- 8 cans chilies
- 6 teaspoons oregano
- 8 tablespoons brown sugar
- 1 teaspoon smoked paprika
- 4 cans tomatoes

- 4 teaspoons garlic
- 4 tablespoons chili powder
- 4 teaspoons cumin

Directions:

1. Pour oil in the Instant Pot. Warm up oil in the pressure cooker. It will take you over 3 minutes on "Sauté" regime.
2. Wash and cut chicken meat on slices.
3. Place chicken meat in the Instant Pot. Pour creams over chicken meat and mix well.
4. Mix cumin, chili powder, garlic, paprika, tomatoes, sugar, oregano, chilies, salt, smoke and essential oil.
5. Pour seasoning mix on top of the chicken meat.
6. Pour salsa over the chicken meat.
7. Cook meat for 30 minutes on "High Pressure" regime.
8. Let the pressure release naturally (10 minutes).
9. Serve hot!

Nutrition:

- Calories: 117
- Fat: 2g

- Carbohydrates: 5g
- Protein: 21g

Chicken with Black Beans and Rice

Super healthy and super satisfying dinner with beans, rice and chicken in one taco bowl!

Prep time: 10 minutes | **Cooking time:** 10 minutes | **Servings:** 10

Ingredients:

- 1 tablespoon olive oil
- 1 tablespoon coconut oil
- 4 cups lettuce
- 2 chicken breasts
- 2 bay leaves
- 2 red onions
- 2 teaspoons garlic powder

- 2 yellow onions
- 2 teaspoons marjoram
- 2 green bell peppers
- 2 teaspoons cayenne pepper
- 2 cups black beans

- 2 teaspoons cumin powder
- 2 cups water
- 2 teaspoons salt
- 2 cups rice
- 2 cups water

Directions:

1. Pour oil in the Instant Pot. Warm it up on "Sauté" regime. It will take you around 3 minutes just to warm up oil and not to overcook it.
2. Mix salt, lettuce, bay leaf, garlic powder, marjoram and cayenne pepper with cumin powder. Divide seasoning mix on two parts. Place one seasoning part on the bottom of the Instant Pot.
3. Place chicken meat over seasoning. Mix well, seasoning should cover all sides of the meat.
4. Add beans to the pressure cooker.
5. Add second part of seasoning to the Instant Pot.
6. Add chopped onions and bell pepper to the mix in the pressure cooker.
7. Cook meat mix for 10 minutes on "High Pressure" regime.
8. Let the pressure release naturally (20 minutes).
9. Pour water in a bowl. Bring water to boil. Place rice in bowling water and cook for 10 minutes.
10. Serve rice with chicken and beans!

Nutrition:

- Calories: 550
- Fat: 16g

- Carbohydrates: 63g
- Protein: 44g

Chili Chicken with Lime

Lime chicken is extra juicy and extra tender, especially after the Instant Pot!

Prep time: 10 minutes | **Cooking time:** 5 minutes | **Servings:** 12

Ingredients:

- 6 pounds chicken breasts
- 2 teaspoons liquid smoke
- 6 limes
- 12 garlic cloves
- 3 teaspoons chili powder
- 1 teaspoon black pepper
- 1 cup rosemary leaves
- 1 cup chopped cherry tomatoes
- 1 cup heavy creams
- 3 teaspoons cumin
- 3 teaspoons salt
- 3 teaspoons onion powder
- 1 teaspoon ginger powder

Directions:

1. Mix onion powder with salt, pepper, cumin and chili powder. Add ginger powder. If you want get more tender and juicy sauce – add 1 teaspoon lime juice and water. Mix seasoning well.
2. Cover chicken meat with seasoning. Add heavy creams. Coat chicken meat with hands.
3. Make lime juice of limes. The same time wash and halve tomatoes. Add tomatoes to the Pot.
4. Pour some oil in the Instant Pot. Warm up oil for 3 minutes on "Sauté" regime. Just warm up oil and don't overcook it.
5. Place chicken meat in the pressure cooker, add lime juice and liquid smoke.
6. Cook chicken in the Instant Pot for 5 minutes on "High Pressure" regime.
7. Let the pressure release naturally (10 minutes).
8. Serve chicken with lemon slices.

Nutrition:

- Calories: 180
- Fat: 10g
- Carbohydrates: 0g
- Protein: 0g

General Tso'c Chicken

Tender chicken meat in sweet sauce with green onion!

Prep time: 15 minutes | **Cooking time:** 5 minutes | **Servings:** 3

Ingredients:

- 1 ½ pound chicken
- 2 cups cooked rice
- 1 teaspoon sesame oil
- 1 green onion
- 6 tablespoons rice vinegar

- Sesame seeds to serve
- 6 tablespoons soy sauce
- ¼ teaspoon red pepper flakes
- ¼ cup Hoisin Sauce

- 1 garlic clove
- 4 tablespoons brown sugar
- ¼ teaspoon ginger
- 2 tablespoons cornstarch

Directions:

1. Cover cornstarch with water and leave for 15 minutes to rest.
2. Mix ginger, sugar, minced garlic clove, soy sauce, rice vinegar, Hoisin sauce, red pepper flakes, chopped onion and cover chicken meat with seasoning.
3. Leave chicken meat to marinate for 15 minutes.
4. Pour oil in the Instant Pot and warm up for 3 minutes on "Sauté" regime.
5. Place chicken meat in the pressure cooker and cook for 10 minutes on "Manual" regime.
6. Do a quick release.
7. Serve chicken meat with cooked rice and sesame seeds.

Nutrition:

- Calories: 413
- Fat: 25g

- Carbohydrates: 31g
- Protein: 18g

Teriyaki Drumsticks with Honey

Teriyaki drumsticks are delicious, light and tender dinner both with potatoes and rice!

Prep time: 15 minutes | **Cooking time:** 15 minutes | **Servings:** 3

Ingredients:

- ¼ cup soy sauce
- Scallions
- 3 tablespoons rice wine

- 1 tablespoon sesame seeds
- 2 tablespoons honey
- 8 drumsticks

- 2 garlic cloves
- 1 teaspoon sriracha
- 1 teaspoon ginger

Directions:

1. Wash and chop scallions.
2. Mix ginger, sriacha, garlic cloves, honey, sesame seeds and rice wine with soy sauce.
3. Wash chicken meat.
4. Cover chicken meat with sauce.
5. Add scallions to the chicken meat.
6. Place chicken with scallions in the Instant Pot.
7. Cook for 20 minutes on "Low Pressure" regime.
8. Change regime on "Poultry" and cook chicken for 15 minutes more.
9. Let the pressure release naturally (20 minutes).
10. Serve hot!

Nutrition:

- Calories: 309
- Fat: 7g

- Carbohydrates: 22g
- Protein: 35g

Bourbon Chicken

Super light sauce for the chicken – something you need to try today!

Prep time: 5 minutes | **Cooking time:** 15 minutes | **Servings:** 3

Ingredients:
- 1 ½ pounds chicken meat
- 1 cup honey
- 1/8 teaspoon salt
- ¼ tablespoon red pepper flakes
- 1/8 teaspoon pepper
- 2 teaspoons garlic
- ½ cup onion
- 2 tablespoons vegetable oil
- ¼ cup ketchup
- ½ cup soy sauce

Directions:
1. Wash and cube chicken meat.
2. Mix garlic, chopped onion, pepper, red pepper flakes and salt.
3. Mix honey, ketchup and soy sauce.
4. Pour oil in the Instant Pot. Turn on pressure cooker and set "Sauté" regime.
5. Place onion mix in the Instant Pot and cook for 3 minutes on "Sauté" regime.
6. Place chicken meat in the pressure cooker and add soy sauce marinade.
7. Cook chicken for 15 minutes on "High Pressure" regime.
8. Let the pressure release naturally (10 minutes).
9. Serve hot!

Nutrition:
- Calories: 351
- Fat: 12g
- Carbohydrates: 28g
- Protein: 43g

Peanut Chicken with Noodles

Get satisfying dinner in hour after the start of cooking – with pressure cooker it is easy to cook juicy chicken meat!

Prep time: 5 minutes | **Cooking time:** 50 minutes | **Servings:** 5

Ingredients:
- 1 1/2lb chicken breasts
- Onions
- Cilantro
- 1 cup peanut sauce
- 1 cup sugar snap
- ¾ cup broth
- 5oz rice noodles
- 1 cup peas

Directions:
1. Place peas in the Instant Pot.
2. Turn on "Sauté" regime and cook peas for 2 minutes. Remove peas from the pressure cooker and set aside.
3. Pour broth in the Instant Pot.
4. Place chicken with chopped onions, peas, peanut sauce, sugar snap, cilantro and noodles in the Instant Pot.
5. Cook for 15 minutes on "High Pressure" regime.
6. Add water to the pressure cooker and shred chicken meat. Cook for 15 minutes more on "High Pressure" regime.
7. Serve!

Nutrition:
- Calories: 550
- Fat: 26g
- Carbohydrates: 51g
- Protein: 13g

Pao Chicken

Only one receipt and all the greatest traditions of East!

Prep time: 15 minutes | **Cooking time:** 25 minutes | **Servings:** 12

Ingredients:

- 3 packs chicken thighs
- 9 tablespoons water
- 1 cup flour
- 3 tablespoons cornstarch
- Salt to taste
- Pepper to taste

- 6 garlic cloves
- 3 tablespoons oil
- 12 tablespoons rice vinegar
- 3 red peppers
- 6 tablespoons honey

- 3 green peppers
- 12 tablespoons soy sauce
- 3 onions
- 3 cups peanuts

Directions:

1. Wash and cut peppers, onion and chicken meat into cubes. Mix well. Place mix in the microwave to warm up for 1 minute.
2. Mix soy sauce, honey, rice vinegar, garlic cloves, water and cornstarch with salt and pepper. Use blender to get tender sauce. Place sauce in the microwave and warm up sauce for 1 minute.
3. Use blender to get light and tender sauce.
4. Pour ½ sauce over the chicken meat with vegetables and rice. Add peanuts to the mix.
5. Leave meat with vegetables for 15 minutes to marinade.
6. Place ingredients in the Instant Pot and cook on "High Pressure" release for 15 minutes. Do a quick release.
7. Pour reminded sauce over the chicken meat and serve!

Nutrition:

- Calories: 85
- Fat: 3g

- Carbohydrates: 9g
- Protein: 4g

Chicken with Rice in Soy Sauce

Enjoy Asia traditions with easy soy sauce recipes!

Prep time: 10 minutes | **Cooking time**: 15 minutes | **Servings**: 2

Ingredients:

- 1/4 pounds chicken meat
- 1 cup light soy sauce
- Salt to taste
- Pepper to taste
- 1 tablespoon oil

- 1 tablespoon melted butter
- 1/2 tablespoons thyme
- 1 shallot
- 1/2 cups chicken broth
- 1/2 cups mushrooms

- 1/2 cups jasmine rice
- 1 cup heavy creams
- 1 cup shredded tomatoes
- 1/2 garlic cloves
- 1 cup soy sauce

Directions:

1. Mix salt, pepper, ½ soy sauce, garlic cloves, thyme and chicken meat in one bowl. Mix with light soy sauce to get more tender juicy sauce. Add tomatoes to the mix. Place seasoning with vegetables in blender and mix well.
2. Mix soy sauce with chopped mushrooms, shallots and broth in another bowl. Pour creams over ingredients. Whisk sauce using mixer on the second speed.
3. Pour chicken stock in the pressure cooker.
4. Place rice in the Instant Pot.
5. Cook rice for 5 minutes on "High Pressure" regime.
6. Let the pressure release naturally (2 minutes).
7. Add chicken meat and vegetable mix to the pressure cooker. Cook on "High Pressure" regime for 10 minutes.
8. Let the pressure release naturally (10 minutes).
9. Serve hot!

Nutrition:

- Calories: 350
- Fat: 4g

- Carbohydrates: 10g
- Protein: 5g

Fall-Of-The-Bone Chicken

Is it possible to cook full chicken without an oven Try this delicious receipt and make sure!

Prep time: 10 minutes | **Cooking time:** 35 minutes | **Servings:** 10

Ingredients:
- 1 chicken
- 6 garlic cloves
- 1 tablespoon coconut oil
- ½ teaspoon salt
- 1 teaspoon paprika
- 2 tablespoons lemon juice
- 1 cup broth
- ¼ teaspoon pepper
- 1 teaspoon thyme

Directions:
1. Mix thyme, pepper, lemon juice, paprika, salt and garlic cloves.
2. Pour broth in the Instant Pot.
3. Place chicken in the pressure cooker.
4. Add seasoning over the chicken.
5. Add coconut oil on top.
6. Cook chicken for 25 minutes on "High Pressure" regime.
7. Let the pressure release naturally (10 minutes).
8. Serve with rosemary!

Nutrition:
- Calories: 330
- Fat: 20g
- Carbohydrates: 13g
- Protein: 24g

Lemon Butter Chicken

Super light and tender chicken slices with herbs and butter for the perfect lunch!

Prep time: 15 minutes | **Cooking time:** 10 minutes | **Servings:** 12

Ingredients:
- 12 bon-in chicken thighs
- 4 cups water
- 2 tablespoons paprika
- 2 cups brown rice
- 2 cups white rice
- 1 teaspoon salt
- 4 cups spinach
- 6 tablespoons butter
- 2 teaspoons thyme
- 6 garlic cloves
- 1 lemon juice
- 1 lime juice
- 1 cup broth
- 1 cup Parmesan
- 1 cup heavy cream
- 2 tablespoons melted butter

Directions:
1. Mix salt, pepper and paprika. Top chicken with seasoning. Add butter and place chicken with seasoning in the microwave. Warm up meat for 1 minute.
2. Place reminded butter in the Instant Pot. It will take you 2 minutes to melt butter.
3. Add chicken meat to the pressure cooker. Cook on "High Pressure" regime for 6 minutes.
4. Mix garlic with creams and lemon juice. Add Parmesan to the mix and top with thyme.
5. Add creamy mix to the chicken meat. Pour broth over the meat. Cook meat with spinach for 10 minutes on "Poultry" regime.
6. Cook rice in bowling water.
7. Serve chicken with rice!

Nutrition:
- Calories: 258
- Fat: 12g
- Carbohydrates: 8g
- Protein: 27g

Chicken and Stuffing

Only 20 minutes and chicken stuffing is ready!

Prep time: 10 minutes | **Cooking time:** 20 minutes | **Servings:** 12

Ingredients:
- 12 chicken breasts
- 3 cups sour cream
- 3 cups chicken broth
- 2 tablespoons butter
- 3 bags green beans
- 3 cans chicken soup
- 3 bags cornbread stuffing

Directions:
1. Pour broth in the Instant Pot. The same time place butter in a cup and place butter in the microwave. Melt butter up for 1 minute. Pour butter in the broth and mix well.
2. Place chicken breasts in the pressure cooker.
3. Cook chicken meat for 15 minutes on "High Pressure" regime. Remove chicken meat from the Instant Pot and shred it.
4. Mix chicken soup, stuffing, beans and corn. Add stuffing mix to the Instant Pot.
5. Cook meat for 6 minutes on "High Pressure" regime.
6. Let the pressure release naturally (10 minutes).
7. Use blender to blend all the cooked ingredients.
8. Serve!

Nutrition:
- Calories: 170
- Fat: 1g
- Carbohydrates: 21g
- Protein: 4g

Jalapeno Popper Chicken Chili

Try tender meat with healthy vegetables and light sauce!

Prep time: 10 minutes | **Cooking time:** 10 minutes | **Servings:** 12

Ingredients:
- 3 ¼ cups onion
- 2 cups cooked bacon
- 4 cups jalapeno
- 14 ounces cornbread
- 9 teaspoons garlic
- 10 ounces tomatoes
- 9 cups chicken breasts
- 6 cups chicken stock
- 6 teaspoons chili powder
- 3 teaspoons oregano
- 3 teaspoons cumin
- 1 teaspoon pepper
- 1 teaspoon salt

Directions:
1. Mix salt, pepper, cumin, oregano, chili powder, tomatoes, garlic, onion and jalapeno. If you want to get more tender mix – just add some lemon juice and water to the seasoning mix.
2. Pour stock in the pressure cooker. Warm it up on the "Sauté" regime. It will take you around 4 minutes.
3. Place chicken meat in the Instant Pot.
4. Add seasoning mix on top of the chicken meat.
5. Cook chicken for 10 minutes on "Soup" regime.
6. Let the pressure release naturally (10 minutes).
7. Add cheese to the chicken meat and cook for 3 minutes on "High Pressure" regime.
8. Do a quick release.
9. Serve chicken with cornbread and bacon.

Nutrition:
- Calories: 282
- Fat: 11g
- Carbohydrates: 25g
- Protein: 21g

Lemon Garlic Chicken

Easy, quick and delicious poultry receipt!

Prep time: 10 minutes | **Cooking time:** 15 minutes | **Servings:** 4

Ingredients:

- 2 pounds chicken breasts
- 4 teaspoon flour
- 1 teaspoon salt
- 1 lemon juice
- 1 onion
- ¼ cup wine
- 1 tablespoon avocado oil
- ¼ teaspoon paprika
- 5 garlic cloves
- 1 teaspoon parsley
- ½ cup chicken broth

Directions:

1. Mix parsley, garlic, paprika, wine, onion, lemon juice and salt.
2. Cover chicken with seasoning.
3. Pour chicken broth in the Instant Pot.
4. Coat chicken with flour.
5. Place chicken meat in the pressure cooker.
6. Cook for 15 minutes on "Poultry" regime.
7. Let the pressure release naturally (10 minutes).
8. Serve hot!

Nutrition:

- Calories: 202
- Fat: 7g
- Carbohydrates: 6g
- Protein: 27g

Lemon Herb Chicken

Juicy chicken will be even more tender with lemon and milk!

Prep time: 10 minutes | **Cooking time:** 15 minutes | **Servings:** 12

Ingredients:

- 12 chicken thighs
- 6 tablespoons milk
- Garlic to taste
- Oregano to taste
- 6 lemons
- 2 onion
- Carrots to serve
- 1 stick butter
- 1 cup chicken stock
- 12 potatoes
- 6 tablespoons oil
- Salt to taste
- Pepper to taste

Directions:

1. Mix garlic, oregano, chopped onion, cubed carrots and cubed potatoes. Add around 1 teaspoon water to the seasoning mix – you will get soft and tender sauce.
2. Pour oil in the pressure cooker. Warm up oil before cooking for 1 minute on "Sauté" regime in the pressure cooker.
3. Place vegetable mix in the Instant Pot. Cook on "Sauté" regime for 4 minutes.
4. Pour milk in the pressure cooker and place chicken on top.
5. Cook chicken for 5 minutes on "High Pressure" regime with onion mix.
6. Add broth with butter to the Instant Pot.
7. Cook meat for 15 minutes on "High Pressure" regime.
8. Let the pressure release naturally (10 minutes).
9. Serve hot!

Nutrition:

- Calories: 150
- Fat: 3g
- Carbohydrates: 0g
- Protein: 35g

Garlic and Sugar Chicken

Brown sugar with garlic over the tender chicken meat – something you will like today!

Prep time: 10 minutes | **Cooking time:** 4 hours | **Servings:** 12

Ingredients:
- 8lb shredded chicken
- 8 teaspoons red pepper flakes
- 4 cups brown sugar
- 8 tablespoons water
- 23 cup apple cider vinegar
- 8 tablespoons cornstarch
- 1 cup lemon lime soda
- 6 teaspoons pepper
- 4 garlic heads
- 8 tablespoons soy sauce

Directions:
1. Mix red pepper flakes, soy sauce, garlic, sugar, soda, vinegar and cornstarch. Add water to the seasoning mix – it will make mix more tender and soft.
2. Pour water in the Instant Pot. Warm up water on "Sauté" regime. It will take you around 3 minutes.
3. Place chicken meat in the pressure cooker.
4. Add seasoning on top of the chicken meat.
5. Cook chicken on "High Pressure" regime for 4 hours.
6. Let the pressure release naturally (20 minutes).
7. Serve with herbs!

Nutrition:
- Calories: 259
- Fat: 14g
- Carbohydrates: 10g
- Protein: 26g

Turkey Verde and Rice

Try extra healthy turkey with satisfying rice!

Prep time: 10 minutes | **Cooking time:** 25 minutes | **Servings:** 5

Ingredients:
- 2/3 cup chicken broth
- ½ teaspoon salt
- 1 cup brown rice
- 1lb turkey tenderloins
- 1 onion

Directions:
1. Pour chicken broth in the Instant Pot.
2. Chop onion and cook on "Sauté" regime for 4 minutes.
3. Mix rice with salt and add to the pressure cooker.
4. Cook rice on "High Pressure" regime for 10 minutes.
5. Add turkey to the Instant Pot and cook for 15 minutes more on "High Pressure" regime.
6. Let the pressure release naturally (20 minutes).
7. Serve with lemon!

Nutrition:
- Calories: 170
- Fat: 1g
- Carbohydrates:
- Protein: 4g

Chicken Sausage with Red Beans and Rice

Really satisfying dinner should include everything – just like this one!

Prep time: 10 minutes | **Cooking time:** 45 minutes | **Servings:** 5

Ingredients:

- 1/2 onion
- 5 cups cooked rice to serve
- 1/2 bell pepper
- 1/2 pound chicken sausage
- 1 celery stalk

- 2 cups water
- 4 garlic cloves
- 2 bay leaves
- 2 cups bell pepper
- 1 tablespoon rosemary
- 3 taco packs
- 1 cup chicken stock

- 1/2 pound beans
- 1/2 teaspoon thyme
- 1/2 teaspoon salt
- 1/2 teaspoon hot sauce
- ½ teaspoon pepper

Directions:

1. Slice chicken sausage and place on the separate plate. Clean chicken sausage of the skin.
2. Mix pepper, salt, hot sauce, thyme, beans, bay leaves, garlic cloves, celery, onion and pepper. Pour water to the seasoning mix – this way you will get tender and soft sauce.
3. Pour water in the Instant Pot.
4. Add onion mix to the Pot and cook for 30 minutes on "High Pressure" regime. Pour stock in the Instant Pot.
5. Let the pressure release naturally (25 minutes). The same time wash and cut bell peppers. Add bell peppers to the Pot and mix.
6. Add chicken sausage and cook on the same regime. It will take you 15 minutes to finish cooking session.
7. Let the pressure release naturally (10 minutes).
8. Serve with tacos!

Nutrition:

- Calories: 180
- Fat: 4g

- Carbohydrates: 29g
- Protein: 9g

Stuffed Turkey Tenderloin

Try tender turkey tenderloin with satisfying stuffing and get dinner that will give you both vitamins and energy!

Prep time: 15 minutes | **Cooking time:** 20 minutes | **Servings:** 12

Ingredients:

- 4 turkey breasts tenderloins
- 6 cups chicken broth
- 4 bacon slices
- 1 cup dry white wine
- 2 cups butternut squash
- 4 springs rosemary
- 1 cup cranberries
- 1 teaspoon fresh rosemary

Directions:

1. Top tenderloins with rosemary. Attentively cover meat from all the sides with hands.
2. Pour broth in the pressure cooker. Warm up broth for 5 minutes on "Sauté" regime. Do not overcook and do not bring broth to boil.
3. Add cranberries with butternut squash and white wine. Cook on "Sauté" regime.
4. Make holes in the turkey meat.
5. Add bacon to the Instant Pot.
6. Cook for 20 minutes on "High Pressure" regime.
7. Let the pressure release naturally (10 minutes).
8. Serve hot!

Nutrition:

- Calories: 204
- Fat: 9g
- Carbohydrates: 1g
- Protein: 29g

Turkey Spinach Lasagna

Try Italian traditional receipt in new variant!

Prep time: 10 minutes | **Cooking time:** 20 minutes | **Servings:** 6

Ingredients:

- 1lb turkey
- 1 cup water
- 1 teaspoon Italian seasoning
- 1 jar pasta sauce
- ½ teaspoon pepper flakes
- 8 lasagna noodles
- 15oz ricotta
- Pepper to taste
- 1 cup mozzarella
- 1 package chopped spinach

Directions:

1. Mix pepper with Italian seasoning.
2. Pour water in the Instant Pot.
3. Prepare baking form suitable for the pressure cooker.
4. Make 1 layer of lasagna noodles. Add turkey meat on top. Add seasoning mix over the turkey meat. Add ricotta, pepper flakes and pasta sauce on top. Make 3 more layers.
5. Add mozzarella cheese and spinach over the layers.
6. Cook lasagna for 20 minutes on "High Pressure" regime.
7. Serve hot!

Nutrition:

- Calories: 274
- Fat: 4g
- Carbohydrates: 31g
- Protein: 27g

Turkey Sausage

Super easy receipt for extra satisfying dinner!

Prep time: 5 minutes | **Cooking time:** 15 minutes | **Servings:** 1

Ingredients:

- 1lb turkey meat
- Salt to taste
- Pepper to taste
- 1 head cabbage
- Olive oil
- 2 teaspoons Dijon mustard
- 1 onion
- 2 teaspoons balsamic vinegar
- 3 cloves garlic
- 2 teaspoons sugar

Directions:

1. Pour oil in the Instant Pot.
2. Wash and chop onion.
3. Mix onion with salt and place in the pressure cooker.
4. Add garlic, sugar, vinegar and pepper to the onion.
5. Cook on "Sauté" regime for 5 minutes.
6. Add mustard, cabbage and turkey meat to the Instant Pot. Make a sausage shape of the meat.
7. Cook for 15 minutes on "High Pressure" regime.
8. Let the pressure release naturally (10 minutes).
9. Serve with herbs!

Nutrition:

- Calories: 90
- Fat: 6g
- Carbohydrates: 0g
- Protein: 9g

Diy Sandwich Meat

Easy to cook and satisfying turkey meat with herbs and light seasoning – receipt for the true poultry lovers!

Prep time: 5 minutes | **Cooking time**: 40 minutes | **Servings:** 4

Ingredients:
- 3 pounds turkey breasts
- 1 cup chicken broth
- ½ cup seasoning
- 1/3 cup avocado oil
- 2 garlic cloves

Directions:
1. Put seasoning over the turkey meat.
2. Pour chicken broth in the Instant Pot.
3. Place meat in the pressure cooker.
4. Make small holes in the turkey meat and add garlic with avocado oil.
5. Cook turkey on "High Pressure" regime for 30 minutes.
6. Let the pressure release naturally (20 minutes).
7. Serve!

Nutrition:
- Calories: 220
- Fat: 2g
- Carbohydrates: 42g
- Protein: 8g

Turkey Breast

The easier juicy receipt with pressure cooker – the more you will like it!

Prep time: 15 minutes | **Cooking time:** 30 minutes | **Servings:** 12

Ingredients:
- 9 1/2 lb bone-in turkey breast with skin
- 12 tablespoons water
- Salt to taste
- Pepper to taste
- 12 tablespoons cornstarch
- 4 cans turkey broth
- 4 springs thyme
- 4 onion s
- 4 stocks celery

Directions:
1. Pour water in the Instant Pot. Warm water for 4 minutes. Set "Sauté" regime just to warm it up and do not bring to boil.
2. Cover turkey meat with celery, thyme, cornstarch and pepper with salt. Set aside. Use hands to cover meat with marinade.
3. Place chopped onions in the Instant Pot and cook for 4 minutes on "Sauté" regime.
4. Add turkey meat to the pressure cooker.
5. Pour broth over the meat.
6. Cook meat on "High Pressure" regime for 30 minutes.
7. Let the pressure release naturally (10 minutes).
8. Serve!

Nutrition:
- Calories: 97
- Fat: 3g
- Carbohydrates: 1g
- Protein:17g

Chicken Florentine

Make today taste like Italy!

| **Prep time:** 10 minutes | **Cooking time:** 15 minutes | **Servings:** 12 |

Ingredients:

- 6 boneless chicken breasts
- Parmesan cheese to serve

- 12 cups chicken broth
- 1 tablespoon creams
- 12oz mozzarella cheese
- 8 cans mushroom soup

- 8 garlic cloves
- 16 cups baby spinach
- 16oz spaghetti noodles

Directions:

1. Pour broth in the Instant Pot. The same time pour creams in the cup and warm up in the microwave. Pour creams in the chicken broth. Warm up broth in the pressure cooker. It will take you around 4 minutes to make broth hot on "Sauté" regime.
2. Break spaghetti in halves. Place spaghetti in the pressure cooker.
3. Mix chicken meat with garlic, spinach, mushroom soup and add to the Instant Pot.
4. Cook for 5 minutes on "Poultry" regime.
5. Add mozzarella to the chicken and cook on "Poultry" regime. Meat should be covered with soft and tender cheese. It will take you 10 minutes.
6. Let the pressure release naturally (10 minutes).
7. Serve hot!

Nutrition:

- Calories: 130
- Fat: 6g

- Carbohydrates: 13g
- Protein: 4g

Tuscan Creamy Garlic Chicken

Real Italian recipes can make you fall in love with poultry!

| **Prep time:** 10 minutes | **Cooking time:** 5 minutes | **Servings:** 4 |

Ingredients:

- 2 pounds chicken breasts
- ½ cup parmesan cheese
- 2 tablespoons olive oil

- 1 teaspoon house seasoning
- ½ cup chicken broth
- ¾ cup heavy creams

- 2 cloves garlic
- ½ teaspoon sea salt
- 2 teaspoons Italian seasoning

Directions:

1. Wash and slice chicken meat to get several thin slices.
2. Mix seasoning with garlic, salt, house seasoning and top chicken with this mix.
3. Pour broth in the Instant Pot.
4. Add chicken mix with seasoning to the pressure cooker.
5. Cook for 5 minutes on "High Pressure" regime.
6. Add creams and olive oil to the chicken and cook for 5 minutes more on "Poultry" regime.
7. Let the pressure release naturally (10 minutes).
8. Serve hot!

Nutrition:

- Calories: 380
- Fat: 21g

- Carbohydrates: 5g
- Protein: 32g

Parmigiana

Enjoy Italy today with light chicken baked in its own juice!

Prep time: 12 minutes | **Cooking time:** 14 minutes | **Servings:** 4

Ingredients:
- 1/3 cups olive oil
- 1 1/3 cups mozzarella cheese
- 1 pound chicken breasts
- 16ounces tomato sauce
- 1/3 cups parmesan
- 1 1/3 tablespoons butter
- 1/8 teaspoons garlic powder

Directions:
1. Pour oil in the Instant Pot.
2. Warm up oil in "Sauté" regime for 3 minutes.
3. Place butter in the pressure cooker.
4. Warm up butter on "Sauté" regime for 3 minutes.
5. Place chicken meat in the Instant Pot.
6. Add garlic powder, tomato sauce and two types cheese.
7. Cook on "High Pressure" regime for 5 minutes.
8. Let the pressure release naturally (10 minutes).
9. Serve!

Nutrition:
- Calories: 360
- Fat: 35g
- Carbohydrates: 0g
- Protein:13g

Crack Chicken with Cheese

Try light and tender, satisfying and full of vitamins receipt!

Prep time: 10 minutes | **Cooking time:** 25 minutes | **Servings:** 4

Ingredients:
- 7 slices cooked bacon
- 4oz cheddar cheese
- 2 pounds chicken breasts
- 3 tablespoons cornstarch
- 1 packet ranch seasoning
- 1 cup water
- 8oz cream cheese

Directions:
1. Pour water in the Instant Pot.
2. Place chicken meat in the pressure cooker.
3. Add seasoning and cornstarch to the chicken in the Instant Pot.
4. Place cheese on top and cook for 25 minutes on "High Pressure" regime.
5. Add cooked bacon and do a quick release.
6. Serve hot!

Nutrition:
- Calories: 210
- Fat: 6g
- Carbohydrates: 4g
- Protein: 36g

MEAT

Flank Steak with Raspberry Salsa

Easy to cook steak with juicy and sweet sauce will be perfect dinner for everybody!

Prep time: 10 minutes | **Cooking time:** 10 hours | **Servings:** 16

Ingredients:
- 5 tablespoons lime juice
- 16 tortillas
- ¼ cup chili sauce
- Cilantro to serve
- 3 drops hot sauce
- 1 crushed raspberry
- 1 pack taco seasoning
- 1 teaspoon cumin
- 1 flank steak
- 1 tablespoon Jalapeno pepper
- ¾ cup scallions
- ½ cup cilantro springs

Directions:
1. Mix lime juice with chili and hot sauces.
2. Add taco seasoning to sauce mix.
3. Place sauce in the Instant Pot.
4. Add steak to the Instant Pot.
5. Cook on "Slow Cook" regime for 60 minutes.
6. Mix scallions with jalapeno and cilantro.
7. Add remaining ingredients and use blender to make tender sauce.
8. Place ½ of the sauce mix in the Instant Pot and cook on the same regime for 9 hours.
9. Serve with ½ remaining sauce!

Nutrition:
- Calories:375
- Fat: 10g
- Carbohydrates:44g
- Protein:29g

Sweet and Spicy Ribs

Asian cuisine is always full of taste and has extra delicious flavor!

Prep time: 5 minutes | **Cooking time:** 60 minutes | **Servings:** 16

Ingredients:
- 4 pounds beef country style ribs
- 4 tablespoons soy sauce
- 2 cups water
- 4 tablespoons lime juice
- 4 cups mirin
- Cooked rice to serve
- 2 cups sweet chili garlic sauce
- 4 teaspoons ginger
- 1 cup agave nectar
- 1 cup brown sugar

Directions:
1. Pour water in the Instant Pot.
2. Place ribs in the Instant Pot.
3. Cook meat on "Meat" regime for 60 minutes.
4. Mix soy sauce, lime juice, mirin, chili garlic sauce, ginger, nectar and sugar.
5. Add seasoning sauce to the Instant Pot.
6. Cook for 20 minutes on "High Pressure" regime.
7. Serve with rice!

Nutrition:
- Calories: 220
- Fat: 72g
- Carbohydrates: 4g
- Protein:22g

Country Steak

Country steak is soft and tender with satisfying sauce and delicious aroma! Meat – source of the health, strength and power! Don't miss it!

Prep time: 15 minutes | **Cooking time:** 30 minutes | **Servings:** 16

Ingredients:
- 4 pounds beef steak
- 4 cups beef broth
- 1 cup flour
- 1 cup celery
- 4 tablespoons vegetable oil
- 1 cup onion
- 2 teaspoons salt
- 12 garlic cloves
- 1/2 teaspoon pepper
- 1 cup ketchup
- 1 teaspoon Worcestershire sauce

Directions:
1. Wash and cut meat into slices. It may be cubes or stripes – as you like the most. If you are choosing stripes it is better to use blender to get shredded meat.
2. Cover meat with flour from the both sides. Place flour in the zip bag and top meat with it.
3. Pour oil in the Instant Pot and warm it up on "Saute" regime. It will take you 5 minutes until oil will start boiling.
4. Place steaks in the Instant Pot and cook on "High Pressure" regime for 6 minutes.
5. Add sauce, ketchup, garlic cloves, oil, celery and broth with stock to the Instant Pot. Mix well to get soup consistence.
6. Cook meat for 30 minutes on "Meat" regime.
7. Serve with hot sauce!

Nutrition:
- Calories: 490
- Fat: 34g
- Carbohydrates: 30g
- Protein:18g

Swiss Steak

Swiss style steak will be full of vitamins and energy for sure!

Prep time: 10 minutes | **Cooking time:** 30 minutes | **Servings:** 10

Ingredients:
- 4 pounds roast
- 2 teaspoons black pepper
- 1/2 cup flour
- 2 teaspoons salt
- 4 tablespoons oil
- 2 bell peppers
- 4 cans tomatoes
- 2 onions

Directions:
1. Wash and chop onion, pepper and tomato.
2. Cover meat with seasoning and flour.
3. Place oil in the Instant Pot and set "Meat" regime.
4. Place meat in the Instant Pot.
5. Blend vegetables to get sauce.
6. Add sauce to the meat in the Instant Pot.
7. Cook meat with sauce on "Meat" regime for 30 minutes.
8. Serve with fresh herbs!

. **Nutrition:**
- Calories: 430
- Fat: 5g
- Carbohydrates: 11g
- Protein:28g

Mediterranean Beef

Satisfying, fresh and healthy meat will be perfect addition to the side or great dinner itself!

Prep time: 10 minutes | **Cooking time:** 40 minutes | **Servings:** 20

Ingredients:
- 20lb shoulder roast
- 10 cups Medjool dates
- 9 tablespoons flour
- 4 cups balsamic vinegar
- 2 teaspoons salt
- 4 cups red wine
- 8 teaspoons pepper
- 6 cups beef broth
- 7 teaspoons oregano
- 10 garlic cloves
- 10 onions
- 8 tablespoons olive oil
- 4 shallots

Directions:
1. Mix spices with herbs and seasoning together.
2. Cut meat into cubes.
3. Cover meat with flour.
4. Top meat with seasoning mix.
5. Pour oil in the Instant Pot. Add vegetables to the Pot.
6. Cook meat in the Instant Pot for 5 minutes on "Saute" regime.
7. Add shallots and dates to the Instant Pot.
8. Cook meat for 40 minutes on "High Pressure" regime.
9. Serve with fresh vegetables!

Nutrition:
- Calories: 275
- Fat: 5g
- Carbohydrates: 34g
- Protein: 25g

Italian Beef

Trust Italian recipes and make perfect dinner today!

Prep time: 5 minutes | **Cooking time:** 45 minutes | **Servings:** 18

Ingredients:
- 18lbs beef roast
- 6 packs spaghetti sauce mix
- 18lbs red potatoes
- 25oz can tomato sauce
- 18 cups carrot
- 2 cups water

Directions:
1. Wash and cut potatoes with carrots.
2. Pour water in the Instant Pot.
3. Place carrots and potatoes in the Instant Pot.
4. Place meat on top of the vegetable layer.
5. Top meat with sauces.
6. Cook on "Stew" regime for 45 minutes.
7. Serve with fresh herbs!

Nutrition:
- Calories: 530
- Fat: 20g
- Carbohydrates: 60g
- Protein: 20g

Chili Lime Steak

Hot chili with fresh lime and satisfying meat with delicious herbs!

Prep time: 5 minutes | **Cooking time:** 15 minutes | **Servings:** 4

Ingredients:
- 2 pounds steak strips
- 3 avocado
- 1 tablespoon water
- 1 teaspoon Cholula
- 1 teaspoon garlic
- ½ teaspoon pepper
- 1 tablespoon EVOO
- ½ teaspoon salt
- 2 teaspoons lime juice
- ½ teaspoon chili powder

Directions:
1. Pour oil in the Instant Pot and turn on "Saute" regime.
2. Place garlic in the Instant Pot.
3. Cook garlic for 3 minutes on "High Pressure" regime.
4. Place strips, avocado slices, Cholua, pepper, EVOO, salt, lime juice and chili powder in the Instant Pot, apart from avocado.
5. Cook for 10 minutes on the same regime.

Nutrition:
- Calories: 266
- Fat: 17g
- Carbohydrates: 3g
- Protein: 24g

Salisbury Steak with Mushroom Sause

Tender and satisfying mushroom sauce over the meat slices will be perfect topping for the satisfying lunch!

Prep time: 15 minutes | **Cooking time:** 30 minutes | **Servings:** 12

Ingredients:
- 3 lbs ground beef
- 2 tablespoon butter
- 6 tablespoons milk
- 1 teaspoon paprika
- 3 tablespoons Worcestershire sauce
- 2 teaspoons pepper
- 2 garlic clove
- 1 teaspoon salt
- 1 cup panko
- 16 ounces mushrooms
- 6 tablespoons cornstarch
- 2 onions
- 6 tablespoons water
- 6 cups beef broth
- 1 teaspoon pepper
- 1 tablespoon tomato paste
- 1 teaspoon thyme
- 1 tablespoon Dijon mustard
- 1 teaspoon salt
- 2 tablespoons parsley

Directions:
1. Place butter in the Instant Pot.
2. Mix milk with Worcestershire sauce, garlic, panko, salt, pepper and paprika.
3. Top meat slices with sauce mix.
4. Peel and slice mushrooms.
5. Mix mushrooms with the chopped onion.
6. Separately mix beef broth, tomato paste, mustard, parsley, salt, thyme, pepper and cornstarch.
7. Place steaks in the Instant Pot and cook for 2 minutes on "Saute" regime.
8. Blend tomato paste mix.
9. Add mushrooms with onion to the meat and cook for 15 minutes on "High Pressure" regime.

Nutrition:
- Calories: 309
- Fat: 18g
- Carbohydrates: 11g
- Protein: 24g

Beef Bourguignon

Roasted vegetables with the beef in its own juice!

Prep time: 20 minutes | **Cooking time:** 50 minutes | **Servings:** 16

Ingredients:

- 4lb stewing steak
- 4 tablespoon maple syrup
- 2 lb bacon
- 8 sweet potatoes
- 20 carrots
- 4 tablespoon olive oil
- 4 red onion
- 2 cup beef broth
- 8 garlic cloves
- 4 cup red wine
- 8 teaspoons salt
- 8 teaspoons pepper
- 8 tablespoons thyme
- 8 tablespoons parsley

Directions:

1. Pour oil in the Instant Pot and warm it up.
2. Wash and peel potatoes. Cut into cubes.
3. Mix parsley, thyme, pepper, salt, garlic, chopped onion, cubed carrot slices and cubes potatoes.
4. Place veggie mix in the Instant Pot. Cook on "High Pressure" regime for 3 minutes.
5. Cover steaks with wine.
6. Cover bacon with maple syrup.
7. Place steaks and bacon to the Instant Pot.
8. Cook ingredients for 30 minutes on the same regime.
9. Serve with sauce!

Nutrition:

- Calories: 461
- Fat: 17g
- Carbohydrates: 11g
- Protein:48g

Egg and Pork Congee

Easy and light Chinese receipt is perfect variant for the super tasty dinner!

Prep time: 10 minutes | **Cooking time:** 70 minutes | **Servings:** 1

Ingredients:

- 1/8 cup rice to serve
- Dash of white pepper
- 2 cold water
- 1/4 teaspoon sesame oil
- 1/5 pound pork shank
- ½ teaspoon salt
- 1/4 pound pork bones
- 1 egg
- 2 slices ginger

Directions:

1. Place pork shanks and pork bones in the bowl.
2. Pour water in the bowl and bring to boil.
3. Remove meat from water.
4. Place pork bones, shanks and rice with ginger in the Instant Pot.
5. Cook ingredients in the Instant Pot for 35 minutes on "High Pressure" regime.
6. Remove pork shank from the Instant Pot.
7. Remove and set aside pork bones – we will need only meat from the pork bones.
8. Mix salt, eggs and pepper.
9. Top pork meat with egg mix.
10. Place meat in the Instant Pot and cook for 35 minutes more on "Meat" regime.
11. Serve with onions!

Nutrition:

- Calories: 256
- Fat: 5g
- Carbohydrates: 40g
- Protein:11g

Braised Pork Hock

Bet you have never tried this tender steak!

Prep time: 5 minutes | **Cooking time:** 60 minutes | **Servings:** 3

Ingredients:

- 2 pounds pork hock
- ¼ teaspoon sugar
- 1 ½ cup master stock
- 2 tablespoons garlic

Directions:

1. Pour water in the bowl and bring to boil.
2. Boil pork hock in water for 5 minutes.
3. Top dried pork meat with stock.
4. Place meat with the stock in the Instant Pot.
5. Cook for 20 minutes on "High Pressure" regime.
6. Add sugar and garlic to the Pot and cook meat for 40 minutes more on the same regime.

Nutrition:

- Calories: 70
- Fat: 3g
- Carbohydrates: 6g
- Protein:0g

Shumai

Super tender shrimps with satisfying pork in dumplings – something for the great dinner!

Prep time: 40 minutes | **Cooking time:** 10 minutes | **Servings:** 2

Ingredients:

- ½ pound tiger prawns
- ½ teaspoon salt
- 1 teaspoon cornstarch
- ½ teaspoon oil
- ½ pound pork
- ½ teaspoon sugar
- 2 tablespoons chicken stock
- ½ teaspoon pepper
- 1 tablespoon cornstarch
- 1 teaspoon sesame oil
- 1 tablespoon wine
- 1 teaspoon fish sauce
- 2 teaspoons light soy sauce
- ¾ stalk onions
- 20 wonton wrappers
- 2 slices ginger
- 2 mushrooms

Directions:

1. Mix oil with the salt and cornstarch.
2. Cover prawns with cornstarch mix.
3. Mix soy sauce with fish sauce and add wine.
4. Cover pork meat with wine.
5. Mix pepper and cornstarch with sugar.
6. Pour chicken stock into the Instant Pot.
7. Set "Saute" regime and warm up chicken stock.
8. Chop onion with mushrooms and mix with ginger.
9. Fry mushroom mix on the frying pan.
10. Add sugar mix to the pork meat.
11. Mix pork meat with the shrimps in marinade and add fried onions.
12. Make one mix of the ingredients.
13. Place wrappers on the flat surface and add 1 teaspoon meat mix in each wrapper.
14. Roll up wrappers and top with oil.
15. Place wrappers in the Instant Pot and cook for 7 minutes on "High Pressure" regime.

Nutrition:

- Calories: 197
- Fat: 11g
- Carbohydrates: 16g
- Protein:10g

Pork Bone Soup

Do you like traditional Asian cuisine? Try this bone soup!

Prep time: 10 minutes | **Cooking time:** 80 minutes | **Servings:** 5

Ingredients:
- 4 pork bones
- Salt to taste
- 2 carrots
- 6 ½ cups cold water
- 2 corns on cod
- 1 piece Chenpi
- 1 slice ginger
- 2 dried dates

Directions:
1. Boil bones for 5 minutes in water.
2. Cover chenpi with water and leave for 20 minutes.
3. Place all the ingredients in the Instant Pot.
4. Cook ingredients for 30 minutes on "High Pressure" regime.
5. Leave soup in the Instant Pot and let the pressure release naturally for 10 minutes.
6. Cook soup for 15 minutes more on the same regime!
7. Serve with fresh herbs!

Nutrition:
- Calories: 240
- Fat: 12g
- Carbohydrates:1g
- Protein: 29g

Katsu Curry

Crispy meat in panko with seasoning and herbs – this dish you will love!

Prep time: 15 minutes | **Cooking time:** 30 minutes | **Servings:** 12

Ingredients:
- 12 pork loin chops
- Salt to taste
- 8 tablespoons olive oil
- Pepper to taste
- 4 tablespoon butter
- 8 tablespoons olive oil
- 4 cup chicken stock
- 4 cup panko
- 8 Japanese roux cubes
- 4 onions
- 8 garlic cloves
- 4 carrots
- 8 potatoes
- 4 cups flour
- 4 eggs
- Panko

Directions:
1. Coat pork with pepper and salt.
2. Place pork chops in the Instant Pot.
3. Add olive oil to the Instant Pot and cook meat for 6 minutes on "Meat" regime.
4. Add onions, salt and pepper with garlic. Cook onion mix for 1 minute on "Saute" regime.
5. Pour chicken stock in the Instant Pot.
6. Add carrots with potatoes to the Instant Pot.
7. Cook mix for 10 minutes on "High Pressure" regime.
8. Melt butter and cover meat with butter and oil.
9. Top meat with panko and cook for 7 minutes not changing the regime.
10. Add eggs with panko to the meat and cook for 5 minutes more on the same settings.
11. Serve with herbs!

Nutrition:
- Calories: 200
- Fat: 10g
- Carbohydrates: 28g
- Protein:4g

Pork Chops with Tomato Sauce

Tender meat with delicious tomato sauce and light seasoning will be extra delicious!

Prep time: 10 minutes | **Cooking time:** 20 minutes | **Servings:** 3

Ingredients:

- 4 pork loin chops
- ½ tablespoon dark soy sauce
- ½ teaspoon white sugar
- 1 tablespoon light soy sauce
- ¼ teaspoon salt
- ¼ teaspoon sesame oil
- 1 onion
- 1 ½ tablespoon cornstarch
- 4 garlic cloves
- Salt to taste
- Pepper to taste
- 1 shallot
- 1 cup water
- 8 mushrooms
- 1 teaspoon Worcestershire sauce
- ½ cup tomato paste
- 1 tablespoon white sugar
- 2 tablespoons ketchup
- 1 tablespoon peanut oil

Directions:

1. Mix two types soy sauce, sugar, salt, oil.
2. Cover meat with soy sauce and leave to marinate.
3. Add mushrooms and peanuts with oil to the Instant Pot. Cook for 6 minutes on "Saute" regime.
4. Add onions with shallots and garlic to the Instant Pot. Cook for 2 minutes more on the same regime.
5. Add remaining ingredients to the Instant Pot and cook for 10 minutes more on "High Pressure" regime.

Nutrition:

- Calories: 216
- Fat: 10g
- Carbohydrates: 6g
- Protein:23g

Chops in Onion Sauce

Satisfying and super tender onion sauce with the delicious pork meat!

Prep time: 15 minutes | **Cooking time:** 15 minutes | **Servings:** 3

Ingredients:

- 4 pounds pork loin chops
- Salt to taste
- 1 onion
- 1 ½ tablespoon cornstarch
- 1 tablespoon olive oil

- ¾ cup chicken stock
- 1 tablespoon vinegar
- 1 teaspoon sugar
- 1 tablespoon light soy sauce
- 1 tablespoon soy sauce

- ¼ teaspoon sesame oil
- 1 tablespoon wine
- ¼ teaspoon white pepper
- ¼ teaspoon salt
- ½ teaspoon sugar

Directions:

1. Mix sugar, white pepper, sesame oil, salt, wine and soy sauce.
2. Cover meat with marinade and leave for 20 minutes to marinate.
3. Place chops with the oil in the Instant Pot and cook for 6 minutes on "High Pressure" regime.
4. Add chopped onion with salt and pepper.
5. Cook meat with onions for 2 minutes on "High Pressure" regime.
6. Mix chicken stock with sauce, soy sauce and sugar.
7. Add sauce mix to the meat.
8. Cook meat in sauce for 7 minutes more on "Meat" regime.

Nutrition:

- Calories: 270
- Fat: 8g

- Carbohydrates: 27g
- Protein: 22g

Char Siu

Try BBQ in Instant Pot – it is easier than you think!

Prep time: 10 minutes | **Cooking time:** 45 minutes | **Servings:** 3

Ingredients:

- 1 pound pork butt meat
- Salt to taste
- 3 tablespoons honey
- 1 cup water
- 2 tablespoons soy sauce
- 1 tablespoons chu hou paste
- 1 tablespoon light soy sauce
- 2 cubes Chinese red bean curd
- 1 teaspoon garlic powder
- 3 tablespoons char siu sauce
- 2 tablespoons wine
- ½ teaspoon sesame oil

Directions:

1. Mix paste, red bean curd, char siu sauce, sesame oil, wine, garlic powder, light soy sauce.
2. Place pork in the plastic bag and add marinade.
3. Marinate meat in the bag for 30 minutes.
4. Pour water in the Instant Pot.
5. Place meat in the Instant Pot.
6. Add remaining ingredients with marinade to the Instant Pot and cook on "High Pressure" regime for 20 minutes.
7. Preheat oven up to 450oF.
8. Place meat in the oven and cook for 5 minutes.
9. Serve meat with fresh herbs!

Nutrition:

- Calories: 558
- Fat: 31g
- Carbohydrates: 33g
- Protein:36g

Savory Waffles

Crispy and hot waffles with the delicious and tender meat!

Prep time: 25 minutes | **Cooking time:** 15 minutes | **Servings:** 12

Ingredients:

- 3 cups BBQ pork
- 1 teaspoon salt
- 1 cup Parmesan cheese
- 3 teaspoons vanilla extract
- 3 eggs
- 6 teaspoons baking powder
- 3 cups flour
- 4 tablespoons honey
- 3 cup smilk
- 1 cup peanut oil
- 1 cup butter

Directions:

1. Mix flour with salt and powder.
2. Mix milk, butter, honey, oil and vanilla extract in the bowl.
3. Pour milk mix on the frying pan and warm up.
4. Beat eggs and mix with hot sauce.
5. Add Parmesan to the egg mix.
6. Pour mix with pork to the waffle maker and cook for 6 minutes on "High Pressure" regime.
7. Place pork with waffles and remaining ingredients in the Instant Pot and cook for 10 minutes on the same regime.
8. Serve with maple sauce!

Nutrition:

- Calories: 159
- Fat: 9g
- Carbohydrates: 17g
- Protein:4g

Ginger Pork Shogayaki

Light meat with the sauce is easy to cook in Instant Pot. Do you want to try?

Prep time: 5 minutes | **Cooking time:** 50 minutes | **Servings:** 20

Ingredients:

- 10 pounds pork shoulder
- Salt to taste
- Pepper to taste
- 10 onions
- 5 heads lettuce
- 10 tablespoons peanut oil
- 2 tcups ginger root
- 5 cup swater
- 10 clove garlic
- 2 cups mirin
- 1 tablespoon soy sauce
- 2 tablespoons cooking sake
- ½ tablespoon miso paste

Directions:

1. Warm up Instant Pot and pour oil inside of the Pot.
2. Mix ginger with garlic and soy sauce, miso paste, sake and mirin.
3. Add water to sauce mix.
4. Place ginger sauce in the Instant Pot and warm up the sauce.
5. Add meat and chopped onion with salt and pepper to the Instant Pot.
6. Cook for 13 minutes on "High Pressure" regime.
7. Slice pork and add ½ of lettuce. Cook for 15 minutes more on the same regime.
8. Serve with lettuce!

Nutrition:

- Calories: 156
- Fat: 1g
- Carbohydrates: 30g
- Protein:4g

Pork Shoulder

Just imagine how tasty it will be – pork with tomato sauce and tender seasoning!

Prep time: 5 minutes | **Cooking time:** 50 minutes | **Servings:** 15

Ingredients:

- 5 pounds pork shoulder meat
- 3 teaspoons honey
- 5 teaspoons melted caramel
- Salt to taste
- Pepper to taste
- 5 onions
- 10 tablespoons peanut oil
- 5 shallots
- 15 mushrooms
- 9 garlic cloves
- 15 tablespoons tomato paste
- 5 cups chicken stock
- 9 tablespoons ketchup
- 3 teaspoons Worcestershire sauce
- 3 tablespoons sugar
- 3 tablespoons light soy sauce

Directions:

1. Top meat with salt and pepper.
2. Pour oil in the Instant Pot. Pour caramel to the Instant Pot.
3. Place pork in the Instant Pot and cook for 10 minutes on "High Pressure".
4. Mix tomato paste, ketchup, soy sauce, sugar, sauce and chicken stock.
5. Mix mushrooms with garlic and onion. Add honey and use mixer to make a tender mix.
6. Place mushroom mix on the frying pan and fry with the shallot and seasoning.
7. Place sauce with mushrooms to the Instant Pot and cook for 15 minutes on "High Pressure" regime.
8. Serve with fresh herbs!

Nutrition:

- Calories: 228
- Fat: 16g
- Carbohydrates: 0g
- Protein:20g

Pulled Pork

Pulled pork is one of the most delicious and tender dishes!

Prep time: 10 minutes | **Cooking time:** 85 minutes | **Servings:** 18

Ingredients:

- 9 pounds pork shoulder
- Salt to taste
- 1 cup chili sauce
- 2 teaspoons white pepper
- 15 garlic cloves
- 3 teaspoons paprika
- 2 onions
- 6 tablespoons peanut oil
- 1 cup chicken stock
- 3 tablespoons Dijon mustard
- 1 cup maple syrup
- 1 tablespoon Worcestershire sauce
- 1 tablespoon light soy sauce

Directions:

1. Mix chicken stock with maple syrup, light soy sauce, Worcestershire sauce and mustard.
2. Pour oil in the Instant Pot. Add chili sauce to the Pot and cook on "Saute" regime for 7 minutes. Add pepper and cook for 2 more minutes.
3. Cover meat with salt and pepper.
4. Place meat in the Instant Pot and cook for 12 minutes on "High Pressure" regime.
5. Mix onions with garlic and add to the Instant Pot.
6. Cook onions in the Instant Pot for 2 minutes not changing setting.
7. Pour sauce in the Instant Pot and cook meat for 30 minutes on the same regime.
8. Cut pork into thin slices and place back to the Instant Pot.
9. Cook for 15 minutes more on "High Pressure" regime.
10. Serve with onions!

Nutrition:

- Calories: 335
- Fat: 5g
- Carbohydrates: 49g
- Protein:21g

Ribs with Black Bean Sauce

Soft meat with satisfying beans and tender sauce!

Prep time: 5 minutes | **Cooking time:** 30 minutes | **Servings:** 15

Ingredients:

- 5 pounds pork ribs
- 1 cup fish sauce
- 1 cup oil
- 2 cups water
- 1 cup cornstarch

- 1 cupblack bean sauce
- Pinch of white pepper
- 5 tablespoons light soy sauce
- 5 teaspoons sugar

- 5 tablespoons wine
- 5 teaspoons sesame oil
- 5 tablespoons ginger
- 16 garlic cloves

Directions:

1. Pour water in the Instant Pot.
2. Mix fish sauce with cornstarch and set aside.
3. Cover pork with the oil.
4. Place garlic in the Instant Pot and cook for 3 minutes on "High Pressure" regime.
5. Mix bean sauce, soy sauce, wine, ginger, sesame oil, sugar and white pepper.
6. Add roasted garlic to sauce mix.
7. Place pork meat in marinade. Leave to marinate for 25 minutes.
8. Place meat in the Instant Pot.
9. Cook meat for 15 minutes on "High Pressure" regime.
10. Top meat with fish sauce and cornstarch.
11. Cook meat for 4 minutes more not changing setting.
12. Serve with fresh herbs!

Nutrition:

- Calories: 282
- Fat: 20g

- Carbohydrates:4g
- Protein: 21g

Ribs

Easy, soft and delicious receipt for the meat lovers!

Prep time: 15 minutes | **Cooking time:** 45 minutes | **Servings:** 15

Ingredients:

- 5 rack baby back ribs
- 15 drops liquid smoke
- 10 carrots
- 10 tablespoons brown sugar
- 3 teaspoon cayenne pepper
- 9 teaspoons chili powder
- 4 teaspoon fennel seed
- 10 teaspoons black pepper
- 5 teaspoon cumin seed
- 5 teaspoon onion powder
- 5 teaspoon kosher salt
- 5teaspoon garlic powder
- 5 teaspoon cinnamon powder
- 7 onions
- 1 cup sugar
- 3 garlic cloves
- 2 tablespoons mustard
- 1 cup ketchup
- 2 tablespoons apple cider vinegar
- ½ cup water.
- ½ cup honey
- ½ cup maple syrup

Directions:

1. Wash and cut carrots.
2. Pour liquid smoke on the meat.
3. Mix sugar, chili powder, pepper, onion powder, garlic powder, cinnamon powder, salt, cumin seed, cayenne pepper and fennel seed.
4. Cover meat with seasoning mix.
5. Pour water in the Instant Pot.
6. Place meat in seasoning in the Instant Pot and cook for 10 minutes on "High Pressure" regime.
7. Mix chopped onion, garlic and sugar.
8. Place onion mix in the Instant Pot and cook for 5 minutes more on "Saute" regime.
9. Mix ketchup, maple syrup, honey, vinegar and mustard.
10. Add sauce to the meat and cook for 15 minutes more on "Meat" regime.
11. Serve with fresh basil leaves!

Nutrition:

- Calories: 120
- Fat: 7g
- Carbohydrates: 4g
- Protein:12g

Chinese Braised Beef Shank

Tender. Light and healthy meat receipt for those who love low calories dishes!

Prep time: 15 minutes | **Cooking time:** 45 minutes | **Servings:** 13

Ingredients:

- 10 pounds beef shank
- Soy sauce
- 6 ½ cups master stock

Directions:

1. Pour water in the bowl.
2. Bring water to boil.
3. Place meat in the boiling water and boil for 5 minutes.
4. Place meat in the Instant Pot and add master stock.
5. Cook meat for 35 minutes on "High Pressure" regime.
6. Serve with fresh peppers and soy sauce!

Nutrition:

- Calories: 110
- Fat: 6g
- Carbohydrates: 6g
- Protein:10g

Meatloaf

Cook super juicy meatloaf in the Instant Pot!

Prep time: 20 minutes | **Cooking time:** 45 minutes | **Servings:** 13

Ingredients:

- 7 ½ pounds beef
- 8 ½ cup cheese
- 13 bacon strips
- 4 ¼ cup milk
- 5 onions
- 2 ¾ cup panko
- 12 garlic cloves
- 4 ¼ teaspoon pepper
- 6 eggs
- 4 ¾ teaspoon salt
- 3 ½ teaspoon oregano
- 2 ¾ teaspoon Worcestershire sauce
- 1 ½ teaspoon fennel seeds
- 6 cups chicken stock
- 8 teaspoon dried oregano
- 6 ½ cup tomato sauce
- 7 teaspoon basil
- 3 cup tomato paste

Directions:

1. Mix chicken stock with tomato sauce, tomato paste, basil and oregano.
2. Mix beef, bacon, chopped onion, garlic, beaten eggs, oregano, fennel seed, sauce, salt, pepper, panko, cheese and milk.
3. Form bread loaf of the meat mix.
4. Place meatloaf in the Instant Pot.
5. Add sauce to the meatloaf.
6. Cook meatloaf with sauce for 20 minutes on "High Pressure" regime.
7. Preheat oven up to 450oF.
8. Place meatloaf in the oven and cook for 15 minutes not changing settings.
9. Serve with fresh herbs!

Nutrition:

- Calories: 241
- Fat: 17g
- Carbohydrates: 0g
- Protein:20g

Congee with Beef

Liquid but satisfying, tender but delicious, healthy but easy!

Prep time: 5 minutes | **Cooking time:** 60 minutes | **Servings:** 3

Ingredients:

- 1 pound beef
- 1 stalk green onion
- ½ cup spinach
- 7 cups water
- ¾ cup rice
- 1/3 teaspoon salt
- 1/3 teaspoon white pepper
- ¼ teaspoon oil

Directions:

1. Mix oil, salt and pepper.
2. Top meat with marinade and leave for 20 minutes.
3. Place rice, water and beef in the Instant Pot.
4. Cook meat with rice for 25 minutes on "High Pressure" regime.
5. Add remaining ingredients to the Instant Pot and cook for 20 minutes more on the same regime.
6. Serve with fresh herbs!

Nutrition:

- Calories: 360
- Fat: 13g
- Carbohydrates: 45g
- Protein:13g

Beef and Broccoli

Do you like healthy food? This receipt is easy and delicious introduction to the healthy lifestyle!

Prep time: 10 minutes | **Cooking time:** 1 hour | **Servings:** 2

Ingredients:
- 1 pound roast steak
- Pepper to taste
- 2 tomatoes
- 2 jalapeno peppers
- Salt to taste
- 1/6 heads broccoli
- 1 tablespoon olivet oil
- 1 garlic clove
- 1/6 tablespoons ginger
- 1/4 cups chicken stock
- ¼ teaspoons sesame oil
- 1/2 tablespoons light soy sauce
- 1/2 teaspoons five spice powder
- 1/4 tablespoons dark soy sauce
- ½ tablespoons oyster sauce

Directions:
1. Mix soy sauces with oyster sauce, powder, sesame oil and chicken stock. Wash and cut peppers with tomatoes. Cover vegetables with powder mix.
2. Pour oil in the Instant Pot.
3. Cover steak with salt and pepper.
4. Place meat in the Instant Pot and cook for 15 minutes on "High Pressure" regime.
5. Add garlic with ginger to the Instant Pot and cook on "High Pressure" for 2 more minutes.
6. Pour liquid in the Instant Pot and add rice.
7. Cook beef for 15 minutes on "High Pressure" regime.
8. Add vegetables and cook for 10 more minutes on the same settings.

Nutrition:
- Calories: 152
- Fat: 8g
- Carbohydrates:9g
- Protein:11g

Beef Curry

Soft and tender Japanese beef curry is one of the most delicious recipes – try and make sure!

Prep time: 10 minutes | **Cooking time:** 65 minutes | **Servings:** 9

Ingredients:
- 4 pounds steak
- 5 tablespoons Japanese soy sauce
- 6 garlic cloves
- 7 Japanese roux cube curry
- 4 ¾ cup chicken stock
- 3 ½ pounds onions and shallots
- Salt to taste
- Pepper to taste
- 9 tablespoons butter
- 3 1/3 tablespoon baking soda

Directions:
1. Place butter in Instant Pot and melt it up.
2. Mix chopped onions with chopped shallots and baking soda.
3. Place onion mix in the Instant Pot and cook for 20 minutes on "High Pressure" regime.
4. Add steak with soy sauce, garlic cloves, curry, stock, salt, pepper and butter to the Pot and cook for 45 minutes on "High Pressure" regime.
5. Serve with rice!

Nutrition:
- Calories: 606
- Fat: 46g
- Carbohydrates: 27g
- Protein:28g

Beef Stroganoff

Classical receipt in the better and more delicious version for the Instant Pot!

Prep time: 15 minutes | **Cooking time:** 40 minutes | **Servings:** 15

Ingredients:

- 4 pounds chick roast
- 3 cups sour cream
- 1 pound mushrooms
- 2 tablespoons flour
- 1 onion
- Salt to taste

- Pepper to taste
- Lime juice
- 8 garlic cloves
- 2 teaspoons paprika
- 3 cups white wine
- 1 tablespoon olive oil

- 3 cups chicken stock
- 1 tablespoon mustard
- 2 tablespoons light soy sauce
- 1 tablespoon Worcestershire sauce

Directions:

1. Mix liquid ingredients with ½ herbs. Add lime juice to the mix.
2. Mix pepper, salt and paprika.
3. Pour oil in the Instant pot. Pour 2 cups water to the Pot.
4. Mix herbs and salts with flour. Place mix in the bowl and add meat. Cook on low fire for 4 minutes.
5. Place meat in the Instant Pot and cook for 15 minutes on "Meat" regime.
6. Wash and cut mushrooms into small pieces and add to the Pot.
7. Add onion to the Instant Pot with garlic cloves.
8. Cook meat for 6 minutes more on "High Pressure" regime.
9. Pour sauce mix over ingredients and cook for 12 minutes more on the same regime.
10. Pour wine in the Pot and cook for 10 minutes on "Low Pressure" regime.
11. Serve beef meat with cheese!

Nutrition:

- Calories: 361
- Fat: 16g

- Carbohydrates: 17g
- Protein: 36g

Irish Beef Stew

One of the best beef stew recipes you have ever tried!

Prep time: 10 minutes | **Cooking time:** 55 minutes | **Servings:** 15

Ingredients:

- 6 pounds chick steak
- 6 tablespoons olive oil
- 18 mushrooms
- 7oz chocolate
- 3 onions
- 1 bay leaf
- 12 garlic cloves
- 1 spring rosemary
- 1 shallot
- 6 springs thyme
- 6 carrots
- 1 potato
- 1 ½ tablespoon flour
- 1 cup Guinness
- 4 cups chicken stock
- 1 tablespoon tomato paste
- 1 tablespoon Worcestershire sauce
- 4 tablespoons fish sauce
- 2 tablespoons light sauce

Directions:

1. Mix tomato paste with fish sauce, soy sauce, Worcestershire sauce and chicken stock. Set aside.
2. Pour oil in the Instant Pot and set "Saute" regime.
3. Cover steak with seasoning from the both sides.
4. Place steak in the Instant Pot for 15 minutes on "High Pressure" regime.
5. Add garlic, onion, shallots and mushrooms to the Instant Pot. Cook onion mix for 4 minutes more on the same regime.
6. Pour Guinness and add remaining ingredients to the Instant Pot.
7. Cook meat for 30 minutes more on "Meat" regime.
8. Serve with fresh herbs!

Nutrition:

- Calories: 220
- Fat: 8g
- Carbohydrates: 19g
- Protein:17g

Beef Shank Soup

Satisfying and light soup with tender meat slices!

Prep time: 15 minutes | **Cooking time:** 2.5 hours | **Servings:** 5

Ingredients:

- 1 1/2 lbs beef shank
- ¼ cup parsley
- 2 tablespoons EVOO
- 2 cups cabbage
- 8 cups water
- ½ teaspoon marjoram
- 1 tablespoon cider vinegar
- ½ teaspoon thyme
- 1 teaspoon salt
- 1 parsnip
- 3 springs of fresh thyme
- 1 ½ cup turnip
- 3 garlic cloves
- 5 carrots
- 2 bay leaves
- 3 celery stalks
- 1 onion

Directions:

1. Pour EVOO in the Instant Pot.
2. Place beef shank in the Instant Pot and cook on "High Pressure" regime for 6 minutes.
3. Pour water over the beef shank.
4. Pour vinegar to the pressure cooker.
5. Add salt, thyme, bay leaf and garlic to the Instant Pot.
6. Cook for 10 minutes on "Soup" regime.
7. Shred beef shank and remove fat.
8. Chop onions – add to the Instant Pot. Add celery, cut carrots, garlic cloves, turnip, thyme, salt, marjoram, parsley and cabbage.
9. Cook for 3 minutes on "High Pressure" regime.
10. Add more water and cook for 2 hours on "High Pressure" regime.
11. Let the pressure release naturally (20 minutes).
12. Serve hot with herbs!

Nutrition:

- Calories: 140
- Fat: 5g
- Carbohydrates:1g
- Protein: 24g

Sausage and Zucchini Stew

Try hot, healthy and satisfying stew with zucchini slices and tender sausage!

Prep time: 10 minutes | **Cooking time:** 6 hours | **Servings:** 6

Ingredients:

- 1lb sausage
- 1 teaspoon basil
- 1 cup celery
- 1 teaspoon oregano
- 1 cup chopped onion
- 1 teaspoon sugar
- 3 cups zucchini
- 1 teaspoon salt
- 28oz tomatoes
- 1 teaspoon garlic powder
- 1 teaspoon Italian seasoning

Directions:

1. Cut sausages on slices.
2. Place sausages in the pressure cooker and cook for 6 minutes on "High Pressure" regime.
3. Add seasoning, garlic powder, cubed tomatoes, salt, zucchini, sugar, chopped onion, oregano, celery and basil to the Instant Pot.
4. Mix ingredients well.
5. Cook stew for 6 hours on "Low Pressure" regime.
6. Serve hot with fresh herbs!

Nutrition:

- Calories: 285
- Fat: 15g
- Carbohydrates: 18g
- Protein: 22g

Lamb Stew

Try satisfying, extra light and meaty lamb stew to get energy for the full day!

Prep time: 10 minutes | **Cooking time:** 35 minutes | **Servings:** 5

Ingredients:
- 2lbs lamb stew meat
- ½ teaspoon salt
- 1 acorn squash
- 3 tablespoons water
- 3 carrots
- 6 garlic cloves
- 1 onion
- 1 bay leaf
- 1 spring rosemary

Directions:
1. Wash and peel acorn squash.
2. Cut acorn squash into cubes.
3. Place acorn squash in the pressure cooker and cook for 1 minute on "High Pressure" regime.
4. Add cubed carrots, chopped onion and rosemary, bay leaf, garlic, salt to the Instant Pot.
5. Pour water over ingredients.
6. Place meat on top of the stew.
7. Cook for 35 minutes on "Stew" regime.
8. Let the pressure release naturally (15 minutes).
9. Serve warm!

Nutrition:
- Calories: 340
- Fat: 11g
- Carbohydrates: 32g
- Protein: 30g

Beef Noodle Soup

Light bullion, tender meat and soft noodles with fresh herbs – easy and juicy receipt in Instant Pot!

Prep time: 10 minutes | **Cooking time:** 50 minutes | **Servings:** 7

Ingredients:
- 1 ½ pounds beef neck bones
- ¼ cup cilantro
- 2 carrots
- Salt to taste
- 2 tablespoons coconut aminos
- 18 ounce yam noodles
- 1 tablespoon fish sauce
- Water
- 3 garlic cloves
- 1 cup mushrooms

Directions:
1. Wash and cut mushrooms on slices.
2. Wash and peel carrots. Cut carrots on cubes.
3. Place bones, carrots aminos, fish sauce, garlic and mushrooms in the Instant Pot.
4. Pour water over ingredients.
5. Cook soup ingredients for 40 minutes on "High Pressure" regime.
6. Let the pressure release naturally (10 minutes).
7. Add noodles and salt.
8. Serve with fresh herbs!

Nutrition:
- Calories: 900
- Fat: 2g
- Carbohydrates: 35g
- Protein: 23g

Curried Rosemary Lamb Rib Stew

Soft, tender lamb stew with herbs and vegetables for the dinner – the best idea!

Prep time: 10 minutes | **Cooking time:** 35 minutes | **Servings:** 4

Ingredients:
- 2lbs lamb ribs
- 3 fresh rosemary springs
- 1 teaspoon pink salt
- 1 teaspoon turmeric
- 7 cups chopped cabbage
- 1 cup chopped carrots
- 1 cup celery
- 2 cups butternut squash
- 5 mint leaves
- 1 cup bone broth
- 1 teaspoon turmeric
- 2 garlic cloves
- ½ teaspoon salt
- Pinch of fresh ginger
- 1 lime juice

Directions:
1. Mix mint leaves, turmeric, salt, lime juice, garlic cloves, bone broth, butternut squash and mix using blender to get tender mixture.
2. Place lamb with pink salt and turmeric in the Instant Pot.
3. Add carrots, celery, cabbage and springs to the Instant Pot.
4. Pour sauce over the stew in the pressure cooker.
5. Cook lamb stew on "Meat" regime for 35 minutes.
6. Do a quick release.
7. Serve!

Nutrition:
- Calories: 399
- Fat: 44g
- Carbohydrates: 3g
- Protein: 12g

Cuban Lechon Asado

Shredded light meat without fat, but with tender and satisfying taste!

Prep time: 10 minutes | **Cooking time:** 90 minutes | **Servings:** 5

Ingredients:
- 5lb pork roast
- 2 tablespoons olive oil
- 1 ½ criollo marinade
- 1 onion

Directions:
1. Wash and chop onion.
2. Wash meat.
3. Cut meat into slices (about 4).
4. Pour oil in the Instant Pot.
5. Place onions in the Instant Pot and cook for 4 minutes on "Sauté" regime.
6. Cover pork with marinade and leave for 15 minutes to marinate.
7. Place pork in the pressure cooker.
8. Cook meat for 90 minutes on "High Pressure" regime.
9. Let the pressure release naturally (30 minutes).
10. Serve hot!

Nutrition:
- Calories: 351
- Fat: 14g
- Carbohydrates: 3g
- Protein: 51g

Soy-free Tau Yew Bak

Sweet sauce over the pork meat with light and tender herbs!

Prep time: 15 minutes | **Cooking time:** 20 minutes | **Servings:** 5

Ingredients:
- 2lb pork
- 1 teaspoon salt
- 3 tablespoons molasses
- 2/3 cup water
- 3 tablespoons coconut aminos
- 1 stick cinnamon
- 6 garlic cloves
- 1 clementine
- 1 inch ginger
- 2 mace strips

Directions:
1. Wash and cut pork meat.
2. Mix mace with ginger, clementine, garlic, cinnamon, aminos, salt and molasses.
3. Use blender to get tender sauce.
4. Pour sauce over the meat and leave for 10 minutes to marinade.
5. Place meat in the pressure cooker.
6. Pour water over the meat.
7. Cook meat for 20 minutes on "High Pressure" regime.
8. Let the pressure release naturally (10 minutes).
9. Serve with herbs!

Nutrition:
- Calories: 344
- Fat: 12g
- Carbohydrates: 0g
- Protein: 41g

Hong Shao Rou

In another words, the name of this receipt is red-cooked pork – try real Asian meat!

Prep time: 15 minutes | **Cooking time:** 35 minutes | **Servings:** 12

Ingredients:
- 8lb pork belly
- 8 springs coriander
- 8 tablespoons maple syrup
- 4 ginger
- 9 tablespoons sherry
- 1cup water
- 4 tablespoons molasses
- 4 teaspoons sea salt
- 8 tablespoons coconut aminos

Directions:
1. Pour water in the Instant Pot. Warm up water in the pressure cooker. It will take you around 4 minutes to warm it up on "Sauté" regime.
2. Mix coriander with maple syrup, ginger, sherry, molasses, sea salt and aminos. Add water to the seasoning mix. It will give a chance to make soft and porridge texture sauce.
3. Pour sauce in the Instant Pot and cook for 10 minutes on "Sauté" regime.
4. Add pork and pour water over the meat.
5. Cook for 25 minutes on "High Pressure" regime.
6. Let the pressure release naturally (10 minutes).
7. Serve with peppers!

Nutrition:
- Calories: 431
- Fat: 43g
- Carbohydrates: 5g
- Protein: 4g

Cajun Sausage Risotto

Satisfying, light and fresh Cajun sausage risotto on your plate for the lunch today – something you need to try!

Prep time: 15 minutes | **Cooking time:** 15 minutes | **Servings:** 4

Ingredients:

- 2 pounds rope sausage
- 2 handfuls greens
- 1 tablespoon Cajun seasoning
- 2 cups scallions
- 1 teaspoon sea salt
- 2 summer squash
- 4 tablespoons butter
- 3 cups water
- 2 cups rice

Directions:

1. Mix squash, salt, seasoning, chopped scallions with greens.
2. Cut sausage on slices.
3. Place seasoning mix with sausage in the pressure cooker.
4. Cook sausages with seasoning for 4 minutes on "Sauté" regime.
5. Add rice with water to the Instant Pot and cook for 8 minutes on "High Pressure" regime.
6. Let the pressure release naturally (10 minutes).
7. Serve hot!

Nutrition:

- Calories: 436
- Fat: 13g
- Carbohydrates: 58g
- Protein: 23g

Pork Taco Salad

Try satisfying and quick salad with pulled shredded pork meat!

Prep time: 6 minutes | **Cooking time:** 15 minutes | **Servings:** 4

Ingredients:

- 1 batch pulled pork
- Dressing to choice
- 2 heads lettuce
- 1 tablespoon avocado oil
- 1 batch pico de gallo
- 1 tablespoon adobo seasoning
- 1 batch guacamole
- ½ onion
- 1 bell pepper

Directions:

1. Wash bell pepper and cut on slices.
2. Cut lettuce on slices.
3. Clean and chop onion.
4. Pour oil in the Instant Pot.
5. Place onion with peppers in the pressure cooker.
6. Cook for 3 minutes on "Sauté" regime.
7. Place pork in the Instant Pot.
8. Cook Instant Pot for 10 minutes on "High Pressure" regime. Let the pressure release naturally (10 minutes).
9. Mix guacamole, adobo seasoning, pico de gallo and add to the meat.
10. Place meat on the plate, mix with lettuce, onions and peppers, add dressing and mix well.
11. Serve cold!

Nutrition:

- Calories: 799
- Fat: 46g
- Carbohydrates: 59g
- Protein: 39g

Maple Balsamic Beef

Can beef can be this tasty and juicy? With Instant Pot it can!

Prep time: 20 minutes | **Cooking time:** 35 minutes | **Servings:** 6

Ingredients:
- 3lb chuck steak
- 1 teaspoon garlic
- 1 ½ teaspoon salt
- 1 cup maple syrup
- 1 teaspoon ginger
- ½ cup vinegar
- 2 tablespoons olive oil
- 1 cup bone broth

Directions:
1. Wash and cut beef meat into slices.
2. Mix ginger, salt and garlic.
3. Place meat in the Instant Pot.
4. Add seasoning mix with oil to the Instant Pot.
5. Cook meat on "High Pressure" regime for 6 minutes.
6. Add broth, vinegar and syrup to the pressure cooker.
7. Cook for 25 minutes on "Meat" regime.
8. Let the pressure release naturally (10 minutes).
9. Serve hot!

Nutrition:
- Calories: 150
- Fat: 14g
- Carbohydrates: 5g
- Protein: 0g

Plantain Curry

Fresh herbs with satisfying bullion and tender meat slices are easy to cook with Instant Pot!

Prep time: 10 minutes | **Cooking time:** 35 minutes | **Servings:** 5

Ingredients:
- 2 tablespoons coconut oil
- 1 tablespoon coriander leaves
- 1 teaspoon garlic powder
- 1 teaspoon ginger powder
- 1 ripe plantain
- 1 teaspoon turmeric powder
- 1 stick cinnamon
- 1 teaspoon sea salt
- 4 lime leaves
- 2 onions
- 2lbs pot roast
- 1 cup coconut milk
- 3 teaspoon coconut oil

Directions:
1. Mix turmeric, garlic powder, ginger powder, sea salt and oil.
2. Pour seasoning mix over the meat and leave to marinate.
3. Marinate meat for 15 minutes.
4. Chop onions.
5. Pour oil in the Instant Pot.
6. Place onions with seasoning in the Instant Pot.
7. Cook onions for 3 minutes on "Sauté" regime.
8. Add meat and cook for 6 minutes more on "Sauté" regime.
9. Add milk, lime leaves, cinnamon, sea salt, coriander leaves.
10. Cook dish for 35 minutes on "High Pressure" regime in the pressure cooker.
11. Let the pressure release naturally (10 minutes).
12. Serve hot!

Nutrition:
- Calories: 290
- Fat: 11g
- Carbohydrates: 50g
- Protein: 2g

Stuffed Peppers

With this dish you can get everything you want – energy, vitamins and taste!

Prep time: 10 minutes | **Cooking time:** 15 minutes | **Servings:** 4

Ingredients:

- 4 bell peppers
- Parsley to taste
- 1 onion
- Garlic powder to taste
- 1 tomato

- 1 teaspoon adobo
- 2 garlic cloves
- 1 pinch cayenne pepper
- 1lb beef
- 1 teaspoon pepper

- 1 bag boiled brown rice
- 2 teaspoons salt
- 1 egg
- 1 cup parmesan
- 1 can tomato sauce

Directions:

1. Wash and clean bell peppers of the insights. Cut off bel peppers head.
2. Wash and chop onions, cut tomatoes and garlic.
3. Mix vegetables with meat, egg and rice.
4. Mix salt, pepper, cayenne pepper, adobo, garlic powder and parsley.
5. Mix onion-meat mix with seasoning.
6. Place mix in peppers.
7. Pour water in the Instant Pot.
8. Place peppers in the pressure cooker.
9. Cook peppers for 15 minutes on "Manual" regime.
10. Let the pressure release naturally (10 minutes).

Nutrition:

- Calories: 238
- Fat: 8g

- Carbohydrates: 28g
- Protein: 14g

Taco Meat

The moment when meat is juicy and crispy the same time!

Prep time: 5 minutes | **Cooking time:** 20 minutes | **Servings:** 12

Ingredients:

- 4 ½ lbs ground beef
- 4 red onions
- 8 tablespoons oregano
- 9 garlic cloves
- 8 tablespoons olive oil

- 1 teaspoon marjoram
- 4 teaspoons oregano
- 4 teaspoons basil
- 4 teaspoons chili powder
- 2 teaspoons cumin

- 2 teaspoons turmeric
- 1 teaspoon pepper
- 1 teaspoon paprika
- 2 teaspoons salt
- 2 tablespoons creams

Directions:

1. Mix salt, paprika, pepper, reminded seasoning, chopped and peeled onion and oregano. Add water to the seasoning mix. Use blender to get sauce. Add creams to the sauce. Place ingredients with creams in blender cup and mix well to get tender texture.
2. Place seasoning mix in the pressure cooker and cook for 4 minutes on "Sauté" regime.
3. Add beef to the Instant Pot.
4. Cook beef on "Manual" for 15 minutes.
5. Let the pressure release naturally (10 minutes).
6. Dry meat.

Nutrition:

- Calories: 85
- Fat: 3g

- Carbohydrates: 1g
- Protein: 12g

Short Ribs

Short ribs with Korean sweet sauce will be meat receipt you love the most!

Prep time: 10 minutes | **Cooking time:** 20 minutes | **Servings:** 4

Ingredients:
- 5 pounds short ribs
- Salt to taste
- Pepper to taste
- 1 onion
- 3 tablespoons vinegar
- 2 shallots
- 1 cup chicken stock
- 2 carrots
- 3 cups red wine
- 5 garlic cloves
- 5 parsley springs
- 1 rosemary spring

Directions:
1. Cover meat with salt and pepper. Make a big layer of seasoning over the meat.
2. Place meat in the pressure cooker.
3. Mix chopped onions, shallots and cubed carrot. Cook meat with veggie mix for 13 minutes on "High Pressure" regime.
4. Add rosemary, parsley, garlic, red wine, chicken stock, vinegar and cook meat for 8 minutes more on "Stew" regime.
5. Let the pressure release naturally (10 minutes).
6. Serve hot!

Nutrition:
- Calories: 164
- Fat: 7g
- Carbohydrates: 1g
- Protein: 25g

Cubes Steak with Gravy

Gravy will add juicy taste to the meat and steak will be tender and soft after the cooking in Instant Pot!

Prep time: 4 minutes | **Cooking time:** 6 minutes | **Servings:** 4

Ingredients:
- 2 pounds cube steak
- 2lbs cornstarch
- 1 can onion soup
- 1lb steak sauce
- 1 packet gravy mix
- 10oz water

Directions:
1. Pour water in the Instant Pot.
2. Place steak with cornstarch in the Instant Pot.
3. Pour onion soup with gravy mix and steak sauce over the meat in the pressure cooker.
4. Cook meat for 5 minutes on "High Pressure" regime.
5. Let the pressure release naturally (10 minutes).
6. Serve hot!

Nutrition:
- Calories: 450
- Fat: 19g
- Carbohydrates: 0g
- Protein: 46g

Korean Chicken Meatballs

Try soft, sweet and juicy Korean meatballs with fresh herbs!

Prep time: 5 minutes | **Cooking time:** 10 minutes | **Servings:** 10

Ingredients:

- 1lb chicken
- 1 teaspoon olive oil
- 1 egg
- ½ cup BBQ sauce
- 2 garlic cloves
- ½ cup breadcrumbs
- 1 tablespoon ginger
- 1/3 teaspoon salt
- 1 teaspoon red pepper flakes
- ½ teaspoon sesame oil

Directions:

1. Pour BBQ sauce on one plate.
2. Place breadcrumbs on the other plate.
3. Place green onions on the third plate.
4. Pour oil in the Instant Pot.
5. Mix pepper flakes with sesame oil, salt, ginger, garlic cloves, beaten egg and chicken meat.
6. Roll up meatballs.
7. Place meatballs in the pressure cooker.
8. Cook meatballs for 5 minutes on "Poultry" regime.
9. Top meatballs with BBQ sauce.
10. Add crumbs to the meatballs.
11. Cook meat for 5 minutes on "High Pressure" regime.

Nutrition:

- Calories: 96
- Fat: 6g
- Carbohydrates: 1g
- Protein: 0g

Corned Beef

Try tender and satisfying beef meat cooked in its own juice!

Prep time: 20 minutes | **Cooking time:** 50 minutes | **Servings:** 12

Ingredients:

- 6 pounds beef brisket
- 4 tablespoons cornstarch
- 20 red potatoes
- 1 teaspoon allspice
- 1 onion
- 20 coriander leaves
- 16 garlic cloves
- 10 peppercorns
- 8 cups beef broth
- 6 whole cloves
- Head cabbage
- 1 bay leaf
- 1 spice packet

Directions:

1. Wash meat. Carefully remove skin and fat.
2. Place meat in the Instant Pot.
3. Mix chopped onion with cubed potato. Add garlic to the onion mix. Place onion mix in the microwave for 4 minutes to warm seasoning. Onions and garlic should be hot.
4. Mix bay leaf with spices, cabbage, cloves, peppercorns, garlic cloves, coriander leaves, allspice, cornstarch and mix with meat.
5. Pour broth in the pressure cooker.
6. Place ingredients in the Instant Pot.
7. Cook ingredients for 40 minutes on "High Pressure" regime.

Nutrition:

- Calories: 71
- Fat: 4g
- Carbohydrates: 0g
- Protein: 8g

Kalua Pig

Have you ever been in Korea? Enjoy Asia with this easy to cook and juicy receipt

Prep time: 15 minutes | **Cooking time:** 100 minutes | **Servings:** 8

Ingredients:
- 3 bacon slices
- 1 cabbage
- 5 pounds shoulder roast
- 1 cup water
- 5 peeled garlic cloves
- 1 ½ tablespoons sea salt

Directions:
1. Pour water in the Instant Pot.
2. Place bacon slices in the pressure cooker and cook on "Sauté" regime with garlic cloves for 6 minutes.
3. Shred bacon meat. Return meat to the pressure cooker.
4. Mix sea salt with shredded roast and cabbage.
5. Mix all the ingredients with bacon and garlic in the Instant Pot.
6. Cook for 90 minutes on "High Pressure" regime.
7. Let the pressure release naturally (10 minutes).
8. Serve hot!

Nutrition:
- Calories: 80
- Fat: 3g
- Carbohydrates: 1g
- Protein: 10g

Bone-in Ham

Tender and sweet meat on the bone with fresh herbs will be perfect dinner for everyone!

Prep time: 5 minutes | **Cooking time:** 25 minutes | **Servings:**4

Ingredients:
- ½ cup maple syrup
- 1 bone-in ham
- ½ cup honey
- 1 teaspoon nutmeg
- ¼ cup brown sugar
- 1 teaspoon cinnamon
- 2 tablespoons orange juice

Directions:
1. Mix orange juice with cinnamon and sugar.
2. Place ham in the Instant Pot.
3. Pour juice mix over the ham in the Instant Pot.
4. Add nutmeg with honey and maple syrup to the pressure cooker.
5. Cook meat for 15 minutes on "High Pressure" regime.
6. Let the pressure release naturally (10 minutes).
7. Serve with fresh herbs!

Nutrition:
- Calories: 80
- Fat: 5g
- Carbohydrates: 3g
- Protein: 8g

Beef Brisket with Tomatoes

Try this juicy beef meat with seasoning and colorful vegetables and enjoy!

Prep time: 10 minutes | **Cooking time:** 6 hours | **Servings:** 12

Ingredients:

- 9 pounds beef brisket
- Salt to taste
- Pepper to taste
- 4 yellow onions
- 8 tablespoons olive oil
- 28 ounces tomatoes
- 12 garlic cloves
- 4 cups beef stock

Directions:

1. Cover meat with salt and pepper well. Use hands to coat meat with seasoning from all sides.
2. Pour oil in the Instant Pot and warm up for 3 minutes on "Sauté" regime. You need just to warm up butter and do not boil it.
3. Add chopped onion, garlic cloves and tomatoes to the Instant Pot.
4. Cook vegetable mix for 4 minutes on "Sauté" regime. They should be golden color.
5. Add beef stock and beef brisket to the pressure cooker.
6. Cook meat for 6 hours on "Slow" regime.
7. Let the pressure release naturally (30 minutes).
8. Serve warm!

Nutrition:

- Calories: 351
- Fat: 17g
- Carbohydrates: 13g
- Protein: 35g

Maple Smoked Brisket

No fat, tender meat and delicious seasoning will be super satisfying with this receipt!

Prep time: 5 minutes | **Cooking time:** 50 minutes | **Servings:** 12

Ingredients:

- 4½ lbs beef brisket
- 9 springs fresh thyme leaves
- 7 tablespoons maple sugar
- 4 tablespoons liquid smoke
- 8 teaspoons sea salt
- 8 cans bone broth
- 4 teaspoons pepper
- 2 teaspoons smoked paprika
- 6 teaspoons mustard powder
- 6 teaspoons onion powder
- 1 tablespoon heavy creams

Directions:

1. Mix onion powder with mustard powder and smoked paprika. Add pepper, sea salt and maple sugar to the mix. Add water to the seasoning mix. It will make sauce creamy. Add creams and use blender to mix sauce.
2. Pour broth in the Instant Pot.
3. Place meat in the pressure cooker and add liquid smoke with thyme leaves.
4. Cover meat with seasoning well.
5. Cook meat for 50 minutes on "High Pressure" regime.
6. Let the pressure release naturally (10 minutes).
7. Serve with fresh green onions!

Nutrition:

- Calories: 250
- Fat: 15g
- Carbohydrates: 6g
- Protein: 23g

Pot Taco Meat

The easiest and the most delicious receipt is up to you!

Prep time: 10 minutes | **Cooking time:** 8 hours | **Servings:** 16

Ingredients:
- 4 pounds beef
- 1 teaspoon sea salt
- 1 onion
- 1 teaspoon coriander
- 10 garlic cloves
- 1 teaspoon cumin
- 1 cup tomatoes
- 1 ½ teaspoon onion powder
- ¼ cup Worcestershire sauce
- 1 ½ teaspoon garlic powder
- 6 tablespoons taco seasoning
- 1 jalapeno

Directions:
1. Wash and cut jalapeno pepper on slices.
2. Mix taco seasoning with garlic powder, onion powder, cumin, garlic cloves and coriander with sea salt.
3. Place chopped onion with seasoning mix in the pressure cooker.
4. Cook for 4 minutes on "Sauté" regime.
5. Add jalapeno, sauce, tomatoes and beef to the Instant Pot.
6. Cook meat with seasoning for 6 hours on "Low Pressure" regime.
7. Let the pressure release naturally (20 minutes).
8. Serve hot!

Nutrition:
- Calories: 72
- Fat: 2g
- Carbohydrates: 1g
- Protein: 13g

Cranberry Pot Roast

Sweet cranberry sauce with tender and juicy meat covered with soft seasoning!

Prep time: 15 minutes | **Cooking time:** 75 minutes | **Servings:** 5

Ingredients:
- 2 tablespoons olive oil
- 2 cups bone broth
- Salt to taste
- Pepper to taste
- 3 garlic cloves
- 1 pound beef
- 2 garlic cloves
- ½ cup white wine
- 1 cinnamon stick
- 1 cup cranberries
- 1 teaspoon horseradish powder
- ½ cup water
- ¼ cup honey

Directions:
1. Cover meat with salt and pepper.
2. Pour oil in the Instant Pot.
3. Place garlic cloves with honey and cranberries in the Instant Pot.
4. Cook cranberries for 4 minutes on "Sauté" regime.
5. Blend mix in the pressure cooker.
6. Place meat in the Instant Pot.
7. Mix powder with cinnamon, garlic cloves and sauce. Place in the Instant Pot.
8. Pour water with wine over the meat in the Instant Pot.
9. Cook for 75 minutes on "High Pressure" regime.
10. Let the pressure release naturally (10 minutes).

Nutrition:
- Calories: 587
- Fat: 36g
- Carbohydrates: 34g
- Protein: 33g

Carne Guisada

Try Spanish national meat receipt to get vitamins, energy and inspiration!

Prep time: 5 minutes | **Cooking time:** 35 minutes | **Servings:** 12

Ingredients:

- 4 tablespoons avocado oil
- 2 tablespoons potato starch
- 2 pounds beef
- 1 cup tomato sauce
- 2 onions
- 2 cups beef broth
- 2 tablespoons garlic
- 1 teaspoon oregano
- 1 serrano pepper
- 1 teaspoon chipotle pepper
- 1 bay leaf
- 1 cup hot sauce
- 1 tablespoon butter
- 1 teaspoon pepper
- 1 teaspoon cumin
- 1 teaspoon salt
- 1 teaspoon chili powder
- 1 teaspoon paprika
- 1 tablespoon heavy creams

Directions:

1. Mix paprika, chili powder, salt, cumin, pepper, bay leaf, chipotle pepper, pepper, oregano, garlic, chopped onion and potato starch. Add creams to the seasoning mix. Pour water over seasoning. Mix well using blender. Pour hot sauce over seasoning. Use mixer on the second speed to mix ingredients well.
2. Mix butter with oil. Pour oil in the pressure cooker. Warm up oil on "Sauté" regime. It will take you around 3 minutes.
3. Place onion mix in the Instant Pot.
4. Cook on "Sauté" regime. Onions need to turn golden color. It will take you 6 minutes.
5. Add tomato sauce, beef broth and beef to the Instant Pot.
6. Cook for 35 minutes on "Meat" regime.
7. Let the pressure release naturally (10 minutes).
8. Serve hot!

Nutrition:

- Calories: 240
- Fat: 7g
- Carbohydrates: 17g
- Protein: 32g

Porcini and Tomato Beef

Try tender tomatoes with beef meat and enjoy Mediterranean cuisine!

Prep time: 15 minutes | **Cooking time:** 50 minutes | **Servings:** 5

Ingredients:

- 5 pounds short ribs
- ¼ cup Italian parsley
- Salt to taste
- 2 tablespoons vinegar
- Pepper to taste
- ½ cup bone broth
- ½ ounce mushrooms
- 1 cup marinara sauce
- 1 cup hot water
- 6 garlic cloves
- 1 tablespoons lard of fat
- 2 celery stalks
- 1 onion
- 3 carrots

Directions:

1. Wash ribs.
2. Cur carrots and chop onion.
3. Mix celery, garlic cloves, pepper, salt and parsley.
4. Place onion mix with seasoning in the pressure cooker.
5. Cook for 5 minutes on "Sauté" regime.
6. Pour broth in the Instant Pot.
7. Add ribs with marinara, vinegar and fat to the Instant Pot.
8. Cook for 30 minutes on "High Pressure" regime.
9. Add chopped mushrooms with hot water to the Instant Pot.
10. Cook meat with mushrooms for 30 minutes on "High Pressure" regime.
11. Let the pressure release naturally (10 minutes).
12. Serve hot!

Nutrition:

- Calories: 290
- Fat: 1g
- Carbohydrates: 60g
- Protein: 12g

Mocha-Rubbed Pot Roast

Try super sweet and juicy meat in the pressure cooker with this easy receipt!

Prep time: 20 minutes	**Cooking time:** 1 hour	**Servings:** 4

Ingredients:

- 2 tablespoons coffee
- 1 teaspoon sea salt
- 2 tablespoons paprika
- 1 teaspoon ginger
- 1 tablespoon pepper
- 1 teaspoon chili powder

- 1 tablespoon cocoa powder
- 1 teaspoon Aleppo pepper
- 2 pounds beef chunk roast
- 3 tablespoons vinegar

- 1 cup broth
- 6 figs
- 1 onion

Directions:

1. Mix coffee with sea salt, paprika, ginger, pepper, chili powder and cocoa powder.
2. Cover beef roast with seasoning.
3. Cook beef for 30 minutes on "Meat" regime.
4. Pour broth in the Instant Pot.
5. Add figs, pepper and vinegar with chopped onion to the Instant Pot.
6. Cook for 30 minutes on "High Pressure" regime.
7. Let the pressure release naturally (15 minutes).
8. Serve hot!

Nutrition:

- Calories: 519
- Fat: 27g
- Carbohydrates: 26g
- Protein: 43g

Bo Kho

Try national Vietnamese receipt with vegetables and tender seasoning!

Prep time: 10 minutes	**Cooking time:** 50 minutes	**Servings:** 6

Ingredients:

- ½ teaspoon ghee
- Salt to taste
- 5 pounds bone-in ribs
- 1 cup bone broth
- 1 onion

- 1 pound carrots
- 1 ½ teaspoon curry powder
- 1 bay leaf
- 2 tablespoons ginger

- 2 star anise
- 2 cups tomatoes
- 1 stalk lemongrass
- 3 tablespoons fish sauce
- 2 tablespoons applesauce

Directions:

1. Place ghee in the Instant Pot and melt it up on "Sauté" regime for 3 minutes.
2. Place ribs in the Instant Pot.
3. Add ginger, applesauce, fish sauce, lemongrass, tomatoes, anise, bay leaf, curry powder, carrots, onion, salt and add to the pressure cooker over the meat.
4. Mix meat well with seasoning.
5. Pour broth over the meat.
6. Cook meat for 50 minutes in the Instant Pot on "High Pressure" regime.
7. Do a quick release.
8. Serve hot!

Nutrition:

- Calories: 528
- Fat: 23g
- Carbohydrates: 29g
- Protein: 53g

Mexi Meatloaf

Try original and tender meatloaf receipt to get minimum calories and maximum pleasure!

Prep time: 10 minutes | **Cooking time:** 35 minutes | **Servings:** 12

Ingredients:

- 8 pounds beef
- 4 tablespoons ghee
- 4 cups salsa
- 1 cup tapioca starch
- 4 teaspoons cumin
- 4 eggs
- 4 teaspoons garlic powder
- 4 onions
- 4 teaspoons chili powder
- 4 teaspoons pepper
- 4 teaspoons paprika
- 4 teaspoons sea salt
- 4 teaspoons onion powder
- 1 tablespoon creams

Directions:

1. Mix onion powder, sea salt, paprika, pepper, chili powder, garlic powder, chopped onion, cumin, starch and salsa. Add creams to the seasoning mix. Pour water over the seasoning. Use blender to mix ingredients.
2. Use blender to get tender sauce.
3. Place ghee in the pressure cooker.
4. Melt ghee on "Sauté" regime for 3 minutes.
5. Place beef in the Instant Pot.
6. Mix sauce with beaten egg and add to the meat.
7. Cook meat in the Instant Pot for 35 minutes on "Stew" regime.
8. Let the pressure release naturally (10 minutes).

Nutrition:

- Calories: 189
- Fat: 5g
- Carbohydrates: 22g
- Protein: 14g

Nightshade Ropa Vieja

Try Mediterranean receipt to get maximum pleasure, tender taste and try really soft meat with satisfying herbs!

Prep time: 10 minutes | **Cooking time:** 35 minutes | **Servings:** 4

Ingredients:

- 2 tablespoons avocado oil
- ½ cup olives
- 1 onion
- ½ lime juice
- 2 tablespoons garlic
- 1 bay leaf
- 2 teaspoons cumin
- 2lbs beef
- 1 teaspoon sea salt
- 1 teaspoon fish sauce
- ½ teaspoon pepper
- ¼ cup apple juice
- ¼ teaspoon turmeric
- ¼ cup coconut aminos

Directions:

1. Pour oil in the Instant Pot.
2. Mix chopped onions with garlic and place in the Instant Pot. Cook for 4 minutes on "Sauté" regime.
3. Mix aminos, turmeric, pepper, salt, cumin, garlic with onion olives and bay leaf.
4. Mix meat with seasoning.
5. Place meat and seasoning mix in the pressure cooker.
6. Add fish sauce, apple juice to the meat.
7. Cook meat for 35 minutes on "Stew" regime.
8. Let the pressure release naturally (20 minutes).

Nutrition:

- Calories: 594
- Fat: 32g
- Carbohydrates: 27g
- Protein: 53g

FISH AND SEAFOOD

Easy Salmon

Only ten minutes and satisfying salmon is on your plate!

Prep time: 5 minutes | **Cooking time:** 5 minutes | **Servings:** 4

Ingredients:

- 3 lemons
- 4 cup green beans
- ¾ cup water
- 1 cup rice
- 4 salmon fillets
- ¼ teaspoon pepper
- 1 bunch dill
- ¼ teaspoon salt
- 1 tablespoon butter

Directions:

1. Pour water in the Instant Pot.
2. Add lemon juice in the Instant Pot.
3. Place salmon fillets in the Instant Pot.
4. Top salmon with dill and lemon.
5. Add remaining ingredients to the salmon, apart from rice.
6. Cook for 8 minutes in the Instant Pot on "High Pressure" regime.
7. Serve salmon with rice and lemon!

Nutrition:

- Calories: 180
- Fat: 11g
- Carbohydrates: 0g
- Protein:19g

Shrimp Risotto

Meet Asia with satisfying shrimp and fresh vegetables will be both perfect appetizer and great lunch idea!

Prep time: 10 minutes | **Cooking time:** 10 minutes | **Servings:** 9

Ingredients:

- 9 tablespoons butter
- 3 ¼ cup parsley
- Onion
- 2 cups milk
- ½ cup creams
- 3 ¼ cup fisiago cheese
- 8 garlic cloves
- 2 pounds shrimp
- 4 ½ cup fibiago rice
- Salt to taste
- Pepper to taste
- 5 tablespoons white wine
- 6 ½ cups stock

Directions:

1. Place butter in the Instant Pot and make it melty.
2. Wash and chop onion and garlic. Place onion slices in the Instant Pot and cook until it turns gold.
3. Add rice and cook for 2 minutes on "High Pressure" regime.
4. Pour white wine, milk and creams on the rice and cook for 2 minutes more on "Saute" regime.
5. Add seasoning and stock to the Instant Pot and cook for 10 minutes on "High Pressure" regime.
6. Place herbs, cheese and shrimps in the Instant Pot.
7. Cook shrimps for 7 minutes on the same regime.
8. Serve risotto hot with herbs!

Nutrition:

- Calories: 560
- Fat: 19g
- Carbohydrates: 56g
- Protein:26g

Country Shrimp Boil

Boil with seafood will not only give you energy for the full day, but give you all the necessary vitamins!

Prep time: 5 minutes | **Cooking time:** 10 minutes | **Servings:** 3

Ingredients:
- 1lbs potatoes
- Cajun seasoning to taste
- 3 ears of corn
- Water
- 2 tablespoons Old Bay seasoning
- 1 1/2 lbs fresh shrimps
- ½ teaspoon salt
- 1lb cooked sausage

Directions:
1. Wash and cube potatoes.
2. Pour water in the Instant Pot.
3. Place potatoes and corn with seasoning, herbs in the Instant Pot.
4. Cook water with seasoning for 5 minutes on "High Pressure" regime.
5. Place sausages and shrimps in the Instant Pot.
6. Cook ingredients for 5 minutes on "High Pressure" regime.
7. Serve in bowl hot!

Nutrition:
- Calories: 207
- Fat: 5g
- Carbohydrates: 33g
- Protein:21g

Shrimp Paella

Try Portugal national dish – paella is super heathy and extra satisfying!

Prep time: 5 minutes | **Cooking time:** 5 minutes | **Servings:** 4

Ingredients:
- 1 pound shrimps
- Lemon juice
- 1 cup rice
- Chopped parsley
- ¼ cup butter
- Parmesan to serve
- 1 teaspoon salt
- Butter to taste
- ¼ teaspoon pepper
- 4 garlic cloves
- 1 pinch pepper
- 1 ½ cup water
- 1 lemon
- 1 pinch saffron

Directions:
1. Mix lemon juice, rice, parsley, butter, parmesan, salt, pepper, garlic cloves, pepper, lemon and saffron.
2. Place shrimps on top of the ingredient mix.
3. Cook paella in Instant Pot for 5 minutes on "High Pressure" regime.
4. Remove shrimps after the cooking and clean of shells.
5. Serve hot!

Nutrition:
- Calories:262
- Fat: 2g
- Carbohydrates: 41g
- Protein:19g

Shrimp with Coconut Milk

Tender and light coconut milk with satisfying shrimps – extra healthy and easy lunch!

Prep time: 10 minutes | **Cooking time:** 10 minutes | **Servings:** 4

Ingredients:
- 1 pound shrimps
- ½ can coconut milk
- 1 tablespoon ginger
- 1 teaspoon masala
- 1 tablespoon garlic
- ½ teaspoon cayenne pepper
- ½ teaspoon turmeric
- 1 teaspoon salt

Directions:
1. Mix seasoning.
2. Cover shrimps with seasoning.
3. Top shrimps with milk and masala.
4. Pour 2 cups water in the Instant Pot.
5. Place shrimps in the Instant Pot.
6. Cook on "Low Pressure" regime for 6 minutes.
7. Serve with extra milk!

Nutrition:
- Calories: 272
- Fat: 10g
- Carbohydrates: 13g
- Protein:30g

Pepper Salmon

Try fish full of vitamins baked in its own juice!

Prep time: 5 minutes | **Cooking time:** 10 minutes | **Servings:** 14

Ingredients:
- 6 ¾ cups water
- 9 carrots
- Parsley
- 8 red bell peppers
- 3 pounds salmon fillet
- 7 zucchinis
- 9 teaspoons ghee
- 3 ½ lemon
- 2 ¼ teaspoon salt
- 1 ½ teaspoon pepper

Directions:
1. Pour water in the Instant Pot.
2. Top salmon with herbs.
3. Place salmon in the Instant Pot.
4. Top salmon with ghee and lemon slices.
5. Sprinkle salt and pepper on the lemon slices. Cook fish for 4 minutes in the Instant Pot on "High Pressure" regime.
6. Wash and chop vegetables.
7. Add remaining ingredients to the Instant Pot.
8. Cook ingredients for 4 minutes in the Instant Pot on the same regime.
9. Serve cooked veggies with fresh herbs!

Nutrition:
- Calories: 410
- Fat: 9g
- Carbohydrates: 50g
- Protein:33g

Shrimp with Grits

This quick and easy receipt will become perfect addition to any lunch and dinner!

Prep time: 5 minutes | **Cooking time:** 45 minutes | **Servings:** 4

Ingredients:

- 1lb shrimp
- ¼ cup scallions
- 2 teaspoons Old Bay seasoning
- ¼ cup heavy creams
- 3 strips bacon
- ¼ teaspoon pepper
- 1/3 cup onion
- ½ teaspoon salt
- ½ cup bell pepper
- ¼ teaspoon tabasco sauce
- 1 tablespoon garlic
- ¼ cup chicken broth
- 2 tablespoons white wine
- 2 tablespoons lemon juice
- 1 ½ cups tomatoes
- ½ cup grits
- 1 tablespoon butter
- 1 cup milk
- Salt and pepper to taste
- 1 cup water

Directions:

1. Clean shrimps and cover with Old Bay seasoning.
2. Cook shrimps on "Saute" regime for 3 minutes.
3. Mix chopped onion with bell pepper and bacon. Place ingredients in the Instant Pot and cook for 3 minutes on the same regime.
4. Add garlic to the Instant Pot and cook for 2 minutes on "Saute" regime.
5. Place shrimps in the plate with white wine and leave to rest.
6. Mix tomatoes, sauce, salt, pepper and lemon juice with broth.
7. Place mixed tomatoes in the Instant Pot.
8. Mix milk with garlic, water, salt and pepper. Add grits to the mix.
9. Place milk mix in the Instant Pot and cook for 10 minutes on "High Pressure" regime.
10. Place shrimp back in the Instant Pot.
11. Cook for 10 minutes on "High Pressure" regime.
12. Top shrimps with bacon and scallions.
13. Serve with sauce!

Nutrition:

- Calories: 296
- Fat: 16g
- Carbohydrates: 21g
- Protein:17g

Crab Legs with Corn

Easy ten minutes receipt to get extra satisfying crab legs with corn!

Prep time: 5 minutes | **Cooking time:** 10 minutes | **Servings:** 1

Ingredients:

- 1 pack crab legs
- 1 corn on cob

Directions:

1. Wash and clean crab legs.
2. Break crab legs in two parts.
3. Pour water in the Instant Pot.
4. Place crab legs in the Instant Pot.
5. Top crab legs with the corn on cob.
6. Cook ingredients on "High Pressure" regime for 10 minutes.
7. Serve hot with herbs!

Nutrition:

- Calories: 370
- Fat: 5g
- Carbohydrates: 35g
- Protein:46g

Cajun Shrimp with Sausages

Perfect mix of meat and seafood – extra light and super delicious dish the same time!

Prep time: 10 minutes | **Cooking time:** 10 minutes | **Servings:** 4

Ingredients:

- ½ pounds smoked sausages
- ½ lemon
- 4 ears corn
- 1/8 teaspoon lemon pepper
- 2 red potatoes
- 5 shakes hot sauce
- 1 tablespoon Louisiana Shrimp
- ¼ teaspoons Old Bay seasoning
- Water
- 1/8 teaspoon Cajun shrimps
- ½ pounds raw shrimps
- 1 tablespoon garlic
- 6 tablespoons butter

Directions:

1. Cut sausages into slices.
2. Wash and cut potatoes.
3. Mix corn with potato slices and sausages.
4. Place corn mix in the Instant Pot.
5. Add Louisiana to the corn mix.
6. Cook corn mix in the Instant Pot for 5 minutes on "High Pressure" regime.
7. Melt butter on the frying pan.
8. Mix butter with remaining ingredients.
9. Top corn mix with sauce and serve hot!

Nutrition:

- Calories: 252
- Fat: 11g
- Carbohydrates:12g
- Protein:41g

Cajun Pasta

Tender shrimps with sausages and chicken breast – you will like the taste!

Prep time: 10 minutes | **Cooking time:** 30 minutes | **Servings:** 14

Ingredients:

- 4 pounds chicken breast
- Parsley to taste
- 2 pounds shrimp
- 2 pounds fettucine pasta
- 1 pound sausage
- 4 cups chicken broth

- 8 tablespoons Cajun Spice Blend
- 4 tomatoes
- 2 red bell peppers
- 9 tablespoons canola oil
- 2 ½ green bell pepper

- 2 ¼ teaspoon pepper
- 3 ½ onion
- 2 ½ teaspoon salt
- 3 garlic cloves

Directions:

1. Mix chopped chicken with shrimp, spices, cut sausages, chopped peppers, onion and pepper with salt and garlic.
2. Pour oil in the Instant Pot.
3. Place chopped ingredients in the Instant Pot.
4. Cook ingredients for 5 minutes on "Saute" regime.
5. Add tomatoes and stock with parsley to the mix in the Instant Pot.
6. Cook tomatoes for 3 more minutes on "High Pressure" regime.
7. Add boiled pasta to the Instant Pot and cook for 3 minutes on the same settings.
8. Serve with seasoning and herbs.

Nutrition:

- Calories: 920
- Fat: 44g

- Carbohydrates: 92g
- Protein:41g

Lobster Bisque

Light and creamy lobster soup will give you power for all the day!

Prep time: 5 minutes | **Cooking time:** 10 minutes | **Servings:** 3

Ingredients:
- 1 cup carrots
- 1 pint whipping cream
- 1 cup celery
- 4 lobster tails
- 29oz tomatoes
- 5 teaspoons paprika
- 2 shallots
- 1 teaspoon pepper
- 1 garlic clove
- 1 teaspoon dill
- 1 tablespoon butter
- 1 tablespoon Old Bay seasoning
- 32oz chicken broth

Directions:
1. Wash and mince shallots.
2. Mix butter with shallots and garlic.
3. Preheat shallots for 4 minutes on the frying pan.
4. Wash and cut tomatoes with carrots and celery.
5. Add vegetables to the Instant Pot.
6. Pour chicken broth in the Instant Pot and add herbs with spices.
7. Add remaining ingredients to the Pot.
8. Cook ingredients for 5 minutes on "High Pressure" regime.
9. Serve hot with fresh herbs!

Nutrition:
- Calories: 160
- Fat: 8g
- Carbohydrates: 5g
- Protein:5g

Alaskan Crab Legs

Crab legs with nothing odd – just boom of vitamins and minimal amount of calories!

Prep time: 5 minutes | **Cooking time:** 10 minutes | **Servings:** 14

Ingredients:
- 6 pounds crab legs
- Melted butter
- 4 cups water
- 7 ½ tablespoon salt

Directions:
1. Pour water in the Instant Pot.
2. Add salt to the Instant Pot.
3. Place crab legs in the Instant Pot.
4. Cook on "High Pressure" regime for 5 minutes.
5. Leave pressure release naturally for 5 minutes.
6. Top crab legs with melted butter.
7. Serve with fresh herbs!

Nutrition:
- Calories: 130
- Fat: 2g
- Carbohydrates: 0g
- Protein:26g

Salmon with Chili Sauce and Lime

Healthy salmon fillets with herbs and seasoning topped with chili sauce and lime slices – boom of vitamins on your plate!

Prep time: 10 minutes | **Cooking time:** 5 minutes | **Servings:** 11

Ingredients:
- 11 salmon fillets
- 2 teaspoons cumin
- 4 cups water
- 2 teaspoons paprika
- Sea salt to taste
- 5 tablespoons parsley
- Pepper to taste
- 4 tablespoons hot water
- 5 jalapeno
- 4 tablespoons olive oil
- 3 limes
- 7 tablespoons honey
- 2 garlic cloves

Directions:
1. Mix jalapeno with lime, cumin, garlic, paprika, honey, parsley, olive oil and hot water.
2. Use blender to combine all the ingredients.
3. Pour water in the Instant Pot.
4. Place salmon fillets in the Instant Pot.
5. Add sauce to the salmon fillets.
6. Cook fillets in the Instant Pot for 5 minutes on "High Pressure" regime.
7. Serve with lemon slices!

Nutrition:
- Calories: 152
- Fat: 5g
- Carbohydrates: 4g
- Protein: 22g

Shrimp Jambalaya with Hot Sauce

Hot sauces with tender seasoning and fresh herbs on the tender shrimps – receipt you will like to try anytime!

Prep time: 10 minutes | **Cooking time:** 20 minutes | **Servings:** 3

Ingredients:
- 2 tablespoons oil
- 3 tablespoons parsley
- 8 ounces sausage
- 1 cup chicken broth
- 8 ounces turkey
- 2 cup tomatoes
- 8 ounces raw shrimp
- 1 cup rice
- 1 teaspoon Creole Seasoning
- 3 celery stalks
- 2 teaspoons thyme leaves
- 1 bell pepper
- 2 dashes cayenne pepper
- 3 garlic cloves
- 1 dash tabasco sauce
- Onion
- 2 teaspoons Worcestershire sauce

Directions:
1. Mix seasoning with cayenne pepper and thyme.
1. Pour oil in the Instant Pot.
2. Place turkey and sausages with seasoning to the Instant Pot.
3. Cook meat for 3 minutes on "High Pressure" regime.
4. Add shrimps with sauces turkey, tomatoes, sausages, celery stalks, chopped onion to the Instant Pot.
5. Cook for 10 minutes on "High Pressure" regime.
6. Cook for 7 minutes on "Low Pressure" regime.
7. Serve with hot sauce!

Nutrition:
- Calories: 380
- Fat: 5g
- Carbohydrates: 9g
- Protein: 19g

Tuscan Shrimp with Alfredo Sauce

Light and healthy shrimps with sweet sauce and seasoning – perfect addition to the dinner and satisfying appetizer!

Prep time: 10 minutes | **Cooking time:** 5 minutes | **Servings:** 14

Ingredients:

- 6lbs shrimp
- 1 tablespoons sugar
- 4 jars alfredo sauce
- 7 tablespoons cayenne pepper

- 2 cups fresh spinach
- 3 ½ tablespoons onion
- 8 ½ cup tomatoes
- 4 tablespoons garlic powder

- 1 box pasta noodles
- 14 tablespoons fennel
- 5 tablespoons paprika
- 2/3 cup oregano
- 6 tablespoons salt

Directions:

1. Mix oregano, salt, paprika, fennel, garlic powder, onion, sugar and cayenne pepper.
2. Pour three cups water in the Instant Pot.
3. Add pasta to the Instant Pot.
4. Cook on "High Pressure" regime for 5 minutes.
5. Add sauce, tomatoes and shrimps with seasoning to the Instant Pot.
6. Cook ingredients for 7 minutes more on the same regime.
7. Serve with sweet sauce!

Nutrition:

- Calories: 210
- Fat: 6g

- Carbohydrates: 32g
- Protein:13g

Cajun Gumbo

Satisfying soup with tender rice and delicious seafood – perfect lunch and great dinner!

Prep time: 10 minutes | **Cooking time:** 25 minutes | **Servings:** 4

Ingredients:

- 1lb beef
- 1 cup rice
- 1lb smoked sausage
- 3 cups chicken broth
- 1lb shrimp
- Salt to taste

- Pepper to taste
- 1 jar roux
- Pinch of thyme
- 1 cups onion
- 3 teaspoons Tony Chachere seasoning

- 1 green pepper
- 2 garlic cloves
- 3 pieces celery
- 1 bag okra

Directions:

1. Mix shrimp with okra.
2. Mix remaining ingredients in the other bowl.
3. Pour two cups of water in the Instant Pot.
4. Place mix of the ingredients (without shrimp and okra) to the Instant Pot.
5. Cook mix for 15 minutes in the Instant Pot on "High Pressure" regime.
6. Add okra and shrimp.
7. Cook gumbo for 10 more minutes on the same regime.
8. Serve with fresh herbs!

Nutrition:

- Calories: 220
- Fat: 11g

- Carbohydrates: 16g
- Protein:14g

King Prawns in Instant Pot

Prawns baked in their own juice with fresh herbs and tender seasoning!

Prep time: 5 minutes | **Cooking time**: 1 minute | **Servings:** 7

Ingredients:
- 28 king prawns
- Salt to taste
- Pepper to taste
- 3 limes
- 2 teaspoons cumin
- 5 tablespoons garlic
- 1 tablespoon coriander
- 3 tablespoons coconut oil
- 2 tablespoons red Thai Curry Paste

Directions:
1. Pour water in the Instant Pot.
2. Mix garlic with lime, curry paste and coconut.
3. Top prawns with lime mix.
4. Place prawns in the Instant Pot.
5. Top prawns with salt, pepper, limes, cumin, garlic, coriander, coconut oil and paste.
6. Cook prawns on "High Pressure" for 1 minute.
7. Serve with fresh basil leaves!

Nutrition:
- Calories: 72
- Fat: 2g
- Carbohydrates: 7g
- Protein:7g

Lobster Tails in Instant Pot

The most satisfying part of lobster and the most delicious seafood – try lobster tails right now!

Prep time: 2 minutes | **Cooking time:** 5 minutes | **Servings:** 2

Ingredients:
- 1 cup water
- Sea salt to taste
- 2lbs lobster tails
- Ghee

Directions:
1. Pour water in the Instant Pot.
2. Cut lobster tails.
3. Sprinkle salt on the lobster meat.
4. Add ghee to the lobster tails.
5. Place lobster in the Instant Pot.
6. Cook on "High Pressure" for 5 minutes.
7. Serve with fresh herbs!

Nutrition:
- Calories: 90
- Fat:1g
- Carbohydrates: 0g
- Protein:19g

Caribbean Style Salmon

Enjoy Caribbean cuisine – try tender and satisfying salmon fillets!

Prep time: 5 minutes | **Cooking time:** 10 minutes | **Servings:** 4

Ingredients:

- 1 pound salmon fillets
- 1 teaspoon lime
- 1 ½ tablespoons Jerk seasoning
- 1 cup avocado
- ¼ teaspoon sea salt
- 2 tablespoons cilantro
- 2 cups rice
- 2/3 cups onion
- 15 ounces black beans
- 2 cups mango
- ¼ teaspoons pepper

Directions:

1. Coat salmon fillets with Jerk seasoning.
2. Add sea salt to the salmon fillets.
3. Pour water in the Instant Pot.
4. Mix boiled rice, beans, salt and pepper.
5. Place salmon in the Instant Pot.
6. Cook salmon for 5 minutes on "High Pressure" regime.
7. Clean and slice salmon after the cooking.
8. Mix avocado, mango, lime juice and cilantro with chopped onion.
9. Serve salmon with rice and salmon. Add avocado mix.
10. Serve!

Nutrition:

- Calories: 109
- Fat: 8g
- Carbohydrates: 10g
- Protein:2g

Parmesan Shrimp

Butten milky shrimps will be not only delicious, but also juicy after baking in Instant Pot!

Prep time: 10 minutes | **Cooking time:** 10 minutes | **Servings:** 10

Ingredients:

- 6 tablespoons butter
- Pepper to taste
- 3 pounds shrimps
- Salt to taste
- 7 garlic cloves
- 5 ½ cup parmesan
- 4 ½ teaspoons red pepper flakes
- 6 ½ cup half and half
- 3 ½ teaspoons paprika
- 8 cups water
- 12 cups carbanada

Directions:

1. Place butter in the Instant Pot. Saute for 1 minute to melt.
2. Mix garlic with pepper flakes.
3. Place garlic mix in the Instant Pot and cook for 2 minutes on "Saute" regime.
4. Mix shrimps with pepper, salt, paprika and noodles.
5. Pour water in the Instant Pot.
6. Add shrimps with seasoning to the Instant Pot.
7. Top shrimps with cheese and serve!

Nutrition:

- Calories: 480
- Fat: 14g
- Carbohydrates: 65g
- Protein:26g

High Protein Shrimp with Tomatoes

Juicy baked shrimp for the real sport lovers to get as much energy as possible!

Prep time: 10 minutes | **Cooking time:** 10 minutes | **Servings:** 4

Ingredients:
- 1 tomato
- 1 pound shrimp in shells
- ½ can coconut milk
- 1 tablespoon minced ginger
- 1 teaspoon masala
- 1 tablespoon garlic
- ½ teaspoon cayenne pepper
- ½ teaspoon turmeric
- 1 teaspoon salt

Directions:
1. Make a mix of a tomato, shrimp, milk, ginger, masala, garlic, cayenne pepper, turmeric and salt.
2. Pour oil on the frying pan.
3. Fry mix for 2 minutes on the frying pan.
4. Place shrimp mix in the Instant Pot.
5. Pour water in the Instant Pot.
6. Cook for 3 minutes on "High Pressure".
7. Serve with fresh basil leaves and toasts.

Nutrition:
- Calories: 329
- Fat: 5g
- Carbohydrates: 19g
- Protein: 47g

Alaskan Cod

Cod fish is one of the most satisfying and tender – try healthy fish with roasted tomatoes!

Prep time: 3 minutes | **Cooking time:** 5 minutes | **Servings:** 13

Ingredients:
- 10 codfish fillets
- 9 tablespoons butter
- 8 cups tomatoes
- Salt to taste
- Pepper to taste

Directions:
1. Prepare baking form for the Instant Pot.
2. Place tomatoes in the Instant Pot.
3. Pour water in the Instant Pot.
4. Top tomatoes with the codfish.
5. Add salt and pepper on top.
6. Pour butter on top of the fish.
7. Cook for 5 minutes on "High Pressure" regime.
8. Serve with rosemary!

Nutrition:
- Calories: 60
- Fat: 1g
- Carbohydrates: 0g
- Protein: 15g

Fish Au Gratin

Try really soft and tender fish in French style!

Prep time: 10 minutes | **Cooking time:** 40 minutes | **Servings:** 9

Ingredients:

- 9 tablespoons butter
- 4 pounds fish fillets
- 6 tablespoons flour
- 4 cups Cheddar cheese
- 5 ½ teaspoon salt
- 5 ½ teaspoon lemon juice
- 4 ½ tablespoon mustard
- 3 ¼ cups milk
- 4 ¼ tablespoon nutmeg

Directions:

1. Place butter in the Instant Pot. Melt it.
2. Mix flour with nutmeg, salt and mustard.
3. Add mustard mix to the Instant Pot.
4. Pour milk with lemon juice to the Instant Pot.
5. Add cheese to the Instant Pot.
6. Place fish in the Instant Pot and mix with cheesy sauce.
7. Cook fish for 40 minutes on "Low Pressure" regime.
8. Serve with fresh basil leaves!

Nutrition:

- Calories: 225
- Fat: 0g
- Carbohydrates: 9g
- Protein:7g

Beer Mussels

Enjoy sea vibes with the mussels with beer and lemon – this taste will make you fall in love with seafood!

Prep time: 5 minutes | **Cooking time:** 5 minutes | **Servings:** 13

Ingredients:

- 8 tablespoons olive oil
- 9 pounds mussels
- 8 onions
- 17oz beer
- 14oz spicy sausages
- 10 tablespoons white pepper

Directions:

1. Pour oil in the Instant Pot.
2. Mix herbs, vegetables and sausages.
3. Cook mix on "High Pressure" regime for 5 minutes.
4. Add mussels and pour beer on top.
5. Cook for 2 minutes on "High Pressure".
6. Serve with lemon slices!

Nutrition:

- Calories: 150
- Fat: 0g
- Carbohydrates: 9g
- Protein:0g

Drunken Clams

Eel sea taste – try clams in wine!

Prep time: 5 minutes | **Cooking time:** 10 minutes | **Servings:** 2

Ingredients:
- ¼ cup olive oil
- 2 tablespoons lemon juice
- 2 garlic cloves
- 3 pounds fresh clams
- ¼ cup fresh basil
- ¼ cup white wine
- 2 cups pale ale
- ½ cup chicken broth
- 1 cup water

Directions:
1. Pour oil in the Instant Pot.
2. Mix garlic with basil and place in the Instant Pot.
3. Mix water with chicken broth, lemon juice and wine.
4. Pour lemon juice mix in the Instant Pot and boil for 3 minutes on "Saute" regime.
5. Place clams with garlic cloves, clams, wine, basil, pale ale and cook on "High Pressure" regime for 5 minutes.
6. Serve with fresh herbs!

Nutrition:
- Calories: 220
- Fat: 11g
- Carbohydrates: 17g
- Protein:13g

Shrimp Stock

Easy, extra light and full of vitamins shrimp stock is easy to cook in Instant Pot!

Prep time: 5 minutes | **Cooking time:** 120 minutes | **Servings:** 3

Ingredients:
- 72oz shrimp shells
- 2 tablespoons apple cider vinegar
- 3 liters water
- 3 bay leaves
- Onion

Directions:
1. Pour water in the Instant Pot.
2. Place shells with vinegar and bay leaves with onion in the Instant Pot.
3. Cook for 120 minutes on "High Pressure" regime.
4. Leave stock in the Instant Pot and let the pressure release naturally for 10 minutes.
5. Serve stock with herbs!

Nutrition:
- Calories: 39
- Fat: 1.2g
- Carbohydrates: 7g
- Protein:1g

Mediterranean Cod

Try fish cooked in Mediterranean traditions!

Prep time: 5 minutes | **Cooking time:** 15 minutes | **Servings:** 6

Ingredients:
- 6 pieces cod
- 28oz tomatoes
- 3 tablespoons butter
- 1 teaspoon oregano
- 1 lemon
- ½ teaspoon pepper
- 1 onion
- 1 teaspoon salt

Directions:
1. Place butter in the Instant Pot and turn on "Saute" function.
2. Add cod, tomatoes, butter, oregano, lemon, pepper, chopped onion and salt to the Instant Pot.
3. Cook ingredients on "High Pressure" regime for 10 minutes.
4. Add more butter to the fish and cook on "High Pressure" for 5 more minutes.
5. Serve fish with herbs!

Nutrition:
- Calories: 150
- Fat: 1g
- Carbohydrates: 12g
- Protein:21g

San Francisco Seafood

Tender, delicious and soft shrimps with the herbs and lemon juice!

Prep time: 20 minutes | **Cooking time:** 40 minutes | **Servings:** 9

Ingredients:
- 6 loaves baguette
- 5 tablespoons parsley
- 6 tablespoons olive oil
- 3 pounds mussels
- 4 cups onion
- 5 ½ pound raw shrimp
- 8 tablespoons garlic
- 7 ½ pound raw scallions
- 3 cups leeks
- 6 ¼ teaspoon pepper
- 3 ½ cup celery
- 4 ½ teaspoon salt
- 3 ½ cup bell pepper
- 9 bay leaves
- 4 ½ cup carrots
- 8 ½ teaspoon thyme
- 10 serrano chili pepper
- 10 tablespoon lemon juice
- 2 ½ cup tomatoes
- 9 cups water
- 6 ounces tomato paste
- 3 ½ cups red wine

Directions:
1. Turn on oven and preheat up to 375oF.
2. Slice baguette and coat with olive oil and salt.
3. Bake bread for 10 minutes in the oven.
4. Pour oil in the Instant Pot.
5. Mix chopped onion, garlic, celery, leeks and carrots with bell pepper. Add serrano chili pepper and tomatoes.
6. Cook onion mix in the Instant Pot for 5 minutes on "High Pressure" regime.
7. Add wine, tomato paste, tomatoes, peppers, carrots, scallions and mussels to the Instant Pot.
8. Cook seafood for 25 minutes more on the same regime.
9. Serve with baked bread!

Nutrition:
- Calories: 210
- Fat: 11g
- Carbohydrates: 19g
- Protein:4g

Thai Salmon with Chili

Fresh basil leaves, chili sauce and tender salmon with herbs – get as many vitamins as possible!

Prep time: 15 minutes | **Cooking time:** 15 minutes | **Servings:** 14

Ingredients:
- 9lbs salmon fillet
- 11 tablespoons oil
- 9 chillis
- 7 ¾ cup chopped basil
- 11 garlic cloves
- 8 teaspoons sugar
- 9 tablespoons soy sauce
- 7 tablespoons fish sauce
- 6 tablespoons oyster sauce

Directions:
1. Turn on oven and preheat up to 392oF.
2. Mix chili with garlic. Bake for 10 minutes.
3. Mix soy sauce, oyster sauce, sugar and fish sauce.
4. Place basil with herbs and sauces with seasoning in the Instant Pot.
5. Add salmon to the Instant Pot.
6. Cook fish for 10 minutes in the Instant Pot on "High Pressure" regime.
7. Serve with herbs!

Nutrition:
- Calories: 240
- Fat: 14g
- Carbohydrates:7g
- Protein:20g

Caribbean Salmon with Salsa

Try Caribbean soft and tender receipt to get maximum vitamins and taste quickly and easy!

Prep time: 5 minutes | **Cooking time:** 5 minutes | **Servings**: 4

Ingredients:
- 1 pound salmon fillet
- 1 teaspoon lime juice
- 1 ½ tablespoon seasoning
- 1 cup avocado
- 2 cups jasmine rice
- 2 tablespoons cilantro
- 15 ounces black beans
- 2/3 cups onion
- ¼ teaspoon sea salt
- 2 cups mango
- ¼ teaspoon pepper

Directions:
1. Cover salmon with seasoning and pepper. Add sea salt.
2. Pour water in the pressure cooker.
3. Place salmon in the Instant Pot.
4. Add rice, beans and lime juice.
5. Mix chopped onion, mango and cilantro with avocado. Set aside.
6. Cook salmon with rice for 5 minutes on "High Pressure" regime.
7. Let the pressure release naturally (10 minutes).
8. Serve with mango mix.

Nutrition:
- Calories: 221
- Fat: 10g
- Carbohydrates: 9g
- Protein: 24g

Lobster Stew

Try something ultra healthy and super exotic – for example, lobster stew!

Prep time: 20 minutes | **Cooking time:** 50 minutes | **Servings:** 5

Ingredients:

- 5 Maine lobsters
- 2 springs parsley
- Salt to taste
- ½ teaspoon lemon juice
- 12 tablespoons butter
- Pepper to taste
- 1 cup sherry
- 2 pinches paprika
- 5 cups milk
- 1 inch cayenne
- 2 cups creams

Directions:

1. Pour water in the Instant Pot.
2. Add salt to some water in the Instant Pot.
3. Place lobsters in the pressure cooker and cook for 5 minutes on "High Pressure" regime.
4. Separate cooked lobsters and divide tails with bodies.
5. Clean lobsters of the shells.
6. Place butter in the empty and dried Instant Pot.
7. Melt butter for 3 minutes on "Sauté" regime.
8. Add lobster bodies and shells to the pressure cooker.
9. Add sherry, salt, pepper and parsley.
10. Add cayenne, milk, lemon juice and creams.
11. Cook lobsters for 25 minutes on "High Pressure" regime.
12. Let the pressure release naturally (10 minutes).
13. Separate mix in bowls and serve!

Nutrition:

- Calories: 280
- Fat: 21g
- Carbohydrates: 14g
- Protein: 10g

Shrimp Po Boy Roll

Easy and satisfying shrimp rolls will be both perfect lunch and delicious appetizer!

Prep time: 15 minutes | **Cooking time:** 2 minutes | **Servings:** 2

Ingredients:

- 1 pound shrimps
- Fresh lemon to serve
- ½ cup Remoulade sauce
- Tomatoes to serve
- 2 stalks celery
- Lettuce to serve
- 2 tablespoons dill pickles
- ½ teaspoon sea salt
- 1 tablespoon pepper

Directions:

1. Pour water in the Instant Pot.
2. Wash shrimps and cut off heads.
3. Place shrimps in the Instant Pot.
4. Cook on "Steam" regime for 1 minute.
5. Do a quick release.
6. Mix sea salt, pepper and cover shrimps. Place shrimps in the fridge.
7. Mix washed and cubed tomato with lemon, celery and lettuce.
8. Mix sauce with dill.
9. Coat shrimps with sauce. Mix with the cubed vegetables.
10. Serve with buns!

Nutrition:

- Calories: 420
- Fat: 27g
- Carbohydrates: 46g
- Protein: 12g

Seafood Boil

The greatest source of vitamins ever for you in one bowl!

Prep time: 10 minutes | **Cooking time:** 5 minutes | **Servings:** 4

Ingredients:
- 3 cups red potatoes
- 1lb shrimp
- 6 corns on cob
- 1 1/2 lb snow crab clusters

Directions:
1. Wash and peel potatoes.
2. Clean corn on cob of the leaves.
3. Cube potatoes.
4. Cut cobs on slices.
5. Wash and clean shrimps of the shells and heads.
6. Clean and wash crab meat.
7. Pour water in the pressure cooker.
8. Place all the potatoes, crab meat, shrimps and corns on cod in the Instant Pot.
9. Cook for 15 minutes on "High Pressure" regime.
10. Let the pressure release naturally (10 minutes).
11. Serve in boils!

Nutrition:
- Calories: 110
- Fat: 2g
- Carbohydrates: 0g
- Protein: 22g

Risotto with Lobster

Try satisfying rice with easy sauce and delicious, tender lobster meat!

Prep time: 15 minutes | **Cooking time:** 10 minutes | **Servings:** 9

Ingredients:
- 6 tablespoons olive oil
- Salt to taste
- Pepper to taste
- 3 tablespoons butter
- 1 cup parmesan cheese
- 6 cups risotto rice
- 9 tablespoons creams
- 9 1/2 cups water
- 12ounces mushrooms
- 3 shallots
- 3 green onions
- 6 garlic cloves

Directions:
1. Wash and chop onion carefully. You should get cup with small onion slices. Remove skin carefully and make super small onion slices.
2. Mix half of butter with oil. Pour oil in the Instant Pot. It will take you 3 minutes to warm up butter. Cook butter on "Sauté" regime.
3. Place onion with garlic in the Instant Pot. Cook for 4 minutes on "Sauté" regime.
4. Add salt, pepper, slices mushrooms, chopped shallot, rice and mix well in the Instant Pot.
5. Pour water in the Instant Pot.
6. Cook for on "High Pressure" regime. It will take you around 3 minutes. The same time place reminded butter in a cup and warm up in microwave.
7. Add creams, cheese and reminded hot butter to the pressure cooker.
8. Cook for 5 minutes on "High Pressure" regime.
9. Let the pressure release naturally (10 minutes).

Nutrition:
- Calories: 339
- Fat: 8g
- Carbohydrates: 43g
- Protein: 22g

Red Lobster Alfredo

Try extraordinary variant of chicken Alfredo with satisfying lobster full of vitamins!

Prep time: 5 minutes | **Cooking time:** 5 minutes | **Servings:** 2

Ingredients:
- 1 pound chicken
- 8oz parmesan cheese
- 1 garlic clove
- 16oz fettucine pasta
- ½ cup breadcrumbs
- 1 cup heavy creams
- 1 tablespoons Cajun seasoning
- 2 tablespoons butter
- 1 egg

Directions:
1. Wash and cube chicken meat.
2. Place butter in the Instant Pot and melt up for 3 minutes on "Sauté" regime.
3. Add chicken to the Instant Pot and mix with pasta.
4. Add garlic, beaten egg, seasoning, creams and cheese. Mix well.
5. Cook chicken meat for 5 minutes on "High Pressure" regime.
6. Let the pressure release naturally (10 minutes).
7. Serve hot!

Nutrition:
- Calories: 560
- Fat: 25g
- Carbohydrates: 47g
- Protein: 0g

Lobster Mac and Cheese

What a delicious mix it is! Just try satisfying and tender lobster with soft cheese and fresh mac!

Prep time: 10 minutes | **Cooking time:** 10 minutes | **Servings:** 3

Ingredients:
- 2 lobster tails
- Pinch of parmesan
- 8oz cavatappi
- 1 tablespoon butter
- 2 cups water
- 1 garlic clove
- 1 teaspoon salt
- 1.4oz bacon
- 1 teaspoon dry mustard
- 1 cup breadcrumbs
- ½ teaspoon chili flake
- Pepper to taste
- ¾ cup milk
- 7oz cheddar cheese

Directions:
1. Pour water in the Instant Pot.
2. Wash and clean lobster.
3. Place lobster in the Instant Pot and cook for 3 minutes on "High Pressure" regime.
4. Clean lobster.
5. Mix bacon, garlic and butter. Cover bacon with breadcrumbs. Add Parmesan.
6. Cook bacon for 5 minutes on "High Pressure" regime.
7. Add pasta, water, salt, mustard, chili flake, milk and cheddar to the pressure cooker. Cook for 5 minutes on "High Pressure" regime.
8. Let the pressure release naturally (10 minutes).
9. Serve!

Nutrition:
- Calories: 540
- Fat: 31g
- Carbohydrates: 37g
- Protein: 29g

Steamed Full Lobster with Beer

Try full big lobster with beer for the lunch today and get as many vitamins as possible!

Prep time: 4 minutes | **Cooking time**: 5 minutes | **Servings**: 1

Ingredients:
- 3 cups water
- 1 lobster
- 1 cup beer

Directions:
1. Pour water in the Instant Pot.
2. Place lobster in the pressure cooker. Add beer over the lobster.
3. Cook lobster for 5 minutes on "High Pressure" regime.
4. Do a quick release.
5. Remove lobster and serve with lemon slices.

Nutrition:
- Calories: 215
- Fat: 18g
- Carbohydrates: 1g
- Protein: 13g

Crab Salad

Super light, satisfying and easy salad for the lunch will be juicy and full of vitamins!

Prep time: 5 minutes | **Cooking time**: 5 minutes | **Servings**: 4

Ingredients:
- 1 pound crab meat
- ¼ teaspoon pepper
- 1 shallot
- ¼ teaspoon salt
- ½ cup mayonnaise
- ½ teaspoon dill
- ½ cup celery
- ½ teaspoon paprika

Directions:
1. Mix paprika, celery, dill and pepper.
2. Wash crab meat and place in the Instant Pot.
3. Add seasoning over the meat.
4. Add chopped shallot.
5. Cook crab for 5 minutes on "High Pressure" regime.
6. Chop crab meat and mix with mayonnaise!
7. Serve with toasts!

Nutrition:
- Calories: 350
- Fat: 2g
- Carbohydrates: 30g
- Protein: 16g

Japanese Seafood Curry

Easy, satisfying, juicy and healthy seafood set will be your private source of vitamins today!

Prep time: 20 minutes | **Cooking time:** 15 minutes | **Servings:** 4

Ingredients:
- 12 manila clams
- Japanese rice cooked
- Sea salt to taste
- ¼ apple
- 3 cups water
- 1 tablespoon soy sauce
- 3 onions
- 1 pack curry roux
- 6 mushrooms
- ¼ cup white wine
- 2 garlic cloves
- 6oz calamari
- 1 inch ginger
- 6oz scallop
- 6oz shrimp
- 1 tablespoon oil

Directions:
1. Pour water with salt over the mussels and leave mussels for 1 hour.
2. Pour oil in the Instant Pot.
3. Place cleaned shrimp in the Instant Pot.
4. Cook on "Sauté" regime for 1 minute.
5. Place scallop, ginger, cut calamari, garlic cloves, sliced mushrooms, curry, chopped onions, rice, manilla and apple in the pressure cooker.
6. Pout wine and soy sauce over the ingredients in the Instant Pot.
7. Cook for 15 minutes on "High Pressure".
8. Let the pressure release naturally (10 minutes).
9. Serve!

Nutrition:
- Calories: 110
- Fat: 5g
- Carbohydrates: 16g
- Protein: 0g

Old Bay Fish Tacos

Try satisfying, easy to cook, tender and crispy fish tacos with sweet sauce!

Prep time: 15 minutes | **Cooking time:** 10 minutes | **Servings:** 7

Ingredients:
- 2 cod fillets
- ½ cup cheese
- 1 tablespoon Old Bay seasoning
- 7 corn tortillas
- 2 tablespoons oil

Directions:
1. Pour oil in the Instant Pot.
2. Place cod fillets with seasoning in the Instant Pot.
3. Cook on "Sauté" regime for 2 minutes.
4. Change regime on "High Pressure" and cook for 8 minutes more.
5. Let the pressure release naturally (10 minutes).
6. Place fish on tortillas and cover with cheese.
7. Serve!

Nutrition:
- Calories: 420
- Fat: 15g
- Carbohydrates: 50g
- Protein: 20g

Bang Bang Pasta with Shrimps

Satisfying Italian receipt in best Mediterranean traditions – something you need today!

Prep time: 5 minutes | **Cooking time:** 5 minutes | **Servings:** 12

Ingredients:

- 6 garlic cloves
- 1 teaspoon onion powder
- 4 teaspoons paprika
- 1 teaspoon red pepper flakes

- 6 tablespoons olive oil
- 8 tablespoons sriracha
- 12 cups water
- 1 cup chili sauce
- 2 cups mussels

- 3 pounds spaghetti
- 1 cup mayo
- 3 pounds shrimp
- 6 minced garlic cloves
- 3 teaspoons lime juice

Directions:

1. Pour oil in the Instant Pot. It will take you 3 minutes to warm up oil. Do not overcook it and don't make it bulbing in the pressure cooker.
2. Place garlic, paprika and pepper flakes in the Instant Pot.
3. Cook seasoning for 1 minute on "Sauté" regime.
4. Place pasta in the Instant Pot. Place mussels over the pasta. Pour some water over mussels and pasta.
5. Pour water in the Instant Pot.
6. Add shrimp, lime juice, mayo, chili sauce, sriracha and onion powder with minced garlic to the Instant Pot.
7. Cook for 5 minutes on "High Pressure" regime.
8. Do a quick release.
9. Serve hot with fresh herbs!

Nutrition:

- Calories: 294
- Fat: 11g

- Carbohydrates: 29g
- Protein: 20g

Easy Juicy Salmon

Find out how to cook salmon only in few minutes! The easiest fish receipt is up to you!

Prep time: 5 minutes | **Cooking time:** 5 minutes | **Servings:** 2

Ingredients:

- 2 skins salmon fillets
- ½ broccoli head

- 1 lemon

- 2 teaspoons chipotle paste

Directions:

1. Wash and slice salmon filets.
2. Make juice of the lemon.
3. Place salmon in the Instant Pot.
4. Cover salmon with lemon juice.
5. Add chopped broccoli to the Instant Pot.
6. Add paste to the Instant Pot.
7. Cook on "Steam" regime for 5 minutes.
8. Do a quick release.
9. Serve with lemon slices!

Nutrition:

- Calories: 42
- Fat: 1g

- Carbohydrates: 8g
- Protein: 1g

Salmon and Spinach Pesto Pasta

Enjoy best Italian traditions with juicy and easy to cook recipes!

Prep time: 5 minutes | **Cooking time:** 5 minutes | **Servings:** 3

Ingredients:

- 16ounces pasta
- 1 cup heavy creams
- 4 cups water
- 1 tablespoon lemon zest
- 12 ounces salmon
- Salt to taste
- Pepper to taste
- 1 lemon
- 1 cup Parmesan
- 1 teaspoon lemon juice
- 1/3 cup olive oil
- ¼ cup walnuts
- 2 garlic cloves
- ½ pound baby spinach

Directions:

1. Wash spinach.
2. Mix spinach with garlic cloves, lemon zest, creams, parmesan cheese, salt, pepper, olive oil and blend well.
3. Add walnuts to some sauce and mix well one more time.
4. Pour water in the Instant Pot.
5. Place pasta in the Instant Pot.
6. Add sauce to pasta and top with salmon, lemon zest.
7. Cook pasta for 5 minutes on "High Pressure" regime.
8. Let the pressure release naturally (5 minutes).
9. Serve hot!

Nutrition:

- Calories: 637
- Fat: 23g
- Carbohydrates: 76g
- Protein: 26g

Mediterranean Rosemary Salmon

Enjoy juicy and delicious fish receipts right now – add more bright colors to the grey weekdays!

Prep time: 5 minutes | **Cooking time:** 5 minutes | **Servings:** 3

Ingredients:

- 1lb salmon
- Salt to taste
- Pepper to taste
- 10oz asparagus
- 1 lemon
- 1 spring rosemary
- 2 tablespoons olive oil
- ½ cup cherry tomatoes

Directions:

1. Wash and cut salmon on slices.
2. Wash and halve cherry tomatoes.
3. Pour olive oil in the Instant Pot.
4. Place salmon in the pressure cooker.
5. Cover salmon with salt, pepper and rosemary. Add lemon juice to the fish.
6. Add asparagus to the fish fillet.
7. Place cherry tomatoes in the Instant Pot.
8. Cook fish with vegetables for 5 minutes on "High Pressure" regime.
9. Let the pressure release naturally (10 minutes).
10. Serve with fresh herbs!

Nutrition:

- Calories: 110
- Fat: 3g
- Carbohydrates: 18g
- Protein: 4g

Fish Chowder with Cod

Try creamy, light and full of vitamins soup with milk and codfish fillets!

Prep time: 10 minutes | **Cooking time:** 25 minutes | **Servings:** 12

Ingredients:

- 4 tablespoons butter
- 10 slices bacon
- 2 cups onion
- 2 cups milk
- 1 mushrooms
- 2 cups flour
- 6 cups cubed potatoes
- 2 cups clam juice
- 8 cups chicken broth
- Salt to taste
- Pepper to taste
- 4lbs cod
- 2 teaspoons Old Bay seasoning
- 2 tablespoons heavy creams
- Lemon slices to serve

Directions:

1. Pour water in the Instant Pot. Add creams to the pressure cooker. Mix well water with creams in the Instant Pot to get milky base for cooking. The same time wash lemon and cut on slices. Set aside.
2. Wash cod fillets and place in the Instant Pot. Cook fillets in the Instant Pot for 9 minutes.
3. Remove fillets from the pressure cooker.
4. Place butter in the Instant Pot and add onion, mushrooms, pepper, salt and potatoes. Cook for 4 minutes on "Sauté" regime.
5. Add chicken broth and cook for 10 minutes on "High Pressure" regime.
6. Add Old Bay seasoning and cod to some soup.
7. Mix flour with juice and use blender to get tender mixture.
8. Pour flour mixture in soup and mix well.
9. Add milk and cook for 4 minutes on "Soup" regime. Place lemon slices on chowder.

Nutrition:

- Calories: 206
- Fat: 3g
- Carbohydrates: 0g
- Protein: 18g

Mussels Fra Diavolo

Try really healthy and hot Spanish receipt right now!

Prep time: 10 minutes | **Cooking time:** 5 minutes | **Servings:** 3

Ingredients:

- 28oz tomatoes
- 1 lemon
- 2 jalapeno peppers
- Sea salt to taste
- ½ cup white onion
- ½ cup basil
- ¼ cup white wine
- 2 pounds mussels
- ¼ cup vinegar
- 2 garlic cloves
- ¼ cup olive oil
- 2 tablespoons pepper flakes

Directions:

1. Wash and cut tomatoes.
2. Mix tomatoes with chopped jalapeno peppers, chopped onion, red pepper flakes and garlic.
3. Place tomato mix in the pressure cooker.
4. Add wine, olive oil and vinegar to the Instant Pot.
5. Add mussels to the mix.
6. Cook mussels on "High Pressure" for 5 minutes. Add basil, salt and pepper.

Nutrition:

- Calories: 375
- Fat: 4g
- Carbohydrates: 63g
- Protein: 19g

Shrimp Biryani

Add Portuguese vibes to your life! Try easy and full of vitamins biryani!

Prep time: 20 minutes | **Cooking time:** 10 minute | **Servings:** 3

Ingredients:

- 1 cup basmati rice
- 2 red onion
- 2 tablespoons ghee
- 1 tablespoon raw cashews
- 1 tablespoon golden raisins
- 4 cardamom pods
- 1 tomato
- 3 whole cloves
- 20 curry leaves
- 1 cinnamon
- 1 serrano pepper
- ½ teaspoon cumin seeds
- 2 teaspoon ginger
- 2 teaspoon minced garlic
- 1 teaspoon garam masala
- 1 pound shrimps
- 1 teaspoon paprika
- 1 cup water
- 1 teaspoon salt
- ½ teaspoon turmeric
- ½ teaspoon pepper

Directions:

1. Place ghee in the Instant Pot.
2. Melt ghee on "Sauté" regime for 4 minutes.
3. Add raisins and chopped onion with cashews to the pressure cooker. Cook for 6 minutes on "High Pressure" regime.
4. Add basmati rice to the Instant Pot.
5. In a separate bowl mix cubed tomato, curry leaves, pepper, ginger, minced garlic, cumin seeds, cinnamon, whole cloves and pods. Use blender to get tender sauce.
6. Pour sauce over the rice in the pressure cooker. Cook rice for 5 minutes on "High Pressure" regime.
7. Mix garam masala, paprika, salt, pepper, turmeric and water. Add shrimps and mix well. Add shrimps with seasoning to the Instant Pot. 8. Cook rice for 8 minutes on "High Pressure" regime.
8. Let the pressure release naturally (10 minutes).
9. Serve!

Nutrition:

- Calories: 393
- Fat: 22g
- Carbohydrates: 45g
- Protein: 9g

Spaghetti Mussels with Basil

Try Mediterranean cuisine, and enjoy energy full and tender dishes!

Prep time: 25 minutes | **Cooking time:** 15 minutes | **Servings:** 10

Ingredients:

- Salt to taste
- Pepper to taste
- 18oz spaghetti
- 5 tablespoon olive oil
- 9 tablespoons oil

- 3 cups basil
- 5 shallots
- 2 lbs tomatoes
- 4 teaspoons red pepper flakes

- 4 teaspoons lemon zest
- 4lbs mussels
- 2 cups white wine
- 1 teaspoon sea salt
- 1/8 teaspoon vinegar

Directions:

1. Mix basil with salt and pepper. Add red pepper flakes and lemon zest to the mix.
2. Pour olive oil in the pressure cooker.
3. Add pasta, tomatoes, cut shallot, seasoning to the Instant Pot. Add sea salt. Sprinkle ingredients with vinegar.
4. Cook for 11 minutes on "High Pressure" regime.
5. Pour wine over the pasta and add mussels. Mix well to cover mussels.
6. Cook mussels for 5 minutes on "High Pressure" regime.
7. Let the pressure release naturally (5 minutes).
8. Serve hot!

Nutrition:

- Calories: 535
- Fat: 2g

- Carbohydrates: 82g
- Protein: 38g

Cheesy Tuna Helper

Satisfying sauce with cheese for the fish and any seafood dishes to make your day bright!

Prep time: 5 minutes | **Cooking time:** 5 minutes | **Servings:** 2

Ingredients:

- 1 can tuna
- 3 cups water
- 16oz egg noodles
- ¼ cup panko
- 1 cup peas
- 4oz cheddar cheese
- 28oz mushrooms

Directions:

1. Wash and cut mushrooms.
2. Pour water in the pressure cooker.
3. Place pasta in the Instant Pot.
4. Add tuna with peas to the pasta.
5. Cook for 5 minutes on "High Pressure" regime.
6. Do a quick release.
7. Add cheese with panko and noodles.
8. Cook for 5 minutes on "Sauté" regime.

Nutrition:

- Calories: 270
- Fat: 12g
- Carbohydrates: 26g
- Protein: 14g

Mussels with Butter Garlic Lemongrass Toast

Try real mussels with toast and fresh herbs – enjoy Mediterranean cuisine and get as much vitamins as possible!

Prep time: 10 minutes | **Cooking time:** 15 minutes | **Servings:** 3

Ingredients:

- 2 ½ pounds mussels
- Fresh lime
- 4 tablespoons butter
- 14 cup basil
- ¼ cup curry paste
- Salt to taste
- Pepper to taste
- 1 can coconut milk
- ½ cup white wine
- 4 tablespoons salted butter
- 1 baguette in slices
- 1 tablespoon lemongrass
- ¼ cup basil
- 2 garlic cloves

Directions:

1. Place butter in the Instant Pot. Melt butter for 3 minutes on "Sauté" regime.
2. Place curry in the Instant Pot. Cook for 1 minute on "Sauté" regime.
3. Mix milk, pepper, salt, wine and pace in the Instant Pot. Cook for 4 minutes on "Sauté" regime.
4. Add mussels to the pressure cooker.
5. Cook for 5 minutes on "High Pressure" regime.
6. Add basil and let the pressure release naturally (10 minutes).
7. Turn on oven and preheat up to 400oF.
8. Mix butter. Lemongrass, garlic, basil, salt and place on toast.
9. Place toast in the oven and cook for 10 minutes.
10. Serve toast with mussels.

Nutrition:

- Calories: 156
- Fat: 9g
- Carbohydrates: 11g
- Protein: 9g

Panko Shrimp

Try crispy, juicy and tender seafood right now!

Prep time: 10 minutes | **Cooking time:** 20 minutes | **Servings:** 4

Ingredients:
- 1 pound shrimp
- Salt to taste
- Pepper to tast
- 1 egg white
- Seasoning to taste
- ½ cup flour
- 1 teaspoon paprika
- ¾ cup crumbs
- 1/3 cup yogurt
- ¼ cup sweet chili sauce
- 2 tablespoons sriracha

Directions:
1. Wash and clean srinps of skins.
2. Cover shrimps with salt, pepper, seasoning and paprika. Leave shrimps to rest.
3. Mix chili sauce with siracha and yogurt. Use blender to get tender sauce. Pour sauce in a cup and set aside.
4. Coat shrimps with flour.
5. Coat shrimps with egg.
6. Coat shrimps with panko.
7. Place shrimps in the Instant Pot and cook for 10 minutes on "High Pressure" regime. Do a quick release. Place shrimps on the oven preheated up to 400oF.Bake for 6 minutes.
8. Serve hot!

Nutrition:
- Calories: 444
- Fat: 13g
- Carbohydrates: 3g
- Protein: 43g

Crab Dip

Perfect appetizer, great addition to the dinner table and delicious light lunch for those who care about the health!

Prep time: 5 minutes | **Cooking time:** 5 minutes | **Servings:** 3

Ingredients:
- 3 packs cream cheese
- Salt to taste
- 3.4 cup mayo
- 1 teaspoon parsley
- 2 packs crab meat
- 1 teaspoon mustard
- ¼ cup white wine
- ¼ cup parmesan cheese

Directions:
1. Mix parmesan with mustard, mayo and salt. Add cream cheese.
2. Place minced crab meat and add white wine with creamy sauce. Add parsley and cheese to the mix.
3. Place crab meat in the Instant Pot and cook for 5 minutes on "High Pressure" regime.
4. Do a quick pressure.
5. Serve cold!

Nutrition:
- Calories: 70
- Fat: 5g
- Carbohydrates: 4g
- Protein: 1g

Mussels with Apple Cider

Try new variant of drunken mussels and get more tender taste!

Prep time: 10 minutes | **Cooking time:** 10 minutes | **Servings:** 3

Ingredients:
- 2 pounds mussels
- Parsley to taste
- 1 tablespoon coconut oil
- 1 tablespoon apple vinegar
- 2 shallots
- 1 cup apple cider
- 1 garlic clove

Directions:
1. Mix garlic with parsley.
2. Pour oil in the Instant Pot.
3. Add mussels.
4. Pour apple vinegar over the mussels.
5. Add garlic and parsley to the Instant Pot.
6. Add shallots to the Instant Pot.
7. Add apple cider to the pressure cooker.
8. Cook for 3 minutes on "High Pressure" regime.
9. Let the pressure release naturally (10 minutes).
10. Serve!

Nutrition:
- Calories: 361
- Fat: 10g
- Carbohydrates: 13g
- Protein: 40g

Zucchini Soup with Jumbo Crab

Extra easy, light and healthy soup with crab for you right today!

Prep time: 10 minutes | **Cooking time:** 25 minutes | **Servings:** 3

Ingredients:
- ½ onion
- Pepper to taste
- 2 garlic cloves
- 2 tablespoon yogurt
- 3 zucchini
- 32oz chicken broth

Directions:
1. Chop onion.
2. Place onion with garlic in the Instant Pot and cook on "Sauté" regime for 4 minutes.
3. Pour broth in the pressure cooker and add pepper with chopped zucchini.
4. Cook for 5 minutes on "High Pressure" regime.
5. Add yogurt and cook or 3 minutes more on "Sauté" regime.
6. Let the pressure release naturally (10 minutes).
7. Serve with fresh herbs!

Nutrition:
- Calories: 460
- Fat: 15g
- Carbohydrates: 0g
- Protein: 10g

Paella with Mussels and Shrimps

Super healthy and extra satisfying paella with seafood is something you need right now – trust us!

Prep time: 5 minutes | **Cooking time:** 40 minutes | **Servings:** 12

Ingredients:

- 1 onion
- 1 teaspoon thyme
- 1 cup bell pepper
- 3 cups chicken broth
- 6 garlic cloves
- 6 cups rice
- 1 teaspoon salt
- 12 lemon wedges
- 1 cup heavy creams
- 1 teaspoon pepper
- 3 pounds mussels
- 1 pound calamari
- 3 pinches saffron
- 3 cups peas
- 3 pounds shrimp

Directions:

1. Mix thyme, pepper, garlic, onion, bell pepper, saffron and peas. Add creams to seasoning mix and mix using blender one more time.
2. Place saffron mix in the Instant Pot and cook for 4 minutes on "Sauté" regime.
3. Add salt, rice and broth. Add calamari cut on slices. Cook for 30 minutes on "High Pressure" regime.
4. Add shrimps and mussels to the mix and cook for 10 minutes on "High Pressure" regime.
5. Let the pressure release naturally (10 minutes).

Nutrition:

- Calories: 558
- Fat: 5g
- Carbohydrates: 62g
- Protein: 62g

Mussel Chowder

Easy, satisfying and delicious receipt for the whole family today!

Prep time: 5 minutes | **Cooking time:** 15 minutes | **Servings:** 4

Ingredients:

- 2 tablespoons butter
- 2 tablespoons parsley
- 1 onion
- 1 cup heavy creams
- 2 celery stals
- 2 pounds mussels
- 1 teaspoon thyme
- 1 cups water
- 3 tomatoes
- ½ cup wine
- 3 potatoes
- 1 clam juice cup
- 1 cup corn

Directions:

1. Melt butter in the Instant Pot (4 minutes on "Sauté" regime).
2. Place chopped onion, thyme, pepper and salt to the Instant Pot.
3. Cook for 5 minutes on "Sauté" regime.
4. Wash and chop potatoes with tomatoes and corn.
5. Place vegetables in the pressure cooker.
6. Add wine, juice and water to the Instant Pot.
7. Cook for 15 minutes on "High Pressure" regime.
8. Add creams with mussels to the pressure cooker.
9. Cook for 3 minutes on "Soup" regime.
10. Do a quick release.
11. Serve hot!

Nutrition:

- Calories: 524
- Fat: 27g
- Carbohydrates: 27g
- Protein: 41g

Shrimp and Crab Bisque

Try super healthy bisque with crab meat – this variant you will like more!

Prep time: 15 minutes | **Cooking time:** 2 hours | **Servings:** 16

Ingredients:

- 2 tablespoons olive oil
- 4 tablespoons parsley
- 4 tablespoons butter
- 2 cups crab
- 6 leeks
- 2lbs shrimp
- 8 garlic cloves
- 2 cups cream

- Pinch of pepper flakes
- 1 cup flour
- 4 tablespoons tomato paste
- 2 teaspoons pepper
- 8 cups fish stock
- 4 teaspoons pepper
- 4 cups water

- 2 tablespoons sugar
- 2 cans tomatoes
- 1 tablespoon hot sauce
- 1 cup green onions
- 1 cup cherry tomatoes
- 2 teaspoons Old Bay seasoning

Directions:

1. Place butter and oil in the Instant Pot.
2. Cook on "Sauté" regime to warm up. It will take you around 3 minutes just to warm up butter and not to bring it to boil. Add green onions, hot sauce and halves cherry tomatoes to the Instant Pot. Mix ingredients well.
3. Add leeks with garlic and salt.
4. Add pepper flakes and sauté seasoning in the pressure cooker. Wait until ingredients will turn golden color. It will take you 5 minutes.
5. Add tomato paste, water, stock, seasoning, tomatoes and sugar to the Instant Pot.
6. Add sherry with flour and cook for 2 hours on "High Pressure" regime.
7. Add shrimps, creams, parsley, crab and cook for 15 minutes on "High Pressure" regime.
8. Do a quick release and serve hot!

Nutrition:

- Calories: 327
- Fat: 18g

- Carbohydrates: 9g
- Protein: 26g

Oysters with Mussels

Try juicy and tender seafood canapes for the lunch today!

Prep time: 10 minutes | **Cooking time:** 25 minutes | **Servings:** 4

Ingredients:

- 5oz butter
- 1 teaspoon herbs
- 12 garlic cloves
- Pinch of cayenne
- 1 cup wine
- Salt to taste
- Pepper to taste
- 1 teaspoon vinegar
- 2 tablespoons creams
- 5 cooked mussels

Directions:

1. Place butter in the Instant Pot.
2. Melt up butter for 3 minutes on "Sauté" regime.
3. Mix pepper, herbs and salt with garlic cloves.
4. Place garlic mix in the pressure cooker.
5. Cook for 5 minutes on "Sauté" regime.
6. Add wine, cayenne, vinegar and creams to the Instant Pot.
7. Cook on "High Pressure" regime for 25 minutes.
8. Let the pressure release naturally (10 minutes).
9. Pour over the mussels and serve!

Nutrition:

- Calories: 90
- Fat: 3g
- Carbohydrates: 4g
- Protein: 12g

Mussels with Beer and Sausage

Try meaty seafood boil with beer and get maximum pleasure!

Prep time: 10 minutes | **Cooking time:** 5 minutes | **Servings**: 3

Ingredients:
- 1 tablespoon olive oil
- 2 pounds mussels
- 1 onion
- 12oz beer
- 8oz sausages
- 1 tablespoon paprika

Directions:
1. Cut sausages on slices.
2. Pour oil in the Instant Pot (warm up for 3 minutes on "Sauté" regime).
3. Place chopped onion and sausages in the pressure cooker.
4. Cook meat for 5 minutes on "Sauté" regime.
5. Add paprika, beer, mussels and cook for 5 more minutes on "High Pressure" regime.
6. Do a quick release.
7. Serve hot!

Nutrition:
- Calories: 237
- Fat: 7g
- Carbohydrates: 23g
- Protein: 18g

Mahi Mahi

Enjoy seafood full of vitamins and energy!

Prep time: 10 minutes | **Cooking time:** 10 minutes | **Servings**: 3

Ingredients:
- 2 mahi mahi fillets
- 1 tablespoon lime juice
- Salt
- 1 tablespoon hot sauce
- 2 garlic cloves
- 2 tablespoons honey
- 1 piece ginger
- ½ lime

Directions:
1. Wash fillets and cover with salt and pepper.
2. Melt honey in the Instant Pot (it will take 3 minutes on "Saute" regime). Mix honey with garlic, ginger, hot sauce and lime juice.
3. Pour water (about 1 cup) in the pressure cooker.
4. Cover mahi mahi with sauce and place in the Instant Pot.
5. Cut lime on slices. Set aside.
6. Cook mahi mahi for 1 minutes on "High Pressure" regime. Do a quick release.
7. Serve hot!

Nutrition:
- Calories: 145
- Fat: 13g
- Carbohydrates: 21g
- Protein: 19g

VEGETABLE DISHES

Curried Chickpea

Chickpea with hot seasoning and vegetable mix will be juicy and healthy vegan dish!

Prep time: 25 minutes | **Cooking time:** 30 minutes | **Servings:** 20

Ingredients:

- 3 cup chickpeas
- Cilantro to taste
- Pepper to taste
- Salt to taste
- 8 cup rice
- 8 teaspoon cayenne pepper

- 9 cups water
- 6 cups greens
- 1 acorn squash
- ½ teaspoon lime juice
- 1 teaspoon oil
- 8 chopped tomatoes
- 2 teaspoon cumin seeds

- 4 teaspoon mango powder
- 3 cup red onion
- 4 teaspoon garam masala
- 4 garlic cloves
- ¼ teaspoon turmeric
- ½ inch ginger

Directions:

1. Cover rice with water. Leave rice in water for 15 minutes until it gets lighter.
2. In the separate bowl cover chickpeas with water and leave for 30 minutes.
3. Pour oil in the instant Pot. Turn on Instant Pot and warm up oil.
4. Place cumin seeds in the Instant Pot and cook for 3 minutes.
5. Mix chopped onion with garlic and ginger. Add salt, pepper and chili to the onion mix. Cook ginger mix in the Instant Pot for 5 minutes on "High Pressure" regime.
6. Add spices and greens with lime juice and tomato and cook for 5 minutes on the same regime.
7. Add water to the Instant Pot.
8. Add remaining ingredients to the Instant Pot and cook for 20 minutes on "High Pressure" regime.
9. Serve with curry sauce!

Nutrition:

- Calories: 270
- Fat: 5g

- Carbohydrates: 51g
- Protein:9g

Black Eyed Pea Curry

Tender roasted vegetables full of vitamins and taste will make any day brighter!

Prep time: 15 minutes | **Cooking time:** 30 minutes | **Servings:** 12

Ingredients:

- 2 cups black eyed peas
- 30 curry leaves
- 3 teaspoons oil
- 2 teaspoon scumin seeds
- 1 cup chopped onion
- Lemon to serve

- 15 garlic cloves
- 6 cups water
- 2 inch ginger
- 2 teaspoons salt
- 2 teaspoons garam masala

- 2 cups chopped veggies
- 2 teaspoons coriander
- 6 tomatoes
- 3 teaspoons turmeric
- 5 tablespoons coconut
- ½ teaspoon cayenne

Directions:

1. Pour oil in the Instant Pot and set saute function.
2. Mix chopped onion, garlic and ginger. Place onion mix in the Instant Pot and cook for 5 minutes on "High Pressure" regime.
3. Place tomato in the Instant Pot.
4. Add remaining vegetables to the Instant Pot and cook on "High Pressure" regime for 15 minutes.
5. Serve with rice or as a soup!

Nutrition:

- Calories: 259
- Fat: 4g

- Carbohydrates: 42g
- Protein:16g

Veg Kolhapuri

Baked vegetables in their juice with bright seasoning and tender taste – you will like this!

Prep time: 10 minutes | **Cooking time:** 30 minutes | **Servings:** 4

Ingredients:

- 1 teaspoon coriander seeds
- Salt to taste
- 2 teaspoons sesame seeds
- Pepper to taste
- ½ teaspoon poppy seeds
- 2 cups water
- ½ teaspoon black pepper corns

- ½ cup chopped bell pepper
- ½ teaspoon mustard seeds
- 2 cups veggies carrots
- ¼ teaspoon Fanugreek seeds
- 1 ½ cup sweet potatoes
- ½ teaspoon cumin seeds
- 2 cups cauliflower
- 4 chillies

- ¼ teaspoon salt
- 2 tablespoons coconut
- 5 garlic cloves
- ¼ teaspoon nutmeg powder
- 1 inch ginger
- ½ teaspoon paprika
- 2 tomatoes
- ¼ teaspoon cinnamon
- ½ onion

Directions:
1. Mix coriander seeds with cinnamon, sesame seeds, paprika, poppy seeds, nutmeg powder, black pepper corns, coconut, mustard corns, red chilies, Fenugreek seeds and cumin seeds.
2. Place seed mix in the Instant Pot and cook on "High Pressure" regime for 5 minutes.
3. Mix onion, tomatoes, ginger, garlic and salt using blender.
4. Place tomato mix in the Instant Pot and cook for 10 minutes on the same settings.
5. Mix chopped cauliflower, salt, cayenne, potato, water, veggie carrots and bell pepper.
6. Add vegetable mix to the ingredients in the Instant Pot.
7. Cook ingredients for 20 minutes on "High Pressure" regime.
8. Serve with fresh herbs!

Nutrition:

- Calories: 224
- Fat: 17g

- Carbohydrates: 11g
- Protein:4g

Veggie Dhansak

Add bright Indian vibes to the grey ration!

Prep time: 15 minutes | **Cooking time:** 30 minutes | **Servings:** 2

Ingredients:

- ¾ cup split dals
- 3 garlic cloves
- 2 cups chopped vegetables
- ½ cup chopped onion
- 1 cup greens

- ½ teaspoon cumin seeds
- 1 tablespoon ginger
- ¾ teaspoon mustard seeds
- 4 garlic cloves
- 1 teaspoon oil

- 1 minced chili
- 1 ½ teaspoon dhana jaera powder
- ½ teaspoon turmeric

Directions:

1. Cover dal with water and leave for 15 minutes.
2. Mix chopped vegetables, turmeric, dhana jaera, greens, turmeric, ginger, minced chili and garlic.
3. Place ginger mix in the Instant Pot and cook for 5 minutes on "Saute" regime.
4. While seasoning is cooking, mix oil, garlic cloves, cumin seeds and chopped onion.
5. Fry onion mix on the frying pan for several minutes.
6. Place all the ingredients in the Instant Pot and cook for 5 minutes more on "High Pressure" regime.
7. Serve with rice!

Nutrition:

- Calories: 505
- Fat: 30g

- Carbohydrates: 10g
- Protein:20g

Masala Eggplant Curry

Tender and spicy curry with bright taste and sweet flavor!

Prep time: 15 minutes | **Cooking time:** 15 minutes | **Servings:** 3

Ingredients:

- 1 tablespoon coriander seeds
- Water
- ½ teaspoon cumin seeds
- 1 teaspoon lime juice
- ½ teaspoon mustard seeds
- ½ teaspoon salt

- 3 tablespoons chickpeas
- ½ teaspoon raw sugar
- 2 tablespoons chopped nuts
- ½ teaspoon turmeric
- 2 tablespoons coconut shreds
- ½ teaspoon cayenne

- 1 inch ginger
- Pinch cinnamon
- 2 garlic cloves
- ½ teaspoon cardamom
- 1 green chili

Directions:

1. Pour oil in the Instant Pot.
2. Mix cumin, coriander and mustard seeds.
3. Place cumin mix in the Instant Pot and cook for 5 minutes on "High Pressure" regime.
4. Add chickpea flour to the mix and nuts with coconut. Cook for 3 minutes more on "Saute" regime.
5. Add water to the Instant Pot and mix chili, cardamom, garlic cloves, cinnamon, cayenne, coconut shreds, turmeric, sugar and salt. Place in the Instant Pot and cook on "High Pressure" for 5 minutes more.
6. Add remaining ingredients to the Instant Pot and pour 1 more cup of water in the processor.
7. Cook on "High Pressure" for 5 minutes.
8. Place stuffed eggplants on the frying pan and fry on olive oil for 20 minutes.
9. Serve hot!

Nutrition:

- Calories: 140
- Fat: 0g

- Carbohydrates: 18g
- Protein:12g

Lentil Bean Chili

Hot chili with bright taste and delicious light smell will be both quick lunch and satisfying dinner!

Prep time: 30 minutes | **Cooking time:** 45 minutes | **Servings:** 8

Ingredients:

- 2 cups lentils
- Jalapeno
- 4 cups beans
- 2 cups frozen corn
- 8 teaspoons oil
- 3 teaspoons salt

- 4 onions
- 8 cups water
- 1 chili
- 1 cup celery
- 3 garlic cloves
- 1 red pepper

- 2 tomatoes
- 3 teaspoons taco spice
- 1 teaspoon pepper powder

Directions:

1. Cover lentils with water and leave for 30 minutes to rest.
2. Pour oil in the Instant Pot and add chopped onion. Cook onion for 5 minutes on "High Pressure" regime.
3. Mix chili with garlic and place in the Instant Pot. Cook for 3 minutes more on the same settings.
4. Mix tomatoes, pepper, taco spice and cook for 5 minutes in the Instant Pot on "High Pressure" regime.
5. Add jalapeno, celery corn and other ingredients to the Instant Pot and pour more water.
6. Cook ingredients for 20 minutes on the same regime.
7. Set "Low Pressure" regime and cook for another 20 minutes.
8. Serve hot with yogurt to taste!

Nutrition:

- Calories: 305
- Fat: 25g

- Carbohydrates: 66g
- Protein:23g

Brown Rice Soup

Satisfying and healthy rice with the delicious vegetables and tender sauce!

Prep time: 15 minutes | **Cooking time:** 50 minutes | **Servings:** 12

Ingredients:

- 3 cups brown lentils
- Lemon juice
- 1 cup brown rice
- 2 cups baby spinach
- 6 teaspoons oil
- 2 teaspoons salt
- 3 teaspoons cumin seeds
- 9 cups water
- 3 teaspoons mustard seeds

- 12 cups veggies
- 6 bay leaves
- 6 teaspoons lemon juice
- 2 onions
- 8 teaspoons ketchup
- 12garlic cloves
- 3 cups tomatoes
- 6 inch ginger
- 4 teaspoon pepper
- 6 green chili

- 2 teaspoon chipotle pepper
- 2 teaspoon turmeric
- 6 teaspoon coriander powder
- 3 teaspoon paprika
- 3 teaspoon garam masala

Directions:

1. Cover lentil with water.
2. Leave lentil in a bowl with water for 15 minutes.
3. Pour oil in the Instant Pot. Add cumin seeds and mustard seeds to the Instant Pot and cook for 3 minutes in the Instant Pot on "High Pressure" regime.
4. Mix chopped onion, bay leaf, chili, ginger and garlic. Cook onion mix in the Instant Pot for 5 minutes on "Saute" regime.
5. Add masala, peppers, tomatoes, ketchup, lentis, lemon juice, veggies, seeds and rice in the Instant Pot.
6. Cook on "High Pressure" regime for 40 minutes.
7. Cook on "Low Pressure" regime for 7 minutes more.

Nutrition:

- Calories: 101
- Fat: 1g

- Carbohydrates: 15g
- Protein:7g

Chana Dal Veggie Soup

Indian cuisine is always full of taste and has super soft smell!

Prep time: 10 minutes | **Cooking time:** 45 minutes | **Servings:** 12

Ingredients:

- 5cup chana dal
- Cilantro to taste
- 14 cups water
- 5 teaspoon salt
- 4 teaspoon oil
- 6 cup chopped veggies
- 6 medium onion
- 9 pureed tomatoes
- 18 garlic cloves
- 5 cayenne
- 4 inch ginger
- 4 teaspoon turmeric
- 4 teaspoon garam masala

Directions:

1. Mix chana dal with water and cook for 30 minutes on the frying pan.
2. Pour oil in the Instant Pot and add onion, ginger and garlic. Cook onion mix for 5 minutes on "High Pressure" regime.
3. Add pureed tomatoes to the instant Pot.
4. Add veggies, salt and water to the Instant Pot and cook for 15 minutes on the same regime.
5. Add cilantro and lemon – serve with rice!

Nutrition:

- Calories: 230
- Fat: 8g
- Carbohydrates: 29g
- Protein: 10g

Potato Curry with Spinach

Potato curry will be delicious both with crackers and fresh herbs!

Prep time: 15 minutes | **Cooking time:** 30 minutes | **Servings:** 12

Ingredients:

- 6 teaspoons oil
- 6 teaspoons lemon juice
- 4 teaspoons cumin seeds
- 8 cups chopped baby spinach
- 2 onions
- 2 teaspoons salt
- 9 cloves garlic

- 6 cups water
- 3 inch ginger
- 1 cup potato
- 4 teaspoon coriander
- 1 can chickpeas
- ½ teaspoon garam masala
- 8 tomatoes

- 2 teaspoon turmeric
- 2 teaspoon cayenne powder
- 2 teaspoon cinnamon
- 2 teaspoon black pepper

Directions:

1. Pour oil in the Instant Pot and add cumin seeds. Cook cumin seeds for 5 minutes.
2. Mix chopped onions, ginger and garlic. Add tomatoes and spices.
3. Pour water in the Instant Pot and cook tomato mix for 5 minutes on "Saute" regime.
4. Add pepper, cinnamon, cayenne powder, turmeric, masala, chickpeas, potato, ginger, cumin seeds, lemon juice, onions and spinach. Whisk in the Instant Pot.
5. Cook ingredients for 25 minutes on "High Pressure" regime.
6. Serve with paprika!

Nutrition:

- Calories: 188
- Fat: 10g

- Carbohydrates: 30g
- Protein:8g

Vegan Dal Makhani

Creamy soup with beans and roasted vegies!

Prep time: 60 minutes | **Cooking time:** 60 minutes | **Servings:** 12

Ingredients:

- 3 cups black gram
- Butter to garnish
- 12 cups water
- 1 cup cashew milk
- 3 cups pineapples
- 3 tablespoons fenugreek leaves
- 3 teaspoons salt

- 3 teaspoons garam masala
- 1 teaspoon cayenne powder
- 1 cups tomatoes
- 2 basil leaves
- 3 tablespoons soy sauce
- 6 teaspoons oil

- 1 teaspoon turmeric powder
- 6 teaspoons cumin seeds
- 1 teaspoon asafetida
- 5 green chilies
- 3 cups chopped onion
- 1 inch ginger
- 6 garlic cloves

Directions:

1. Cover lentils with water and leave for 60 minutes.
2. Place lentils in the Instant Pot with the water, add pineapples, salt and cayenne powder.
3. Cook lentils for 30 minutes on "Low Pressure" regime.
4. Mix cumin seeds, chopped onion, chili, ginger, asafetida and garlic. Fry on the frying pan for 6 minutes.
5. Add seasoning mix to the Instant Pot. Mix tomatoes with the turmeric and add to the Instant Pot. Mash ingredients and cook for 10 minutes on "High Pressure" regime.
6. Add masala, beans, fenugreek leaves and milk with butter. Cook for 30 minutes more on "Low Pressure" regime.
7. Add basil with soy sauce and cook for 6 minutes more on the same settings!
8. Serve!

Nutrition:

- Calories: 318
- Fat: 9g

- Carbohydrates: 0g
- Protein: 16g

Eggplant Sambar

Bright, light and delicious – this soup tastes like paradise – check it!

Prep time: 10 minutes | **Cooking time:** 30 minutes | **Servings:** 12

Ingredients:

- 3 teaspoons safflower
- Cilantro to taste
- 1 teaspoon mustard seeds
- 6 teaspoons tamarind paste
- 1 teaspoon fenugreek seeds

- 12 cups water
- 6 red chilies
- 2 cans chili sauce
- 3 cups peas
- 15 curry leaves
- 3 teaspoon salt
- 6 garlic cloves
- 4 basil leaves

- 2 cups green bell pepper
- 2 cups chopped onion
- 6 cups eggplant
- 3 tablespoons Sambhar Powder
- 1 teaspoon turmeric
- 2 tomatoes

Directions:

1. Pour oil in the Instant Pot. Pour chili sauce with chopped basil leaves in the Instant Pot.
2. Add mustard seeds and cook for 3 minutes on "Saute" regime. Remove mix from the Instant Pot and blend with the mixer. Place mix back in the Lid.
3. Mix fenugreek seeds, curry leaves, red chilies, and chopped onion. Cook for 6 minutes in the Instant Pot.
4. Add powder, turmeric, tomatoes and cook for 10 minutes on "High Pressure".
5. Add remaining ingredients in the Instant Pot for 15 minutes on the same settings.
6. Serve with rice!

Nutrition:

- Calories: 152
- Fat: 1g

- Carbohydrates: 25g
- Protein:11g

Chana Saag

Curry with spinach and traditional Asian seasoning will make your weekdays taste special!

Prep time: 10 minutes | **Cooking time:** 40 minutes | **Servings:** 12

Ingredients:

- 3 cup chickpeas
- Cayenne to taste
- 6 teaspoon oil
- 6 tablespoon lemon juice
- 4 onion

- 6 cup milk
- 6 hot green chili
- 7 packs spinach
- 12 garlic cloves
- 3 teaspoon salt

- 4 inch ginger
- 2 cups water
- 5 teaspoon cumin
- 2 cans tomatoes
- 1 teaspoon coriander

Directions:

1. Pour oil in the Instant Pot and turn on "Saute" regime.
2. Mix chopped onion, garlic, ginger and chili. Place chili in the Instant Pot and cook on "High Pressure" for 5 minutes.
3. Add tomatoes and lemon juice, salt, coriander and cumin. Saute until tomato mix will start boiling.
4. Add chickpeas to the tomato mix.
5. Cook mix for 30 minutes on "High Pressure" regime.
6. Add greens and milk – cook for 3 more minutes on the same regime.
7. Serve with the lemon and cayenne.

Nutrition:

- Calories: 360
- Fat: 12g

- Carbohydrates: 54g
- Protein:9g

Mushroom Tacos

Crispy tacos with satisfying and tender mushrooms will give you energy for the full day!

Prep time: 10 minutes | **Cooking time:** 30 minutes | **Servings:** 3

Ingredients:

- 2 chilies
- Avocado to serve
- 1 teaspoon oil
- 8oz mushrooms
- 1 bay leaf
- ¼ teaspoon sugar

- 1 onion
- 3 teaspoons lime juice
- 7 garlic cloves
- 1 teaspoon apple cider
- 2 chipotle chilies
- ¾ cup water

- 1 teaspoon ground cumin
- ¼ teaspoon salt
- ½ teaspoon oregano
- ¼ teaspoon cinnamon
- ½ teaspoon paprika

Directions:

1. Cover chilies with water and leave for 15 minutes.
2. Pour oil in the Instant Pot and add chopped onions, bay leaves, salt and garlic. Cook herbs for 5 minutes on "High Pressure" regime.
3. Separate onion mix in two parts and place one part in the blender.
4. Add mushrooms to the onion mix in the Instant Pot.
5. Place chili to the onion mix in the blender and top with cider vinegar, paprika, cinnamon, oregano, cumin, chilies, apple cider, garlic and avocado. Blend mix well.
6. Add blended mix to the Instant Pot and cook on "High Pressure" regime for 30 minutes with mushrooms.
7. Add lime to the mix and cook for 5 more minutes on the same regime.
8. Serve with greens!

Nutrition:

- Calories: 310
- Fat: 12g

- Carbohydrates: 41g
- Protein:11g

Mung Bean Stew

Satisfying rice, delicious vegetables and fresh green herbs – this receipt collected everything you like!

Prep time: 20 minutes | **Cooking time:** 20 minutes | **Servings:** 12

Ingredients:

- 3 cups mung beans
- 5 teaspoons salt
- 3 cups basmati rice
- 6 teaspoons lemon juice
- 3 teaspoons oil
- 12 cups water

- 3 teaspoons cumin seeds
- 3 teaspoons black pepper
- 3 cups red onion
- 3 teaspoons cayenne pepper
- 7 tomatoes

- 3 teaspoons garam masala
- 9 garlic cloves
- 1 inch ginger
- 2 teaspoons coriander
- 3 teaspoons turmeric

Directions:

1. Cover beans with rice with water and leave for 15 minutes.
2. Mix chopped onions, tomatoes, water, turmeric, coriander, ginger, garlic cloves, garam masala, peppers, cumin seeds and salt. Use blender to mix ingredients well.
3. Heat up oil in the Instant Pot and add blended mix.
4. Cook for 17 minutes on "High Pressure" regime.
5. Place rice, lemon juice and beans in the Instant Pot.
6. Cook on "High Pressure" regime for 20 minutes.
7. Serve with fresh herbs!

Nutrition:

- Calories: 174
- Fat: 1g

- Carbohydrates: 38g
- Protein:7g

Vegan Lasagna Soup

Try new version of lovely satisfying lasagna!

Prep time: 15 minutes | **Cooking time:** 4 hours | **Servings:** 12

Ingredients:
- 8 cups vegetable broth
- Salt to taste
- Pepper to taste
- 2 onions
- 2 tablespoons lemon juice
- 6 garlic cloves
- 8 tablespoons vegan pesto
- 2 cups brown lentils
- 1 pound firm tofu
- 2 teaspoons basil
- 1 cup almond milk
- 2 teaspoons oregano
- 2 cups raw cashews
- 2 cans tomatoes
- 6 cups spinach leaves
- 1 can crushed tomatoes
- 8 lasagna noodles

Directions:
1. Pour broth in the Instant Pot.
2. Mix chopped onion, oregano, garlic, lentils and basil and add to the Instant Pot. Cook on "High Pressure" for 2 hours.
3. Add tomatoes to the Instant Pot ingredients and blend. Cook for 2 hours more for "Low Pressure" regime.
4. Add noodles with spinach to some soup and cook for 15 minutes on "High Pressure" regime.
5. Place cashews with milk in the blender and blend well. Add remaining ingredients to the blender and mix one more time.
6. Add remaining ingredients to the Instant Pot and cook for 7 minutes more on the same settings.

Nutrition:
- Calories: 332
- Fat: 13g
- Carbohydrates: 42g
- Protein: 15g

White Bean Stew

Satisfying beans with seasoning and herbs will not only surprise you with the taste, but also give energy and vitamins for the full day!

Prep time: 30 minutes | **Cooking time:** 50 minutes | **Servings:** 12

Ingredients:
- 2 pounds yellow beans
- 1 cup chopped basil
- 2 onions
- 2 cups fresh corn
- 8 garlic cloves
- 2 bunches kale leaves
- 10 cups water
- 2 teaspoons salt
- 8 teaspoons paprika
- 2 cans tomatoes
- 4 teaspoons oregano
- 2 peppers
- 2 teaspoons cumin
- 2 bell peppers
- 2 teaspoons dried basil
- 2 pounds pilled pumpkin

Directions:
1. Boil beans for 1 hour in hot water and leave to rest.
2. Place onions with oil in the Instant Pot. Add garlic and cook for 3 minutes.
3. Mix basil, corn, garlic cloves, kale leaves, salt, paprika, tomatoes, oregano, peppers, cumin and basil with pumpkin and cook for 30 minutes on "High Pressure" regime in the Instant Pot.
4. Add squash to the Instant Pot and cook for 10 more minutes on "High Pressure" regime.

Nutrition:
- Calories: 106
- Fat: 2g
- Carbohydrates: 18g
- Protein: 5g

Light Minestrone Soup

Fresh and satisfying minestrone will be not only bright dinner, but also lunch full of vitamins!

Prep time: 15 minutes | **Cooking time:** 30 minutes | **Servings:** 16

Ingredients:

- 1 cup olive oil
- Parmesan cheese for topping
- 10 garlic cloves
- 2 teaspoons Italian seasoning
- 4 onions
- 4 cups tubular pasta
- 16oz pancetta
- Salt and pepper to taste
- 8 carrots
- 2 tablespoons sage
- 6 stalks celery
- 2 chunks parmesan
- 4 cups fresh beans
- 1 bunch Italian parsley
- 3 cans Italian tomatoes
- 16 cups water
- 3 potatoes
- 4 can beans
- 2 zucchini
- 8 cans red beans
- 2 ½ cups spinach
- 1 can cannellini beans
- 1 cups fresh cabbage

Directions:

1. Pour oil in the Instant Pot and set saute function.
2. Mix onions with garlic and place in the Pot.
3. Add carrots, pancetta and celery. Cook carrot mix for 5 minutes in the Instant Pot on "Saute" regime.
4. Mix zucchini with beans and potatoes, add spinach, tomatoes and cabbage with parsley to the Instant Pot.
5. Add remaining ingredients to the Instant Pot and cook on "High Pressure" regime for 30 minutes.
6. Serve with fresh herbs!

Nutrition:

- Calories: 80
- Fat: 2g
- Carbohydrates: 20g
- Protein:4g

Marinara Sauce

Marinara will be not only easy sauce receipt, but also perfect addition for any meat plate!

Prep time: 10 minutes | **Cooking time:** 20 minutes | **Servings:** 12

Ingredients:

- 6 28oz cans crushed tomatoes
- 5 cups water
- 6 potatoes
- 6 teaspoons salt
- 2 cups red lentils
- 9 garlic cloves

Directions:

1. Wash and cut lentils.
2. Mix cubes potato, lentils, salt and garlic.
3. Place veggie mix in the Instant Pot and cook for 5 minutes on "High Pressure" regime.
4. Add tomatoes, salt and garlic and blend the mix well.
5. Cook sauce for 15 minutes more on "High Pressure" regime.
6. Serve with fresh basil leaves.

Nutrition:

- Calories: 450
- Fat: 10g
- Carbohydrates: 70g
- Protein:15g

Split Pea Soup

Super easy creamy and satisfying soup in Instant Pot with crackers will make your dinner special!

Prep time: 10 minutes | **Cooking time:** 20 minutes | **Servings:** 16

Ingredients:
- 20 cups water
- Salt to taste
- Pepper to taste
- 4 potatoes
- 2 cups yeast
- 1 cup split peas
- 2 teaspoons liquid smoke
- 2 cups navy beans
- 12 bay leaves

Directions:
1. Pour water in the Instant Pot.
2. Mix potato, peas, bay leaves, beans and liquid smoke.
3. Place potato mix in the Instant Pot and cook on "High Pressure" for 20 minutes.
4. Add yeast and salt with pepper to the mix and blend well.
5. Serve with fresh herbs!

Nutrition:
- Calories: 130
- Fat: 1g
- Carbohydrates: 21g
- Protein:9g

Cauliflower Rice

Easy and delicious cauliflower rice will be perfect vegie entrée for those who like healthy food!

Prep time: 5 minutes | **Cooking time:** 15 minutes | **Servings:** 16

Ingredients:
- 4 medium cauliflowers
- Lime wedges
- 8 tablespoon olive oil
- Cilantro to taste
- 1 teaspoon salt
- 1 teaspoon paprika
- 1 teaspoon parsley
- 1 teaspoon turmeric
- 1 teaspoon cumin

Directions:
1. Wash and cut cauliflowers.
2. Place cauliflowers in the Instant Pot.
3. Pour water on cauliflowers.
4. Add wedges, olive oil, paprika, parsley, turmeric and cumin to the Pot and cook for 15 minutes on "High Pressure" regime.
5. Mash potatoes using blender and serve with herbs!

Nutrition:
- Calories: 108
- Fat: 3g
- Carbohydrates: 14g
- Protein:9g

Squash Soup

Creamy, healthy, easy to cook and quick soup – dinner full of vitamins is easy to prepare with Instant Pot!

Prep time: 10 minutes | **Cooking time:** 40 minutes | **Servings:** 4

Ingredients:

- 1 teaspoon olive oil
- Cranberries
- 1 onion
- Pumpkin seeds

- 2 garlic cloves
- ½ cup coconut milk
- 1 tablespoon curry powder

- 3 cups water
- 1 butternut squash
- 1 ½ teaspoons sea salt

Directions:

1. Mix olive oil with the chopped onion and place in the Instant Pot. Cook onions for 10 minutes on "High Pressure" regime.
2. Add garlic and curry powder to the Instant Pot and cook for 2 minutes more.
3. Mix salt with water and butternut squash.
4. Place butternut mix in the Instant Pot and cook on "Soup" regime for 30 minutes.
5. Blend cooked mix.
6. Mix blended ingredients with cranberries, pumpkin seeds, milk, curry powder and sea salt and place in the Instant Pot.
7. Cook soup for 25 minutes more on the same regime.
8. Serve soup with fresh herbs!

Nutrition:

- Calories: 90
- Fat: 1g

- Carbohydrates: 18g
- Protein:3g

Spinach Chana Masala

Easy and quick Indian dish – something fresh and satisfying!

Prep time: 15 minutes | **Cooking time:** 25 minutes | **Servings:** 7

Ingredients:

- 1 cup raw chickpeas
- Lemon to serve
- 3 tablespoons cooking oil
- Cilantro to taste
- 1 cup chopped onions
- Salt to taste
- 1 bay leaf
- 2 cups baby spinach
- 1 tablespoons grated garlic
- 1 tablespoons chana masala
- ½ tablespoon grated ginger
- 2 teaspoon chili powder
- 1 ½ cups water
- 1 teaspoon coriander powder
- 2 cups tomato paste
- ½ teaspoon turmeric
- 1 tablespoon flour
- 1 green chili

Directions:

1. Wash chickpeas and blend.
2. Coat chickpeas with water and leave for 10 hours to rest.
3. Pour oil in the Instant Pot and add onions. Cook onion for 5 minutes on "High Pressure" regime.
4. Add ginger, garlic paste, chili and bay leaf to the Instant Pot and cook for 2 minutes more on "Saute" regime.
5. Add turmeric, chili powder, water, coriander powder, chana masala and water to the Instant Pot. Cook for 2 minutes more on "Saute" regime.
6. Add flour to the Instant Pot and cook for 1 minute more on the same settings.
7. Add tomato paste, spinach and remaining ingredients and cook for 20 minutes on "High Pressure" regime!
8. Serve with fresh herbs!

Nutrition:

- Calories: 423
- Fat: 14g
- Carbohydrates: 60g
- Protein:19g

Asian Dumplings

Soft and tender dumplings with the Asian seasoning will make lunch healthy and full of vitamins!

Prep time: 25 minutes | **Cooking time:** 10 minutes | **Servings:** 12

Ingredients:
- 1 tablespoon oil
- 12 dumpling wrappers
- 1 cup mushrooms
- 1 teaspoon sesame oil
- ½ cup minced cabbage
- 1 teaspoon ginger
- ½ cup carrot
- 1 tablespoon wine vinegar
- 2 tablespoons soy sauce

Directions:
1. Pour broth in the Instant Pot.
2. Add mushrooms to the Instant Pot.
3. Mix cabbage, soy sauce, vinegar and carrot. Add to the Instant Pot and cook for 5 minutes on "High Pressure" regime.
4. Mix ginger with sesame oil.
5. Cut round circles of the wrappers.
6. Place 1 teaspoon filling to the center of the dumplings and roll up.
7. Pour water in the Instant Pot.
8. Place dumplings in the Instant Pot and cook on "High Pressure" regime for 10 minutes.
9. Serve with herbs!

Nutrition:
- Calories: 360
- Fat: 5g
- Carbohydrates: 69g
- Protein: 8g

Lentil Bolognese

Only 15 minutes and Italian traditional paste is ready!

Prep time: 10 minutes | **Cooking time:** 15 minutes | **Servings:** 16

Ingredients:
- 4 cups black lentils
- Balsamic vinegar
- 4 cans roasted tomatoes
- 4 onions
- Pepper flakes to taste
- 16 garlic cloves
- 8 tablespoons Italian seasoning
- 12 carrots
- 16 cups water
- 4 cans tomato paste

Directions:
1. Pour water in the Instant Pot.
2. Mix lentils, vinegar, tomatoes, onions, pepper flakes, garlic cloves, seasoning, carrots and tomato paste.
3. Use blender to mix ingredients well.
4. Cook sauce for 15 minutes on "High Pressure" regime.
5. Leave sauce in the Instant Pot and let the pressure release naturally for 10 minutes.
6. Serve over pasta!

Nutrition:
- Calories: 50
- Fat: 10g
- Carbohydrates: 10g
- Protein: 3g

French Fries

Can we cook crispy French Fries in the Instant Pot? Yes! It will be same crispy, same golden color and same delicious, but with more light and juicy taste!

Prep time: 5 minutes | **Cooking time:** 15 minutes | **Servings:** 15

Ingredients:
- 15oz potatoes
- Salt to taste
- 5 teaspoons kosher salt
- Oil
- 2 teaspoons baking soda
- 4 cups water
- 4 teaspoons chili powder
- 2 teaspoons pepper
- 1 teaspoon ginger

Directions:
1. Wash and slice potatoes. You may slice them into stripes or into quarters – as you like more.
2. Place water, salt and soda in the Instant Pot and cook for 2 minutes on "High Pressure". You may bring water to boil with the oil.
3. Heat up cooking oil and pour in the Instant Pot.
4. Place potatoes in the oil and cook for 10 minutes on "High Pressure" regime. Cover potatoes with powder, pepper and ginger.
5. Place potatoes on the dry frying pan and cook for 5 minutes not changing the regime.
6. Serve with ketchup or sauce paste!

Nutrition:
- Calories: 198
- Fat: 11g
- Carbohydrates: 22g
- Protein:2g

Veggie Burgers

Soft, easy and super delicious vegetarian burgers will be light and easy dinner for everyone!

Prep time: 5 minutes | **Cooking time**: 20 minutes | **Servings:** 9

Ingredients:
- 1 cup minces onion
- 1 tablespoon flour
- 2 teaspoons ginger
- 1 cup quick oats
- 1 cup minced mushrooms
- 1 tablespoon curry powder
- 1 cup red lentils
- ¼ cup cilantro
- 1 ½ sweet potatoes
- ¼ cup parsley
- 2 ½ cup vegetable stock
- ¼ cup hemp seeds

Directions:
1. Mix chopped onions, mushrooms, potatoes, lentils and stock with ginger.
2. Saute ingredients in the Instant Pot for 5 minutes.
3. Add flour, ginger, oats, curry powder, cilantro, parsley and hemp seeds. Cook for 6 minutes more on "High Pressure" regime.
4. Turn on oven and preheat up to 375oF.
5. Form patties of the ingredients.
6. Bake ingredients for 20 minutes on the same regime.
7. Serve with buns!

Nutrition:
- Calories: 370
- Fat: 9g
- Carbohydrates: 58g
- Protein:17g

Night Easy Pasta

This pasta is so healthy and low in calories, that you can eat it even in the night!

Prep time: 10 minutes | **Cooking time:** 5 minutes | **Servings:** 5

Ingredients:
- 16oz Truth Pasta
- 10oz broccoli
- 4 cups water
- 25oz tomato sauce

Directions:
1. Place pasta, broccoli, tomato sauce in the Instant Pot. Pour water on top.
2. Cook pasta for 5 minutes on "High Pressure" regime.
3. Leave pasta for 15 minutes to rest after the cooking in Instant Pot for the natural pressure release.
4. Place pasta on the plate and top with cheese and herbs to taste.
5. Serve hot!

Nutrition:
- Calories: 426
- Fat: 18g
- Carbohydrates: 45g
- Protein:20g

Lentil Dal with Spinach

There is never enough Asian vibes! Lentil Dal includes everything necessary for the healthy lifestyle and can be super delicious!

Prep time: 10 minutes | **Cooking time:** 20 minutes | **Servings:** 2

Ingredients:
- 1/2 teaspoons butter
- 1 onion
- ¼ cup fresh cilantro
- 1 garlic cloves
- Handful of spinach
- 1/2 teaspoon ground cumin
- 1/2 tomato
- 3 jalapeno peppers
- 2 potatoes
- 1/2 teaspoon coriander
- ½ teaspoon salt
- 1 teaspoon turmeric
- 1 cup water
- ¼ teaspoon cayenne powder
- 1 ½ cups red lentils

Directions:
1. Pour water in the Instant Pot. Wash and peel onions. Cut onion into slices. Wash and peel potatoes. Mix onions with potatoes in one plate. The same time bring water to boil in the Instant Pot on the "Saute" regime.
2. Add onions to the Instant Pot and cook for 3 minutes on "High Pressure" regime. Add salt and pepper to the onions. Sprinkle veggies with oil to get more crispy and golden color.
3. Add turmeric, garlic, coriander, cumin and cayenne to the Instant Pot. Wash and chop tomatoes with spinach.
4. Cook for 4 minutes more on "High Pressure" regime. Add peppers and cook for 5 more minutes.
5. Add water, lentils, salt and tomato wedges to the Instant Pot.
6. Cook for 10 minutes on "High Pressure" regime. Add more water if needed.
7. Whisk mix with the spinach and lentils. You may use blender.
8. Serve with fresh herbs!

Nutrition:
- Calories: 195
- Fat: 9g
- Carbohydrates: 22g
- Protein:8g

Shepard's Pie

Quick and satisfying pie is easy to cook in Instant Pot!

Prep time: 10 minutes | **Cooking time:** 10 minutes | **Servings:** 20

Ingredients:
- 10 cups chopped onion
- 1 cup tomato paste
- 5 cups chopped carrots
- 8 cups mashes potatoes
- 5 cups chopped celery
- 4 cups tomatoes
- 4 cups peeled sweet potatoes
- 1 cup tamari
- 5 cups French lentils
- 5 tablespoons Worcestershire sauce
- 5 cups vegetable stock

Directions:
1. Place onion, celery and carrot to the Instant Pot.
2. Cook vegie mix on "Saute" regime for 3 minutes.
3. Add seasoning and herbs with stock to the Instant Pot.
4. Cook on "High Pressure" regime for 10 minutes.
5. Add flour, Worcestershire sauce, tomatoes, tamari, tomato paste and with mashed potatoes to the Instant Pot.
6. Cook for 8 minutes on "High Pressure" regime!
7. Serve with herbs!

Nutrition:
- Calories: 303
- Fat: 6g
- Carbohydrates: 37g
- Protein:25g

Coconut Curry

Feel Thai taste – try sweet coconut curry with vegetables!

Prep time: 20 minutes | **Cooking time:** 50 minutes | **Servings:** 7

Ingredients:
- 1 potato
- ½ teaspoon chili flakes
- 1 broccoli crown
- 1 teaspoon miso
- 1 broccoli
- 2 teaspoons tamari sauce
- 1.2 onion
- 1 tablespoon turmeric
- 1 can chickpeas
- 1 tablespoon ginger
- 1 can tomatoes
- 2 garlic cloves
- 1 cans coconut milk

Directions:
1. Mix potato, chili flakes, broccoli, miso, tamari sauce, chopped onion, turmeric, chickpeas, ginger, tomatoes, garlic cloves and milk.
2. Turn on Instant Pot and set "High Pressure" regime.
3. Place all the ingredients to the instant Pot.
4. Cook ingredients for 50 minutes on "High Pressure" regime.
5. Serve!

Nutrition:
- Calories: 303
- Fat: 19g
- Carbohydrates: 27g
- Protein:9g

Carrot Soup

Try light, satisfying and easy carrot soup with heavy creams and herbs!

Prep time: 10 minutes | **Cooking time:** 15 minutes | **Servings:** 4

Ingredients:

- 1 tablespoon butter
- Cilantro to serve
- 1 tablespoon oil
- 1 tablespoon sriracha
- 1 onion
- 1 can milk
- 1 garlic clove
- 2 cups broth
- 1 piece ginger
- Pepper to taste
- 1 pound carrots
- Salt to taste
- ¼ teaspoon sugar

Directions:

1. Place butter and oil in the Instant Pot.
2. Warm up butter and oil for 3 minutes on "Sauté" regime.
3. Chop onions and mix with garlic, ginger.
4. Place garlic ginger mix in the Instant Pot.
5. Cook on "Sauté" regime for 1 minute.
6. Wash and cut carrots on slices.
7. Mix carrots with brown sugar.
8. Add salt, pepper and milk with sriracha sauce.
9. Mix milky mix with broth.
10. Place mix in the pressure cooker.
11. Cook for 6 minutes on "High Pressure" regime.
12. Let the pressure release naturally (10 minutes).
13. Place cooked mix in a bowl.
14. Use blender to mix all the ingredients.
15. Serve with heavy creams and fresh herbs!

Nutrition:

- Calories: 348
- Fat: 89g
- Carbohydrates: 45g
- Protein: 21g

Peanut Tofu Pineapple Curry

Try sweet and full of vitamins curry right today – get maximum vitamins and energy!

Prep time: 10 minutes | **Cooking time:** 15 minutes | **Servings:** 3

Ingredients:

- 2 cups tofu
- 1 lime juice
- 1/3 cup pineapple cubes
- Salt to taste
- ¼ cup raw cashews
- ¼ teaspoon turmeric
- 14oz milk

- 1 ½ teaspoon sriracha
- 2 tablespoons curry paste
- 1 teaspoon coconut sugar
- ½ cup water
- 3 teaspoons vinegar
- 3 tablespoons butter
- 1 teaspoon soy sauce

- 1 tablespoon olive oil
- 2 teaspoons grated ginger
- 2 red chili
- 2 teaspoons garlic
- 1 onion

Directions:

1. Cut tofu on cubes.
2. Pour oil in the Instant Pot.
3. Place chili in the pressure cooker.
4. Chop onion and place in the Instant Pot.
5. Add cashew nuts and ginger.
6. Add garlic to the Instant Pot.
7. Cook for 3 minutes on "Sauté" regime.
8. Add butter, milk, water and red curry paste to the pressure cooker.
9. Add soy sauce, sriracha, vinegar, sugar and salt with turmeric powder to the Instant Pot.
10. Add tofu and cook for 2 minutes on "High Pressure" regime.
11. Do a quick release.
12. Add pineapple and lime juice.
13. Cook for 2 minutes on "High Pressure" regime.
14. Serve with rice and cilantro.

Nutrition:

- Calories: 200
- Fat: 9g

- Carbohydrates: 23g
- Protein: 8g

Brussels Sprouts with Pork

Satisfying pork meat can be several times healthier with Brussels sprouts!

Prep time: 10 minutes | **Cooking time:** 15 minutes | **Servings:** 4

Ingredients:

- 1 pound pork chops
- 1 chunk carrot
- 1 teaspoon salt
- 2 cups Brussels sprouts
- 1 tablespoon coconut oil
- ½ teaspoon thyme
- 1 cup onion
- 2 teaspoons garlic
- 1 cup chicken broth
- 1 tablespoon flour

Directions:

1. Wash pork chops.
2. Wash and cut sprouts with onion and carrot.
3. Cover pork meat with salt.
4. Pour oil in the Instant Pot.
5. Melt oil for 3 minutes on "Sauté" regime.
6. Place pork chops in the Instant Pot and cook for 6 minutes on "High Pressure" regime.
7. Remove pork chops from the pressure cooker.
8. Place chopped onion with garlic and thyme in the Instant Pot.
9. Add pork chops and pour broth over the ingredients in the Instant Pot.
10. Cook for 15 minutes on "High Pressure" regime.
11. Do a quick release.
12. Remove pork from the pressure cooker.
13. Place carrots with sprouts in the Instant Pot.
14. Cook for 3 minutes on "High Pressure" regime.
15. Do a quick release.
16. Mix ingredients well and serve hot!

Nutrition:

- Calories: 330
- Fat: 22g
- Carbohydrates: 10g
- Protein: 24g

Red Curry

Try hot, spicy and full of taste curry in vegan style!

Prep time: 5 minutes | **Cooking time:** 15 minutes | **Servings:** 6

Ingredients:

- 3 tablespoons red curry paste
- 12 basil leaves
- 1 can coconut milk
- 4 lime juice

- 1lb tofu
- ½ cup bamboo shoots
- ¼ cup chicken broth
- ½ cup onion
- 2 tablespoons fish sauce

- 1 cup carrots
- 2 teaspoons sugar
- 1 cup red bell pepper
- 1 tablespoons lime juice

Directions:

1. Place curry paste in the Instant Pot.
2. Pour milk in the Instant Pot and cook or 1 minute on "Sauté" regime.
3. Cut tofu on cubes.
4. Place tofu in the pressure cooker. Pour broth over the ingredients.
5. Cook for 5 minutes on "High Pressure" regime.
6. Do a quick release.
7. Mix fish sauce, lime juice, carrots, bell pepper, bamboo shoots, onions and cook for 5 minutes on "Sauté" regime.
8. Add sugar and basil leaves!
9. Let the pressure release naturally (10 minutes).
10. Serve hot!

Nutrition:

- Calories: 420
- Fat: 23g

- Carbohydrates: 44g
- Protein: 9g

Tomato Basil Soup

Try tender tomato soup with fresh herbs and satisfying seasoning for the lunch today!

Prep time: 15 minutes | **Cooking time:** 5 minutes | **Servings:** 16

Ingredients:

- 1cup olive oil
- 4 tablespoons basil leaves
- 16oz carrots
- 2 teaspoons pepper
- 16oz onion

- 4 teaspoons salt
- 2 tablespoons basil
- 2 cups half and half
- 6 cans pureed tomatoes
- 2 cups chicken broth

- 1 cucumber
- 1 cup shredded turkey meat

Directions:

1. Wash and chop onions. Add cucumber to the onions.
2. Mix chopped onion with carrots.
3. Place vegetables in the Instant Pot and cook on "Sauté" regime for 4 minutes. Add shredded turkey meat to the vegetables. Mix ingredients well.
4. Pour oil in the Instant Pot and add basil.
5. Cook ingredients on "Sauté" regime for 4 minutes more.
6. Add tomatoes and broth to the blender cup. Pour blended mix in the pressure cooker.
7. Cook for 5 minutes on "High Pressure".
8. Let the pressure release naturally.
9. Add cream, salt, pepper and basil. Cook for 3 minutes on "Sauté" regime.
10. Do a quick release and serve!

Nutrition:

- Calories: 155
- Fat: 6g

- Carbohydrates: 21g
- Protein:6g

Mashed Cauliflower with Spinach

Soft, delicious and tender cauliflower with spinach leaves and soft taste seasoning!

Prep time: 10 minutes | **Cooking time:** 15 minutes | **Servings:** 14

Ingredients:

- 2 heads cauliflower
- 4 tablespoons butter
- 4 tablespoons olive oil
- 1/4 teaspoon garlic powder
- 2 cups onion
- 1/2 teaspoon pepper
- 4 cups spinach
- 1 teaspoon salt
- 1 teaspoon sea salt
- 1 teaspoon rosemary
- 1 teaspoon cardamom

Directions:

1. Mix salt, pepper and garlic powder. Add sea salt, cardamom and rosemary to seasoning mix. You may add a little bit oil to taste to make seasoning mix more soft and more render.
2. Wash and cut cauliflower with spinach. You should get small size cubes.
3. Place water in the Instant Pot. Warm up water – it will take you around 2 minutes. Do not overcook.
4. Place cauliflower in the Instant Pot.
5. Cook for 10 minutes on "Sauté" regime.
6. Add oil to the pressure cooker.
7. Add spinach, chopped onions and cook for 5 minutes on "Sauté" regime.
8. Add seasoning to the Instant Pot and let the pressure release naturally.
9. Remove ingredients from the Instant Pot and use blender to mix well.
10. Serve warm!

Nutrition:

- Calories: 465
- Fat: 40g
- Carbohydrates: 18g
- Protein: 5g

Garlic Butter Potatoes

Try soft and delicious potatoes with seasoning and butter light sauce!

Prep time: 10 minutes | **Cooking time:** 10 minutes | **Servings:** 4

Ingredients:

- 3 pounds red potatoes
- 2 tablespoons parsley leaves
- 1 stick butter
- ¼ cup parmesan
- 4 garlic cloves
- ½ cup vegetable broth
- ½ teaspoon oregano
- Salt to taste
- Pepper to taste
- ½ teaspoon basil

Directions:

1. Wash and cut potatoes on slices.
2. Mix basil with oregano, garlic, salt, pepper and parsley leaves.
3. Place butter in the pressure cooker and warm up for 3 minutes on "Sauté" regime.
4. Place potatoes in the Instant Pot.
5. Add seasoning mix to potatoes.
6. Add broth and cook potatoes for 7 minutes on "High Pressure" regime.
7. Add cheese and let the pressure release naturally (10 minutes).
8. Serve hot!

Nutrition:

- Calories: 140
- Fat: 5g
- Carbohydrates: 21g
- Protein: 2g

Detox Turmeric Veggie Soup

Enjoy truly heathy lifestyle with detox bright soup full of vitamins!

Prep time: 10 minutes | **Cooking time:** 20 minutes | **Servings:**3

Ingredients:

- 4 cups butternut squash
- 1 tablespoon coconut oil
- 2 cups carrots
- 1 can coconut milk
- 1 sweet potato
- 3 cups vegetable broth
- 1 onion
- 1 teaspoon sea salt
- 2 teaspoons garlic
- ¼ teaspoon cayenne pepper
- 1 teaspoon ginger
- 1 teaspoon curry powder
- 2 teaspoons turmeric powder
- 1 teaspoon garam masala

Directions:

1. Mix garam masala with turmeric powder, curry powder and cayenne pepper. Add ginger.
2. Pour vegetable broth in the Instant Pot.
3. Place chopped onion in the Instant Pot.
4. Add seasoning mix to the chopped onions.
5. Add sea salt, chopped potato and milk with squash, cut carrots and oil.
6. Mix ingredients well inside of the pressure cooker.
7. Cook for 20 minutes on "High Pressure" regime.
8. Remove ingredients from the Instant Pot.
9. Use blender to get pureed mix in the Instant Pot.
10. Serve with heavy creams and fresh herbs!

Nutrition:

- Calories: 276
- Fat: 0g
- Carbohydrates: 60g
- Protein: 12g

Vegan Chickpea Curry

Try real vegan menu and start with this delicious, light and healthy receipt!

Prep time: 5 minutes | **Cooking time:** 25 minutes | **Servings:** 12

Ingredients:

- 3 cups chickpea curry
- 9 tablespoons pepper
- 3 cups tomatoes
- Salt to taste
- 2 cups onion
- 6 teaspoons lemon juice

- 6 tablespoons oil
- 6 bay leaves
- 6 garlic
- 3 tablespoons curry powder
- 1 teaspoon garam masala

- 1 cup heavy creams
- 1 lime
- 1 teaspoon turmeric

Directions:

1. Pour water over chickpeas. Wash and cut lime on slices. Place lime in the Instant Pot.
2. Pour oil in the pressure cooker. Add heavy creams and mix well. You should get tender milky mixture.
3. Add chopped onion and garlic to the Instant Pot.
4. Cook garlic on "Sauté" regime. It will take you around 5 minutes.
5. Add tomatoes with salt and bay leaves to the Instant Pot.
6. Cook for 1 minute on "High Pressure" regime.
7. Place chickpeas in the pressure cooker and add water.
8. Mix chili powder, garam masala, turmeric and curry powder with lemon, salt, pepper and cilantro.
9. Cook ingredients on "High Pressure" regime for 10 minutes.
10. Do a quick release.
11. Serve hot!

Nutrition:

- Calories: 360
- Fat: 21g

- Carbohydrates: 41g
- Protein: 8g

Veggie Stew

Try light, satisfying and tender stew with delicious seasoning and colorful roasted vegetables!

Prep time: 30 minutes | **Cooking time:** 15 minutes | **Servings:** 8

Ingredients:

- ½ onion
- 2 tablespoons cornstarch
- 1 celery stalk
- 4oz peas
- 1 carrot
- ¾ cup onions
- 2 garlic cloves
- ¼ teaspoon pepper
- ¼ cup vegetable broth

- ½ teaspoon bouquet seasoning
- 8oz white mushrooms
- ½ teaspoon salt
- 8oz portobello mushrooms
- 1 tablespoon vinegar
- 8oz button mushrooms
- 2 potatoes
- 1 cup green beans

- 1 teaspoon Italian seasoning
- 1 celery stalk
- 1 teaspoon rosemary
- 2 carrots
- ½ teaspoon rubbed sage
- 3 cups vegetable broth
- ½ cup wine
- 1 can tomato sauce
- 1 can tomatoes

Directions:

1. Select "Sauté" regime on the interface of the Instant Pot.
2. Mix chopped onion, garlic, celery and cubed carrot.
3. Place vegetable mix in the pressure cooker.
4. Cook for 4 minutes on "Sauté" regime.
5. Mix Italian seasoning with sage and rosemary.
6. Wash and slice mushrooms (all types).
7. Add mushrooms with seasoning to the Instant Pot.
8. Pour wine over the ingredients.
9. Mix tomatoes with sauce and broth.
10. Add potatoes, vinegar, salt, bouquet, pepper and cook for 15 minutes on "High Pressure" regime.
11. Do a quick release.
12. Serve with peas and cornstarch!

Nutrition:

- Calories: 224
- Fat: 8g

- Carbohydrates: 33g
- Protein: 16g

Scalloped Potatoes

Pureed potatoes with milk and tender seasoning will be the dinner you want to try for sure!

Prep time: 25 minutes | **Cooking time:** 15 minutes | **Servings:** 6

Ingredients:
- 7 potatoes
- ½ teaspoon thyme
- 1 cup vegetable broth
- ½ teaspoon garlic powder
- 2 tablespoons broth
- ¼ teaspoon pepper
- 3 teaspoons creams
- 8oz cheddar cheese
- ½ teaspoon salt

Directions:
1. Wash and clean potatoes.
2. Mix salt with pepper, garlic powder and thyme.
3. Place seasoning over the potato slices.
4. Pour broth in the Instant Pot.
5. Place potatoes in the pressure cooker.
6. Pour creams over potatoes and cook for 15 minutes on "High Pressure" regime.
7. Mash potatoes with milk using blender.
8. Add cheesy sauce to the potatoes.
9. Serve!

Nutrition:
- Calories: 190
- Fat: 7g
- Carbohydrates: 26g
- Protein: 5g

Ghee

Try homemade ghee for the satisfying and delicious dinner!

Prep time: 10 minutes | **Cooking time**: 2 hours | **Servings:** 2

Ingredients:
- 24oz butter

Directions:
1. Place butter in the Instant Pot.
2. Set "Slow Cooker" regime.
3. Cook butter for 2 hours on the "Slow" regime.
4. Change regime on "Sauté" and cook for 10 minutes.
5. Place ghee in the fridge and cool it down.
6. Pour ghee in jars and add to the dishes cold!

Nutrition:
- Calories: 123
- Fat: 14g
- Carbohydrates: 0g
- Protein: 1g

Vegetable Chowder with Cheese

Your favorite chowder without meat but with more vitamins and Is calories!

Prep time: 15 minutes | **Cooking time:** 30 minutes | **Servings:** 7

Ingredients:

- 5 tablespoons butter
- 2 cups cheddar cheese
- 3 carrots
- ½ cup half and half
- 3 celery stalks
- 3 cups milk
- 1 onion
- 6 tablespoons flour
- 4 garlic cloves
- Pinch cayenne pepper
- 4 cups chicken broth
- ½ teaspoon pepper
- 3 potatoes
- 1 teaspoon salt
- 1 celery root
- ¼ teaspoon thyme
- 2 broccoli heads
- 1 cauliflower head

Directions:

1. Wash and cut on slices cauliflower, carrot, broccoli.
2. Place butter in the pressure cooker.
3. Melt it up for 3 minutes on "Sauté" regime.
4. Add chopped carrots with celery and onions.
5. Cook vegetable mix for 4 minutes on "Sauté" regime.
6. Add garlic with chicken broth and cubed potatoes.
7. Add thyme, celery, pepper, salt, paprika, cayenne pepper and mix well.
8. Cook for 15 minutes on "High Pressure" regime.
9. Add broccoli and cauliflower to the vegetable mix.
10. Cook for 10 minutes on "High Pressure" regime.
11. Add flour with butter, milk, half and half and cheese.
12. Cook for 6 minutes on "High Pressure" regime.
13. Let the pressure release naturally (10 minutes).

Nutrition:

- Calories: 400
- Fat: 26g
- Carbohydrates: 24g
- Protein: 18g

Sweet Acorn Squash

Try sweet vegetable meal for the lunch right mow – only 5 minutes and dinner is ready!

Prep time: 4 minutes | **Cooking time**: 5 minutes | **Servings:** 2

Ingredients:

- 1 acorn squash
- Pinch pf pepper
- 1 tablespoon butter
- Pinch of salt
- 1 tablespoon sugar
- ¼ teaspoon cinnamon

Directions:

1. Halve acorn and wash it up.
2. Clean acorn from the filling.
3. Pour water in the Instant Pot.
4. Place acorn in the pressure cooker.
5. Place inside of the acorn butter, sugar, salt and cinnamon.
6. Place acorn with filling in the Instant Pot.
7. Cook for 5 minutes on "High Pressure" regime.
8. Let the pressure release naturally (10 minutes).
9. Cover acorn with nutmeg and serve!

Nutrition:

- Calories: 560
- Fat: 10g
- Carbohydrates: 90g
- Protein: 10g

Potato Medley with Carrot

Healthy, juicy and delicious medley with satisfying vegetables is easy to cook with pressure cooker!

Prep time: 5 minutes | **Cooking time:** 10 minutes | **Servings:** 12

Ingredients:

- 4 tablespoons olive oil
- Parsley to taste
- 2 onions
- 2 teaspoons seasoning
- 6 garlic cloves
- 2 teaspoons Italian seasoning
- 8 pounds carrots
- 1 cup vegetable broth
- 1 cup shredded chicken meat
- 1 cup heavy creams

Directions:

1. Pour oil in the Instant Pot. Add heavy creams to the pressure cooker. Mix well and warm up for 1 minute on "Sauté" regime.
2. Wash and chop onion with carrots. Add shredded turkey.
3. Place onion in the Instant Pot.
4. Cook onions for 5 minutes on "Sauté" regime. Wait until ingredients turn golden color.
5. Add carrots, garlic cloves parsley, seasoning with Italian seasoning to the Instant Pot.
6. Pour broth to the Instant Pot.
7. Cook for 10 minutes on "High Pressure" regime.
8. Let the pressure release naturally (10 minutes).

Nutrition:

- Calories: 208
- Fat: 3g
- Carbohydrates: 43g
- Protein: 5g

Mega Vegan Chili

Try delightful, easy to cook and quick chili with minimum calories and maximum vitamins!

Prep time: 10 minutes | **Cooking time:** 30 minutes | **Servings:** 12

Ingredients:

- 2 onions
- Lime wedges
- 4 carrots
- Seasoning to taste
- 1 cup grain wheat
- 4 bell peppers
- 4 cups corn
- 2 jalapeno chili peppers
- 2 cans tomatoes
- 8 garlic cloves
- 2 cups water
- 4 cans beans
- 2 teaspoons cumin
- 1 teaspoon salt
- 1 teaspoon chili powder
- 1 teaspoon chipotle chili powder
- 1 teaspoon cardamom
- 1 cup heavy creams
- 1 lemon

Directions:

1. Wash and cut tomatoes with onion, carrots and peppers. Add sliced lemon to the vegetable mix. Pour creams over the ingredients. Mix well.
2. Place vegetables with corn in the Instant Pot. Add cardamom over the vegetables.
3. Add pepper, salt, cumin, chili powder, chipotle chili powder, garlic cloves, chili and wheat with seasoning to the Instant Pot.
4. Add beans with water to the pressure cooker.
5. Cook on "High Pressure" regime. It will take you around 3 minutes.
6. Let the pressure release naturally (10 minutes).

Nutrition:

- Calories: 214
- Fat: 4g
- Carbohydrates: 24g
- Protein: 20g

Mexican Corn on Cob with Lime Sauce

Try bright, colorful, juicy and delicious corn right now!

Prep time: 15 minutes | **Cooking time:** 15 minutes | **Servings:** 24

Ingredients:

- 24 ears corn
- 6 tablespoons lime juice
- 2 cups hemp hearts
- 2 teaspoons salt

- 12 tablespoons yeast
- 2 teaspoons cayenne pepper
- 8 tablespoons rice flour

- 8 garlic cloves
- 2 red onions
- 2 cups sea salt

Directions:

1. Wash corn and clean of the leaves. Place corn in the Instant Pot. The same time wash and peel red onion. Cut red onion on small slices. Cut corn on slices and mix with onion.
2. Add water, garlic, cayenne pepper, salt, lime juice and hemp hearts to the Instant Pot. Add sea salt to the seasoning mix.
3. Cook on "High Pressure" regime. It will take you 5 minutes to finish cooking session.
4. Mix yeast with four and add to the pressure cooker.
5. Cook for 5 minutes more on "High Pressure" regime.
6. Let the pressure release naturally (10 minutes).
7. Serve hot!

Nutrition:

- Calories: 165
- Fat: 8g

- Carbohydrates: 22g
- Protein: 4g

Vegan Chou Farci

Try satisfying filled cabbage with delicious and tender stuffing! His good looking dinner will be bright addition to any table!

Prep time: 40 minutes | **Cooking time:** 70 minutes | **Servings:** 4

Ingredients:

- ½ cup barley
- 1 cabbage
- 1 ½ cup water
- Salt to taste
- Pepper to taste
- 1 teaspoon boullion

- ½ cup tomato sauce
- 1 onion
- ¼ teaspoon cayenne pepper
- 2 carrots
- ¼ teaspoon allspice

- 1 ½ cup lentils
- ½ teaspoon ginger
- 4 garlic cloves
- 1 teaspoon paprika
- 1 teaspoon thyme
- 1 bay leaf

Directions:

1. Place barley with water in the Instant Pot.
2. Pour boullion in the pressure cooker.
3. Cook for 20 minutes on "High Pressure" regime.
4. Chop onions, carrots and add to the Instant Pot.
5. Cook carrots for 5 minutes on "High Pressure" regime.
6. Add garlic, lentils, thyme, bay leaf and all spices.
7. Add tomato sauce, salt and pepper.
8. Cook for 9 minutes on "High Pressure" regime.
9. Add cabbage to the Instant Pot.
10. Cook for 8 minutes on "High Pressure" regime.
11. Turn on oven and preheat up to 350oF.
12. Place leaves on the baking plate and add filling.
13. Roll filling with leaves.
14. Bake for 40 minutes.
15. Serve hot!

Nutrition:

- Calories: 200
- Fat: 15g

- Carbohydrates: 3g
- Protein: 9g

Cranberry Beans and Kale

Try light and satisfying cranberry soup right now!

Prep time: 15 minutes | **Cooking time:** 60 minutes | **Servings:** 16

Ingredients:

- 4 cups cranberry beans
- Pepper to taste
- 6 tablespoons yeast
- 4 ribs celery
- 10 ounces kale
- 14 garlic cloves
- 4 cups pasta
- 2 teaspoons rosemary
- 4 teaspoons salt
- ½ teaspoon paprika
- 1 teaspoon sea salt
- 1 teaspoon Italian herbs
- 1 cup green bell pepper
- ¼ teaspoon red pepper flakes
- 2 teaspoons oregano
- 26 ounces tomatoes
- 3 teaspoons basil

Directions:

1. Cover beans with water and leave for 60 minutes to rest.
2. Chop onion. Mix onion with bell pepper. Add creams over the onion mix. Mix vegetables with sea salt and herbs.
3. Mix onion with celery, garlic, red pepper flakes and rosemary. Place in the pressure cooker.
4. Cook on "Sauté" regime. It will take you around 5 minutes. Wait until ingredients turn golden color.
5. Mix tomatoes with basil, oregano, paprika and place in the Instant Pot.
6. Cook for 4 minutes on "High Pressure" regime.
7. Add beans, broth, salt and cook for 10 minutes on "High Pressure" regime.
8. Let the pressure release naturally (15 minutes).
9. Add pasta, kale and pepper. Cook for 6 minutes on "High Pressure" regime.
10. Let the pressure release naturally (10 minutes).
11. Serve hot!

Nutrition:

- Calories: 235
- Fat: 10g
- Carbohydrates: 22g
- Protein: 7g

Dal Tadka

Satisfying and easy lentil soup with vegetables and herbs – the best lunch idea ever!

Prep time: 10 minutes | **Cooking time:** 25 minutes | **Servings:** 12

Ingredients:

- 1 cup lentils
- 1 teaspoon red pepper flakes
- 1 cup moong dal
- 1 onion

- 1 tablespoon vinegar
- 1 cup chicken stock
- 6 cups water
- 1 teaspoon garam masala
- 2 tomatoes

- 1 teaspoon salt
- 6 garlic cloves
- 1 teaspoon turmeric
- 2 teaspoons ginger
- 2 teaspoons cumin seeds

Directions:

1. Mix lentils with moong dal, water, vegetable, seeds and seasoning. Pour vinegar over the ingredients. Mix ingredients well and leave for 15 minutes to rest in sauce.
2. Place mix in the Instant Pot. Pour stock over the ingredients.
3. Cook for 10 minutes on "High Pressure" regime.
4. Let the pressure release naturally (10 minutes).
5. Add masala, salt, onion, pepper flakes and turmeric to the mix.
6. Cook for 15 minutes on "Sauté" regime.
7. Do a quick release.
8. Serve hot!

Nutrition:

- Calories: 106
- Fat: 4.4g

- Carbohydrates: 12g
- Protein: 5g

Collard Green Soup

Try healthy, fresh, satisfying soup full of vitamins and low in calories!

Prep time: 60 minutes | **Cooking time:** 60 minutes | **Servings:** 8

Ingredients:
- 1 pound beans
- 1 orange
- 1 onion
- ½ cup orange juice
- 3 ribs celery
- 12 ounces greens
- 4 garlic cloves
- Salt to taste
- 2 tablespoons ginger
- Chili powder
- 1 teaspoon thyme
- ¼ teaspoon pepper
- 1 teaspoon paprika
- 1 ½ teaspoon chili powder
- 2 garlic cloves
- ¼ teaspoon cayenne powder
- 1 cup carrots
- ¼ teaspoon allspice
- 3¼ teaspoon nutmeg

Directions:
1. Pour water over the beans and leave for 1 hour to rest.
2. Pour oil in the Instant Pot. Warm up oil for 7 minutes on "Sauté" regime.
3. Chop onion and mix with celery. Add ginger to the onion mix.
4. Place onion mix in the pressure cooker. Cook for 5 minutes on "Sauté" regime.
5. Add beans with thyme, chili powder, cayenne powder, nutmeg and allspice to the Instant Pot.
6. Cook for 6 minutes on "High Pressure" regime.
7. Add ginger, carrots, paprika, pepper, salt, greens and juice with orange to the Instant Pot.
8. Cook for 10 minutes on the "High Pressure" regime.
9. Let the pressure release naturally (10 minutes).
10. Serve hot!

Nutrition:
- Calories: 192
- Fat: 6g
- Carbohydrates: 23g
- Protein: 12g

Celeriac Soup

Tender and juicy light soup with flowers aroma and soft taste!

Prep time: 10 minutes | **Cooking time:** 60 minutes | **Servings:** 4

Ingredients:
- 2 celery roots
- ½ teaspoon lemon juice
- 1 onion
- ½ teaspoon salt
- 4 garlic cloves
- ½ teaspoon thyme
- 3 cups vegetable broth
- 1/8 teaspoon white pepper

Directions:
1. Wash and cut celery in cubes.
2. Place chopped onion with thyme, celery, garlic cloves, salt and pepper in the Instant Pot.
3. Pour broth in the Instant Pot.
4. Add lemon juice to the pressure cooker.
5. Cook for 30 minutes on "High Pressure" regime.
6. Use bender to get soft and tender mixture.

Nutrition:
- Calories: 275
- Fat: 20g
- Carbohydrates: 6g
- Protein: 16g

Rasedar Rajma

Try beans with sauce and seasoning! Add herbs and taste tender and delicious dinner

Prep time: 20 minutes | **Cooking time:** 90 minutes | **Servings:** 12

Ingredients:

- 4 cups beans
- Cilantro to taste
- 12 cups water
- 1/4 teaspoon chili pepper
- 2 tablespoons root
- 2 teaspoons garam masala

- 2 teaspoons salt
- 1 teaspoon turmeric
- 2 onions
- 2 teaspoons fenugreek
- 2 teaspoons garlic
- 4 tablespoons coriander
- 1 teaspoon thyme

- 1 cup yogurt
- 4 cups tomatoes
- 3 tablespoons heavy creams

Directions:

1. Pour water over the beans. Add ginger and salt to the beans. Leave beans to soak for 15 minutes. Dry beans well in 15 minutes.
2. Cook for 6 minutes in the Instant Pot for 6 minutes.
3. Leave beans to rest for 60 minutes.
4. Mix onion with garlic and add to the pressure cooker.
5. Cook for 1 minute on "Sauté" regime.
6. Wash and cut vegetables. Add tomatoes with fenugreek, turmeric, coriander, garam masala and chili pepper. Add heavy creams to the vegetable mix. Mix well using fork.
7. Cook for 5 minutes on "High Pressure" regime.
8. Add thyme, tomatoes, yogurt, cilantro and cook for 20 minutes on "Sauté" regime.
9. Let the pressure release naturally (10 minutes).
10. Place ingredients on the plate and mix well using blender.
11. Serve!

Nutrition:

- Calories: 240
- Fat: 1g

- Carbohydrates: 44g
- Protein: 16g

Green on Green Soup

Extra fresh, healthy and light green soup for the true lovers of healthy lifestyle!

Prep time: 30 minutes | **Cooking time:** 90 minutes | **Servings:** 12

Ingredients:

- 3 onions
- Soy yogurt
- 12 garlic cloves
- Lemon slices to serve
- 9 carrots
- Salt to taste
- 3 potatoes
- 3 tablespoons lemon juice
- 1 cup peas
- 3 tablespoons cashew butter
- 10 cups water
- 1 cup basil
- 12 ounces mushrooms
- 9 tablespoons yeast
- 12 pounds greens
- 1 teaspoon thyme
- 1 cup halved cherry tomatoes
- 1 cup Parmesan cheese
- 1 lime
- 2 teaspoons oregano
- 1 teaspoon salt

Directions:

1. Mix oregano with salt, thyme, greens, basil, salt, onion and garlic. Add cherry tomatoes and lime slices to seasoning mix and mix well.
2. Add peas, carrots, potato to seasoning mix and place in the pressure cooker.
3. Pour water over the ingredients in the Instant Pot.
4. Cook for 10 minutes on "High Pressure" regime.
5. Let the pressure release naturally (30 minutes).
6. Add sliced mushrooms and cook for 30 minutes on "High Pressure" regime.
7. Add yeast, butter, lemon juice and cook for 5 minutes on "High Pressure" regime.
8. Let the pressure release naturally (15 minutes). Put cheese over the ingredients and wait until it starts melting.
9. Serve with soy yogurt!

Nutrition:

- Calories: 191
- Fat: 6g
- Carbohydrates: 23g
- Protein: 11g

Dal Bhaji

Try how real India tastes with this easy and satisfying receipt!

Prep time: 45 minutes | **Cooking time:** 45 minutes | **Servings:** 6

Ingredients:

- 1 cup masoor dal
- ½ teaspoons lemon juice
- 3 cups water
- Salt to taste
- 1 cup cubed vegetables
- 3 tomatoes
- ½ cup peas
- ¼ teaspoon turmeric powder
- 1 onion
- ½ teaspoon cayenne
- 1 teaspoon ginger
- 3 teaspoons masala
- 1 teaspoon garlic
- 1 bell pepper

Directions:

1. Place dal in the Instant Pot.
2. Add water to the pressure cooker.
3. Cook for 15 minutes on "High Pressure" regime.
4. Mix green beans with cubed vegetables and cook for 5 minutes on "High Pressure" regime in the Instant Pot.
5. Add onions, ginger, garlic, bell pepper and cook for 6 minutes on "High Pressure" regime.
6. Add masala, cayenne, and turmeric powder, tomatoes, salt and lemon juice.
7. Cook for 20 minutes on "Low Pressure" regime.
8. Do a quick release.

Nutrition:

- Calories: 169
- Fat: 1g
- Carbohydrates: 31g
- Protein: 12g

Taco Salad

Try crispy, easy, fresh and juicy taco salad with light seasoning and fresh sauce!

Prep time: 15 minutes | **Cooking time:** 40 minutes | **Servings:** 8

Ingredients:

- 1 pound beans
- 1 green bell pepper
- 3 cups water
- Salt to taste
- 1 onion
- 3 teaspoons chili powder
- 2 garlic cloves
- 2 tablespoons tomato paste
- 2 teaspoons oregano
- 2 red chilies
- ½ teaspoon cumin

Directions:

1. Pour water over the beans.
2. Cook for 10 minutes on "High Pressure" regime in the pressure cooker.
3. Let beans to rest for 60 minutes.
4. Mix chopped onion with garlic, oregano, chilies, cumin, chili powder, salt and bell pepper.
5. Add tomato paste with vegetables and seasoning to the Instant Pot.
6. Cook taco salad for 5 minutes on "High Pressure" regime.
7. Add oil and cook for 30 minutes on "Sauté" regime.
8. Serve with tacos and yogurt!

Nutrition:

- Calories: 550
- Fat: 24g
- Carbohydrates: 18g
- Protein: 26g

Hummus Ghanoush

Try spicy, light, satisfying and easy humus for the lunch today!

Prep time: 10 minutes | **Cooking time:** 5 minutes | **Servings:** 16

Ingredients:

- 2 eggplants
- Sumac to serve
- 6 garlic cloves
- 1 teaspoon paprika

- 2 cans chickpeas
- 2 teaspoons salt
- 6 tablespoons lemon juice
- ½ teaspoon paprika

- 6 tablespoons tahini
- 1 teaspoon cumin

Directions:

1. Wash and cut eggplant. You should get like 5 cm cubes.
2. Mix cumin with tahini, paprika, lemon juice, salt and paprika. Use spoon to mix all the seasoning well.
3. Place eggplant in the pressure cooker. You may pour a little bit oil of the bottom – it will give golden color to the eggplant.
4. Cook eggplant for on "High Pressure" regime. It will take you around 2 minutes to make eggplant cooked enough.
5. Add seasoning mix and chickpeas to the Instant Pot.
6. Cook on "High Pressure" regime. It will take you around 3 minutes.
7. Do a quick release.
8. Serve with lemon slices over the dish and add fresh basil leaves!

Nutrition:

- Calories: 79
- Fat: 5g

- Carbohydrates: 9g
- Protein: 3g

Pav Bhaji

Try sandwich and burger filling in best vegan traditions right now!

Prep time: 15 minutes | **Cooking time:** 60 minutes | **Servings:** 12

Ingredients:

- 2 onions
- Buns to serve
- 2 teaspoons ginger
- 1 teaspoon lemon juice
- 2 teaspoons garlic
- Salt to taste
- 4 chilies

- 1 teaspoon turmeric powder
- 2 bell peppers
- 2 teaspoons chili powder
- 6 tomatoes
- 6 tablespoons masala
- 2 cups beans

- 2 cups carrots
- 2 cups cabbage
- 2 cups cauliflower
- 1 cup green peas
- 4 cups potatoes
- 1 cup cucumbers

Directions:

1. Wash and cut potatoes on cubes.
2. Chop onions.
3. Mix cubed carrots with green beans, cut cabbage, cauliflower ad potatoes. Wash and cut cucumber on 1 cm cubes. Add cucumber to the vegetable mix.
4. Place vegetables with peas in the Instant Pot and cook for 5 minutes on "High Pressure" regime.
5. Place onions with ginger, garlic, bell peppers and cook for 8 minutes on "High Pressure" regime.
6. Mix masala, chili powder, turmeric and salt with tomatoes.
7. Add vegetables and cook for 20 minutes in the pressure cooker.
8. Add lemon juice. Mix ingredients with lemon juice.
9. Place mix in the plate and mix using blender.
10. Place vegetable mix on buns and serve!

Nutrition:

- Calories: 120
- Fat: 3g

- Carbohydrates: 17g
- Protein: 3g

Thai Traditional Vegetable Curry

Try the most satisfying and tender vegetable curry with delicious seasoning and bright fresh herbs!

Prep time: 20 minutes | **Cooking time:** 10 minutes | **Servings:** 12

Ingredients:
- 2 bunches broccoli
- 15basil leaves
- 4 teaspoons garlic
- 2 cups chickpeas
- 2 cups milk
- 1 pound mushrooms
- 4 tablespoons soy sauce
- 2 pounds sweet potatoes
- 2 teaspoons lemongrass
- Pinch of red pepper flakes
- 2 teaspoons basil
- 1/2 teaspoon cardamom
- 1 teaspoon coriander
- ¼ teaspoon cinnamon
- 1 teaspoon sea salt
- 1 teaspoon rosemary

Directions:
1. Wash and cut broccoli. You should get small slices.
2. Add coriander and rosemary with sea salt to the broccoli slices. Mix ingredients well to cover broccoli from all sides with seasoning.
3. Place water in the Instant Pot. Warm up water for 3 minutes on "Sauté" regime.
4. Add broccoli with garlic, milk, soy, sauce, lemongrass and potatoes, mushrooms, red pepper flakes, potatoes, basil, cardamom, coriander to the pressure cooker.
5. Cook for 7 minutes on "High Pressure" regime.
6. Add chickpeas and cook for 5 minutes more on "High Pressure" regime.
7. Do a quick release.

Nutrition:
- Calories: 340
- Fat: 10g
- Carbohydrates: 56g
- Protein:6g

Lime-Chipotle Tortilla Chips

Try bright, colorful and delicious veggie dinner right today!

Prep time: 30 minutes | **Cooking time:** 20 minutes | **Servings:** 12

Ingredients:
- 1cup barley
- Tortilla chips for serving
- 6 cups tomatoes
- Salt to taste
- 6 tablespoons water
- 2 cups beans
- 6 cups onions
- 2 cup black beans
- 6 garlic cloves
- 4 cups corn
- 2 teaspoons cumin
- 4 green bell peppers
- 2 teaspoons chili powder
- 2 tablespoons Tabasco sauce
- 2 tablespoons hot sauce
- 2 tablespoons lemon juice

Directions:
1. Pour water in the Instant Pot. Warm up water – do not bring it to boil. Add lemon juice to the Instant Pot and mix well with water. Add water if there is not enough.
2. Add garlic, cumin, chili powder and sauce to the pressure cooker. If you want more tender sauce – warm it up for 2 minutes in microwave with seasoning.
3. Wash and clean bell peppers of seeds. Add chopped bell peppers to the Instant Pot.
4. Add tomatoes and corn to the Instant Pot. Add hot sauce and mix well with ingredients.
5. Add barley, salt, beans and cook for 20 minutes on "High Pressure" regime.
6. Do a quick release.

Nutrition:
- Calories: 570
- Fat: 27g
- Carbohydrates: 73g
- Protein: 8g

DESSERTS

Layered Cheesecake

Tree soft layers with the creamy basis – easy and quick cheesecake in the Instant Pot!

Prep time: 60 minutes | **Cooking time:** 60 minutes | **Servings:** 13

Ingredients:

- 4 tablespoons butter
- Sugared cranberries
- 1 ½ cup chocolate cookie crumble
- 4oz chocolate

- 8oz cream cheese
- 4oz white chocolate
- 1 cup sugar
- 4oz milk chocolate
- 2 tablespoons cornstarch

- 1 tablespoons vanilla extract
- 3 eggs
- ½ cup Greek yogurt

Directions:

1. Cover Instant Pot with the foil.
2. Place melted butter on the bottom of the cups for the baking in Pressure Cooker.
3. Top melted butter with the cookie crumbs.
4. Mix eggs, sugar, cornstarch, yogurt and vanilla extract with the cream cheese. Lay on the crumbs layer in the Instant Pot.
5. Place melted milk chocolate in the Instant Pot.
6. Add melted white and dark chocolate.
7. Place mix in the fridge for 20 minutes.
8. Pour water in the Instant Pot.
1. 9. Place cups with the   cheesecake in the Instant Pot and cook on "High Pressure" regime for 45 minutes.
9. Let cheesecake rest after the baking for 30 minutes.
10. Serve with berries!

Nutrition:

- Calories: 277
- Fat: 18g

- Carbohydrates: 23g
- Protein:5g

Chocolate Chip Cake

Crispy cake with chocolate slices in the Instant Pot – delicious pies are easy to cook with the Instant Pot!

Prep time: 15 minutes | **Cooking time:** 45 minutes | **Servings:** 12

Ingredients:

- ¾ cup wheat flour
- 2 cups chocolate chips
- ¾ cup flour
- ½ teaspoon vanilla extract
- ½ teaspoon salt
- Egg
- 1 teaspoon baking soda
- 15 ounce can pureed pumpkin
- ½ teaspoon baking powder
- ½ cup Greek yogurt
- ¾ teaspoon pumpkin pie spice
- 2 tablespoon canola oil
- ¾ cup sugar
- 3 bananas

Directions:

1. Clean and mash banana with water using blender.
2. Mix baking powder, baking soda, flour, salt, pumpkin pie spice and set aside.
3. Warm up puree in microwave and mash in a blender with banana.
4. Mix banana with yogurt, beaten egg, vanilla, oil and sugar using mixer.
5. Add all the ingredients, apart from the chips to the blended mix and mix one more time.
6. Make crisps of the chocolate chips. Add chocolate chips to the mix.
7. Pour 2 cups water in the Instant Pot.
8. Place cup with the pie in the Instant Pot and cook for 35 minutes on "High Pressure" regime.
9. Leave pie in the Instant Pot and let the pressure release naturally for 10 minutes!

Nutrition:

- Calories: 100
- Fat: 4g
- Carbohydrates: 22g
- Protein:2g

Peanut Butter Cheesecake in Cup

Small, easy and super tender cheesecake in the cup will be small happiness for you!

Prep time: 10 minutes | **Cooking time:** 60 minutes | **Servings:** 8

Ingredients:

- 1 cup crushed Oreo cookies
- 2/3 cup peanut butter chips
- 2 tablespoons melted butter
- 1/3 cup heavy creams
- 12 ounces cream cheese
- 6oz milk chocolate
- ½ cup sugar
- ¾ cup chocolate chips
- ½ cup peanut butter
- 1 egg yolk
- ¼ cup heavy cream
- 2 eggs
- 1 ½ teaspoon vanilla extract
- 1 tablespoon flour

Directions:

1. Cover Instant Pot with the foil. Prepare cup for the baking in the Instant Pot.
2. Mix butter with the crushed Oreo cookies.
3. Place mix in the fridge for 10 minutes.
4. Mix cream cheese with sugar, butter, creams, flour, vanilla and eggs.
5. Add chocolate chips to the creamy mix.
6. Add cheese, chocolate, yolks, vanilla extract and remaining ingredients to the creamy mix and mix one more time using blender.
7. Pour water in the Instant Pot.
8. Place cup with creamy mix and Oreo with butter on top in the Instant Pot.
9. Cook cheesecake for 50 minutes on "High Pressure" regime.
10. Place cheesecake in the fridge for 5 hours after the cooking.
11. Serve with chocolate cookies!

Nutrition:

- Calories: 220
- Fat: 10g
- Carbohydrates: 32g
- Protein:4g

Banoffee Pie

Soft banana with caramel and creamy layers – light and easy pie!

Prep time: 10 minutes | **Cooking time:** 40 minutes | **Servings:** 16

Ingredients:

- 4 cups biscuits
- Paleo caramel sauce
- 4 cups Greek yogurt
- 1 teaspoon vanilla essence
- 5 bananas
- 5 tablespoons butter
- 1 can prepared caramel

Directions:

1. Pour water in the Instant Pot.
2. Pour caramel in the Pot and warm up.
3. Crush biscuits in the blender.
4. Place crumbs, butter and caramel in the Instant Pot and cook for 3 minutes on "Saute" regime.
5. Peel and slice bananas.
6. Mix yogurt, vanilla essence and mashed bananas in the bowl.
7. Make a layer of the crumbs. Add ingredients on top and cover with caramel sauce!

Nutrition:

- Calories: 678
- Fat: 33g
- Carbohydrates: 90g
- Protein:11g

Bundt Cake

Crispy and tender, healthy and easy – all these about one chocolate cake!

Prep time: 5 minutes | **Cooking time:** 25 minutes | **Servings:** 4

Ingredients:
- 1 ½ cup flour
- 1/3 cup chocolate chips
- 2 bananas
- ½ teaspoon cinnamon
- ¼ cup honey
- 2 drops essential oil
- 1 teaspoon vanilla
- 1 teaspoon baking soda
- 2 eggs
- 1 tablespoon vinegar
- 2 tablespoons coconut oil
- ½ cup milk

Directions:
1. Mix flour with melted butter.
2. Cover Pot with the foil.
3. Mix vinegar with and milk and cook to get buttermilk.
4. Mix mashed bananas with eggs, oil, honey, vanilla, oil and milk.
5. Blend banana mix with the remaining ingredients.
6. Add chocolate chips to the mix.
7. Pour water in the Instant Pot.
8. Place buttermilk mix on the bottom of the cup for the baking. Add banana mix.
9. Bake pie for 25 minutes on "High Pressure" regime in the Instant Pot.
10. Serve with powdered sugar!

Nutrition:
- Calories: 280
- Fat:11g
- Carbohydrates: 43g
- Protein:0g

England Blueberry Pudding

Super delicious and full of vitamins pudding is easy to cook in Instant Pot!

Prep time: 15 minutes | **Cooking time:** 50 minutes | **Servings:** 12

Ingredients:
- 3 cups flour
- 1lb blueberries
- 1 teaspoon baking powder
- 10oz milk
- 1 teaspoon salt
- 3 beaten eggs
- 1 cup butter
- 1 cup sugar
- 3 tablespoons breadcrumbs

Directions:
1. Mix flour with baking powder.
2. Place butter in the Instant Pot. Bring to the melting condition. Put crumbs in the Por.
3. Mix eggs with milk and blueberries.
4. Unite all the mixtures.
5. Cover Instant Pot with the foil.
6. Cook pie for 15 minutes on "High Pressure" regime.
7. After that cook on "Low Pressure" for 35 minutes.
8. Serve with creams!

Nutrition:
- Calories: 232
- Fat: 7g
- Carbohydrates: 42g
- Protein:3g

Espresso Flan

Natural coffee taste with the soft almond flavor and tender texture on your plate!

Prep time: 10 minutes	**Cooking time:** 20 minutes	**Servings:** 7

Ingredients:

- 4 eggs
- Ground espresso
- 1 can condensed milk
- 1/2 cup toasted almonds
- 14oz milk
- ½ cup cane sugar
- ¾ cup espresso
- ½ teaspoon espresso salt
- 1 teaspoon pure vanilla extract

Directions:

1. Mix beaten eggs, condensed milk and espresso salt. Add espresso with whole milk to the mix. Use blender to mix ingredients.
2. Place foil in the Pot.
3. Place sugar in the Instant Pot and cook for 5 minutes on "Saute" regime.
4. Add vanilla extract, cooked milk, salt, cane sugar and almonds.
5. Place pie ingredients in the Instant Pot and cook for 15 minutes on "High Pressure" regime.

Nutrition:

- Calories: 110
- Fat: 3g
- Carbohydrates: 18g
- Protein: 3g

Key Lime Pie

Fresh taste, crispy bottom of the pie and tender flavor! Key Lime is one of the most favorite pies nowadays! Try it in the new, more tasty and juicy variant – cooked in Instant Pot!

Prep time: 10 minutes	**Cooking time:** 15 minutes	**Servings:** 3

Ingredients:

- 1/2 cup graham crackers
- 1/2 teaspoon key lime zest
- 2 tablespoons melted butter
- 1/2 can caramel
- ¼ cup sugar
- 1 cup lemon juice
- 3 tablespoons honey
- 1 egg yolk
- ½ cup heavy creams
- 1 cup key lime juice
- 1 tablespoon sugar
- 1/2 tablespoons lemon zest

Directions:

1. Crush crackers in the blender. Add sugar to the crushed crackers to make them sweet.
2. Mix melted butter with the crackers. Use fork to make a mix – it will be the base of the cake.
3. Cover Instant Pot with the foil. The same moment mix lemon juice with the melted honey. The same time – prepare special baking form for the Instant Pot to cook your cake in.
4. Mix egg yolks with sugar and place in the Instant Pot. Use blender to get sweet and the same time light mix.
5. Place lime zest in the blender and mix with the yolks and sugar.
6. Add caramel, creams, sugar and remaining zest to make mix tender. Blend well with the base of the cake.
7. Place lime mix in the Pot.
8. Pour water in the Instant Pot.
9. Cook pie in the Instant Pot for 15 minutes on "High Pressure" regime.

Nutrition:

- Calories: 310
- Fat: 17g
- Carbohydrates: 36g
- Protein: 6g

Rice Pudding

Easy, tasty and healthy pudding will be extra quick to cook with Instant Pot!

Prep time: 10 minutes | **Cooking time:** 15 minutes | **Servings:** 10

Ingredients:
- 5 cups rice
- 6 cans caramel
- 15 cups coconut milk
- 15 strips orange zest
- 5 cups almond milk
- 5 vanilla beans
- 5 cups water
- 3 teaspoon ground cloves
- 10 cinnamon sticks

Directions:
1. Pour water over the rice and leave for 20 minutes to rest.
2. Mix milk, coconut milk, almond milk and water.
3. Add cloves, vanilla. Cook for 5 minutes more. Pour milk mix in the Instant Pot and cook for 5 minutes more on "Saure" regime.
4. Add rice to the mix and cook for 15 minutes on "High Pressure".
5. Serve with cloves and zest!

Nutrition:
- Calories: 140
- Fat: 6g
- Carbohydrates: 19g
- Protein:3g

Crusted Cream Cheesecake

Crumbs with soften cheese and light creams will taste special!

Prep time: 10 minutes | **Cooking time:** 25 minutes | **Servings:** 6

Ingredients:
- 1 cup cream buisquits
- ½ cup double cream
- 3 tablespoons melted butter
- Few drops almond extract
- 3 cups cream cheese
- 1 teaspoon vanilla extract
- ½ cup caster sugar
- 2 eggs
- 2 tablespoons custard powder

Directions:
1. Make crumbs of the biscuits.
2. Mix melted butter with the biscuits.
3. Prepare cake tin and cover with the foil.
4. Place butter mix on the bottom of the tin.
5. Mix cream, almond extract, cream cheese, vanilla extract, caster sugar, eggs and powder. Place on the butter mix.
6. Pour water in the Instant Pot.
7. Cook cake for 25 minutes on "High Pressure".
8. Cook cake in the fridge for 4 hours.
9. Serve with creamy biscuits!

Nutrition:
- Calories: 239
- Fat: 2g
- Carbohydrates: 22g
- Protein:3g

Chocolate Cake

Crispy outside and softy tender inside – just try and you will like it!

Prep time: 5 minutes | **Cooking time:** 40 minutes | **Servings:** 6

Ingredients:
- ¾ cup flour
- 1 teaspoon xanthan gum
- ¾ cup cocoa powder
- 1 teaspoon vanilla extract
- 1 ½ cups powdered sugar
- ½ teaspoon baking powder
- ½ cup butter
- 3 eggs

Directions:
1. Beat eggs and separate yolks from the whites.
2. Blend egg whites.
3. In the other cup, blend egg yolks.
4. Mix flour, baking and cocoa powders.
5. In the other cup, mix melted butter and sugar.
6. Add vanilla extract to the united mixtures.
7. Stir in egg white and mix.
8. Pour in egg yolk and mix.
9. Add flour to the mix and place baking form with the dough in the Instant Pot.
10. Cook on "High Pressure" regime for 35 minutes.
11. Serve hot!

Nutrition:
- Calories: 104
- Fat: 5g
- Carbohydrates: 15g
- Protein:1g

Apple Cider

Liquid dessert can be even better than any cakes – check it out!

Prep time: 5 minutes | **Cooking time:** 15 minutes | **Servings:** 6

Ingredients:
- 10 apples
- Water
- 1 orange
- 1 teaspoon cardamom
- 2 cinnamon stalks
- 2 teaspoon cloves
- 1 cup brown sugar

Directions:
1. Wash and cut fruits.
2. Pour water in the Instant Pot.
3. Place cut fruits in the Instant Pot.
4. Cook fruits for 10 minutes on "High Pressure" regime.
5. Mash fruits in the Instant Pot.
6. Cook fruits for 5 more minutes on "High Pressure" regime.
7. Strain mixture and serve warm!

Nutrition:
- Calories: 120
- Fat: 0g
- Carbohydrates: 28g
- Protein:0g

Thai Coconut Rice

Asian dessert can not only give you vitamins, but also add colors to the grey weekdays!

Prep time: 10 minutes | **Cooking time:** 10 minutes | **Servings:** 4

Ingredients:

- 1 cup thai sweet rice
- Sesame seeds
- 1 ½ cups water

- 1 mango
- 1 can coconut milk
- ½ teaspoon cornstarch

- 4 tablespoons pure sugar cane
- 1 punch salt

Directions:

1. Pour water in the Instant Pot.
2. Place rice in the Instant Pot.
3. Cook rice on "High Pressure" regime for 10 minutes.
4. Warm up milk.
5. Add salt and sugar to milk.
6. Pour milk on the rice and cook for 10 minutes on the same settings in the Instant Pot.
7. Mix cornstarch with water and add to the rice.
8. Serve rice with mango slices and coconut sauce with sesame seeds!

Nutrition:

- Calories:440
- Fat: 12g

- Carbohydrates: 82g
- Protein:12g

Upside-Down Pie

Soft and sweet apples with crispy dough – upside down pie will make you fall in love with apple desserts! What can be better that delicious cake/ But can something be better than super juicy cake in the Instant Pot?

Prep time: 10 minutes | **Cooking time:** 15 minutes | **Servings:** 2

Ingredients:

- 1/2 cups water
- 1/4 teaspoon baking soda
- 1/2 apples
- 1/4 teaspoons baking powder
- 1/2 tablespoon lemon juice

- 1 orange
- ½ teaspoon cinnamon
- ¼ cup raw sugar
- 1 cup honey
- ½ cup lemon marmalade
- ½ teaspoon cinnamon
- 1 egg

- 1 cup flour
- 1 cup ricotta cheese
- 1 teaspoon vanilla essence
- 1/3 cup sugar

Directions:

1. Pour water in the Instant Pot. Bring it to boil on the "Saute" regime for 5 minutes.
2. Slice apple. Mix with marmalade and honey. Warm up this mix in the Instant Pot for 5 minutes on "High Pressure" regime.
3. Cover orange slices with lemon juice. Add apples with marmalade sauce.
4. Mix sugar with flour. You may use blender to get more tender texture.
5. Mix all the ingredients together.
6. Place mix in the baking forms and place it in the Instant Pot. It is better to cook in the small round shape caking cups.
7. Cook pie in the Instant Pot for 15 minutes on "High Pressure" regime.
8. Serve with the powdered sugar!

Nutrition:

- Calories: 522
- Fat: 34g

- Carbohydrates: 0g
- Protein:45g

Samoa Cheesecake

This ricotta dessert is one of the most delicious ones!

Prep time: 15 minutes | **Cooking time:** 80 minutes | **Servings:** 12

Ingredients:
- 32oz Ricotta cheese
- 2 cups shredded coconut
- 1 cup lemon juice
- 1 cup pineapple juice
- 1 cup chopped pineapples
- 32oz cream cheese
- 2 cups melted chocolate
- 24oz sour cream
- 2 cans condensed milk
- 12 eggs
- 6 cups crumbled oreos
- 6 tablespoons cornstarch
- 1 teaspoon vanilla extract

Directions:
1. Mix cream cheese with Ricotta cheese.
2. Mix flour, cornstarch and eggs.
3. Mix eggs, pineapple juice and chipped pineapples with the cheese mix. Use blender to mix well.
4. Add Oreo to the mix.
5. Pour water in the Instant Pot.
6. Place foil and add cheesecake mix.
7. Cook cheesecake for 40 minutes on "High Pressure" regime.
8. Remove cheesecake from the Instant Pot and place can of condensed milk inside.
9. Cook milk on "High Pressure" for 40 minutes.
10. Pour caramel on the cheesecake and add remaining ingredients as a topping.

Nutrition:
- Calories: 198
- Fat: 14g
- Carbohydrates: 12g
- Protein:25g

Chocolate Muffins with Zucchini

Extraordinary, super sweet and super satisfying muffins – exactly what you wanted to try!

Prep time: 30 minutes | **Cooking time:** 10 minutes | **Servings:** 25

Ingredients:
- 2 eggs
- ½ teaspoon baking soda
- 1 cup juice
- 1 cup flour
- 2 teaspoons vanilla extract
- 3 tablespoons cocoa powder
- 1 tablespoon butter
- ¼ teaspoon salt
- 1 cup water
- ¾ teaspoon cinnamon
- 1 cup zucchini
- 1/3 cup chocolate chips

Directions:
1. Mix eggs with oil and vanilla extract. Add juice to the mix.
2. Melt butter.
3. Add melted butter with cocoa powder to the mix.
4. Mix flour, baking soda and salt with cinnamon.
5. Add flour mix to the chocolate mixture.
6. Add zucchini and chocolate chips to the mix.
7. Pour water in the Instant Pot.
8. Form muffins.
9. Place muffins in the Instant Pot.
10. Bake muffins for 10 minutes on "High Pressure" regime.

Nutrition:
- Calories: 255
- Fat: 9g
- Carbohydrates: 20g
- Protein:23g

Applesauce

Healthy, tender and satisfying applesauce is super sweet and delicious sauce!

Prep time: 5 minutes | **Cooking time:** 5 minutes | **Servings:** 3

Ingredients:
- 12 apples
- 1 cup water
- 2 tablespoons butter
- ¼ teaspoon salt
- 1 tablespoon cinnamon
- ½ lemon juice
- 1 tablespoon honey

Directions:
1. Wash and cut apples.
2. Mix butter, cinnamon, honey, lemon juice, salt and water.
3. Add apples to the honey mix.
4. Use blender to mix apples.
5. Place apples in the Instant Pot.
6. Cook on "High Pressure" regime for 5 minutes.
7. Serve with waffles!

Nutrition:
- Calories: 90
- Fat: 0g
- Carbohydrates: 22g
- Protein:0g

Vanilla Butter Cheesecake

Make easy and low carb dessert in few minutes!

Prep time: 5 minutes | **Cooking time:** 20 minutes | **Servings:** 8

Ingredients:
- 16 ounces cream cheese
- ½ cup sugar substitute
- 2 eggs
- 1 tablespoon vanilla extract
- 2 tablespoons butter
- 1 tablespoon cocoa

Directions:
1. Place beaten eggs with cheese in the blender and mix well.
2. Pour water in the Instant Pot.
3. Add vanilla extract, cocoa and sugar to the cream cheese. Mix well.
4. Place cheesecake mix in the Instant Pot.
5. Cook cheesecake for 20 minutes on "High Pressure" regime.
6. Add butter to the dessert and serve!

Nutrition:
- Calories: 870
- Fat: 38g
- Carbohydrates: 72g
- Protein:11g

Chip Bundt Cake

Easy chocolate cake with banana!

Prep time: 5 minutes | **Cooking time:** 25 minutes | **Servings:** 12

Ingredients:
- 3 cups flour
- 1cup chocolate chips
- 6 bananas
- 1 teaspoon cinnamon
- 1 cup raw honey
- 6 drops nutmeg oil
- 3 teaspoons vanilla
- 3 teaspoons baking soda
- 6 eggs
- 3 tablespoons vinegar
- 9 tablespoons coconut oil
- 1 cup milk

Directions:
1. Pour water in the Instant Pot.
2. Place foil in the Instant Pot.
3. Mix vinegar with milk.
4. Mash bananas.
5. Mix bananas with eggs, oil, vanilla, milk and other ingredients, apart from chips.
6. Add chocolate chips to the mix.
7. Cook cake for 25 minutes in the Instant Pot on "High Pressure" regime.
8. Serve with heavy creams.

Nutrition:
- Calories: 400
- Fat: 22g
- Carbohydrates: 48g
- Protein:5g

White Chocolate Cheesecake with Raspberry

Good looking, healthy, sweet and satisfying!

Prep time: 10 minutes | **Cooking time:** 25 minutes | **Servings:** 16

Ingredients:
- 8 tablespoons melted butter
- 4 tablespoons cream
- 4 cups soft cheese
- 8 strawberries
- 1 cup lime juice
- 3 tablespoons sugared powder
- 3 egg
- 1 cup sugar
- 1 tablespoon honey
- 1 teaspoon vanilla essence
- Handful raspberries
- 2 tablespoons white chocolate

Directions:
1. Melt butter.
2. Mix butter with biscuit crumbs. Add lime juice to the mix.
3. Mix sugar with soft cream using blender.
4. Add beaten egg, honey and vanilla essence to the cheese mix.
5. Add white chocolate and raspberries to the cheesecake mix.
6. Pour water in the Instant Pot. Add blended strawberries and mix well in the hot Instant Pot.
7. Place cheesecake in the Instant Pot.
8. Cook cheesecake in the Instant Pot for 25 minutes on "High Pressure" regime.
9. Serve with berries and sugared powder!

Nutrition:
- Calories:412
- Fat: 28g
- Carbohydrates: 34g
- Protein:7g

Toffee Pudding

Sweet, crispy and satisfying dessert with minimal amount of calories!

Prep time: 5 minutes | **Cooking time:** 15 minutes | **Servings:** 2

Ingredients:
- ½ cup butter
- ½ teaspoon ginger
- ½ cup sugar
- Caramel sauce
- 1 cup flour
- 1 tablespoon cocoa powder
- 2 eggs
- 2 tablespoons milk

Directions:
1. Mix melted butter with sugar.
2. Add cocoa powder and ginger to butter mix.
3. Add eggs and milk to cocoa mixture.
4. Add flour and caramel sauce to the mix.
5. Pour water in the Instant Pot.
6. Place cake mix in the Instant Pot.
7. Cook dessert for 15 minutes on "High Pressure" regime.
8. Serve with fresh mint leaves!

Nutrition:
- Calories: 300
- Fat: 5g
- Carbohydrates: 0g
- Protein:3g

Sour Cream Mug Cake

Vitamins, cream and sweet berries in a mug!

Prep time: 5 minutes | **Cooking time:** 5 minutes | **Servings:** 20

Ingredients:
- 4 cups flour
- 3 tablespoons vanilla extract
- 1 1/2 cup sugar
- 9 tablespoons milk
- 8 teaspoons baking powder
- 12 tablespoons sugar
- 10 tablespoons vegetable oil
- 19 raspberries
- 4 tablespoons sour cream
- 1 tablespoon lemon juice
- 4 tablespoons milk

Directions:
1. Pour water in the Instant pot.
2. Mix flour, sugar and baking powder.
3. Mix oil, sour cream, lemon juice and milk.
4. Add raspberries to the mix.
5. Place mixture to the Instant Pot and cook for 3 minutes on "High Pressure" regime.
6. Mix powdered sugar, milk and vanilla.
7. Add vanilla mix to the cake.
8. Serve with fresh mint leaves!

Nutrition:
- Calories: 420
- Fat: 25g
- Carbohydrates: 43g
- Protein:5g

Milky Lava Cake

Crispy caramel with the light and sweet melting sugar mix inside!

Prep time: 5 minutes | **Cooking time:** 11 minutes | **Servings:** 3

Ingredients:
- 1 egg
- 1 2/3 cups caramel sauce
- 2 egg yolks
- 2 tablespoons flour

Directions:
1. Whisk egg yolks with the mixer.
2. Add caramel with the yolks.
3. Pour water in the instant Pot.
4. Add flour and sauce to the caramel mix.
5. Cook cake for 11 minutes on "High Pressure" regime.
6. Serve hot in a cup!

Nutrition:
- Calories: 340
- Fat:14g
- Carbohydrates: 53g
- Protein:4g

Strawberry Cheesecake

Super tender cheesecake? In Instant Pot you can cook whatever you want!

Prep time: 10 minutes | **Cooking time:** 50 minutes | **Servings:** 7

Ingredients:
- ½ cup butter
- ½ cup cream
- 2 cups soft cheese
- 2 teaspoons cinnamon
- 1 cup sugar
- 2 eggs
- 1 teaspoon vanilla essence
- 3 tablespoons honey
- 12 strawberries
- Biscuit crumbs

Directions:
1. Mix biscuit crumbs with cinnamon.
2. Mix butter with cheese and sugar.
3. Place biscuit crumbs on the bottom of the Instant Pot.
4. Mix eggs with creams and vanilla essence.
5. Add egg mix to the cheesy mixture.
6. Add honey and mashed berries to the cheesy mix.
7. Place cheesy mix on top of the crumbs.
8. Bake cheesecake for 40 minutes on "High Pressure" regime.
9. Serve with fresh berries!

Nutrition:
- Calories: 170
- Fat: 7g
- Carbohydrates: 23g
- Protein:20g

Nutella Fudge

The most delicious creamy chocolate dessert you have ever tried!

Prep time: 5 minutes | **Cooking time:** 5 minutes | **Servings:** 16

Ingredients:
- 2 ½ cups marshmallows
- 5 cracker sheets
- 10 ounces chocolate chips
- ½ cup Nutella
- 10 ounces milk chocolate chips

Directions:
1. Place marshmallows on the bottom of the Instant Pot.
2. Mix chips with Nutella.
3. Place cracker sheets with Nutella mix on top of marshmallows.
4. Cook dessert on "High Pressure" regime for 2 minutes.
5. Serve with chocolate creams!

Nutrition:
- Calories: 95
- Fat: 5g
- Carbohydrates: 12g
- Protein: 1g

Pumpkin Cheesecake

Soft and tender juicy pumpkin cheesecake will be perfect dessert!

Prep time: 15 minutes | **Cooking time:** 60 minutes | **Servings:** 7

Ingredients:
- ½ cup melted butter
- Pinch of nutmeg
- 2 cups soft cheese
- ½ cup cream
- 1 cup sugar
- 1 cup pumpkin pie filling
- 1/3 cup brown sugar
- 3 eggs
- 1 teaspoon vanilla essence
- 2 tablespoons honey
- 12 digestives

Directions:
1. Make crumbs of the digestives.
2. Mix crumbs with melted butter.
3. Place butter mix on the bottom of the Instant Pot.
4. Mix eggs, vanilla and nutmeg, pumpkin filling with honey.
5. Mix sugar with cream and cheese.
6. Place creamy mix on top of the crumbs.
7. Pour honey mix over the cheesy mixture.
8. Place cheesecake in the Instant Pot and cook for 1 hour on "High Pressure" regime.
9. Serve with the caramel topping.

Nutrition:
- Calories: 330
- Fat: 13g
- Carbohydrates: 26g
- Protein:5g

Cheesecake Bites

The most delicious dessert ever – you need to try it right now!

Prep time: 20 minutes | **Cooking time:** 30 minutes | **Servings:** 18

Ingredients:
- 7 graham crackers
- 2 teaspoons brown sugar
- 4 tablespoons butter
- Pinch of salt
- 16 ounces cream cheese
- 2 teaspoons vanilla extract
- 2 eggs
- 2 tablespoons cornstarch
- 2/3 cup sugar
- ½ cup sour cream
- 3 tablespoons coconut oil
- 3 cups melted chocolate

Directions:
1. Mix crackers with sugar and salt using blender.
2. Melt butter.
3. Mix butter with the cracker mix.
4. Mix sour cream with sugar, cornstarch and eggs.
5. Mix cheese with vanilla extract.
6. Mix vanilla and cheese with the sugar mixture.
7. Prepare baking cupcake forms.
8. Pour ½ chocolate in the baking form.
9. Place crumbs over the chocolate.
10. Place cheesy mix over the crumbs.
11. Pour chocolate on top of the cheesy mix.
12. Place cheesecake in the Instant Pot.
13. Cook dessert for 30 minutes on "High Pressure" regime.
14. Place dessert in the fridge for 60 minutes.
15. Serve!

Nutrition:
- Calories: 40
- Fat: 3g
- Carbohydrates: 4g
- Protein:1g

Apple Crisp

Really crispy and juicy apple dessert on your plate – something you will adore!

Prep time: 5 minutes | **Cooking time:** 10 minutes | **Servings:** 15

Ingredients:
- 15 apples
- 3 teaspoon salt
- 6 teaspoons cinnamon
- 1 cup brown sugar
- 3 teaspoon nutmeg
- 1 cup flour
- 1 cup water
- 5 cup rolled oats
- 4 tablespoon maple syrup
- 12 tablespoons butter

Directions:
1. Place slices apples in the Instant Pot.
2. Cover apples with cinnamon and nutmeg.
3. Cover apples with maple syrup.
4. Mix butter, salt, sugar and flour.
5. Place mix in the Instant Pot and cook for 10 minutes on "High Pressure" regime.
6. Serve with vanilla ice cream!

Nutrition:
- Calories: 110
- Fat: 1g
- Carbohydrates: 30g
- Protein:0g

Cheesecake Pops

So small and beautiful, but so delicious and satisfying the same time!

Prep time: 10 minutes | **Cooking time:** 30 minutes | **Servings:** 18

Ingredients:
- 16 ounces cream cheese
- ½ cup sugar
- 1lb chocolate
- 2 tablespoons sour cream
- 2 eggs
- 1 teaspoon vanilla extract

Directions:
1. Prepare baking form for the Instant Pot.
2. Mix cream cheese with sugar using blender.
3. Mix cream, vanilla and eggs.
4. Add eggs with vanilla and cream to the cheesy mix.
5. Pour 1 cup of water to the Instant Pot.
6. Melt chocolate.
7. Place cheesy mix in the baking form.
8. Top with chocolate.
9. Cook dessert in the Instant Pot for 30 minutes on "High Pressure" regime.
10. Serve!

Nutrition:
- Calories: 210
- Fat: 12g
- Carbohydrates: 23g
- Protein:3g

Nian Gao

Try national Chinese New Year cake!

Prep time: 5 minutes | **Cooking time:** 55 minutes | **Servings:** 1

Ingredients:
- 2 cups rice flour
- Pinch of sea salt
- ½ cup of wheat starch
- 1 ½ cup cane sugar
- 1 ½ cup cold water
- 1 piece brown sugar
- ¾ cup coconut milk
- 1 1/3 tablespoon sesame paste

Directions:
1. Mix flour with starch and salt.
2. Mix brown sugar with water and cane sugar. Warm up mix on the frying pan to get caramel.
3. Mix sesame paste with coconut mix.
4. Pour water in the Instant Pot.
5. Bring water in the Instant Pot to boil.
6. Mix all the ingredients for the cake in layers.
7. Place trivet in the Instant pot.
8. Place cake on the trivet.
9. Cook for 30 minutes on "High Pressure" regime.
10. Serve hot!

Nutrition:
- Calories: 181
- Fat: 11g
- Carbohydrates: 19g
- Protein:3g

Lavender Crème Brule

Make it feel like France and try extra tender and light lavender dessert!

Prep time: 10 minutes | **Cooking time:** 15 minutes | **Servings:** 1

Ingredients:

- 1 egg yolk
- 1 teaspoon sugar
- 1/3 cup heavy cream
- A pinch of lavender buds
- 1 teaspoon sugar
- 1 teaspoon vanilla extract

Directions:

1. Whisk eggs with sugar.
2. Add creams to milky mixture and mix using blender.
3. Mix milky mixture with lavender buds.
4. Pour in the baking form suitable for the Instant Pot.
5. Pour water in the pressure cooker.
6. Place baking forms in the pressure cooker.
7. Cook Brule for 10 minutes on "High Pressure" regime.
8. Let the pressure release naturally (20 minutes).
9. Cook dessert for 45 minutes.
10. Serve!

Nutrition:

- Calories: 300
- Fat: 25g
- Carbohydrates: 20g
- Protein: 11g

Blueberry Compote

Only 5 minutes and light sweet drink is in your cup!

Prep time: 3 minutes | **Cooking time:** 5 minutes | **Servings:** 10

Ingredients:

- 15 cups blueberries
- 10 tablespoons water
- 3 cups sugar
- 8 tablespoons cornstarch
- 8 tablespoons lemon juice
- 1 cup cherries

Directions:

1. Wash blueberries. Mix blueberries with cherries using blender.
2. Mix blueberries with lemon juice.
3. Add sugar to the blueberry mix.
4. Use blender one more time to get tender mixture.
5. Pour mixture in the baking cup and cook for 3 minutes in the pressure cooker on "High Pressure" regime.
6. Let the pressure release naturally (10 minutes).
7. Pour water over cornstarch.
8. Mix cornstarch with blueberry mix.
9. Cook for 5 minutes on "Sauté" function.
10. Do a quick release.
11. Serve warm.

Nutrition:

- Calories: 306
- Fat: 1g
- Carbohydrates: 78g
- Protein: 0g

Peach Cobbler

Try soft and satisfying peach cobbler for true sweet lovers!

Prep time: 10 minutes | **Cooking time:** 20 minutes | **Servings:** 9

Ingredients:
- 1cup sugar
- 1 teaspoon cinnamon
- 1 cup brown sugar
- 3 teaspoons vanilla
- 6 teaspoons lemon juice
- 9 tablespoons butter
- 9 tablespoons cornstarch
- 1 cup milk
- 1 cup water
- 6 cups baking mix
- 2 tablespoons flour
- 1 teaspoon lime juice

Directions:
1. Wash and cut peaches into slices. Place flour over peach slices and mix with lime juice.
2. Mix water, peach slices, cornstarch, lemon juice, sugar and cinnamon with brown sugar.
3. Prepare baking form suitable for your pressure cooker.
4. Pour peach mix in the baking form. You should fill ½ of each baking form, not full cup.
5. Mix vanilla with butter, baking mix and milk.
6. Add to the baking powder. Do not mix with peach mixture.
7. Cook for 20 minutes on "High Pressure" regime.
8. Let the pressure release naturally (10 minutes).
9. Serve warm!

Nutrition:
- Calories: 150
- Fat: 5g
- Carbohydrates: 40g
- Protein: 3g

Pecan Praline Cheesecake

Try crispy, soft, tender and light cheesecake with delicious and satisfying praline topping!

Prep time: 10 minutes | **Cooking time:** 20 minutes | **Servings:** 8

Ingredients:
- 2 blocs cream cheese
- Sugar syrup
- 2/3 cup sugar substitute
- ½ cup pecans
- 1 teaspoon vanilla extract
- 2 eggs

Directions:
1. Mix sugar with vanilla extract.
2. Add sugar mix to the cream cheese.
3. Use blender to mix cheese with vanilla and get tender sauce.
4. Prepare baking form for the pressure cooker.
5. Pour caramel syrup (sugar syrup) on the bottom of the baking form.
6. Add pecans to the Instant Pot.
7. Cover baking form with butter.
8. Pour water in the pressure cooker.
9. Mix eggs with sugar substitute.
10. Mix egg mixture with cheese sauce.
11. Pour cheese sauce over the pecans.
12. Cook for 20 minutes on "High Pressure" regime.
13. Let the pressure release naturally (20 minutes).
14. Serve cold!

Nutrition:
- Calories: 400
- Fat: 26g
- Carbohydrates: 40g
- Protein: 6g

Candied Lemon Peels

Covered in sugar and caramel sauce these lemon peels will be your favorite sweets!

Prep time: 10 minutes | **Cooking time:** 15 minutes | **Servings:** 8

Ingredients:

- 1 pound lemons
- 5 cups water
- 2 ¼ cups sugar

Directions:

1. Wash lemons.
2. Clean lemon skin using scrub.
3. Slice lemons into quarters and clean of the edges.
4. Make strips of the quarters.
5. Place lemon strips in water.
6. Pour water with lemons in the pressure cooker.
7. Cook for 5 minutes on "High Pressure" regime.
8. Let the pressure release naturally (10 minutes).
9. Add sugar to the Instant Pot and cook strips for 10 minutes on "High Pressure" regime.
10. Let the pressure release naturally (10 minutes).
11. Dry lemon strips and place in the fridge for 4 hours.
12. Serve cold!

Nutrition:

- Calories: 303
- Carbohydrates: 73g
- Fat: 1g
- Protein: 1g

Chocolate Pudding Cake

As crispy as a pie, as tender as natural chocolate pudding!

Prep time: 10 minutes | **Cooking time:** 10 minutes | **Servings:** 4

Ingredients:

- 2/3 cup sweet chocolate morsels
- Powdered sugar to serve
- ½ cup applesauce
- 3 tablespoons cocoa powder
- ¼ cup arrowroot
- 2 eggs
- Pinch of salt
- 1 teaspoon vanilla

Directions:

1. Prepare baking form suitable for your pressure cooker.
2. Pour water in the Instant Pot.
3. Place chocolate in the Instant Pot.
4. Melt chocolate for 6 minutes on "Sauté" regime.
5. Mix beaten eggs with applesauce and vanilla.
6. Mix salt, arrowroot, cocoa powder and add to the melted chocolate.
7. Add some butter to taste.
8. Bake cake for 5 minutes on "High Pressure" regime.
9. Let the pressure release naturally (10 minutes).
10. Serve with powdered sugar.

Nutrition:

- Calories: 300
- Carbohydrates: 51g
- Fat: 2g
- Protein: 3g

Corny Cornbread Casserole

Can cornbread become your favorite dessert? With this receipt for sure!

Prep time: 5 minutes | **Cooking time:** 25 minutes | **Servings:** 6

Ingredients:

- ½ cup butter
- 1 box Muffin mix
- 1 cup sour cream
- 4oz can green chilies
- 1 egg
- 1 can cream style corn
- Corn
- 2 cups honey

Directions:

1. Mix corn with cream style corn, beaten egg, chopped chilies, Muffin mix and add sour cream.
2. Add honey to the corn mix and use blender.
3. Place butter in the Instant Pot and melt up for 4 minutes on "Sauté" regime.
4. Place corn mix in the pressure cooker.
5. Cook for 25 minutes on "High Pressure" regime.
6. Do a quick release.
7. Serve with powdered sugar.

Nutrition:

- Calories: 200
- Fat: 12g
- Carbohydrates: 19g
- Protein: 4g

Lemon Cookie Cups

Soft lemon sauce inside of the crispy cookies – just try and you will fall in love with this receipt!

Prep time: 10 minutes | **Cooking time:** 15 minutes | **Servings:** 4

Ingredients:

- 1 ¾ cups flour
- Powdered sugar to serve
- ½ cups wheat flour
- ¾ cups lemon curd
- ½ teaspoon salt
- ½ teaspoon vanilla extract
- ½ teaspoon baking soda

- ½ teaspoon lemon extract
- ½ teaspoon cream of tartar
- 1 egg
- ½ cup butter
- ½ cup canola oil
- ½ cup sugar

- ½ cup powdered sugar
- 6 tablespoons butter
- 1 teaspoon lemon zest
- 1 cup sugar
- 1/3 cup lemon juice
- 2 eggs
- 2 egg yolks

Directions:

1. Place butter in the plate.
2. Add sugar to some butter and mix using sugar.
3. Mix beaten eggs with egg yolks.
4. Add egg mixture to the butter mix.
5. Add lemon juice to some egg mixture.
6. Mix well using mixer.
7. Place curd in the pressure cooker.
8. Cook for 10 minutes on "High Pressure" regime. Add lemon zest.
9. Let the pressure release naturally (10 minutes).
10. Mix salt with flour, baking soda and cream of tartar.
11. Mix in the separate bowl butter with sugar and fluffy.
12. Add oil to the butter mix.
13. Add canola oil, four mix, powdered sugar, lemon, vanilla extract.
14. Place dough on the bottom of the baking form.
15. Place curd in the cookie.
16. Bake for 10 minutes on "High Pressure" regime.
17. Let the pressure release naturally (10 minutes).
18. Serve cold!

Nutrition:

- Calories: 150
- Fat: 5g

- Carbohydrates: 23g
- Protein: 1g

Cinnamon Poached Pears

Sugar and tender pears with chocolate sauce on top of the caramelized skin!

Prep time: 10 minutes | **Cooking time:** 5 minutes | **Servings:** 6

Ingredients:

- 1 lemon
- 6 pears
- 3 cups water
- 6 cinnamon stalks
- 2 cups white wine
- 2 cups cane sugar
- 2 tablespoons maple syrup
- 9 ounces chocolate
- ¼ cup coconut oil
- ½ cup coconut mil

Directions:

1. Wash and clean lemon.
2. Mix water with sugar and wine.
3. Add cinnamon to some sugar mixture.
4. Pour mixture in the Instant Pot.
5. Set "Keep Warm" regime.
6. Wash pears and place in the pressure cooker.
7. Add lemon juice to the pears and mix with wine syrup.
8. Cook for 5 minutes on "High Pressure" regime.
9. Do a quick release.
10. Mix maple syrup with milk, coconut oil and chocolate.
11. Remove pears from the Instant Pot.
12. Melt up chocolate mix on the "Sauté" regime. It will take around 5 minutes.
13. Pour chocolate sauce over the pears.
14. Serve hot!

Nutrition:

- Calories: 302
- Fat: 1g
- Carbohydrates: 70g
- Protein: 10g

Cranberry Sauce

This sauce will be perfect addition to the toast or morning dessert – just try and you will fall in love with it!

Prep time: 5 minutes | **Cooking time:** 15 minutes | **Servings:** 1

Ingredients:

- 12 ounces cranberries
- White sugar
- 2 ½ teaspoons orange zest
- Pinch of salt
- ¼ cup orange juice
- 2 tablespoons honey

Directions:

1. Wash cranberries and clean from the leaves.
2. Mix maple syrup with orange juice using blender.
3. Mix orange zest with cranberries and add orange juice sauce.
4. Place mixture in the Instant Pot.
5. Cook for 1 minute on "High Pressure" regime.
6. Let the pressure release naturally (7 minutes).
7. Mix cranberries with sugar using blender.
8. Add salt to the cranberries.

Nutrition:

- Calories: 418
- Fat: 0g
- Carbohydrates: 14g
- Protein: 0g

Black Forest Cheesecake

Good looking and sweet cheesecake with satisfying sauce and tender berries!

Prep time: 15 minutes | **Cooking time:** 30 minutes | **Servings:** 7

Ingredients:

- 4 tablespoons butter
- 1/8 teaspoon salt
- ¼ teaspoon baking powder
- ½ teaspoon vanilla extract
- 3 tablespoons cocoa
- 1 egg
- 2 tablespoons flour
- 16 ounces cream cheese
- 2 eggs
- ½ cup sugar
- 1 tablespoons flour

Directions:

1. Mix flour with cocoa powder, baking powder and salt.
2. Mix butter, sugar and vanilla in the separate bowl.
3. Add eggs to some flour and whisk well.
4. Add cocoa powder mix to the flour mix.
5. Add salt to the flour mix.
6. Pour water in the Instant Pot.
7. Prepare baking form suitable for your Instant Pot.
8. Place dough in the baking form.
9. Cook brownie for 7 minutes on "High Pressure" regime.
10. Let the pressure release naturally (5 minutes).
11. Mix cream cheese with sugar using mixer to get tender cream.
12. Mix cheese with vanilla extract.
13. Place on the brownie and cook for 25 minutes on "High Pressure" regime.
14. Let the pressure release naturally (10 minutes).
15. Leave to rest after the cooking and serve cold with grated chocolate!

Nutrition:

- Calories: 320
- Fat: 19g
- Carbohydrates: 32g
- Protein: 4g

Chocolate Pots de Crème

Small cups with satisfying chocolate dessert and crème topping!

Prep time: 10 minutes | **Cooking time:** 15 minutes | **Servings:** 6

Ingredients:

- 1 ½ cup heavy creams
- Whipped cream for topping
- ½ cup whole milk
- 8 ounces bittersweet chocolate
- 5 egg yolks
- Pinch of salt
- ¼ cup sugar

Directions:

1. Mix milk with cream using blender.
2. Mix egg yolks with sugar and salt using blender.
3. Pour milk and creams in the Instant Pot. Warm up mix for 4 minutes on "Sauté" regime.
4. Add warm milk mix to eggs with sugar.
5. Add melted chocolate and mix using blender.
6. Pour chocolate muss into 6 separate cups.
7. Pour water in the pressure cooker.
8. Place cups with chocolate dessert in the Instant Pot.
9. Cook for 6 minutes on "High Pressure" regime. Let the pressure release naturally.

Nutrition:

- Calories: 352
- Fat: 28g
- Carbohydrates: 21g
- Protein: 4g

Flan

This easy dessert conquered hundred hearts – let yours be the next one!

Prep time: 25 minutes | **Cooking time:** 25 minutes | **Servings:** 12

Ingredients:
- 1 cup white sugar
- 6 eggs
- 4 tablespoons water
- 2 pinches sea salt
- 2 cups milk
- 4 teaspoons vanilla extract
- 2 cups heavy cream
- 1 cup sugar
- 1 cup caramel to serve
- 1 tablespoon white chocolate

Directions:
1. Mix sugar with water. Warm up mix in the Instant Pot. Do not over cook – it should not start boiling.
2. Pour sweet water in the pressure cooker and warm up on "Sauté" regime for 4 minutes. Remove caramel from the Instant Pot. Place white chocolate in the pressure cooker. Melt up chocolate for 4 minutes not changing the regime. Set chocolate aside.
3. Mix milk with creams and pour in the Instant Pot. Mix sugar with vanilla extract and sea salt. Add to milk mixture.
4. Pour milk mixture in the Instant Pot. Warm up for 3 minutes on "Sauté" regime.
5. Add water to the pressure cooker. Cook for 10 minutes on "High Pressure" regime.
6. Let the pressure release naturally (10 minutes). Pour caramel and chocolate over the dessert.
7. Place dessert in the fridge for 4 hours.
8. Serve with caramel!

Nutrition:
- Calories: 108
- Fat: 3g
- Carbohydrates: 17g
- Protein: 3g

Berry Compote

One of your favorite additional sweet sauces for every day!

Prep time: 10 minutes | **Cooking time:** 15 minutes | **Servings:** 2

Ingredients:
- 2 cups strawberries
- 1 tablespoon water
- 1 cup blueberries
- 1 tablespoons cornstarch
- ¾ cup sugar
- 2 tablespoons lemon juice

Directions:
1. Wash blueberries and strawberries.
2. Mix berries in blender with sugar.
3. Add lemon juice to the berry mix.
4. Pour berry mix in jars and place in the Instant Pot.
5. Cook for 5 minutes on "High Pressure" regime.
6. Let the pressure release naturally (10 minutes).
7. Mix water with cornstarch and add to the berry mix.
8. Serve cold!

Nutrition:
- Calories: 28
- Fat: 0g
- Carbohydrates:7g
- Protein: 1g

Berries and Cream Cake

Light enough to try in the evening and satisfying enough for the breakfast!

Prep time: 10 minutes | **Cooking time:** 25 minutes | **Servings:** 12

Ingredients:

- 10 eggs
- 4 tablespoons powdered sugar
- 1/2 cup sugar
- 1/2 teaspoon milk
- 2 tablespoons cut strawberries
- 1 tablespoon berries
- 1 tablespoon butter
- 1 cup ricotta cheese
- 1 teaspoon vanilla extract
- 1 cup vanilla yogurt
- 1 cup yogurt
- 2 cups flour
- 1 cup berry compote
- 1 teaspoon salt
- 4 teaspoons baking powder

Directions:

1. Mix eggs with butter, cheese, vanilla and yogurt. Wash berries, place berries in the blender cut and mix with strawberries. Set aside.
2. Use mixer to mix all the ingredients well and get tender sauce.
3. Mix flour with baking powder and salt separately.
4. Mix flour with egg mixture. Use mixer on the second speed to mix well.
5. Pour water in the Instant Pot.
6. Prepare baking form suitable for the Instant Pot.
7. Place dough in the baking form.
8. Make drops in the dough with berry compote.
9. Cook dough in the pressure cooker for 25 minutes.
10. Mix sugar, milk, yogurt and vanilla.
11. Let the pressure release naturally (10 minutes).
12. Cover cake with yogurt sauce and serve!

Nutrition:

- Calories: 430
- Fat: 20g
- Carbohydrates: 65g
- Protein:6g

Japanese Cheesecake

Try only one Japanese dessert and fall in love with Asian cuisine!

Prep time: 15 minutes | **Cooking time:** 20 minutes | **Servings:** 3

Ingredients:

- 3 eggs
- 4oz cream cheese
- 4oz white chocolate chips

Directions:

1. Separate whites from egg yolks.
2. Place chocolate in the Instant Pot.
3. Melt up chocolate for 5 minutes on "Sauté" regime.
4. Mix cream cheese with egg yolks and chocolate.
5. Use mixer to get tender cream.
6. Mix egg whites on high speed with mixer.
7. Place egg yolk mixture in the baking form suitable for the pressure cooker.
8. Add egg whites over the dough.
9. Cook for 20 minutes on "High Pressure" regime.
10. Let the pressure release naturally (10 minutes).

Nutrition:

- Calories: 260
- Fat: 14g
- Carbohydrates: 28g
- Protein:6g

Peach Jam

Make this day colorful and bright with orange bright jam!

Prep time: 5 minutes | **Cooking time:** 15 minutes | **Servings:** 4

Ingredients:
- 2 ½ pounds peaches
- 1 tablespoon vanilla extract
- ½ cup honey
- 1 lemon

Directions:
1. Wash peaches.
2. Mix honey with vanilla extract and lemon juice.
3. Cut peaches on slices.
4. Add honey sauce to peach slices.
5. Cook for 1 minute on "High Pressure" regime.
6. Cook for 15 minutes on "Sauté" regime.
7. Do a quick pressure release.
8. Pour jam in jars and serve cold!

Nutrition:
- Calories: 20
- Fat: 0g
- Carbohydrates: 14g
- Protein: 0g

Lemon Pudding Cups

Tender pudding flavor with light taste and satisfying texture!

Prep time: 5 minutes | **Cooking time:** 5 minutes | **Servings:** 7

Ingredients:
- 3 cups milk
- 2 tablespoons sources gelatin
- ¼ cup lemon juice
- 3 drops oil
- 1 ½ tablespoon lemon zest
- 3 eggs
- ½ cup honey
- 3 tablespoons coconut oil

Directions:
1. Mix lemon juice with lemon zest.
2. Add coconut oil with beaten eggs to the lemon mix and mix using blender.
3. Use blender to get really tender sauce.
4. Mix flour with lemon.
5. Blend one more time.
6. Add milk, honey, coconut oil, gelatin and add to lemon sauce.
7. Pour pudding in jars.
8. Place in the Instant Pot.
9. Cook pudding for 5 minutes on "High Pressure" regime.
10. Let the pressure release naturally (10 minutes).
11. Serve cold!

Nutrition:
- Calories: 130
- Fat: 3g
- Carbohydrates: 25g
- Protein: 1g

Chocolate Sourdough Cake

Crispy cake with hot chocolate topping on your plate – something for the good day!

Prep time: 15 minutes | **Cooking time:** 30 minutes | **Servings:** 1

Ingredients:

- ½ cup sourdough starter
- 1 teaspoon coffee substitute
- ½ cup milk
- ¾ teaspoon baking soda
- 7/8 cup pastry
- ½ teaspoon sea salt
- ½ cup Rapadura
- 3/8 cup cocoa powder
- ½ cup coconut oil
- 1 egg
- 1 teaspoon vanilla extract
- 2 tablespoons chocolate sauce

Directions:

1. Mix starter with milk and flour.
2. Lave to rest for several hours.
3. Pour water in the pressure cooker.
4. Prepare baking form suitable for your Instant Pot.
5. Place dough in the baking form.
6. Mix beaten egg with coconut oil, Rapadura and cocoa powder.
7. Mix egg mixture with dough and add salt, baking soda, coffee.
8. Use mixer to get soft and tender dough.
9. Cook pie for 25 minutes on "High Pressure" regime.
10. Let the pressure release naturally (10 minutes).
11. Do a quick release.
12. Serve with chocolate sauce!

Nutrition:

- Calories: 695
- Fat: 46g
- Carbohydrates: 70g
- Protein: 6g

Christmas Pudding

Everybody love Christmas! With this receipt you will love this celebration even more!

Prep time: 10 minutes | **Cooking time:** 15 minutes | **Servings:** 12

Ingredients:

- 1 orange
- 1 cup flour
- 1 cup water
- 2 tablespoons coconut flour
- 1 ¼ cup pitted dates
- ¼ teaspoon sea salt
- 1 ¼ cup whole prunes
- ½ teaspoon nutmeg
- 1/3 cup coconut oil
- 1 teaspoon allspice
- 2/3 cup dried cranberries
- ¼ teaspoon clove
- 2/3 cup apricots
- 1 teaspoon cinnamon
- 1 ½ cups currants
- 1 teaspoon vanilla extract
- 2/3 cup prunes
- 4 eggs
- ½ cup potato
- 2 tablespoons honey
- ½ cup carrots

Directions:

1. Wash and scrub orange.
2. Mix orange with water using blender.
3. Add dates, prunes and mix one more time using blender.
4. Pour orange mix in the pressure cooker.
5. Cook for 10 minutes on "Saute" function.
6. Add coconut oil to orange mixture.
7. Wash and peel potatoes.
8. Wash and clean carrot. Cut carrot on slices.
9. Mix potato with carrot, honey, beaten eggs, vanilla, orange mix and spices.
10. Add flour to the mix.
11. Use mixer on the second speed to get nice dough.
12. Cook pudding for 15 minutes on "Steam" regime.
13. Change regime on "High Pressure" and cook pudding for 35 minutes more.
14. Let the pressure release naturally (40 minutes).

Nutrition:

- Calories: 306
- Fat: 8g
- Carbohydrates: 55g
- Protein: 4g

Raspberry Curd

Soft and juicy dessert in Instant Pot won't make you feel disappointed!

Prep time: 5 minutes	**Cooking time:** 5 minutes	**Servings:** 3

Ingredients:

- 12 ounces raspberries
- 2 tablespoons butter
- 1 cup sugar
- 2 egg yolks
- 2 tablespoons lemon juice

Directions:

1. Wash raspberries.
2. Mix berries with sugar using blender.
3. Add lemon juice to berry mixture.
4. Pour in the Instant Pot.
5. Cook curd for 1 minute on "High Pressure" regime.
6. Let the pressure release naturally (5 minutes).
7. Do a quick release in 5 minutes.
8. Add whisked yolks and butter to the curd.
9. Cook for 5 minutes on "Sauté" regime in the pressure cooker.
10. Serve cold!

Nutrition:

- Calories: 40
- Fat: 1g
- Carbohydrates: 7g
- Protein: 1g

Borlotti Bean Brownie

You have never expected to try this delicious and sweet brownie!

Prep time: 10 minutes	**Cooking time:** 20 minutes	**Servings:** 14

Ingredients:

- 2 cups Borlotti beans
- 8 cups water
- 1/2 cup sliced almonds
- 1 cup cocoa powder
- 2 teaspoons baking powder
- 1 cup honey
- 4 pinches sea salt
- 1 teaspoon pure extract
- 4 eggs
- 6 tablespoons olive oil
- 1 tablespoon melted dark chocolate

Directions:

1. Cover beans with water.
2. Place beans in the Instant Pot.
3. Cook beans for 15 minutes on "High Pressure" regime.
4. Let the pressure release naturally (10 minutes).
5. Blend beans using blender to get puree consistence. Add chocolate to the beans.
6. Pour water in the pressure cooker.
7. Mix oil with cocoa powder. You may use blender to make mixture more tender.
8. Mix beans cream with eggs, cocoa powder, sea salt, almonds and honey. Place in the Instant Pot.
9. Cook for 20 minutes on "High Pressure" regime.
10. Let the pressure release naturally (10 minutes).
11. Serve hot!

Nutrition:

- Calories: 115
- Fat: 1g
- Carbohydrates: 14g
- Protein: 9g

Lemoncello

Try sweet Italian drink and make this day special!

Prep time: 15 minutes | **Cooking time:** 30 minutes | **Servings:** 3

Ingredients:
- 8 lemons
- 1 cup sugar
- 2 jars
- 1 ½ cup water
- 120 proof grain liquor

Directions:
1. Wash lemons.
2. Using scrub peel lemons and clean skin.
3. Cut lemons on slices.
4. Mix lemon slices with liquor.
5. Pour water in the Instant Pot.
6. Place lemons in liquor in the pressure cooker.
7. Add sugar and mix lemon well.
8. Cook for 30 minutes on "High Pressure" regime.
9. Let the pressure release naturally (10 minutes).
10. Pour liquor in jars and serve!

Nutrition:
- Calories: 230
- Fat: 7g
- Carbohydrates: 39g
- Protein: 2g

Ice Tea

What can be better than ice tea in sunny summer day? With this receipt, you can make ordinary weekend bright and soft!

Prep time: 5 minutes | **Cooking time:** 5 minutes | **Servings:** 8

Ingredients:
- 8 apples
- Maple syrup to taste
- 20 tea bags
- Pinch of baking soda
- 4 teaspoons sugar
- 1 teaspoon honey
- 24 cups water

Directions:
1. Wash apples.
2. Cut apples into slices.
3. Pour water in the Instant Pot. Add honey to the pressure cooker.
4. Warm up water for 5 minutes on "Sauté" regime. Honey also should be melted.
5. Place tea bags in the Instant Pot and add baking soda. Add sugar to the pressure cooker.
6. Add apple slices in the pressure cooker.
7. Cook for 5 minutes on "High Pressure" regime.
8. Do a quick pressure release.
9. Add maple syrup with baking soda to the Instant Pot and mix well.
10. Remove tea bags and add ice. Serve cold!

Nutrition:
- Calories: 2
- Fat: 0g
- Carbohydrates: 1g
- Protein: 0g

Apple Hand Pies

Small, nice looking and easy to cook hand pies will be both sweet dessert and nice addition to the celebration table!

Prep time: 10 minutes | **Cooking time:** 10 minutes | **Servings:** 4

Ingredients:

- 1 red apple
- 1 tablespoons cider vinegar
- 1 green apple

- 3 tablespoons brown sugar
- 1 tablespoon cinnamon
- 3 tablespoons white sugar
- 1 cup flour

- 4 tablespoons ice water
- ½ teaspoon salt
- 3 tablespoons shortening
- ½ tablespoon sugar
- 3 tablespoons butter

Directions:

1. Wash and peel apples.
2. Cut apples into slices.
3. Mix apples with cinnamon, white and brown sugar and vinegar.
4. Mix flour with shortening, butter and salt with sugar on the separate plate.
5. Add water to flour mix and form dough.
6. Make pie shapes of dough.
7. Place apple mix in dough.
8. Roll up pies.
9. Place pies in the pressure cooker.
10. Cook for 10 minutes on "High Pressure" regime.
11. Do a quick release.

Nutrition:

- Calories: 310
- Fat: 6g

- Carbohydrates: 19g
- Protein: 1g

Infused Water

We are what we drink – cook best party infused water right now!

Prep time: 5 minutes | **Cooking time:** 5 minutes | **Servings:** 5

Ingredients:

- 1 cup copped mango
- 2 knobs ginger
- 1 apple

- 5 cinnamon stalks
- 1 cup chopped peaches
- Zest and juice of 1 lemon

- ½ cup raspberries

Directions:

1. Mix chopped mango with ginger using blender.
2. Place fruit mix in the icing form and add water.
3. Mix washed and pilled apple with cinnamon using blender.
4. Place apple mix in the icing forms and add water.
5. Mix washed raspberries with peaches and lemon juice.
6. Place peach mix in the icing form and add water.
7. Place icing forms in the pressure cooker.
8. Cook for 5 minutes on "High Pressure" regime.
9. Do a quick release.
10. Place in the fridge to cool down.

Nutrition:

- Calories: 0
- Fat: 0g

- Carbohydrates: 0g
- Protein: 0g

Velvet Lava Cake

Crispy and soft the same time with tender aroma and satisfying filling – cake for true food lovers!

Prep time: 10 minutes | **Cooking time:** 15 minutes | **Servings:** 6

Ingredients:
- 3 eggs
- 8oz cream cheese
- Oil
- ¼ cup sugar
- Water
- Box of red velvet cake mix

Directions:
1. Mix eggs with cheese using mixer on the second speed.
2. Pour water in the Instant Pot.
3. Prepare baking form suitable for you pressure cooker.
4. Mix sugar with cheese and egg mix.
5. Mix with cake mix and forms balls.
6. Pour oil over the balls.
7. Place cakes in the baking form.
8. Cook for 15 minutes on "High Pressure" regime.
9. Do a quick release.
10. Serve warm!

Nutrition:
- Calories: 440
- Fat: 26g
- Carbohydrates: 51g
- Protein: 5g

Maple Flan

Tender and butter taste pie with vanilla sauce!

Prep time: 10 minutes | **Cooking time:** 75 minutes | **Servings:** 16

Ingredients:
- 1 cup maple syrup
- 2 tablespoons vanilla extract
- 6 eggs
- 1 teaspoon sea salt
- 1 cup milk
- 1 cup caramel
- 1 cup heavy cream

Directions:
1. Pour water in the Instant Pot.
2. Warm up water for 3 minutes on "Sauté" regime. Add caramel and melt it on the same regime for 2 more minutes.
3. Prepare baking dish suitable for your pressure cooker.
4. Place maple syrup in the baking form and cook for 10 minutes on "Sauté" regime.
5. Mix eggs with syrup. Use mixer on the second speed to get tender cream.
6. Mix milk with creams and salt, add vanilla extract.
7. Pour pie mix in the baking form.
8. Cook for 75 minutes on "Steam" regime.
9. Place pie in the fridge to cool down for 1 hour. Cut pie on slices.
10. Serve with maple syrup on top!

Nutrition:
- Calories: 260
- Fat: 10g
- Carbohydrates: 38g
- Protein: 5g

Peppermint Cheesecake

Try fresh and satisfying cheesecake with chocolate syrup!

Prep time: 20 minutes | **Cooking time:** 35 minutes | **Servings:** 9

Ingredients:

- 16 ounces cream cheese
- ½ teaspoon sea salt
- 2 eggs
- ¼ teaspoon peppermint extract
- ½ cup maple sugar
- ½ teaspoons vanilla extract
- ¼ cup heavy cream
- 1 tablespoon flour
- 1 cup almond flour
- 2 tablespoons ghee
- 2 tablespoons maple sugar
- 6 ounces chocolate
- Sea salt to taste
- 1/3 cup cream
- ¼ teaspoon sea salt

Directions:

1. Place chocolate in the Instant Pot. Melt it up for 4 minutes on "Sauté" regime.
2. Mix chocolate with sea salt and cream. Use blender.
3. Place ghee in the pressure cooker and melt it up.
4. Mix ghee with maple sugar and flour using mixer on the second speed.
5. Mix cream cheese with eggs using blender.
6. Add sugar and cream with vanilla extract to cheese mix.
7. Mix peppermint extract, sea salt and flour with cheese mix.
8. Prepare baking form suitable for the pressure cooker.
9. Pour water in the Instant Pot.
10. Place baking form in the pressure cooker and place cheese mix inside of it.
11. Place crust over cheesecake.
12. Cook for 35 minutes in the Instant Pot on "High Pressure" regime.
13. Do a quick release.

Nutrition:

- Calories: 340
- Fat: 25g
- Carbohydrates: 21g
- Protein: 6g

Tapioca Pudding

Time to try low in calories pudding!

Prep time: 10 minutes | **Cooking time:** 10 minutes | **Servings:** 10

Ingredients:

- 1 cup tapioca pearls
- 1 lemon
- 2 cups milk
- 1 cup sugar
- 1 cup water
- 10 rosemary leaves to serve
- 1 teaspoon coffee

Directions:

1. Pour water in the Instant Pot. Warm up water for 3 minutes – do not bring it to boil.
2. Prepare baking form for pudding.
3. Mix tapioca with milk, sugar and lemon. Mash using blender. Add coffee and mix one more time using blender.
4. Pour tapioca mixture in the pressure cooker.
5. Cook for 10 minutes on "High Pressure" regime.
6. Let the pressure release naturally (30 minutes). Pour pudding in the serving cups and add rosemary leaves.

Nutrition:

- Calories: 100
- Fat: 0g
- Carbohydrates: 22g
- Protein:

BONUS GIFT PAGE

Dear friend!
Thank you so much for buying my book and supporting my next cookbooks which I hope you will enjoy as well. In order to thank you I am very happy to present you a gift cookbook: "365 Recipes for Whole Year".

Press this button to get instant access and DOWNLOAD your BONUS:
https://goo.gl/T6iP4m
(No subscription or other additional actions required)

58037686R00213

Made in the USA
San Bernardino, CA
25 November 2017